FREE
RADICAL

ALBERT SZENT-GYORGYI
AND
THE BATTLE OVER VITAMIN C

Ralph W. Moss

WITH A FOREWORD BY
Studs Terkel

PARAGON HOUSE PUBLISHERS
NEW YORK

First edition
Published in the United States by
Paragon House Publishers
90 Fifth Avenue
New York, New York 10011

Library of Congress Cataloging-in-Publication Data

Moss, Ralph W.
  Free radical.

  Includes index.
  1. Szent-Györgyi, Albert, 1893-1986. 2. Biochemists—
Biography. I. Title.
QP511.8.S94M67 1987   574.1'92'0924 [B]   87-8865
ISBN 0-913729-78-7

CONTENTS

Illustrations follow pages 44, 108, and 172

FOREWORD

I vividly recall the first time I met Albert Szent-Gyorgyi. It was during the Vietnam War and he was in Chicago for a scientific convention. Young scientists and students were protesting the war, and on that day Albert and a fellow Hungarian, Edward Teller, tangled publicly. Teller was, and is, a distinguished physicist, known as "the father of the H-bomb," and proud of it. He was very hawklike during the Vietnam War and justified his position eloquently and, I think, madly. Albert Szent-Gyorgyi quietly disputed him. It was a remarkable debate between two fellow Hungarians who had two diametrically opposed visions of the world.

It so happened that, on that day, the distinguished physicist had as a bodyguard two Chicago policemen. These Chicago detectives carried sidearms to protect the physicist from those terrible students who were protesting the war. Albert Szent-Gyorgyi, on the other hand, came by himself, unarmed and unafraid.

To me, that seemed like the metaphor of our times. One man, brilliant, represented the garrison state mentality. He was surrounded by power, by military, by guns. The other was a man of humanity, of peace, and unarmed. This is what the difference of their two outlooks was all about.

I also recall the letters and articles of Albert Szent-Gyorgyi, in the *New York Times,* about that insane adventure called the Vietnam War. There were excerpts from a little book he wrote called *The Crazy Ape.* Now, the "crazy ape" of the name is none other than the human species. We are told the human is the highest of all animal species, sitting on the topmost rung. Yet, ethically, morally, it is the lowest. As Mark Twain used to say, "Man is the only animal that can blush, or has reason to do so." Mankind is the only member of the animal kingdom that kills without necessity, or has wars without necessity.

In a sense, this is what Albert Szent-Gyorgyi was crying out in his many books, articles, and speeches. Yet he did not believe that man is inherently bad. We simply have not yet fulfilled our possibilities. "Fulfilling possibilities" is what Albert Szent-Gyorgyi's long life was about. That is why he remained a maverick who defied convention, that is why, past ninety, he went on looking for a new way of unlocking the door that tells us about cancer, as he did with ascorbic acid, which cured scurvy. He is the prototype of the maverick who eternally searches and questions.

But, to me, he was more than that, something different. He was what Einstein was, what all great scientists are—a poet. He leaped in his imagination, as Einstein did, as Newton did, as Galileo did, as Nils Bohr did . . . as Szent-Gyorgyi did. That is what it's all about: a leap of the imagination.

At the moment we are in the hands of technicians. Technicians are pedestrian, dull people, who say two plus two is four and so on. And what they do, I believe, will lead ultimately to the destruction of our species. But that is of no interest to them, because they are simply technicians.

The poet and the scientist, who are in fact one, say "the human species is something else, not yet fulfilled."

There is one other aspect. One of the great dangers of our time, more dangerous than the bomb, is *banality*. Banality means, I suppose, the suppression of the imagination. Banal people stunt their imagination and try to function without this faculty.

Hannah Arendt described the Nazis in her book *Eichmann in Jerusalem*. She subtitled it *The Banality of Evil*. The Germans were not a different species. Some were good, some were bad, as there are in all societies. But banality took over. They stunted their imaginations and when banality takes over, anything horrendous is possible. I would reverse that, however, and refer not to the banality of evil, but to the *evil of banality*. Banality itself is the evil.

I bring this up because, to me, Szent-Gyorgyi was the antithesis of mind-stunting banality. He represented the imagination of the "free radical," unhampered by convention. Those rebellious kids in Paris in 1968 may have been cockeyed and crazy, but they had a wonderful slogan: "Long live imagination!" And in a sense this is what the life and career of Albert Szent-Gyorgyi was about: "Long live imagination!"

Szent-Gyorgyi's career was extraordinary, both in its scientific and its human dimensions. He worked with the great biochemist, Frederick Gowland Hopkins, in Cambridge and then returned to resuscitate science in Hungary. He won the Nobel Prize and became a leading

Hungarian man of science. But he never was simply a "Hungarian" or "Hungarian-American" scientist. Albert Szent-Gyorgyi was more than a Hungarian. Ultimately, he was a world figure who knew no boundaries.

Because he was opposed to the "evil of banality" he naturally fell afoul of the fascist regimes, both in Germany and in his native land. With his courage and his prestige, he became a leader of the Hungarian underground during Hitler times. He was the man in Hungary that Hitler most wanted to kill. Hitler screamed his name, demanding Szent-Gyorgyi's head. This was not just because Szent-Gyorgyi was of practical importance to the movement, but because his outspoken opposition to fascism kept up the morale of all the decent people opposed to the regime. His life was in danger every day.

Albert Szent-Gyorgyi saw the world, he saw hope, despite developments that were incredible. As scientist, poet, and maverick, he always defied the "institutional truths." He was an independent thinker, a poet/scientist, looking for a key to cancer's prevention and its cure. But I suspect he was not simply looking to cure cancer, the *medical* problem. For cancer itself is the metaphor for something much broader in its implications—the cancer in the world itself. Albert Szent-Gyorgyi wanted to open that door, to see what it can be.

If my attitude toward Albert Szent-Gyorgyi seems a bit worshipful, it is a human, not a godlike figure, that I worship. I deeply respect him not for some supernatural quality, but exactly *because* he is human in the fullest sense of the term. When I think of Albert Szent-Gyorgyi I think of what *could be* in all of us.

Recently, I found a poem of Pablo Neruda that might easily apply to the subject of this book. From Pablo Neruda to Albert Szent-Gyorgyi, one laureate to another:

I'll figure out as best I can.
And do it. If I don't make mistakes
who will believe my errors?
I'll change my whole person
and when no one can recognize me
I'll keep doing the same as I did
since I could not do otherwise.

He could not do otherwise! That was Albert Szent-Gyorgyi—the man, scientist, poet, and friend, whose friendship went beyond all boundaries. I salute the spirit of Albert Szent-Gyorgyi, and warmly welcome this biography.

STUDS TERKEL

PREFACE

The inception of this book was peculiar. In the spring of 1980, I was publicizing my first book, *The Cancer Syndrome,* and was scheduled to appear on the Larry King radio show. The producers wanted to find someone from the "cancer establishment" to debate me, and chose Franklin C. Salisbury of the National Foundation for Cancer Research (NFCR) as my opponent. Both the tiny NFCR and the massive National Cancer Institute (NCI) were based in Bethesda, Maryland. Someone apparently mistook the two and thought that NFCR was a branch of the government.

It was no debate. Frank Salisbury did not disagree with my criticisms of the establishment in which I had served. Rather, he spent his portion of the show singing the praises of one Albert Szent-Gyorgyi, scientific director of his foundation. He seemed to be trying to increase public exposure to a new and rather oddly-named product.

At the time, Frank Salisbury offered me a chance to meet the great Szent-Gyorgyi. I declined, but we kept in touch and soon afterwards I received an assignment from the *Saturday Evening Post* to write an article on this wayward genius, and so I went to his laboratory in Woods Hole, Massachusetts.

From the start, Albert seemed like a storybook character. He came bounding across the room, a big wide-open smile on his face. He grabbed my shoulder, looked into my eyes, and I was lost. It was a most exhilarating experience, very like love. Linus Pauling recalls that his five year old daughter thought that the Szent-Gyorgyi who entered into conversation with her, treating her as an adult was, in fact, someone named "Saint" Gyorgyi. But, as Pauling remarks (and readers of this biography will soon discover) Szent-Gyorgyi's sainthood was in doubt, although he could be, as Pauling also said, "the most charming scientist in the world."

My thinking about Albert Szent-Gyorgyi went through three phases. At first, I was honored to find myself included in his circle and flattered by the degree of confidence he showed in me. When I decided to write his biography I was welcomed into his home and laboratory. At the time I conceived of the job as essentially recording and collating the various wonderful stories he told about his life. This constituted the first draft of the book, which was called, quite reverentially, "One Step Ahead."

There came a point, however, when I realized that Albert could use these very enchanting stories as a mask to hide from the scrutiny of the world. The basis of his success, in fact, seemed to be this appealing, self-dramatizing myth of Albert Szent-Gyorgyi which he had created and perpetuated for sixty years. Not that I doubted his outstanding record of achievement. My own researches bore that out. But I came to think that this personality, this myth, had more than a little to do with his winning of the Nobel Prize—he had been hailed as the "new conquistador from Szeged," and he had truly conquered the hearts of many otherwise sober people.

Albert, I also found, sometimes surrounded himself with people who accepted this myth—people who "bought into it" and in one way or another benefitted from their association with him. In fact, I realized that I myself was in danger of becoming just such a person.

No man is a hero to his valet, or his biographer, I suspect. Some parts of his dealings with colleagues, supporters, and family surprised or even shocked me. I began to doubt the accuracy of some of his claims, and even the importance of what he was doing. This was accentuated by the difficulty of understanding exactly what he was up to. At a certain point I put down the book and felt little desire to complete it—or rather, would have liked just to have been rid of it.

But as more time passed, I realized that neither of these attitudes was correct. The various views needed to be reconciled or synthesized to produce a truer picture of the man. I went back to work with new enthusiasm and hopefully a more balanced picture.

His death in late 1986, although a sad event, allowed me and others who knew him to put his life into greater perspective. I still find it difficult to believe that he is gone. As Viktor Polgar, an official of the Hungarian embassy wrote me, his passing at the age of ninety-three was "unexpected because there are certain individuals one cannot imagine losing and Professor Szent-Gyorgyi was such a man."

Perhaps writing about Albert Szent-Gyorgyi is a way of saving something of that wonderful personality, for those who did not have the good fortune of knowing him.

Jeremy Bernstein has written, "By now we have become accustomed to reading biographies of artists, actors, writers, and even statesmen which discuss the most intimate details of their personal life. But there is, I think, something disturbing—or, at least, unfamiliar—about reading a comparable biography of a scientist."[1] Disturbing or not, such details are part of the complete picture. In Albert's case, sexual complications lay at the heart of his divorce and other personal problems. My uncensored approach may upset some, but I could not portray Albert without telling the whole story. I think he wanted it that way.

♦ ♦ ♦

It may seem overly familiar or presumptive of me to call this great man by his first name. "Prof. Szent-Gyorgyi" would be more respectful and a simple "Szent-Gyorgyi" would, of course, be adequate and correct. In the first draft I tried that, but that made the book seem stiff and formal.

To his colleagues, such as Zoltan Bay, he was "Albi." To Geoffrey Pollitt and his children he was "Grandfather." To Peter Gascoyne and the group at Woods Hole he was always reverentially "Prof."

In the course of the various rewrites I developed complicated naming formulas. At first, he was Albert as a child, becoming Szent-Gyorgyi at the time he graduated from medical school. Then I made him "Albert" in his personal life, and Szent-Gyorgyi in his professional life. Then I suddenly abandoned Albert altogether and switched to Szent-Gyorgyi, then switched it around and instructed the computer to search and replace all Szent-Gyorgyis with Alberts! Finally, I gave up all attempts at logic.

Would one feel comfortable calling the great Dr. Schweitzer by his first name? (In his biography, Norman Cousins calls him "The Doctor.") But "Albert" is what this "Doctor" asked me and many others to call him. I wanted the reader to share this closeness. And so I simply call him Albert most of the time, and Szent-Gyorgyi or "Prof." wherever that seems more appropriate. The result is inconsistent but I think more natural.

♦ ♦ ♦

Research for this book was carried out over a period of seven years and many individuals contributed to its progress and completion. My first debt is, of course, to Albert Szent-Gyorgyi himself for his generous gift of time. Every moment away from his work was painful for him, and he put up with my incessant visits and questions. His wife Marcia was always gracious and helpful to me.

At the National Foundation for Cancer Research I received help from many members of the staff, both past and present. In addition to

Frank Salisbury and his wife Tamara, Charles C. Pixley, M.D., the vice president for scientific administration, was always kind, generous, and understanding. Pat Dunigan, Walter Durr, Anna Belle Fulmer, as well as some past staff members—Gerry Snyder, Janet Greenbaum, Wayne Gray, John Beaty, Ann Greenstein and Sean Kane—all helped me in many ways.

I am also especially indebted to Mr. and Mrs. Henry Rolfs, whose kind interest in Prof. Szent-Gyorgyi and in this project has been unwavering for many years. Their help was invaluable, as it was in making the film about Szent-Gyorgyi's life, *A Special Gift,* which I produced with Pacific Street Films. These two projects and our Public Broadcasting film, *The Cancer War,* overlapped and much of my perspective on the book was gained in working on these films. My thanks to Steven Fischler and Joel Sucher for their insight, help, and good times on the road.

Many scientists aided this project and guided me through the complexities of Szent-Gyorgyi's research (as well as their own). These have included Dr. Bruce Ames, Berkeley; Dr. Zoltan Bay, Chevy Chase; Dr. Carmia Borek, New York; Dr. Enrico Clementi, Poughkeepsie; Dr. Mario Comporti, Siena, Italy; Dr. Mario Dianzani, Turin, Italy; Dr. Harold F. Dvorak, Boston; Dr. Laszlo Fesus, Debrecen, Hungary; Dr. Gabor Fodor, Morgantown; Dr. Sidney Fox, Coral Gables; Dr. James E. Girard, Washington, D.C.; Dr. Csaba Horvath, New Haven; Dr. Alan M. Kaplan, Lexington; Dr. Michael Kasha, Tallahassee; Dr. Per Olov Lowdin, Gainesville and Uppsala, Sweden; Dr. Thomas Merigen, Palo Alto; Dr. Lester Packer, Berkeley; Dr. Ilya Prigogine, Austin, Texas, and Brussels, Belgium; Dr. William A. Pryor, Baton Rouge; Drs. Alberte and Bernard Pullman, Paris, France; Dr. Graham Richards, Oxford, England; Dr. Leonard Rosenthal, Washington, D.C.; Dr. Leo Sachs, Rehovot, Israel; Dr. Ramaswamy Sarma, Albany; Dr. Jeffrey Sklar, Palo Alto; Dr. Trevor Slater, Uxbridge, England; Dr. Martyn Smith, Berkeley; Dr. Colin Thomson, St. Andrews, Scotland; and Dr. Robert W. Veltri, Rockville.

Many of these scientists welcomed me into their laboratories or homes and showed me exceptional hospitality—a reflection, in good part, of their respect and love for Albert Szent-Gyorgyi. In particular, the Pullmans provided me with office space in Paris during the sweltering summer of 1982. Per Lowdin facilitated my contacts with the Nobel Prize committee. And Graham Richards and Harold Dvorak went to bat for me when I was looking for a publisher.

At Woods Hole, I also received the generous assistance of Dr. Peter Gascoyne, Ms. Jane McLaughlin, and Dr. Ron Pethig. These were among the people who knew Albert best, and they provided me with facts, documents, stories, and occasionally gossip. It added up to a unique perspective on Szent-Gyorgyi's life and especially the last phase of his work on bioelectronics. Peter Gascoyne was particularly helpful in trying to explain the theory of quantum biology. Prof. Benjamin Kaminer made detailed comments on the final chapters of the manuscript. Homer Smith, the former director of Marine Biological Laboratory was informative and cooperative.

Prof. Andrew Szent-Gyorgyi (Albert's cousin) and his wife, Eva, both scientists, read this manuscript in an early draft and made many valuable comments. Two other well-known scientists, Profs. Linus Pauling and George Wald, were generous in their comments and reflections. Dr. James. D. Ebert, president of the Carnegie Institution of Washington, D.C. promptly replied to all my questions about his time at Woods Hole.

In May 1984 I followed the trail of Albert's life to Hungary and England. In Hungary, Dr. Ilona Banga and Prof. F. Bruno Straub were my hosts. They both made me feel at home, in the city my mother and her family had left many years before. Prof. Straub, in particular, interrupted a busy schedule to talk to me at length and escort me to Szeged. His insights into Albert Szent-Gyorgyi's work and character were indispensable and show up at many points in the book.

Other former students of "Prof" who warmly welcomed me included Prof. A. Biro, Eotvos Lorand University; Prof. Pal Elodi, Debrecen University; and Prof. Ferenc Guba, Atilla Joszef University, Szeged.

I also received assistance from Albert's cousin Dr. Maria Szent-Gyorgyi, herself an archivist and family historian; Prof. Gyula Juhasz, a historian with the Hungarian Academy of Sciences; Prof. Tibor Donat, Professor of Anatomy, Semmelweis University; Miklos Szanto, editor, and Peter Sos, correspondent of *Magyar Hirek;* Prof. Daniel Bagdy; David Biro, translator; Prof. Laszlo Muszbek and Dr. Olivia Veress, NFCR laboratory, Debrecen; Dr. Janos Perenyi, director of the Technical High School, Szeged; Dr. Andor Zaller, director of the library, Szeged Medical School; Dr. Ivan Nagy, Director of the Central Laboratory, Heim Pal Hospital; Dr. Imre Olah, Second Department of Anatomy, Semmelweis University Medical School; and finally, my own long-lost cousin, Dr. Eva Kardos. She shared her hospitality and insight into Hungarian life.

I was also assisted stateside by Dr. Vencel Hazi, the ambassador of the Hungarian People's Republic, who always took an affectionate interest in Albert Szent-Gyorgyi, and his two lively and intelligent associates, Viktor Polgar, second secretary for cultural affairs, and Istvan Szemenyei, the erstwhile science attaché.

Prof. Gyorgyi Ranki, the Hungarian Chair Professor at Indiana University, Bloomington, kindly read the manuscript for historical accuracy.

In Cambridge, England, I was the guest of one of this century's great scholars, Sir Joseph Needham. Sir Joseph, the retired Master of Grenville and Caius College, Cambridge, is the preeminent author in the West on the history of Chinese technology and science. Before becoming a historian, however, he had a career as a biochemist, as did his wife, Dorothy, author of a history of muscle research. In the 1920s and 1930s they worked at the Dunn laboratory in Cambridge and knew Albert Szent-Gyorgyi. They also looked after Albert's daughter when she came to Cambridge in the 1930s. Their charm rivalled that of Szent-Gyorgyi himself. Through them I learned what a seductive place Cambridge could be.

In England I had the help of Mary Nicholas, librarian of the Medical Research Council, Regent's Park; Robert Moore, National Institute for Medical Research, Mill Hill; and Dr. Philip Tubbs and Jackie Annis, at the Biochemical Laboratory, Cambridge, all of whom helped me with grace and generosity. (Mary Nicholas, in particular, tracked me down at my hotel late one night to inform me that she had located some of the crucial papers I had come to England seeking.) In addition, Jeannette Alton of the Contemporary Scientific Archives Center, Oxford, was extremely helpful in making available to me the papers and correspondence of Prof. Hans Krebs, with the permission of Lady Krebs.

I am especially indebted to Geoffrey Pollitt, the husband of Albert's daughter, and his three children, David, Lesley, and Michael, for their help. They have been a source of insight and advice. Also Csilla Felker provided much information about an otherwise obscure time in Albert's life. Dr. Joseph Svirbely and Prof. and Mrs. C. G. King were equally cooperative in helping me understand the circumstances of vitamin C's discovery.

I would like to offer special thanks to my friends, Alec Pruchnicki, M.D. and Pam Orsini for reading and commenting on this manuscript.

I also wish to thank J. William Hess, associate director of the Rockefeller Archives Center, Pocantico Hills, N.Y., for allowing me to work at the Center and for permission to reprint quotations from its voluminous files; librarians of the National Library of Medicine in Bethesda; and Clement J. Anzul of Fordham University Libraries who allowed me access to his library so that I could finish my research.

As always, my wife Martha gave me her love, help, and support. My gratitude is immeasurable.

◆ ◆ ◆

I have one apology to make to my Hungarian friends and to all lovers of accuracy. Hungarian is a highly accented language. Thus, Szent-Gyorgyi is actually Szent-Györgyi. Pal is Pál, and so forth. In fact, almost every name is accented. For the sake of simplicity, however, I have followed the *New York Times* style book, and left off all these diacritical marks. I am sure this makes for barbaric reading in Hungarian, but I felt Hungarian names are difficult enough for an English speaker, without adding extra difficulties. In addition, these names are difficult to pronounce. Albert always encouraged visitors to pronounce his name "Saint Georgie," which is a fair approximation of the original.

Unless otherwise noted, most of the unattributed quotations come from my own interviews with Albert Szent-Gyorgyi. These were begun in the summer of 1980 and continued until September, 1985. During most of that time I journeyed to Woods Hole four or five times a year and spent a week or so with him and his colleagues each time. In addition, I have greatly profited from two other sources. The first were interviews conducted in the late 1970s by William J. Coughlin for an intended biography which never got written; I inherited Mr. Coughlin's notes through the NFCR. Occasionally, Coughlin came up with quotes from other sources which I could not verify, but which I believed from the context to be accurate. I have used these several times, but each time indicated their source. Other interviews were conducted for the National Library of Medicine in 1967 by Mr. Harlan B. Phillips. I thank them both for the use of their work. At Albert's suggestion, I occasionally corrected the grammar of some of these quotes. (More often than not I left them alone to retain the full flavor of his highly-seasoned speech.) I have also occasionally borrowed from various versions of an anecdote to patch together a single comprehensive version of a story.

The ninety-three-year-long life of Albert Szent-Gyorgyi covered a broad canvas and I have necessarily been dependent on my sources, written or otherwise, for thousands of facts and anecdotes. I thank them all for their help, but they are in no way responsible for any errors which have crept into this narrative in the course of its transmission or interpretation.

Frank and Tamara Salisbury suggested that I write a biography of Albert when I first met him. For seven years they provided every kind of counsel, encouragement, and support. Despite Albert's later difficulties with the NFCR, the Salisburys were always eager to help me complete this work and to see it be accurate and fair. The whole project, like so many things, would probably never have happened without their drive and enterprise. Any book, especially a biography, is in a sense a collaboration among many individuals, including, when lucky, the subject. I cannot speak for these others, but I would like to dedicate my portion of these labors to this unique couple.

RWM
New York, New York

FREE
RADICAL

1

A CRAVING TO KNOW

Surveying the course of his life in the 1960s, Albert Szent-Gyorgyi was puzzled. He noted a "complete dichotomy." On the one hand, he said, his inner story was "exceedingly simple, if not indeed dull." His life was devoted to science and his only real ambition was to contribute to it and live up to its standards.

In this, he succeeded. He isolated vitamin C, helped discover the citric acid cycle, and fathered the whole field of modern muscle physiology. For these achievements he won the Nobel Prize and the Lasker Award. He was teacher and mentor to three generations of biochemists. Later, when most scientists his age were sitting on their laurels, he pioneered a highly original way of looking at the cancer problem and life itself. After three quarters of a century of achievements, Albert Szent-Gyorgyi died in his home at the age of ninety-three. His passing was noted on the front page of the *New York Times*.

This is the life of Albert Szent-Gyorgyi for the history books. But the course of his private life was surprisingly different and often at odds with received notions of the scientific calling. It was a life marked by conflict, drama, and more than occasionally, melodrama.

Born into a privileged family, he was decorated for bravery during World War I—and then deserted the Hungarian Army by shooting himself in the arm. A wandering scholar, he brought his family to the brink of starvation. At thirty-six, feeling himself an utter failure, he sent his wife back to her parents and prepared to commit suicide.

Later, when he was already famous, he fell in love with a colleague's wife and divorced his own companion of twenty years to marry her. During World War II he became an Allied intelligence agent operating

1

behind the Axis lines "involved in secret diplomatic activity with a
setting," as he put it, "fit for a cheap and exciting spy novel." He lived
for years with a finger on the trigger instead of fingering test tubes.

After the War he turned down a chance at the presidency of
Hungary, but created a new Academy of Sciences and founded the
Hungarian-Soviet Friendship Association. In Moscow he was feted on
caviar three times a day. Soon after, he was declared "a traitor to the
people" and he left his homeland in disgust.

Finally, he settled in Woods Hole, Massachusetts, from where he
kept up a one-man war with the U.S. government over atomic policy,
the direction of medical research, and especially the Vietnam War. He
was repeatedly investigated by the FBI and the CIA and hounded by
the IRS. In the last years of his life he twice married women fifty years
his junior. Surveying this eventful life, he said he felt "lost in the
twentieth century":

> All this, in itself, would have no interest. There are many who did more
> for science, were braver, suffered more agony and even paid the penalty of
> death. What may lend interest to my story is that it reflects the turbulence
> of our days. So to give sense to my story I will have to start by asking: why
> all this trouble and what is its relation to science?

Beyond this very evident dichotomy, one seeks for hidden, unifying
threads. Could it be that the same qualities of character that made
Albert Szent-Gyorgyi a great scientist also impelled him into problem-
atic entanglements? Where, if anywhere, did he locate the boundary
between his personal and his political life? Why did he always long for
an ivory tower, yet wind up so unerringly on the barricades? How is it
that this man, whose goal was to show people how to "work together
instead of snatching small advantages from one another," became
embroiled in one bitter quarrel after another—culminating in an
acrimonious legal battle in his ninety-second year?

In a memorable poem, "The Choice," William Butler Yeats wrote:

The intellect of man is forced to choose
Perfection of the life or of the work.
And if it take the second must refuse
A heavenly mansion raging in the dark.

Albert Szent-Gyorgyi rejected such wisdom, or could not or would
not make such a choice. A child of the romantic nineteenth century, he
wanted it all—both monumental scientific achievement and a glorious

adventure of a life. In this, he was more nearly like the Promethean figures of art and literature than almost any other scientist.

Amazingly, he almost succeeded.

There was already a dichotomy in his family when Albert Imre Szent-Gyorgyi von Nagyrapolt was born in Budapest, Hungary, on 16 September 1893.

His father was a conservative businessman, with a 2,000-acre farm approximately fifty miles from the capital. He came from a "titled" family, which traced its ancestry back to the seventeenth century [see Appendix A].

It was a staid family—rather boring. On his mother's side, however, there was real talent. For Josefine Szent-Gyorgyi (nicknamed Fini) was descended from one of the leading scientific dynasties of the age, the Lenhosseks.

Albert grew up in a split family. His parents kept up the appearance of a marriage, but in fact they lived apart. Miklos (Hungarian for Nicholas), Albert's father, lived on his farm in the country while the rest of the family, including Albert, his two brothers, his mother, and maternal grandmother, lived in a large apartment in downtown Pest, the busiest part of the capital.

His mother's brother, Mihaly Lenhossek, who had his own bachelor apartment in the hills of Buda, spent most of his spare time at his sister's apartment. He was a professor at the University, which was nearby, and in time he became an indispensable part of the household, a kind of surrogate father to the boys.[1]

Mihaly was learned and important, the greatest Hungarian physiologist of his day. He himself was the son and grandson of famous Hungarian scientists who formed an unbroken line of eminent anatomists and physiologists reaching back to the late eighteenth century. (Today there is even a street near the University named after him.) Here, then, was a true scientific dynasty, a mixture of natural ability and family traditions, with perhaps a little nepotism mixed in.

Mihaly Lenhossek was nobody's idea of a warm or jovial uncle. His conversation was factual and precise, but fascinating all the same to Albert and his family. Although Budapest in 1900 was cosmopolitan and the fastest growing metropolis in Europe, Hungarians traditionally looked to more advanced Western countries for the latest trends. And Uncle Mihaly was the family's link with the outside world: he read the most important European journals and corresponded with eminent scholars all over the Continent and beyond.

Although daring in the field of neurology, in some areas, at least, Mihaly's views were conservative and cautious. Albert, for example, vividly remembered his uncle holding forth at great length—the year was 1902—on the impossibility of heavier-than-air flights. He had read this opinion in a French journal and passed it on to his eager family. "Everybody felt relieved," Szent-Gyorgyi recalled, suppressing a smile, "because the idea of flying had begun to bother people."

"Our whole later career is decided by the scale of values we receive as children," Albert said. "What is important and what is not important. My uncle was a research scientist, and creativity was the great thing."

Religion was a powerful force in turn-of-the-century Hungary, but it had little or no influence in this "enlightened" family. His father was a Protestant, and Albert was baptized in the upper-class Calvinist church in Pest. His mother was born a Roman Catholic but had mixed feelings about the efficacy of prayer.

"My beloved mother was an enlightened agnostic who just smiled when people talked about religion," Albert recalled. "But if any of her sons were in trouble, she hastened to church to bribe St. Peter with a *forint* [i.e., a quarter] so that he would lobby for her."

About his maternal grandmother, Emma Bossonyi, and her beliefs little is known. During the Nazi era, there was a rumor that she was of Jewish ancestry. There is one piece of evidence to support this, but this idea was never proven and Albert himself rather vehemently denied it [see Appendix A].

At one point in his childhood, because of the pervasiveness of religious sentiment all around him, Albert himself became an ardent believer:

> If one is honest, one believes other people. The more honest you are, the more you believe other people. If an adult says that there is a God who created everything in seven days, you accept it.

This changed when he entered high school, or *Gymnasium:*

> There was one teacher in high school who had much influence on me, who was very intellectual and awoke my interests. And this teacher was an atheist.

In the summertime, the family would head for the countryside. Their farmhouse—grandiloquently called "the palace"—was surrounded by a spacious garden and a big iron fence. There were orchards, stately avenues of trees, a tennis court and, always, two watchdogs to keep out intruders.

The surroundings seemed idyllic, but it did not take long for a sensitive boy to discover that all was not as it seemed. "The palace" was also Albert's introduction to the rigid class divisions of Hungarian society. The foreman and chief mechanic had decent houses, but the average peasant lived in a tiny shack, in a slumlike section of low single-story dwellings called a *puszta*.[2]

Albert once asked a peasant how much he was paid. The answer was "fifty forints a year"—enough to buy a single pair of boots. "They had good lives," Albert later commented, ironically, "like a dog has a good life."

One incident from these times particularly stood out. A family friend drove his automobile up from Budapest. A car was then something newfangled and strange in the Hungarian countryside. When his father's peasants saw the machine they all stopped work and gathered round. The owner explained, as best he could, the workings of the mechanism, but as he talked, the peasants became increasingly agitated. Finally they insisted that there had to be an animal of some sort under the hood and threatened to go on strike—a desperate measure for the times—unless the hood were opened and the "swindle" exposed!

But the backwardness of these peasants, and the rigid class divisions that kept them apart, passed without question in the Szent-Gyorgyi household, "because it was so natural to me that I belonged to the leading class, and the peasants had a simple life. They were peasants, and that was that." Nevertheless, the fact that these peasants sweated for his father did not escape his notice. This formed part of the bill of particulars that Albert accumulated against this father who had scorned *him* as well. No one can say exactly what makes a person liberal or conservative, radical or reactionary, in his or her attitudes. But this early brush with rural exploitation undoubtedly contributed to Albert's growing anti-establishment point of view.

"He had no intellectual interests whatsoever," Albert recalled about his father. "His single interest in life was making money and he spent much time thinking about the sheep, the hogs, and the manure."[3]

Eating, said Albert, was most important to Miklos, and this once slim athlete grew fatter by the year. Every morning during the summer visits the *pater familias* called a solemn family council to decide on the menu of the day. Asked what he wanted to eat, Albert once had the temerity to reply, "It doesn't matter."

His father became irate. "Then you eat 'doesn't matter' and we'll eat the rest," he thundered.

Hunting and horseback riding were Albert's two main diversions at the "palace." The only other children he was allowed to play with were his two brothers, Pal and Imre, and the children of the foreman. During this time Albert developed a jealous dislike for both his older and younger brother which lasted all his life.

Relief came in September when the family, minus Miklos, returned to their Calvin Square (Kalvin Ter) apartment. There they could visit the National Museum, the University, or stroll the great boulevards which imitated (without seriously rivaling) those of Paris. This was a world of lilac trees, of *palacsinta* at Gundel's or ice cream at Gerbaud's—for those who had the money to enjoy such things. Budapest was an advanced European capital in the sea of the backward Hungarian countryside. Its Chain Bridge was considered a miracle of engineering, and Budapest had the first subway system on the Continent, which served as the model for other cities, including faraway New York.

The Hungarians have always been a highly musical people and all the Lenhosseks were musically talented. Albert's mother, a tiny woman, had started out to be an opera singer. Her family had been distressed by this choice and sent her to audition with the great composer Gustav Mahler who was conductor of the Budapest Opera that year. Mahler listened carefully and then told her to get married instead, since her voice was not "big enough" for the concert stage. She still sang and played the piano in private. Her brother Mihaly accompanied her on the cello, and Albert's older brother Pal (Paul, in English) played the violin. He was so good that he eventually became a professional musician, whose specialty was a tour-de-force in which he performed two concertos in a single program. Albert loved music too, but had no special talent. When he practiced the piano and made a mistake, his grandmother would call in the correct note from three rooms away. The Lenhosseks could be so intolerably gifted!

The boys enjoyed teasing their grandmother, who was a very clever, but proper lady. Emma Bossonyi was still studying French when she was past seventy. (The Hungarian literati were incurable Francophiles.) She never went anywhere without a French dictionary in her pocket. The boys also had their own very complete lexicon.

> We would look up some dirty word in French, a real dirty one, and ask my grandmother, innocently, "What does this word mean?"
>
> She didn't know, and said, enthusiastically, "I'll look it up in my dictionary."
>
> A few minutes later she became very red in the face and said, "I just can't find it."

It was during these early teenage years that Albert developed a feeling of inferiority that he never was quite able to shake, and that provided part of his drive for success. Everyone around him was so brilliant and talented. By contrast with them, he himself was decidedly slow. Like Albert Einstein, he did not do well in school. "The fact is," he recalled,

> I must have been a very dull child. Nothing much happened to me. When I was in school I had to cram and cram. I hated books. I hated everything. Nobody taught me how to live and open up my brain, and how wonderful it is to know and to learn and to understand the world and create something.

He reacted by becoming blasé. "I said, 'What the hell shall I do in life? Shall I go abroad and study? What the hell for?' " He was doing so poorly in school that his family had to provide him with a tutor just so he could pass his courses.

Occasionally, without his uncle knowing it, Albert would sneak a look at his big physiology books. Lenhossek was an ardent disciple of the Spanish physiologist (and Nobel laureate) Ramon y Cajal. One of these big books was Ramon y Cajal's pioneering work on the structure of the human brain. "Of course, I didn't understand a word, but I had a craving to know what was in it."

When he reached sixteen, "Something suddenly changed in my brain." It was a kind of intellectual puberty and he lusted after knowledge. Within a few weeks, he read twenty books—simultaneously, he claimed. In his last two years of the Gymnasium (high school) he became an outstanding student. Uncle Mihaly was too wrapped up in his own career, however, to notice the remarkable change in his nephew. He had type-cast Albert as a dullard—a Szent-Gyorgyi perhaps, but not a real Lenhossek. One evening, at dinner, Albert screwed up his courage and announced that he had decided on a career. He would become a medical researcher. If he thought he would please his uncle with this announcement, he was in for a terrible shock. Mihaly stopped eating. There was simply no place in science for such a dim-wit, he explained to the family. The fourth generation would undo the reputation of the previous three!

Albert was wounded by this insensitive frankness, but persisted. He intended to become a scientist. As a compromise, Mihaly finally suggested a career as a cosmetologist, manufacturing women's makeup. "No, I want to be a medical researcher!" Albert insisted. After much arguing back and forth, Lenhossek conceded that pharmacy was a distinct possibility. Or perhaps—just perhaps—dentistry. But medical science was out of the question. "No! No! No!" he screamed.

Arguments like this cut Albert to the quick, and were to leave him with a lifelong defensiveness about his own intelligence. But they also spurred him on to even greater efforts to prove himself to his family, and especially to his accomplished uncle: he was the principal male role model in Szent-Gyorgyi's life. In defense of Lenhossek, it has been suggested that his comments were meant to urge Albert on, a cunning (if brutal) example of reverse psychology in action.

When Albert actually graduated from the Gymnasium with honors, Lenhossek relented even further. Albert would be allowed to study medicine at the Budapest Medical School where he himself was a professor. But there was a catch: he had to agree to specialize in proctology, the study of the human anus and rectum. The reason for this odd choice was that Mihaly himself suffered from hemorrhoids and was desperately seeking relief. He had finally found a use for his dull nephew.

And so, in September 1911, days before his eighteenth birthday, Albert Szent-Gyorgyi entered Budapest Medical School. It was not long before he was doing original research and writing up his results. His first scientific paper, published in a German anatomy journal when he was still a teenager, dealt, predictably, with the epithelium of the anus.[4]

It was not what he would have chosen for himself, but it was a start. In later years, he often quipped: "Because of my uncle I started science at the wrong end."

2

RISKY BUSINESS

By the time Albert reached medical school he was a remarkably determined young man. He now believed he could achieve great things, and acted accordingly. In part, of course, this new self-confidence was based on pride in his illustrious background. The Lenhosseks formed part of the aristocracy of science and it seemed only natural that he would follow in their footsteps. In part, it was simply the arrogance of youth. But it was around this time that Albert first recognized what he referred to as his "special gift." This was his intuitive ability to look at a problem and divine, if not the solution, then the correct question to ask. It was almost as if he could speak directly to nature, "hear her voice," as he later put it, and translate that feeling into action. This almost mystical feeling, akin to a poet's or artist's inspiration, was to remain the basis of his "scientific method" for the rest of his life. It was why he was never overawed by scholarship. Other people's opinions mattered little to him. What did matter was to get his hands on the materials and set to work.

In helping him to do this, medical school was a disaster. It was designed to produce medical practitioners, not brilliant scientists. And Albert scorned medicine. Later on, in desperate circumstances, he would try to turn this early training to account, but at no time did he seriously entertain the idea of becoming a dedicated physician. In fact, he looked down on doctors as being largely uneducated and uninterested in the science of the human body.

Nor had any of his illustrious ancestors been interested in humdrum medical practice either. To be a Lenhossek meant solely to be interested in biological questions at the highest, most theoretical level.

Albert was in medical school because there was nowhere else to go to get training in the biological sciences. There were no Ph.D. programs in biology in Hungary at the time. If one wanted to be a researcher, one became a medical doctor. It was that simple. But Albert hated the rigmarole and when Albert Szent-Gyorgyi hated something, he simply did not do it. After a few months of torturous boredom at the University's main campus on Muzeum St., he stopped going to classes. Instead, he began to take the tram to the outskirts of Pest, showing up at the pathology laboratory of his uncle Mihaly.[1]

Budapest's medical school was rather lax. As long as a student passed his exams—and Albert was always smart enough to do that—he did not really have to attend classes. Since the teaching was pedantic and predictable, he missed little by reading the textbooks instead. Besides, if any teacher noticed his absence, he would also note that this was the nephew of a most distinguished colleague.[2]

By contrast, Albert found work in Lenhossek's laboratory exciting. Here was what he was looking for. Uncle Mihaly was a demigod in his department. There was only one Professor in each university department, and his word was law. Albert wandered the long, green-and-white corridors and drank in the atmosphere: the medical texts in many languages, the heavy oak desks heaped high with papers, the tall windows shuttered from the traffic of the street. Most impressive of all were the laboratory rooms adjacent to his uncle's office on the second floor of the solid building. Here Albert studied the scientific instruments: dissecting and staining kits; scalpels, scissors, and microtomes for cutting tissues; and the various wonderful microscopes. (It was part of the family legend that his own grandfather, Imre Lenhossek, had brought the first microscope to Budapest.)

Uncle Mihaly was pleased by his nephew's sudden enthusiasm for science, but he retained some residual mistrust. He was not about to be swept up by Albert's adolescent mood. He had watched this boy change from a rather dull, inward child into a vibrant young man, but his job was to give some ballast to his sister's family, which had essentially been deserted by her husband. Lenhossek allowed Albert to work in the lab, but kept his distance. If Albert turned out to be flighty or ungifted then Mihaly himself would be untouched by embarrassment.

Albert found this attitude insulting and provocative. Nothing he said seemed able to convince his stolid uncle how much he had changed. For Albert had discovered himself, to an extent that few people ever do. A combination of factors (natural talent, latent insecurities, a desire to please) had led him to experimental science, not just as a career, but as a real *vocation*. He was not following this path because it was expected for a Lenhossek. Instead he seemed to have rediscovered in himself the same gift that had led his ancestors to the same subject. And this discovery brought him an exhilarating self-confidence. He was no longer the awkward teenager. In his white lab coat, handsome and rather dapper, he would mount the yellow electric tram for the long ride down Ulloi Avenue. In his spare time he would stroll down Budapest's spacious boulevards, looking at old volumes in the bookshop windows.

But the study of the anus—this was Lenhossek's grim little joke on his nephew! It was his testing-ground, his rite of passage for the would-be scientist. Here, surely, was a subject designed to discourage any dilettante, by emphasizing the earthy, prosaic, even repulsive nature of so much work in anatomy. Albert hardly seemed to notice. He revelled in the chance to work with slides and microscopes and show off his own intelligence by asking the right questions. He may have started science at "the wrong end," but this was soon to be righted.

After working on proctological problems for almost a year, Albert was allowed to move on to subjects of greater delicacy. He chose the structure of the eyeball. In fact, he performed this complex anatomical work so well that by his third year of medical school he had produced several excellent scientific papers on the subject. These were written in German, then the obligatory language for Central European scientists. (Hungarian *scientists* were as pro-German as their literary counterparts were pro-French.) He studied what are called the hyaloidal, or glassy, bodies in the eyes of amphibians, reptiles, pigs, and finally man. With their insightful comments, and exact engravings, these articles by a student of twenty, published in leading journals, created quite a stir in Budapest's scientific circles. Albert seemed well on his way towards becoming an outstanding anatomist in the Lenhossek tradition.[3]

Beneath the surface, however, all was not well. There were many unseen conflicts and problems in Albert's life. Like most twenty-year-olds, he was caught in a hormonal hurricane. He brooded on sex—or, rather, his lack of opportunity. He had a very strong drive and was himself attractive to women, with his curly hair, open smile, and bright blue eyes. There was simply very little he could do about it. Hungary was part-Catholic, part-Protestant, part-Jewish—and all-Puritan. All religious factions united on one thing: that pre-marital sex was taboo, so taboo that it could not even be discussed.

In my class of society one was not even supposed to talk to a "decent" girl, even in her parents' home, without the presence of a chaperone, usually some elderly lady. Girls were considered the more attractive the less they knew about sex.

All of these customs had the pretense of morality, and caused no end of suffering, creating unbalanced minds and psychopathic aberrations.

Of course, so-called good society turned a blind eye to wide-scale prostitution and the wholesale seduction of working-class women. Many Hungarian men of the time (including his older brother, Pal) cultivated reputations as playboys. But Albert simply could not patronize prostitutes or form a liaison with a shop girl. He was a sensitive young person, who dreamed of romantic love. Brothels were for brawling soldiers. He was trapped.

Another social problem was his negative feeling about his fellow medical students. He had acquaintances, but made no lasting friends in college. The other students at the medical school seemed to him absurdly self-inflating. Doctors-in-training (himself included) were allowed to practice on the poor clinic patients:

> We had no end of useless drugs and we prescribed them in the most complex formulas, all in Latin, so that our patients would not understand them. The patients would thus be kept in the dark about our business, which we tried to keep a mystery.

After two years in the anatomy laboratory (1911–1913), however, Albert was dissatisfied. Not that his work there had not been remarkably successful. Yet there was something static about the study of anatomy; it dealt with dead tissues. What made biology so exciting for him was that it dealt with a subject of endless fascination: the phenomenon of life itself.

Life, he felt, was a kind of miracle. Why should inert materials—atoms and molecules—move, respond, and eventually become self-conscious organisms? This was the question he wanted to answer, the same question, really, that motivated the great artists and writers throughout the ages. Now, he thought, science provided a way of answering it.

"Morphology told me little about life," he complained. Neither anatomy nor morphology could ever answer the question 'What is life?' They were just pedantic disciplines, brilliant exercises that would never get at the core of the problem. To understand life one had to study the actual functioning of living systems. In other words, one had to study *physiology*. Thus in 1913, Albert left his uncle's laboratory and went to work in the physiology department, back on the main campus of the University.[4]

The move marked a break between Albert and his youthful model. To Lenhossek this desertion of anatomy was a confirmation of his worst fears. Albert was flighty, poetic, and unreliable. For Albert, however, it was decisive. At twenty, intellectually speaking, he was on his own. And despite Lenhossek's reservations, there was nothing erratic about this change. In fact, it was dictated by the intellectual currents of the times.

In the late nineteenth century there had been major breakthroughs in the study of organic chemistry. Urea and carbohydrates had been synthesized, and such substances as fats, blood, and bile were analyzed. Justus von Liebig, Friedrich Wohler, and Emil Fischer, obscure names today, were heroes to the young intellectuals of that day. But the greatest hero of all was Claude Bernard (1813–1878), an outstanding experimental scientist and provocative philosopher. Metabolism, Bernard had taught, was more than just the mechanical destruction of foodstuffs by the animal's digestive system. "Animals in the physiologic state," Bernard had said, "are able, like the vegetables, to *create* and destroy sugar."[5]

Claude Bernard was to remain Albert's life-long hero, whose portrait always would grace his laboratory walls. This was not only because of Bernard's intense dedication to experimental science, but also his ability and willingness to combine keen observations with bold philosophical ideas.[6]

Before Albert could accomplish much in physiology, however, his career—along with almost everyone else's—was calamitously interrupted. On 28 June 1914 Archduke Franz Ferdinand of Austria-Hungary and his wife were assassinated by a Serbian nationalist at Sarajevo. World War I had begun.

As it happened, that summer found Albert already in uniform. All students had to serve in the armed forces, and he was doing his obligatory three-month stint when the war was declared. With thousands of other raw recruits he was quickly dispatched to the Eastern front, as Austria-Hungary and its Central Powers partners went on the offensive.

Life had taken an incredible turn. From the cloistered laboratories of the university, and the cultured world of lilac-scented Budapest, Albert suddenly found himself knee-deep in the mud and blood of Poland. The boy who had scorned the practical lessons of anatomy and surgery found himself desperately trying to patch the shattered bodies of wounded soldiers, many of them boys younger than himself.

Budapest had given its soldiers a rousing send-off. Strange as it may seem, the onset of war brought "an immeasurable sigh of relief" to some people.[7] The lingering "peace that was not a peace" of the prewar years was now over. Nearly hysterical mobs greeted the out-break of the war and posters went up everywhere, showing the elderly Emperor Franz Josef kneeling in prayer or the Hungarian cavalry charging forward on their famous horses. But the war did not go as planned, and soon became mired down in a horrendous series of bloody battles. Tacticians called this the "war of attrition" but to Albert and many of his contemporaries, it was a reversion to barba-rism and a sweeping negation of all the values they had been taught. The seeds of radicalism were being planted in an entire generation.

How could such a catastrophe have occurred, they wondered, in a world that had, a short while before, seemed so orderly and pro-gressive? Albert, not alone, eventually discovered the cause of the war in the greed of the ruling elites. All the mentally-sclerotic rulers of Europe seemed to blame, but the Austro-Hungarian ruling class seemed especially culpable. And the fact that his father's family was, in a sense, part of that class made the betrayal seem quite personal [see Appendix A.].

Albert never studied political economy, but his own explanation of the war's origin was based on a crude understanding of economic factors:

> In those days, the Austro-Hungarian Empire was very powerful and rich. The Austro-Hungarians cut off the Serbs' lifeline by forbidding the export of hogs through Hungary. The Serbs became restive. A Serbian student shot the Archduke and his wife while they were driving through Sarajevo. This was a most welcome opportunity for the militarist cliques in Vienna, Berlin and St. Petersburg. Our secretary of defense put before the Emperor fake telegrams according to which the Serbian army had broken into Hungary. This left no alternative to the Emperor and he had to mobilize the army. Berlin followed suit and so did the Russian Tsar, and World War I was on.

Certainly there was more to it than that, but by 1915, Hungarians were becoming disgusted with the war and seeking solutions. Writers such as Endre Ady spoke out courageously against the military. The nobility, financiers, even the royal family were widely rumored to be moving their bank accounts to Switzerland. In 1916–1917 a strike wave broke out across Hungary. That year the Russians advanced rapidly and soon controlled most of the passes of the Carpathian Mountains. The Hungarian plains and Budapest itself lay before them, an untouched plum less than two hundred miles away.

But the tide of battle suddenly turned, as it often did throughout that terrible conflict. The Tsar's troops, with their weak supply lines, soon ran short of ammunition. Hungary's German allies began a fresh offensive to the north and the Russians were forced to retreat. It was now the Hungarians' turn to take the offensive. Two huge armies soon faced one another across the Dnestr River in the Ukraine.

That summer, the river flooded, sending water six or seven feet over its banks. The Hungarian generals believed that no fighting was now possible in these muddy conditions, and consequently moved a large part of their reserves elsewhere. The Russians, realizing the Hungarians' weakness, attacked with ferocious determination. Their heavy guns pounded the west bank of the river and they even bombed the Hungarian trenches with primitive aircraft. The final attack, when it came, was led by Cossack cavalrymen who stripped naked and swam the swollen river, guns held high above their heads. It was a terrifying sight. The Cossacks seized a beachhead and held it for the arrival of the regular troops.

The Hungarians fled in terror, and were cut down right and left. Those who did not die from the bullets, shells, and bombs soon succumbed to septic infections or the waves of cholera, typhoid, smallpox, and typhus. In fact, all those plagues which an earlier generation, typified by the Lenhosseks, had banished with vigorous public health measures, now reasserted themselves with a vengeance. "It is surprising how swiftly history can progress," the Hungarian writer Gyula Illyes reflected bitterly, "whenever it can do so in an inhuman direction."

It was therefore almost miraculous that Albert survived at all. In fact, in this and previous battles he had distinguished himself for bravery and was decorated with the Silver Medal for Valor—not for killing, but for risking his life to save wounded soldiers. But his heart was never in such heroics. In fact, he was filled with a bitter hatred for such medals and especially for the old men who gave them to dying youth.

At this point, something inside him snapped. He had survived the carnage of the Dnestr catastrophe but had to ask himself what possible reason he could have to go on fighting? This was his personal dilemma, but it was also the thought running through the minds of millions of soldiers and civilians, on both sides of the conflict. The faith in authority that normally held society together was coming unglued. Soon, in fact, whole legions would throw down their weapons in disgust, or turn them on their officers. Revolution was in the air.

"About the third year of the war [i.e., 1916]," Albert said, "I could see that the whole war was a swindle of a little clique and that they were sacrificing the whole nation for nothing. We had lost the war, but still they sent us into battle with the idea that 'something may happen.' "

A few days after the Dnestr rout, Albert made his own decision. He stood alone in a pine forest on the west bank of the river. He knew that if he rejoined his shattered unit it would just be a matter of time before he himself would be dead in a ditch. His duty was no longer to a military clique that had managed so efficiently to ruin his beloved nation, but to science. Slowly he lifted his rifle to his left underarm and fired, smashing the humerus bone.

This was risky business. If he were caught disabling himself, his officers would have gladly hanged him as a deserter. Yet he had planned his move carefully. As a medic he knew that a simple flesh wound would only have warranted local treatment. A shot in the hand might get him sent back home, but would also make it impossible for him to do medical research in the future. The foot, he knew, contained too many small bones—foot wounds rarely healed properly. And so, by a process of elimination, he decided on his target.

Bleeding, he ran back to the trenches. Fortunately for him, no one detected the deception, and he was put on a hospital train to Budapest. He had spent almost two years in the trenches, under almost continual fire.

The wound itself was not serious—it healed quickly—but the significance of the deed was great. To shoot yourself to get out of battle went against everything Albert had been taught to believe. "Like many others," he reflected, "I was born and brought up in a feudalistic world. It was deeply ingrained in us that dying for the Emperor was the greatest honor."

In a world in which the smallest slight to one's honor might result in a duel, desertion was the very height of cowardice. Yet Albert had proven that he was no coward by his previous actions and honors. The war had simply wrought a tremendous change in his mind. Like others of his generation he had become radicalized, although he was almost devoid of any revolutionary theory. And once Albert Szent-Gyorgyi became convinced of something, he acted—regardless of the consequences.

While nursing his broken arm, Albert was able to re-enter Budapest Medical School to complete the one year of schooling that remained. But so much had changed. The elegant city was now filled with demoralized soldiers and desperate civilians. Restaurants were forbidden to serve sugar, and grains were strictly rationed. The newspapers were carefully censored but, all the same, contained disquieting rumors of the impending break between Austria and Hungary. The city was strangely quiet, for the church bells had all been melted down to make bullets and shells.

To complete his medical degree, Albert had to pass some surgical examinations. But more than ever, he hated practical medicine. At the university, discipline and, to a certain extent, integrity had broken down. "In that great disorganization," he said, "if one paid the attendant of the surgical clinic fifty pengos [ten dollars] he would tell you which patients were going to be presented at the oral exam that day."

On the afternoon Albert was scheduled to take the exam there were only two patients left for examination, one with a hernia, the other with breast cancer. Albert was sitting in the hall and the attendant motioned to him in sign language what sort of cases were coming up. Albert quickly checked his anatomy text and found fifty pages on hernias of every description. It was impossible for him to read all that. But for breast cancer there were only ten pages. "So I motioned to him, 'Give me the breast cancer case.'" Albert quickly read the ten pages, took the exam, and passed. "But that was all due to the war," he said. "And to me it was a great relief because I could never have studied surgery. It's such a stupid subject, has no intellectual meaning or connections, so I just somehow got through the exams owing to the war."

The school authorities were, in fact, looking the other way. The army needed doctors, and so the university turned a blind eye to such practices. In June 1917 Albert Szent-Gyorgyi, twenty-three years old, graduated as a doctor from Budapest Medical School.

And while this was happening the Russian front collapsed. But this did not mean an end to the fighting for the Hungarians. The government decided to use its Eastern front troops to attack Italy, in the hope of regaining the lost provinces of Lombardy and Venezia. Albert was remobilized.

The previous fall, he had met a beautiful young woman and set his mind on marrying her. Her name was Cornelia (Nelly) Demeny. According to the physicist Zoltan Bay, who knew her as a student, Nelly was the most beautiful and intelligent girl he had ever met. She was also underage for marriage, but Albert used all of his considerable charm to get her away from her worried parents. He showered her with gifts, and on Christmas Day 1916 he showed up at her doorstep with a pony and cart to take a romantic drive.

The Demenys fully intended their daughter to get a good education. Albert promised that he would see to her further development just as solicitously as they would have. On 15 September 1917 his persistence won out and the young couple was married in the Calvinist Church in Pest, where his own parents had been married and where he and his brothers had been baptized.

Albert and Nelly were a handsome, well-matched couple. Nelly was energetic, loving, and outgoing. She was an excellent athlete—a professional-level tennis player. They enjoyed swimming, hiking, and mountaineering together. She came from a wealthy and influential family, her father then being Postmaster General of Hungary. He was a man of "good social feeling," Albert said, and like his daughter a prominent sportsperson. He is best remembered for having introduced skiing into Hungary. In all, it was a good and proper marriage.

In late September 1917 young Dr. Szent-Gyorgyi was sent off to northern Italy. Here he was assigned to a clinic well behind the front lines, near the Italian city of Udine. Since he was an officer now, Nelly was allowed to accompany him. It was certainly a strange honeymoon: Albert and Nelly set up housekeeping in a little cottage right in the midst of the war.

Although their life was tranquil, fifty miles away nine Austro-Hungarian and six German divisions were pushing the Italians across the Tagliamento and the Piave rivers in a particularly bloody campaign.

Albert's passionately anti-war attitudes came out in many ways. For instance, next to his house there lived an Austrian general. Albert knew the man was a general because of the wide red stripe on his pants. But the general had a problem of incontinence, and every day his trousers had to be washed and hung out on the line to dry.

Contemplating these pants, Albert reflected that "even if the general is a stupid fool, the essential thing about him is his red stripe." And so he would facetiously break into a march step and salute every time he passed those pants. If the general had seen him, Albert might have been court-martialed for disrespect to a pair of trousers, but luckily Albert was never caught. "But that just tells me that I was already completely a revolutionary by then," he later recalled.

In the fall of 1918, his anti-establishment attitude finally caught up with him. Next to the building in which he worked there was a large hospital. The administrator of the hospital was a *Privatdocent* (a kind of adjunct professor) from Vienna, who was trying to make a name for himself in the medical field. Some of the 250,000 Italian casualties from this campaign were housed in this hospital, and the Viennese teacher decided to use some of them for gruesome human experiments.[8]

Although it was not his direct concern, Albert could not keep silent once he learned what was going on. He protested to the *Privatdocent*.

"They are only prisoners, only Italians," the administrator told him, nonchalantly. Shocked by the inhumanity of this reply, Albert immediately went to headquarters and denounced the man. The *Privatdocent* in question had three bars on his uniform, however, while Albert had only one. As a consequence it was Albert, not the administrator, who was transferred. As a punishment, he was sent to a malaria-ridden swamp in northern Italy. Nelly, already pregnant, was sent back to Budapest.

"Everyone got tropical malaria in those swamps and died within a few months," he recalled. "It was a virtual death sentence." Just then, however, the southern front collapsed and the Austro-Hungarians retreated in headlong flight. Officers abandoned their troops and whole armies of soldiers flooded into the railroad stations, trying to get home. In all, forty-five Central Powers divisions disintegrated or were captured by the Allies.

Albert fortuitously avoided this debacle. For on 3 October 1918 Nelly had given birth to a daughter, Cornelia, or "Little Nelly," named after herself. Since officers were allowed to visit home if their wives had given birth, Albert invoked this right to get out of his swampy hell-hole. "They allowed me to go to see my own daughter, and while I was at home, the war collapsed."[9]

By November the great conflict was over, the European combatants exhausted. The Austro-Hungarian Empire split apart and lay in ruins. One set of statistics, chosen from many, gives a hint at the devastation experienced in those war years. The Empire as a whole had mobilized 7,800,000 men. Of these, 1,200,000 were killed or died; 3,620,000 were wounded; and 2,200,000 were missing or made prisoner.[10]

Whatever relief was brought by the end of the war was tempered by widescale hunger, disease, and social unrest. The Szent-Gyorgyis were simply happy to be alive. They could hardly imagine that for them, as for most Hungarians, the worst was yet to come.

3

1919

Albert returned to Budapest to find his family in turmoil. On 17 December 1916 his father had died of a stroke, leaving his affairs in the hands of Albert's older brother, Pal.[1]

To hear Albert tell it, Pal was an unreliable adventurer, who had captured his family's trust with his abounding charm. Above all, Albert resented the place Pal occupied, as first-born, in their mother's heart. Relations between the two boys had never been good. While Albert had to plug away at his classes, trying to win his mother's favor with hard work, Pal breezed through everything. He got expelled from one school after another as a "good for nothing." Like their father, he managed to finish his courses at the university, but his real interest in life was gambling.

"He was a big society playboy," Albert said. "He played cards, lost enormous sums, and my poor mother had to stick up for him always, borrowing money here and there from moneylenders to get him out of trouble."

This gambling streak showed up in his response to the political crisis which wracked Hungary after the war. Late in 1918 a revolution broke out in Budapest. The immediate cause was the loss of the war, but the revolt unleashed pent-up social conflicts, of class against class and nationality against nationality, which dated back hundreds of years.

In January 1919 Hungary became a Republic and Count Mihaly Karolyi became its first president. Despite his noble origins, Karolyi was a dedicated radical—the "Red Count," as he was called. His program included a declaration of independence from Austria; an end to Hungary's semi-feudal social system; and a better deal for the Serbs, Romanians, Czechs, and other national minorities, who had constituted half the population in the prewar period. Karolyi inaugurated the reform by dividing his own huge estate among the former peasants.

Albert's sympathies were with Karolyi's reformist brand of socialism, but he himself belonged to no political party. He was unimpressed when he actually heard Karolyi speak. "He had a cleft palate and was hard to understand. He meant well, but I was not interested at all." All Albert wanted was a chance to get on with his scientific work.

Not so brother Pal, a dashing officer who now became a fervent socialist and follower of the Count. Pal, the political gambler, moved north of Budapest and started a socialist newspaper in Esztergom. This charming town is called the "Vatican of Hungary," for historically it is the seat of the Roman Catholic Church. Needless to say, the clergy did not appreciate Pal's invasion of their territory.

Karolyi was pro-Western, but when he reached out a hand of friendship to the Allies he was spurned and betrayed. Most of the new Republic—with French connivance—was soon occupied by Serbian, Romanian, and Czechoslovakian troops. Hungary was simply being dismembered.[2]

Pal was also something of a financial speculator. Toward the end of 1918 he foresaw that the Bolsheviks would soon come to power in Hungary. "Communism is coming," he told a hastily-called family meeting, "and they will take everything we have. So I'll sell it and at least we'll have the money." The country estate had been sold during the war, when their father had become too ill to farm. The proceeds had been reinvested in Budapest real estate. Pal now sold this property at bargain rates. The prices were painfully low, but at least, he said, the family had cash in hand. No sooner had he done this, however, than spiraling inflation began to take hold. Eventually this "hard cold cash" was useful only as wallpaper.

At the end of 1918, Karolyi resigned in disgrace and the government fell into the hands of the fledgling Communist party, led by a fiery agitator, Bela Kun.[3] From January to August 1919 the Communists ran Hungary or, at least, the capital. When they came to power they sent a squad to arrest Pal, a rival socialist. He jumped out of a window and hid all night in a railway car as the Communist patrol searched for him in vain. Finally, a combination of emigré reactionaries and Allied powers overthrew the short-lived Red regime, and Bela Kun fled.

The leader of the right-wing forces entered Budapest on his stallion—quite literally the "man on the white horse." His name was Miklos Horthy. Officially, he was simply the "regent" of the king, but

Horthy refused to allow the royal pretender to enter the country. Instead, he himself ruled Hungary as a virtual dictatorship for the next twenty-five years.[4] Horthy had been an admiral in the old Austro-Hungarian Empire, in the days when Hungary still had access to the sea. Now it had only Lake Balaton in which to sail. Under Horthy, Hungary became derisively known as "the kingdom without a king led by the admiral without a navy."

"Horthy," Albert reflected, sardonically, "was a good soldier and narrow, as a soldier should be. He said, 'You must take these Communists and shoot them!' That is how a soldier solves social problems."

Pal was arrested by the clergy's representatives and denounced as a dangerous Communist, which he was not. "He sat several months in jail and was released because they found that he had done nothing wrong."

In fact, it was his family name and social standing that saved him. Many ordinary working people, who had done far less than he, were summarily slaughtered in the reprisals. The Jews, who constituted a fifth of Budapest's population, were a special target (Kun and many members of his Central Committee were Jewish). Horthy decreed the notorious Numerus Clausus of 1920 which set a strict limit on the number of Jews allowed in the universities.[5]

While Horthy restored confiscated property to its original owners, this did nothing for the Szent-Gyorgyis, for they had sold their real estate of their own free will. Pal, through his financial maneuvering, had managed to lose almost everything.

Pal became desperate. He had several "fantastic ideas," most of which involved black- or gray-marketeering. For instance, since food in the capital was terribly scarce, he used some of the remaining money to buy a truck. With this, he intended to purchase food in the countryside and sell it at a big profit in the city. His truck wound up in a ditch, however, and the produce rotted by the side of the road. "Everything he did," Albert said, with a bit of barely-concealed glee, "turned out wrong."

The younger brother, Imre, was little better in Albert's eyes. He eventually left the city and went to work as a forester. Albert never spoke about him except with apathy or disdain, in terms very similar to those reserved for his father. The one thing about Imre which Albert did find interesting, however, was that he was a dowser, who could locate hidden subterranean water. "I feel things," he used to say, "I can feel water underground." When pressed for an explanation he would add, "I know how things are," which sounded remarkably similar to one of Albert's own pronouncements about science. Imre eventually became a successful lumber dealer. He and Albert soon lost touch.[6]

Not surprisingly, Albert decided to get out of Budapest as soon as possible. He applied for a small research position in Poszony, which was still part of Hungary. From 1 January till 21 September 1919 he was an assistant at the Pharmacological Institute of the Hungarian Elizabeth University, working under Prof. G. Mansfeld.

Only about one hundred miles from Budapest, Poszony was a cultured and pleasant city on the Danube, where Mozart and Liszt had spent time. It was the first city to the west of Budapest with an important old university, founded in 1465. Albert and Nelly took baby Nelly with them, travelling light, with hardly any possessions. Albert found a small apartment. In other times, this might have been an enjoyable interlude in their lives but now poverty made everything difficult.

Mansfeld was professor of pharmacology and Albert was interested in learning something about drugs. It was coincidental that Albert's great-grandfather, the first Mihaly Lenhossek, had started out in just this city—as a druggist's apprentice. Now his descendant was returning to the scene to study drugs. Pharmacology was first developing as a science. From an intellectual point of view, the appeal of drugs was that they were relatively uncomplicated. Physiology now seemed to him too vast and complex a field to be conquered:

> I wanted to understand life. But I found the complexity of physiology overwhelming. And so I shifted to pharmacology, where at least one of the two partners, the drug, was simple.[7]

Together, he said, he and Mansfeld produced "a quite amusing paper in pharmacology." Albert demonstrated an ability to pick up new fields quickly, and to work well as a collaborator with more senior scientists.[8]

There was another young assistant in Mansfeld's lab, Carl F. Cori. Cori at twenty-three was a bit younger than Albert (who had turned twenty-five that fall). Cori's father had been a zoologist and director of the Marine Biology Station in Trieste, his home city. They had much in common. Both had also served in the Austro-Hungarian army on the Italian front. Cori became Albert's first real scientific colleague, and Poszony was the start of a friendship that would last sixty years.

Mansfeld's lab was a good place to be. Mansfeld himself was always full of new ideas. "Most of them were wrong," Albert later quipped, "but they were ideas all the same." This was quite a change from Budapest, where many of the medical school professors seemed to have no ideas at all. The problem was that Mansfeld and his young student were *too* alike; they were both dreamers. Albert had fantastic notions, wild schemes, and grandiose plans. What he needed was intellectual ballast. Instead, Mansfeld would get inspired by the younger man and join in his flights of fancy. "He had a very bad influence on me because I like fantasies. I'm carried away much too easily by these fantasies."

Not all the excitement was of the scientific variety.

In 1919 war broke out between Hungary and the newly-created Republic of Czechoslovakia. The Hungarians resisted, but the Czechs seized Poszony, renaming it Bratislava. The Szent-Gyorgyis, with their Hungarian passports, suddenly found themselves strangers on their native soil.[9]

To visit his beloved mother now became a life-and-death proposition. The only way to return to Hungary was to cross the Danube, which is rather wide at that point. Such crossings were illegal and the new Czech government ordered its border guards "to shoot on sight any Hungarian crossing the Danube in either direction." And so the Hungarians in Bratislava operated a spy network to tell them where the crossing was relatively safe.

One dark winter evening in 1919 Albert left his family and set out to cross the river. Twelve people crowded into a little ferry boat. As they plowed through the water the gunwall of the overburdened craft hung just inches above the water line. In the darkness, Albert became aware of the presence of a beautiful young woman next to him. Looking closer he realized she was a nun. He spoke to her and she answered shyly. Her name, she said, was Sister Angelica and she was trying to return to Hungary to visit her Mother Superior. The boat swayed menacingly and Angelica spontaneously grabbed hold of Albert's arm for support.

Albert was handsome, not tall, but athletic, with curly hair and piercing eyes. He was also incurably romantic. The two young people spent the next hour or two together arm-in-arm, huddled on that little boat. The fact that he was married, and that she taken vows of celibacy, only added piquancy to the relationship. Albert was stimulated by this "quite unusual" scene, but "didn't abuse her confidence." Instead, he comforted her with calming words. When they reached the Hungarian side of the river they parted company. In wartime there were many such brief, intense friendships, which flared up and just as suddenly died.

Upon his return trip, Albert was not so lucky, and had to stand all night in deep snow to avoid the Czech patrols. When he finally got home he came down with an attack of pneumonia. This was serious. A year before several million people had died of this disease in the great pandemic. Pneumonia then had a sixty percent mortality rate.

Albert was taken to the hospital and was soon given up for lost by his friends and family. Even Prof. Mansfeld shrugged his shoulders in painful resignation.

One day, a feverish Albert opened his eyes and saw a vision: a beautiful angel smiling down at him. Since he was a freethinker, this was a shock. He soon realized that this angel was not a hallucination, but the real thing—his friend, Sister Angelica. She was a nurse at this very hospital and tended him day and night, giving him injections, and eventually helping him pull through. This was, he reflected, "his reward for being so generous to her."

On 10 September the treaty of St. Germain was signed and the short war was over. Poszony formally became a part of Czechoslovakia. Elizabeth University was rebaptized the University of Bratislava and Mansfeld, along with the other Hungarian professors, was dismissed. (He eventually found a post at the new University of Pecs, in western Hungary.) The Szent-Gyorgyis, Coris, and hundreds of thousands of other Austro-Hungarians were summarily ordered out of the country. Their own scientific equipment, formerly Hungarian property, was simply expropriated by the new state.

Szent-Gyorgyi and Cori had been through years of trench warfare and were unimpressed by the new decree. They decided they had more claim to their laboratory equipment than the Czechs did. If they had to leave, their microscopes, Bunsen burners, and retorts would leave with them. And so they devised a scheme, noteworthy for its youthful recklessness, to move the entire laboratory, swan-necked glassware and all, back onto Hungarian soil.

First they packed everything in enormous wooden crates. Then they themselves dressed up in old, soiled workclothes and, masquerading as movingmen, got it onto handcarts. In the darkness, they pushed these carts across the campus, down the cobblestone streets of the old city, and through the Fisherman's Gate to the water's edge. Going down an unanticipated flight of stairs, however, one of the cases got loose and slipped out of its straps. It came crashing down with an enormous racket and Cori and Szent-Gyorgyi stared at each other in horror. They expected to hear whistles and the tramp of hobnailed boots on the cobblestones at any moment. Instead, there was only the silence of the old town. They laughed quietly to themselves, continued on their way, and loaded the crates onto a river steamer for the ten-hour trip to Budapest.

"That was quite amusing," Albert later commented. "Life was full of this nonsensical danger; to be able to work at science, you sometimes had to risk your life." If they had been caught, world science would never have known the loss: for not just Albert, but Carl Cori and his young wife, Gerty, all went on to win Nobel Prizes in medicine.[10]

Back in Budapest, Albert found his family in disarray. By going to Poszony, he had avoided the turmoil of the "Budapest Soviet." But things were still chaotic. The currency was shrinking. Although he despised his father's financial dealings, Albert now showed some business acumen himself: he gathered what was left of the family's wealth and converted it into British currency. Britain (or at least the pound) seemed like a beacon of stability in a storm-tossed world. This was, in fact, the first sign of Albert's Anglophilia, his deep love and faith in everything British.

The remains of the estate came to about 1,000 British pounds. He gave his mother 400 and kept 600 for himself, his wife, and daughter to live on during the next few years. No provision was made for his brothers, both of whom had already left the capital.

At this point Albert could conceivably have settled down in Budapest; he had his medical degree and his family had connections. But he was unwavering in his determination to be a research scientist, and a *great* scientist at that. To do so, however, he would need real scientific training, something he certainly had not gotten at Budapest or even at Poszony.

To excel in science, it was assumed, a Hungarian had to go abroad. Albert decided to take the time-honored route of voluntary exile. So many Magyar intellectuals had already done this, that one found more distinguished Hungarian scientists and artists in Germany, England, or (eventually) the United States than in Hungary itself. Leo Szilard, Edward Teller, Eugene Ormandy, John von Neumann—these were just some of the outstanding Hungarians who left Hungary to make their names in the West.

Albert's plans were not clear. But, in his fantasies at least, he may have had in mind to return in triumph to his homeland after a period of wandering. This, after all, was what uncle Mihaly, his grandfather, and great-grandfather had done. Leaving Hungary was an old Hungarian tradition. Not everyone made it home, however.[11]

Although Albert later played down her role, his wife was an unusually devoted and courageous woman to embrace this life of poverty and wandering. Nelly was something of a dare-devil, who regarded physical hardship as an adventure. Perhaps only someone brought up in comfort and security could feel that carefree. In any case, despite the uncertainties and difficulties of their life together, the young couple managed to enjoy themselves. All in all, at least in recollection, these were happy years.

Albert and Nelly shared a devotion to what he later called "that muscular romanticism." An old photo album shows Albert and his friends high up in snowy mountains, all of them dressed in Tyrolean costumes. The photo inscriptions are in German. This seems to have been a college camping trip, perhaps to the Carpathian mountains. Nelly came later, but she was "a very good companion" in this sort of life. "Women are very different," he later reflected. "A really 'femalish' woman would not have done for me then because I had this great urge to go out and have an intense physical life—to enjoy Nature."

Nevertheless, one suspects it was Albert's personality which motivated Nelly more than the life style. He had the kind of charm that attracted women and made them want to take care of him. This charisma not only made people follow him, but *want* to follow him. His young wife at this time proved herself ready to go with him to the ends of the earth. What was Albert's response? He needed and expected a woman's devotion and it is not difficult to see that this was precisely the kind of attention he had always sought, but rarely obtained, from his own mother.

In the last month of 1919, Albert and Nelly, with their baby, joined the exodus of intellectuals from war-torn Hungary. A decade of wandering—of obscurity, struggle, and privation—would ensue before Albert Szent-Gyorgyi would return in triumph to his native land.

4

DIGGING THE FOUNDATIONS

The next stop in Albert Szent-Gyorgyi's westward odyssey was Prague, the capital of the new republic of Czechoslovakia. A cosmopolitan center, Prague had a famous German university, and Albert went to study there. His teacher had a reputation as formidable as his name: Armin von Tschermak von Seysenegg.[1]

Why Tschermak?

The latest thing in physiology was measuring the electric potentials in cells. "I knew that if I wanted to be a physiologist," he said, "I must learn that. The mercury electrode was new, and Tschermak knew it, and he had a first laboratory assistant who taught me all that."

Albert spent only a few weeks there, but it was enough to kindle a lifelong fascination with the role of electricity in biology. In fact, it is impossible to understand Albert's later formulation of "electronic biology" without realizing that in his early, formative years bioelectricity was a topic of the greatest excitement.

Unlike Mansfeld, Tschermak had no personal influence on Albert. In fact, Szent-Gyorgyi hardly ever saw "Herr Professor." When he did, the German Tschermak insisted on calling him "Mr. Petofi." He apparently had the idea that all Hungarians were named after their greatest lyric poet, Sandor Petofi. This was almost certainly a national slight—Germans in general considered Hungarians quite inferior—but Albert never rose to the bait.

Carl Cori was also in Prague at this time, finishing up work for his medical degree. Albert and Carl saw a great deal of each other in those weeks. A persistent problem was the scarcity of tobacco. Almost all young men smoked, and these two were no exceptions. Tobacco not only was hard to come by after the war, but also not everyone in Czechoslovakia wanted to sell it to lowly Austro-Hungarians.

The Czechs felt that since they had been allies of the French and English, they wouldn't sell tobacco to anybody whom they thought was Hungarian or German.

Carl and I worked out a method which consisted of both of us going into a tobacco shop independently. Then I began to blubber in Italian, and of course, the storekeeper didn't understand.

He would ask, "Is there a customer who speaks Italian?"

Cori would then pop up and say, "I understand Italian."

The storekeeper then asked him to translate. Cori would listen and say, finally, "He wants cigarettes." In this way we'd get all the tobacco we wanted.

In December 1919 Albert and his family left Prague and moved to Berlin. He had been accepted to do postdoctoral research with a far more significant figure, Leonor Michaelis.

Michaelis was an interesting person. He had been born in 1875 and was thus forty-five when Albert met him. He had received his medical degree from Berlin and done postgraduate work at Freiburg where he had studied with the great Ehrlich. In 1913 he had developed the very important "Michaelis-Menten equation" which has been called one of the "earliest precise and quantitative laws applying to biochemical systems."

Michaelis, like Szent-Gyorgyi, was a highly intuitive person. His "insight into the working of the enzyme-substrate complex," it has been said, "was quite remarkable, as no hard evidence was to emerge of its existence" until the year of his death.[2]

Michaelis, however, had a problem.

He was a wonderful man with an enormous knowledge of all fields. He had an enormous memory. He was a great musician, a great organ player, a great mathematician. He was just a wonderful, fine fellow, but he was a Jew, which meant that he couldn't make a career in Berlin, which was already strongly anti-Jewish then.

Albert had grown up in a city that was one-fifth Jewish, and in which the Jews formed a prominent and by-and-large accepted part of the cultured middle class. This was Albert's first introduction to the growing anti-Semitism in postwar Europe and it made a deep impression on him.

Michaelis also had another problem: he was a self-proclaimed "biochemist" at a time when that field was not yet recognized as a real scientific specialty. Biochemists were thought to be useful mainly for carrying out routine laboratory tests to help practicing clinicians, not to make original scientific discoveries.[3]

Because of such prejudices, this great scientist was only allowed to work in a little room in the Krankenhaus am Urban hospital in Berlin. To compound matters, Michaelis was a pacer, who walked up and down like a caged lion as he ruminated. The problem here was that his newly-arrived Hungarian student also paced. Since the room was too narrow for both of them to walk in at the same time, they solved this by taking turns at walking up and down—one pacing, the other listening. It must have been quite a sight.

"I was in very close touch with him," said Albert, "but no special friendship developed. I was too young. I was just a nobody then, a young man, but he was very kind, taught me everything from which I profitted; but I developed no special ties."

The main thing Szent-Gyorgyi wanted to learn from Michaelis was how to work with the pH system, the variations in hydrogen ion concentration which is used as a measure of acidity. "Michaelis was the Pope of pH," said Albert, and he soaked up everything the older man had to say on the subject. But Albert acquired more from Michaelis than his knowledge of pH.

> If I learned something from him, it was especially on the human side—how one could have an enormous amount of knowledge and stay very modest. He was in fact excessively modest and withdrawn. How one could know more than all the rest and be more modest than all the rest—that I have learned from him.

The Weimar period in Berlin could have been exciting but Albert was running out of money. Six hundred pounds did not go very far, even with stringent economizing.

Albert asked Michaelis for a job, but the assistantship he offered paid next to nothing. In fact, Michaelis himself was about to leave Germany for Japan and then the United States, where ironically, this most basic of basic scientists would gain immortality as the inventor of the "Toni Home Permanent."[4]

Before leaving Hungary, the Szent-Gyorgyis had devised a fall-back plan. Albert would certainly try to get a decent-paying research position but if that failed to materialize, he would seek a job as a tropical doctor. Colonial physicians were the Foreign Legion of medicine. There were always positions available for M.D.s ready to stake out a new life in the jungle. Albert, reluctantly, was ready to make some use of his Budapest medical degree. And, after all, he might be able to do some research, too. Christiaan Eijkman had discovered the cause of beriberi in Indonesia, and Walter Reed had tracked down yellow fever in Cuba. These examples were fresh in everyone's mind. Perhaps Albert could become a "microbe hunter."

But the *reason* for the shortage of tropical doctors—that, the colonial authorities rarely spoke about. "They went down there to cure those epidemics," Albert said, "and died themselves of the infection. There were always empty places, especially in the Dutch colonies."

When he saw that he could never support his family on an assistant's meager allowance, Albert applied for admission to the prestigious Institute of Maritime and Tropical Diseases in Hamburg and was accepted. The Hamburg Institute was something of an anomaly: the Germans had built this outstanding colonial-medicine center and then promptly lost their budding colonial empire at Versailles.

From 1920 to 1921, therefore, Albert and his family lived in the northern German port city while he studied tropical medicine. He soon discovered that the course was quite demanding and he had no more interest in tropical medicine than in surgery or other practical problems.

At the same time, he tried to continue his own research. He published a paper on Avogadro's number—a paper which was hailed many years later by Linus Pauling for its originality.[5]

Trying to conserve their dwindling nest egg, the Szent-Gyorgyis rented a little basement room. Since most of their food budget went to feed the two Nellies, within about a year Albert had developed hunger edema, a swelling in his arms which was the first stage of overt starvation. In addition, as Hungarians, they were sometimes treated quite badly by their neighbors. "They looked upon us as Eastern European rubbish."

As their money ran out, Albert spent his last pounds on a pith helmet, tropical kit, box of scalpels, and other medical equipment. Without these tools he could hardly hope to take up his lucrative position. He was now, he reported, "ready to sell myself out for tropical medicine."

The whole episode was an act of desperation. In his self-dramatizing way, he later claimed that if he had followed through, "in the tropics I would have been lost forever." What saved him from a life—and possibly a death—in the jungle, was a chance meeting with another Hungarian emigré.

The Dutch Physiological Society held its 1921 annual meeting in Hamburg and Albert attended. At one of the sessions he ran into Frederick "Fritz" Verzar, who was returning to Hungary to take up a professorship in Debrecen. He heard about Szent-Gyorgyi's plight and, one Hungarian to another, offered to recommend him to his former boss, Storm van Leeuwen, of the Pharmaco-Therapeutical Institute of the University of Leiden. Albert grabbed at the chance.

The position paid little, but compared to the near-starvation of

Hamburg, it seemed like a small fortune. He and his family now packed their meager belongings and took the train to Leiden, a city of about 70,000 on the southern coast of Holland. They found a small house in a working-class neighborhood. In his own eyes, he was now a "well-to-do Dutch assistant." Albert felt a wonderful relief at having a regular income, no matter how small, after the uncertainties of impoverishment. The University was a prestigious scientific center and by July 1921, he was proudly publishing papers using his Leiden affiliation.

> It was a good post and for me, as a poor Hungarian, it was wonderful. I felt I had a future there that did not exist in Hamburg.

Of course, he did not know the language but since he spoke and wrote German he thought he could learn Dutch, another Germanic language, in short order. To do so, he hired a tutor and the lessons went well. In fact, Albert was amazed at the similarity of Dutch to German, and the ease with which he picked it up. One puzzle, however, was that when he tried to *use* his newly-learned Dutch nobody understood him. After a few weeks, however, this mystery was cleared up; he discovered that the tutor did not know Dutch either. He was an impostor. But Albert had become quite fluent in Yiddish!

When Albert finally did learn Dutch he enjoyed the experience:

> The Dutch language is very good to express yourself clearly. In German, you can always express yourself in an obscure, fuzzy way, and if it's not fuzzy, it's not German. In Dutch it must be yes or no—very clean-cut, like English.

However, at first, cultural differences caused some problems:

> One of the first Sundays there, Storm van Leeuwen invited me to come to his house and I said, "All right, I will come." For some reason I didn't go. He really resented it. He said, "You lied to me." Well, I learned to be very exact in my speech.
>
> One thing I learned from van Leeuwen was to talk straight. You see, yes, or no has a different meaning in different countries. If in Hungary you say, "Yes," that means "perhaps." If you say "perhaps" that means "no." In Holland yes means yes.

Now began a period of intense productivity. Albert quickly produced seven papers on pharmacology for van Leeuwen. Three of these were in the Dutch language, but most were in English, a language which he had picked up through self-study. Even Dutch scientists, he learned, often wrote in English to gain a wider audience for their work. Holland, of course, had special historical ties to England, and by going there, Albert had brought himself closer to the English-speaking world.

He had developed no special interest in pharmacology, however. These papers were done merely to secure his job with van Leeuwen. Albert later approvingly quoted Nobel Laureate Otto Loewi's witticism, "A drug is a substance which, injected into a rabbit, produces a paper."[6]

In his spare time, at night, Albert began the serious study of chemistry.

> I had seen that the explanation of life must be on the molecular level. So it's no use just working with animals and hearts. You must work with molecules, and that is chemistry.

Nor did study mean locking himself in his room, poring over a textbook.

> If you take up a new subject, the way to do it is not to take books and learn them, but to start research—anything. Get any silly idea and begin to work at it, and then things begin to become alive and interesting, and then you read up. Then come the books, the reading, the knowledge, and all that.

At first, life seemed almost idyllic; but Prof. van Leeuwen turned out to be "a very funny fellow." Nelly, beautiful and chic, loved social gatherings, entertainment, and sports of all kinds. Van Leeuwen was a rather dashing figure, a mercurial captain of the hussars during the war who "got into science somehow."

The ex-cavalry officer quickly sensed an opportunity in his underling's restless and beautiful wife. While Albert was busy with his test tubes, van Leeuwen was off propositioning Nelly. Albert was so obsessed by his work and his career that, by his own admission, he tended to neglect his family.

To a "lady's man" like Storm van Leeuwen, this must have seemed like a golden opportunity, a dream-come-true. Perhaps he also thought that Albert's subordinate position would induce him to turn a blind eye to the affair.

His obvious and forward behavior towards Nelly, however, made the whole situation humiliating for Albert. Even if nothing actually happened, the very suggestion of impropriety was a blow to Albert's

Magyar pride. After a screaming match with his boss, Albert abruptly and bitterly resigned.

So once again, the family had to pack up and move. Albert's decision to quit had been unanticipated and he had no other job to fall back on. Nor did he have much in savings. A second time, he reverted to tropical medicine. Since he had not completed the course at Hamburg, his idea was to go to a small university in the north of Holland, a place called Groningen, pass his Dutch medical exams, and sail for the East.

In 1922 the little family, with their scanty possessions, took the train north to Groningen. Albert was now almost twenty-nine years old. He had written nineteen research papers, had studied with some fairly important scientists, and knew four or five languages (not counting Yiddish). But, to his amazement, he was not able to pass the Dutch medical exams. He completed the first part easily enough and was certified a "semi-Artz," or half-doctor, as the Dutch put it. "But I knew so little about practical medicine that I didn't know how little I knew," Albert quipped. He was now desperate, with "practically no money, no diploma, nothing—but my wife and daughter."

What saved him at this point was an old professor of physiology at Groningen, H. J. Hamburger (1859–1924). "He didn't do great things, but he was well-known in science." The professor needed a technician who could perform a certain operation on dogs. This involved creating a permanent fistula in their intestines, so that various substances could be inserted and removed. It was a basic physiological technique, but when his own assistants tried it, the dogs all died. Not even the local surgeons could perform this operation successfully.

Hamburger had heard that a young Hungarian doctor, a nephew of the great Lenhossek, knew something about physiology and might be able to perform the operation. Albert himself thought the operation meaningless, but it was a job and he was willing to try. And, indeed, the dogs he operated on stayed alive "because I knew the trick of how to do it." The trick, remembered from some earlier laboratory experience, was to eliminate antiseptics in the operation. For some reason, the dogs seemed better able to fight infection without receiving the powerful antiseptics. They survived and so did Szent-Gyorgyi; Hamburger offered him a position as his assistant.

"The salary was very low, but allowed for a very modest life, which was happy and quiet." Little Nelly started school and Big Nelly went out to work to supplement Albert's salary—an unusual step for a middle-class Hungarian woman. Albert became the equivalent of a non-tenured assistant professor, and for the first time began teaching classes in addition to doing research.

Their Dutch neighbors were "exceedingly good and nice people." They did not care that the Szent-Gyorgyis were Hungarians and members of a defeated nation. For example, when the Szent-Gyorgyis first moved into their flat they did not have any furniture, yet "within a few days' time the house was completely furnished" as if by magic. All the poor people around were happy to share the little they had.

Albert rarely had contact with Prof. Hamburger. "He had no influence on me," he recalled. "He was an old fellow with a great name, but it was not very justified. He was one of those people who was everywhere, at all the Congresses as chairman and whatnot, very well known. But if you looked at it, it didn't mean much." The high point of his career had, in fact, come in 1913 when the International Physiological Congress had come to Groningen and he had been the chairman.

Albert did form one significant friendship in northern Holland, with an assistant professor by the name of R. Brinkman. They were to write almost a dozen scientific papers together. Brinkman, he says, "was a very first-rate genius. He had an enormous memory, the most enormous memory I ever met." For example, he would read the daily paper in Groningen and note in passing what babies were born to whom on that day. "If you walked with him, and he saw a little child on the street he would ask the child, 'What's your name?' When they would tell him, he would then tell them the day on which they were born."

Brinkman was also a "first-rate scientist with an enormous imagination." But he provided Albert with an important negative lesson which lasted his whole life.

> He was deeply interested in science, but never achieved much in life because he was much too good a family man. He spent most of his time earning money. He gave physiology courses in high school just to earn a little extra money. Naturally, if you do that, then you have to neglect research.

Albert was more than ever determined not to make the same "mistake" and spend too much time with his own family. At this point he was seeking "perfection of the work," in Yeats's phrase. Groningen was a market town of about 100,000 people, neat and clean in the Dutch way. Through Nelly's charm and good looks the Szent-Gyorgyis were soon admitted to the "best society," despite their poverty. They played tennis with the country club set, although after hours they went back to their simple flat in the working-class section of the town. Albert did not mind. "I had a good life," he recalled, "and these poor millionaires had a very dreary life."

This created "a very funny situation," however. Nelly's attractive sister, Sari, came to stay with them. (Sari eventually married a Dutchman and still lives in Holland.) Fashionable young people, in expensive cars, were constantly pulling up in front of their little house. This was a puzzle to their simple neighbors, and puzzles need solving. "The idea got around that we were running a bordello, a whorehouse," Albert remembered, laughing. "There was a revolution already starting to kick us out." Actually, Albert was too busy with his work to notice. He only learned about this impending scandal after he had already left Groningen in 1926:

> We had a very nice old building attendant, Boom was his name, a very good-hearted fellow. I talked to old Boom when I went back a little bit later, and he said to me, "Oh, it was really too bad how little salary you had, and it's easy to understand how your wife became a whore."

By day Albert performed his operations on dogs, while at night he continued the work on biochemistry he had begun in Hamburg. He was remarkably productive. From 1922 to 1925, in fact, he published thirty-three scientific papers.

At first, this work was eclectic, brilliant but unfocused. Just as he had been slow to develop as a teenager he was slow to develop into scientific maturity. To an outsider, it might have looked as if he were dabbling, jumping from physiology to pharmacology, from bacteriology to biochemistry. On a subconscious level, however, there was a direction:

> Looking at this muddled career with hindsight, I can see my plan. My problem was: was the hypothetical Creator an anatomist, physiologist, chemist, or mathematician? My conclusion is that he had to be all of these, and so if I wanted to follow his trail, I had to have a grasp on all sides of nature. Jumping from one science to the other, I had a rather individual method. I did not try to acquire a theoretical knowledge before starting to work. I went straight to the laboratory, cooked up some senseless theory, and started to disprove it.

He later said, "If you want to build a house, you have to dig a foundation. The bigger the house, the deeper the foundation. I want to build the skyscraper of modern medicine." He was digging deeply now to prepare himself for that task.

At Groningen, he finally found himself. In 1924, at the age of thirty-one, he published the first in a series of epochal papers on biological oxidation. This was the start of a lifelong preoccupation with the question of intracellular respiration. This topic, reduced to its simplest form, involved the way in which food is transformed into energy through a series of steps—oxidation and reduction reactions. Here was the old problem raised by his idol, Claude Bernard, but approached with the far more subtle tools of biochemistry.

The question of intracellular respiration was, at the time, regarded as the central problem of biochemistry. As one Cambridge wit put it:

When biochemists first began
To know a bit about the tale
Of what goes on inside a man
To keep him hearty, whole and hale,
They soon had fearful ructions
Upon the subject of Reductions!

No sooner had they settled that,
And handed round congratulations,
Than off they went like dog and cat
And had a row on Oxidations!
For scientific minds are bent
On never-ceasing argument![7]

And the bitterest of the "never-ceasing arguments" on this topic raged between the two titans of biochemistry, Otto Warburg and Heinrich Wieland.

Otto Warburg (1883–1970) and Heinrich Wieland (1877–1957) for all their greatness, were a bit like the blind men, in the Indian fable, trying to describe an elephant. To the one who got hold of the tail, the elephant was long and stringy. To the one who felt the leg, it was stout and muscular. The elephant, in this case, was intracellular respiration. Each of them had gotten hold of a piece of the truth, without being able to see the bigger picture.

Early investigators of biological oxidation, between 1900 and 1920, had discovered many "dehydrogenases," which seemed to act by removing hydrogen atoms from their substrates in the absence of oxygen. Wieland, a German biochemist then at the height of his influence, postulated that this "dehydrogenation of substrates was the basic process involved in biological oxidation and that oxygen reacts directly with such activated hydrogen atoms."[8]

However, in 1913 Otto Warburg, generally regarded as the greatest of all continental biochemists, had discovered that cyanide in very small concentrations almost completely inhibited the oxygen consumption of respiring cells and tissues. Since cyanide forms a very stable complex with iron (called ferricyanide), Warburg claimed that some iron-containing enzyme, capable of activating oxygen, was essential for biological oxidation.

The two views seemed mutually contradictory, and the battle raged violently between them for years, splitting the new field of biochemistry into hostile camps. Warburg's adherents dogmatically championed the role of oxygen, Weiland's group that of hydrogen.

Enter Albert Szent-Gyorgyi. "Nobody knew what was what," he said. "I got interested in the controversy and found a very simple way to show that both were right, that *active* oxygen oxidized *active* hydrogen. I wrote a very nice little paper about it." This "very nice little paper" is now considered a landmark of twentieth century biochemistry.[9]

It is important not just because it helped end the bitter controversy, but because for the first time Albert put forward the idea that certain intermediary substances—in particular succinic acid—were necessary for respiration to take place. Technically speaking, they served as "intermediate electron carriers between the dehydrogenases and the cytochromes." Here, in embryo, was the whole concept of the respiratory "cycle," later to become so centrally important in biochemistry as the citric acid, or Krebs, cycle.[10]

Another point of entry into the "never-ceasing argument" was Addison's disease. This is a metabolic illness caused by the decreased activity of the adrenal gland. One of its most prominent symptoms is a darkening, or bronzing, of the victim's skin. Albert was not particularly interested in the clinical problem, but he was most curious about the cause of this bronzing.[11]

> I was interested in the function of the adrenal cortex. If the function of this organ is suppressed, life, too, is suppressed (Addison's disease). But before life is extinguished, there appears in man a brown pigmentation, similar to that of certain fruits: apples, pears, bananas, etc. which, in withering, likewise assume a brown color.[12]

On a hunch—an intuition with no immediate rational basis—Szent-Gyorgyi thought the bronzing in Addison's disease might be related to the browning of these familiar plants. As a biochemist, he had long wondered why some plants turned brown in this way and others did not. Of course millions of people had noticed this, but few had thought deeply about it.

Other researchers might have sought the answer directly in a study of Addison's disease patients. Such patients were unavailable to him, however, and he still shunned the complexities of clinical research. To

Albert it did not matter where in the chain of being he worked—the simpler the better. What could be simpler (and cheaper) than the humble potato?

> It was known that this brown coloring of plants is connected with the damaged oxidative mechanism. Since I myself was convinced . . . that in the basic functions, as represented, too, by oxidation, there exist no differences in principle between animal and plant, I undertook the study of the oxidative system of potatoes, browning of the plants depending on its damage. I did this in the hope of finding through these studies the key to the understanding of adrenal function.[13]

In his study of such plants, he made some very basic and interesting discoveries.[14] But this work did not give him any information about adrenal function. He therefore turned to those plants which did *not* turn brown when cut, such as lemons and oranges. These obviously dealt with oxidation in a different way. For instance, it was known that such fruits contained a very active chemical called a peroxidase. In the presence of another chemical, called a peroxide, this peroxidase was able to change various substances to colored pigments. It was a neat little test, ideally suited for chemistry class demonstrations, because it immediately resulted in a dramatic color change. Without peroxidase this color reaction would simply not take place.

"If, for example, benzidine is added to a peroxide in the presence of peroxidase, a deep blue color appears at once, produced by the oxidation of the benzidine." Without peroxidase this reaction would not take place. Therefore, the addition of peroxide and one of these (aromatic) substances served as a color test for the presence of this peroxidase enzyme.

When Albert substituted orange, lemon, or cabbage *juice* for the purified peroxidase in the test, and then added benzidine and peroxide, a curious thing happened. "The blue pigment appeared, but only after a slight delay of about a second." Many others had observed this delay, but few had ever thought to investigate. Albert's lifelong credo however was "to see what everyone else has seen, but think what no one else has thought" and so he pushed forward.

By analysis, Albert determined that there was some other chemical—a strong reducing (anti-oxidant) agent—present in these juices, which prevented the oxidation of the benzidine for about a second. After that delay, the anti-oxidant would be overwhelmed or exhausted and the reaction would proceed.

This was interesting. On a hunch he now turned his attention to actual adrenal glands from cows, bought fresh and fairly cheap in the butchershops of Groningen. When he added silver nitrate to a mince of these glands the mixture quickly turned black. Such a color reaction normally indicated the presence of a strong reducing agent, as well.

> It was a moment of great excitement, when, in my little cellar room in Groningen, I found that the adrenal cortex contains an analogous reducing substance in relatively large amount.

He now set out to isolate this reducing agent from the adrenals, compare it to the plant reducing agent, describe it, and explain their role in oxidative metabolism. It was a job which, with twists, turns, and delays, would take him almost ten years. And the answer, when it came, would say little about Addison's disease or adrenal glands, but make him world-famous in an unexpected way.

Although Albert was mainly interested in making basic scientific discoveries, it did not escape his notice that his discoveries might have some practical applications as well. In particular, he thought he might have stumbled onto the trail of an adrenal hormone, different from adrenalin. (Such a hormone existed and would later be called 'cortisone'.[15])

To test out this idea, Albert began a very limited animal experiment with a crude extract containing his reducing agent—a very limited experiment, indeed, since it was limited to a single alley cat. The cat's adrenal glands were surgically removed, simulating Addison's disease, and then it was given back some of Szent-Gyorgyi's extract. The dying cat responded by jumping off the table.

What is most interesting here is how haphazard Szent-Gyorgyi's approach was. As he himself later admitted almost gleefully, "I was led into the field of oxidations by a false assumption." His whole theory about the origin of bronzing in Addison's disease was questionable; there was little rational basis for believing it had anything to do with the spoiling of a cut apple or pear, for instance.

But that did not matter: Albert did not brood over such technicalities. He leaped from experiment to experiment, leaving it for others to nitpick at the details. And in this way, so infuriating to neat and narrow minds, he was able to find interesting and provocative things in the midst of the turmoil.

Sometimes Albert would seize on a detail which seemed quite trivial to other investigators. He could very well have echoed Agatha Christie's Inspector Poirot, "It is completely unimportant. That is why it is so interesting."

He would fall into a deep depression when things went wrong, would sulk and ruminate. Then suddenly he would grasp some new possibility in the midst of a failure and become elated. After all, he reflected, even experiments that do not pan out can be accurate reflections of nature, if they are performed and interpreted correctly. The important thing was to be daring and conscientious, and never to give up, but to pursue the truth with imagination and passion:

> I make the wildest theories, connecting up the test tube reaction with the broadest philosophical ideas, but spend most of my time in the laboratory, playing with living matter, keeping my eyes open, observing and pursuing the small detail. By working in this way, usually something crops up, some small discrepancy which, if followed up, may lead to basic discoveries.

And it was this method—joyful, spontaneous, and optimistic—that would lead Albert Szent-Gyorgyi to make some very basic discoveries in biochemistry in just a few years' time.

5

"I AM SZENT-GYORGYI"

When the silver nitrate turned black in the presence of minced adrenals, Albert felt he had made a major discovery—a hormone possibly equal in significance to adrenalin itself. But he was frustrated, for no one in Groningen seemed capable of appreciating the importance of this development nor of giving him the assistance he needed. And so he boldly reached out for help.

On 20 December 1924 he wrote to H. H. Dale, one of the most prominent British physiologists, explaining the nature of his latest finding.[1] Dale, who would win the Nobel Prize for his studies of nerve transmission chemicals, wrote in turn to Sir Walter Fletcher, another eminent British scientist:

> I received today a letter from Dr. Szent-Gyorgyi, a Hungarian physiologist, who has been working some years in Holland. I have heard good accounts of him from his Dutch colleagues. He writes to say that he has obtained a new active principle from the suprarenal [i.e. adrenal] gland, having nothing to do with adrenalin and no resemblance in action. He finds that it has a pronounced influence on oxidative metabolism. . . . He wants to know whether I would allow him to come and complete the work here, and whether, in that case, some remuneration could be made available, to enable him to live for the necessary period of some months in London, with a wife and one child.

Dale was well-disposed toward the idea: "On the face of it the proposal seems worthy of further consideration." He therefore wrote back to Szent-Gyorgyi for further details and also made some personal inquiries to Storm van Leeuwen and Prof. Rudolph Magnus "who have both had him in their laboratories." (This was mistaken. Albert had met Magnus, but had never worked for him.)

Around the end of the year, Dale received a fuller account of Szent-Gyorgyi's work plans. It was, he said, "an involved and long-winded" reply, running to ten pages. Dale's sympathy, or "benevolence," as Albert called it in his quaint self-taught English, had opened a floodgate of ideas from the young scientist.

Albert's verbose letter—he had not yet mastered that Dutch directness—was filled with a wealth of ideas. Dale remained skeptical. "I do not attach great importance to the theoretical considerations," he wrote Fletcher. What *did* impress him was the fact that Albert seemed to have something that was new.

"The important part of his rigmarole begins at the bottom of page 6, in which he describes a method by which he has apparently obtained, from the suprarenal gland, a substance giving a very peculiar color reaction." Albert had the temerity to mention how his one experimental cat, "dying of suprarenal deprivation," was revived. Dale commented to Fletcher, "He may be on the verge of something very important."[2]

"To have Szent-Gyorgyi here would, in any case, be something of a speculation," Dale wrote candidly. All the more so since "there may be difficult questions of principle involved in making a personal grant to a citizen of a foreign, and ex-enemy, state."

Dale's reasons for wanting Szent-Gyorgyi to come to England were straightforward. Insulin had been discovered just a few years before, creating worldwide excitement:

> I should not like to turn down, without full discussion, the possibility of our association with something which might prove to be another insulin, in interest and importance. His evidence as it stands is not good, but it is certainly not worse than the earliest evidence with regard to insulin.
>
> There is a pretty clear indication of his having stumbled on something which may have real importance, either as a precursor of adrenalin or a genuine cortical hormone, or possibly as both.

Nevertheless, he wrote to Albert about the difficulty of supporting his work. On 7 January 1925 an excited Szent-Gyorgyi wrote back to Dale, suggesting a compromise. He would come to England and work on the practical aspect of his compound—"whether the substance isolated is the specific internal secretion of the adrenal cortex or not?" He felt he could do this work in three months. If he were successful, then his grant could be extended. "But if the substance does not represent the product searched [for] . . . further expense could be stopped at this point."

It was a modest suggestion, of exactly the kind that Dale himself was about to propose to Fletcher: "We should give him the opportunity of trying to convince us, within a strictly limited period, that he really has got an active principle from suprarenal cortex."

Note the subtle shift in Albert's position. Without Dale, he feared he would get nowhere with his compound. But Dale was interested in practical results, or at least that was the only way he could "sell" the research to his colleagues. It is certain that Albert himself was not interested in searching for a particular "product." That was beneath him, as a pure scientist. The only reason to do research was to satisfy scientific curiosity, to understand how the world works, specifically the components of the cell's oxidation/reduction system. But that was not necessarily of practical importance to anyone.

And so now he confronted the scientist's basic dilemma. Practical people had great difficulty in understanding why they should support such endeavors. Yet without convincing practical people one could not get funds to work (unless one were named Otto Warburg, scion of the famous banking family). At the age of thirty-two, Albert finally discovered what most other scientists already knew: that without funding a scientist was like a fish out of water. And so he made a strategic compromise, promising Dale and Fletcher some immediate, practical results in exchange for their support.

It was a seemingly harmless compromise, hardly a pact with the Devil, but it initiated Albert into the sometimes demeaning world of scientific funding. And this formula—'give me the money and I will come up with a drug,' to put it in its crudest form—would be one he would use many times in the future.

In his internal correspondence with Fletcher, Dale showed that before he met Albert he had little faith in his ability or theories. At this time, for instance, Albert still thought that Addison's disease was caused by an aberration in the oxidative processes. Time would prove him wrong, and Dale immediately sensed the weaknesses in his reasoning:

> Szent-Gyorgyi has done what appears to be quite sound, but not very original work on the mechanism of tissue oxidation. On the basis of this work, he has built up what seems to be a rather flimsy theory, which has led him to examine suprarenal tissue, and particularly the cortex, for the presence of a substance having certain postulated properties. So far as I understand his description, there is no real evidence that he has found anything answering to his theory.

Albert as a boy, c. 1913.
Albert Szent-Gyorgyi's personal collection.

Albert, with his two brothers, Pal (seated) and Laszlo, c. 1917. Note Albert's medal of valor.
National Library of Medicine.

On top of the hospital,
Undine, Italy, 1917.
*Albert Szent-Gyorgi's personal
collection.*

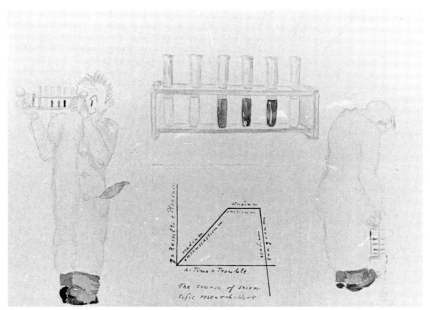

First visit to England, 1924. Albert's self-caricature. From "studium
enthusiasticum" to "studium tragicum" in two months.
Medical Research Council.

Big Nelly at the wheel, and Little Nelly in the sidecar. Cambridge, 1927.
Geoffrey Pollitt.

Gathering of friends, Cambridge, 1927. Albert at far right. Big Nelly fourth
from right (others unknown). *Albert Szent-Gyorgyi's personal collection.*

Albert at work. Possibly Cambridge, 1927.
Albert Szent-Gyorgyi's personal collection.

First laboratory in Szeged, 1932. *Author's collection.*

Prof. C. G. King. (n.d.)
Courtesy Prof. and Mrs. King.

Laboratory staff, 1933, at time of mass production of vitamin C from paprika. Front row (seated): Margaret Zetenyi, secretary; Bela Gozsi, pharmacological chemist; Albert with favorite dog; Dr. Erno Annau, senior research associate. Second row: Edit Joo, laboratory aide; Dr. Joseph Svirbely, research guest from USA; Ilona Banga; Mrs. Nelly Szent-Gyorgyi. Back row: Bruno Straub, medical student (unpaid assistant); Koloman Laki, medical student (unpaid assistant); Dr. Alexander Szalay, physicist.
Photo and Caption Courtesy of Dr. Szalay.

Cathedral Square laboratory, Szeged, 1935. *National Library of Medicine*.

Albert with his wife and mother, Fini (foreground),
c. 1935. *Geoffrey Pollitt*.

With Big Nelly, Little Nelly, and dog, 1936. *Geoffrey Pollitt.*

Playing tennis in New Szeged park, 1930s.
*Albert Szent-Gyorgi's
personal collection.*

In addition, his view of Albert's ability was rather negative:

> I am also pretty clearly convinced that he has not the kind of experience, and technique, which would enable him to get hold of this substance—if it really exists—in such form and quantity as to be able to study it. If we leave matters where they are, Szent-Gyorgyi will presently publish something unconvincing, but suggestive. Meanwhile, in the circumstances of his confidential communication to me, we should have to leave the subject severely alone, until he has published the results of his own efforts.

Dale therefore suggested to Fletcher a "limited speculation," a three-month trial, at twenty-five pounds per month, with no provision for the two Nellies who were to remain in Holland.

Fletcher wrote back with some understated British humor that "the only experimental evidence he quotes, about the cat jumping off the table, in support of his findings, is so slight that his actually quoting it at all has impressed me with his honesty." Fletcher knew far less biochemistry than Dale. But he realized that "the thing is urgent. . . . We ought at least to negotiate at once with St. George. . . ." (Szent-Gyorgyi's name was always too much for Fletcher; he dealt with the difficulty by anglicizing it back to its English roots.)

Just as the negotiations were about to be concluded a "storm cloud" appeared on the horizon: Albert's old nemesis, Storm van Leeuwen. In response to Dale's request for a recommendation, van Leeuwen sent a "mixed account," mingling some praise of Albert's ability with negative comments about his personality. Dale had the wisdom to discount these remarks. "Storm van Leeuwen," he wrote Fletcher, "is a person of a neurotic, artistic temperament, and had had some purely private quarrel, as he frankly admitted, which made it difficult for him to do Szent-Gyorgyi justice."[3]

On the other hand, Prof. Rudolph Magnus of Utrecht sent a glowing letter of praise:

> I can recommend Szent-Gyorgyi to you in every respect, and believe you will have great joy from him. I also regard it as very desirable for him if he could work with you for a time. He is still young, and extraordinarily intelligent, inspired by a great enthusiasm for Science, works very diligently, and is full of ideas. I would very gladly have had him with me, if I had had a position as an assistant vacant. In my opinion, he is through and through an upright man.[4]

And so, on Sunday, 15 February 1925 Albert Szent-Gyorgyi left his family in Groningen and took the ferry across the North Sea to

Britain. He set to work the next day in a room right under the eaves of the laboratory building in Hampstead, a London suburb. Sir Henry had the foresight, in anticipation of his coming, to buy up "all the adrenal glands which were on the Atlantic on their way from Argentina to Europe."

Albert proved himself to be a very energetic worker. Just two days later, Dale wrote, with evident surprise, "he has already prepared a sample of his substance from the suprarenal, and convinced me that he has, at any rate, probably got something hitherto undescribed, which may be of great interest."

Albert worked with furious enthusiasm, trying to both isolate an important chemical and prove himself to these senior scientists. One humorous incident occurred when Albert tried to precipitate his new substance by using lead picrate (picric acid). He had a large mortar and was mincing up this salt when Sir Henry happened to drop by the lab.

"So, what's going on?" he asked.

Szent-Gyorgyi answered, nonchalantly, "I'm just using some lead picrate."

"For heaven's sake," Dale yelled, "stop that immediately! It's very explosive. That will kill you." Lead picrate was most commonly used in the manufacture of high explosives.

"I don't care about that," Albert answered, calmly, "But I am interested in finding this substance."

"I don't mind *you* being killed," Dale answered, "but I don't want the roof of my laboratory blown off."

That afternoon, Albert—who, among his other talents, was a fine amateur caricaturist—drew a cartoon depicting this incident. In it was a humorous portrait of the horrified Dale. He put this in an envelope and took it to Sir Henry's office.

"I have written up the first preliminary results of my studies," he said, soberly. "I would like you to examine them."

Dale frowned at Szent-Gyorgyi's forwardness. But on the following morning, after he had examined the contents of the envelope, he came into Szent-Gyorgyi's lab, beaming with glee. This was the real beginning of their lifelong father-son relationship.

This visit to Dale's laboratory in Hampstead had a profound effect on Albert. In the presence of Dale and his colleagues, Albert matured. He found a *style* of doing science which suited him perfectly, serious in its aims but light-hearted in manner. He shook off the Germanic pedanticism that was his intellectual heritage and, after Hampstead, generally wrote and spoke English in a charmingly simple and straight-forward way. England gave him the luxury of being himself, in public as well as in private.

The visit also gave some of the leading British biochemists a chance to get to know him. Their doubts largely vanished, because his personal magnetism was so palpable. As Magnus predicted they had "great joy from him."

The insurmountable problem, however, was that Albert could not isolate what had become known as "his substance," much less show its therapeutic properties. In fact, his whole visit was summed up in another comic watercolor he drew at the time. It shows a rack of brightly colored test tubes. On one side is a mad-looking scientist—young Szent-Gyorgyi himself—glowing with delight in his discovery. In a second drawing he is hunched over in evident depression, his chemicals dripping to the floor.

This little sketch, he recalled, summed up his feelings at the time. There was also a graph which illustrated in scientific fashion what had happened to him in England. The y-coordinate represented "results and pleasure." The x-coordinate "time and trouble." The graph proceeds from a rapidly ascending "stadium enthusiasticum," or course of enthusiasm, to a flat "stadium criticum," and then rapidly descends into "stadium tragicum." It is a vivid illustration of that manic-depressive thread which ran through his personality.[5]

What led to this "stadium tragicum" was an absolute debacle; in fact, the collapse of the whole premise of his trip. For it turned out that the peculiar and promising color change of the silver nitrate was nothing but a well-known color reaction of adrenalin with iron. And the iron was coming not from the glands but from the sides of the meat mincer in which he ground them up! For an up-and-coming young scientist it was a colossal and embarrassing blunder.

At the end of March 1925, a deflated Szent-Gyorgyi left England, his three month visit cut short to a mere six weeks. This failure did not mean that his substance did not exist; but the silver nitrate test for it was a bust. Once back in Holland, he confronted a deteriorating situation. On 5 January 1924, just days before his own departure for England, Prof. Hamburger had died. By the time Albert returned to Holland a new physiological laboratory head had been appointed: Dr. F. J. J. Buytendijk.

Buytendijk was a fairly prominent scientist, but "he thought all biochemists were washouts, and biochemistry was stupid nonsense. Only psychology was interesting." This view of biochemistry was not uncommon at the time. Buytendijk resented a good research position being "wasted" on a biochemist and proceeded to make life difficult for his Hungarian assistant. He obviously was looking for an opportunity to force him out.[6]

Albert continued to work, but in a worsening atmosphere. In July 1925 he wrote what he called "a little paper on the respiration of plants." Actually, it was his paper on the respiration in the potato, now considered to be one of his most important contributions to science. He showed it to Prof. Buytendijk to get his formal approval before publication, and hopefully to impress him as well. But Buytendijk was not about to be impressed.

"You can do with it what you like," he told Szent-Gyorgyi. "Publish it, throw it in my wastepaper basket, it doesn't matter." Then, Albert recalled, the professor became even more crude and hostile, telling him in no uncertain terms that he did not need him around the lab. Shocked, hurt, and indignant, Albert resigned.[7]

Now in his early thirties, he still had not found a steady way to support his family or himself. Nelly's part-time employment was certainly not enough. He had no job, no prospects, little money, no Dutch diploma, no important connections. His one great chance in England had ended in a fiasco. And he certainly could not expect any glowing recommendation from Prof. Buytendijk. Even his papers on plant respiration, although duly published, were greeted with silence. Maybe, he thought, Buytendijk was right: it made little difference if he published or not.

Prone to depression, he summed up his life as a failure. His grandiose plan to take the scientific world by storm now seemed like a bitter joke. Sensitive and proud, like many Hungarians, he brooded over his insults and injuries. And unable to support his wife Nelly and their seven-year-old daughter he finally decided to send them home by train.

"I sent them to Budapest to her parents," he recalled, "thinking you can have them back and feed them and I'll make an end to the whole story. I was ready to completely check out, to commit suicide."

No one who knew Albert believed that he really would have killed himself. His enthusiasm for work always won out in the end. Yet if he toyed with the idea of suicide it was because life seemed to offer him no other options. He lived for science. Unlike his Dutch friend Brinkman, his family was never the focus of his emotional life. If science were taken away from him, he felt there was nothing worth living for.

From 3–6 August 1926 the International Physiological Society was to hold its triennial Congress in Sweden. "One last time in my life I wanted to have a good time, so I went up to Stockholm where there was a big international meeting. Once more I really wanted to be among scientists." Albert gathered his "last few pennies" for the trip. The chairman that year was Sir Frederick Gowland Hopkins, "the greatest living biochemist of his day" and one of the major intellectual figures of the twentieth century.[8]

The audience hushed as Hopkins, an almost pathologically-shy eccentric rarely seen outside his laboratory in Cambridge, began the presidential address. Lost in thought, Albert sat in the huge auditorium, surrounded by his fellow scientists. This was the international, intellectual fraternity he had longed to join, since the days in Budapest when he had stared in rapt fascination at his uncle's textbooks. Now, he mused, this meeting was to be his farewell to it all.

Hopkins had chosen as his topic "the mechanism of biological oxidation." Midway through the address, a despondent Szent-Gyorgyi was suddenly shocked out of his reveries. He could have sworn that Hopkins had mentioned his name. Yes, it was true. Three times in the course of his speech, Hopkins referred to the fine work of an obscure researcher at an obscure university in northern Holland. He was referring to Szent-Gyorgyi's paper—"On the Oxidation Mechanism of the Potato"—the same one Buytendijk had told him he could throw in the wastebasket! No other scientist's work received this kind of attention from the dean of English biochemists.[9]

Despite his isolation in northern Holland, despite his individualistic way of working, Albert had made a major contribution to a topic of great importance to some of Europe's leading minds. Some years later, also in Stockholm, Dr. E. Hammarsten poetically summed up Szent-Gyorgyi's contribution to this question: "The manner in which the life-giving active oxygen's dramatic encounter in the darkness of the cell ensued had been unknown ever since the morning in time until . . . Szent-Gyorgyi carried out some experiments which proved to be the prelude of the secret."

There was irony here, for, at the time, Hopkins was citing Szent-Gyorgyi mainly to *disagree* with him. He and his colleagues at the Dunn laboratory in Cambridge had experimented with the same enzymes as Szent-Gyorgyi but had come to quite different conclusions—"with this view [of Szent-Gyorgyi's] I entirely disagree," Hopkins had even said. But Hopkins was so much the gentleman, and so absolutely fairminded in that particularly British way, that he could sincerely pay deep homage to the insights of an opponent.

The speech made Szent-Gyorgyi a momentary celebrity at the Congress. Screwing up his courage, he made his way to the podium after the lecture and blurted out, "I am Szent-Gyorgyi."

Hopkins' eyes lit up. He studied the open-faced young man in front of him and said, simply, "Why don't you come to Cambridge?"

"How can I?" Szent-Gyorgyi asked. "I have no money."

"Well, then, I'll get you a fellowship," Hopkins declared. So great was his influence that one letter sufficed to set the Rockefeller Foundation (RF) in motion. On 15 October 1926 a still-dazzled Szent-Gyorgyi received a grant to study with Prof. Hopkins and Dale.

Albert returned to Holland, hastily packed his few belongings, then wired for the two Nellies to rejoin him in Cambridge. His first monthly stipend check arrived at the beginning of January 1927: $182. There were also liberal allowances for travel and other expenses. This was a lordly income for a man who was practically bankrupt at the time and had spent the previous eight years in dire poverty, flirting with starvation a number of times.

The Szent-Gyorgyis rented an ancient cottage at 35 Oldstone Road, and Albert immediately set to work. Holland, even Hungary, seemed very distant. He relished the intense intellectual atmosphere of Cambridge and its no-holds-barred approach to knowledge. There was a cross-fertilization of ideas in Cambridge among people of many different viewpoints. Here he could work, free of money worries, teaching responsibilities, or humiliating appeals for funds.

"For the first time I could devote myself to chemistry in earnest," he said. And for that reason he was happier than he had ever been before. His wanderings, it seemed, were over. In Cambridge, Albert Szent-Gyorgyi had finally found his intellectual home.

6

A SCIENTIFIC HOME

Albert came to Cambridge to isolate finally that mysterious chemical he had found in the adrenal cortex. At the time he thought of this as a "highly reducing substance which is specific for the interrenal system," i.e., a kind of hormone. He surprised his colleagues when he announced that this same (or a very similar) substance was also present in citrus juices and the watery extract of cabbages. Here was a strange hormone indeed. Adrenalin, for instance, was not found in cabbages.

As a chemist, what Albert had to do first was to purify this substance in crystalline form, analyze it chemically, and then determine its biological properties. At first, his attempts were marked by repeated failures and frustration, as they had been in Dale's laboratory. The main problem was that it existed in only microscopic amounts within the adrenal cortex, and he simply did not have enough adrenals. Prof. August Krogh (1874–1949), the 1920 Nobel laureate, generously sent him fresh adrenals from Copenhagen by plane, but these too perished in transit.

Albert finally extracted less than a gram's worth of crystals of his substance from orange juice and the watery extract of cabbage—about enough to fit on the tip of his finger. With this, he learned that the substance was a carbohydrate, probably a sugar acid, having the chemical formula $C_6H_8C_6$. Then his meager supply ran out.

Prof. Hopkins urged Szent-Gyorgyi to publish his findings, which had begun to arouse interest among biochemists around the world. When he submitted his work to the prestigious *Biochemical Journal* he finally had to decide on a name for what had simply been called "Szent-Gyorgyi's substance." With a pixyish sense of humor Albert proposed calling it "Ignose." This was a neologism fashioned from the

51

Latin "Ignosco," "I don't know," and an "-ose" ending, meaning "sugary," tacked on for good measure.

The editor of the journal, Arthur Harden, was not amused. He was a "superb critic," Hopkins warned, "but unduly suspicious of adventures into the realm of the imagination." Harden predictably reprimanded the eccentric Hungarian for his levity. Undeterred, Albert resubmitted the paper, rechristening his compound "Godnose." Harden was scandalized and threatened to reject the paper entirely unless a suitable name was found.

"Godnose" had a nice Edward Learian ring to it, typical of Albert's creative manipulation of English. Harden suggested the much less poetic "hexuronic acid" for the compound, if Albert wanted to see it published.[1]

Albert reluctantly accepted Harden's designation and it was for the isolation of this "hexuronic acid" that Albert Szent-Gyorgyi received his doctor of philosophy degree from Cambridge University in 1927. It had taken him one year. This was an impressive achievement and Albert now could write "Ph.D." after his name as well as "M.D." He would have given all his credits, however, in exchange for a clear identification of his new substance.

The main significance of Albert's stay in Cambridge was the change it wrought in his character and outlook. In some ways, he became very British, but without ever losing his humorous, artistic, emotional Hungarian temperament. For instance, he now wore tweeds and smoked a pipe. He not only wrote in English, but the whole family spoke English at home as well.

Life in Cambridge, from 1926–1931, was pleasant for the three of them—probably their happiest time together as a family. An old Chinese curse says, "May you live in interesting times." In that sense, these were very uninteresting times for the Szent-Gyorgyis in contrast to what was to come.

Albert's day was measured out by his daily bicycle trips to the brick laboratory on Tennis Court Road. On the weekends there were get-togethers with his colleagues, or car rides in the lovely green countryside of Cambridgeshire.

Especially important was the tolerance that surrounded them. "For a Hungarian," Albert reflected, "life in the postwar years in Europe was very unpleasant because political hatred lingered long in the atmosphere, and it made traveling very difficult and humiliating. I found a really international outlook in Cambridge, which I still regard as my scientific homeland." From the vantage point of Cambridge, Hungary looked pathetically backward and intolerant, an impoverished country personified by the menacing and slightly ludicrous figure of Admiral Horthy.

To Albert, and many of his colleagues, Cambridge was undoubtedly the greatest university in the world. The town (unlike urban Oxford) was pure charm: its winding, cobblestone streets lined with solid stone buildings; the well-groomed stores, in which Cornelia could shop; students and dons in flowing black academic robes bustling about. There was an invigorating atmosphere here, a mixture of seriousness and lightheartedness, that seemed akin to the university towns of François Villon's day.

It was not unusual to see a world-famous professor energetically bicycling down Jesus Lane or Newmarket Road. Albert himself soon adopted this means of transportation. To those brought up in the British or American academic traditions, this may not seem like much. But such a sight would have been shocking—in fact, unimaginable—in Budapest or almost any other continental city where the "dignity" of the professor tended to be his most closely-guarded asset.

Once enrolled in Fitzwilliam College, he was given laboratory bench space in the large Sir William Dunn Laboratory, which had been dedicated just a few years before on Tennis Court Lane, behind Pembroke College. It was one of the few biochemical laboratories in the world.[2]

And it was now that Szent-Gyorgyi came under the influence of that remarkable man, Frederick Gowland Hopkins (1861–1947). Hopkins became Albert's mentor. From Cambridge days on, a portrait of Hopkins at work, complete with drooping walrus moustache, would always hang in Albert's laboratory regardless of where he wandered. Yet it would be of interest to a psychologist that Hopkins was able to exert this influence on Albert (and many others) by speaking hardly a word, for Hopkins was "excessively modest." He avoided his colleagues whenever possible, not out of malevolence, but perhaps because he knew he could never deny a request:

> He was, and still is, a mystery to me. He was the man who had the most influence on my scientific development, though I never talked to him about science and heard him speak but once or twice. His papers were not especially fascinating, yet he had a magic influence on the people around him.

Albert enjoyed this paradox and probably exaggerated it for the sake of the telling. Yet attempts to communicate with the Professor were certainly difficult. If a visitor knocked on his door, he would quietly slip out the back way. If it were urgent for Albert to speak to him, therefore, he would knock on the front door of his office, then take off wildly down the corridor and catch Hopkins as he tried to sneak out the rear exit.

One day in the late twenties, an American visitor to the Dunn was startled to hear noises coming from the library stacks. He found Hopkins pacing up and down, mumbling to himself in obvious distress. "I'm terribly upset," he confided. "I've wasted my life. And yet I feel that *somehow* I might have done something useful, if only I'd had the chance." Then he sulked off. A few weeks later Hopkins received the Nobel Prize for Medicine and Physiology.[3]

The key to Hopkins's character was that he had been extremely poor as a child and had worked for many years as a humble lab chemist, a technician; this was as close as he thought he would ever get to science. Then a small inheritance enabled him to enter medical school and he blossomed. Although Albert had certainly not been deprived, he saw parallels with his own erratic career:

> Hopkins never had a scientific education, and he knew very little. He was just as shy as I in talking to scientists because he was ashamed of his ignorance. I do not dare talk to scientists because I am ashamed. I know so little, and they catch me immediately because I know so little.

Like Szent-Gyorgyi, Hopkins loved basic research. Not that he was opposed to practical advances; they just did not motivate him. He did science the way others do music or painting—simply for the joy of discovery.

> That little, unassuming man, with all his childish vanity, was a humble searcher for truth. What his individuality proclaimed was that in spite of all the hard work involved, research is not a systematic occupation but an intuitive artistic vocation.

Ironically, by pursuing science just out of sheer curiosity, Hopkins made immensely important practical contributions to knowledge. It was he who, essentially, discovered vitamins (although he failed to come up with a catchy name for them). He also found the essential amino acids, and laid the basis for muscle physiology with his studies of lactic acid production. Yet all of these earth-shaking results were simply the by-products of his own pleasurable quest to find new things. It is perfectly characteristic that one of his greatest discoveries came from asking what caused the brilliant color of a butterfly's wings! This example of an almost hedonistic attachment to basic research was to inspire Albert throughout his life.[4]

Without being a martinet in the lab, Hopkins was able to elicit great work from his junior colleagues. The Dunn laboratory and library were kept open twenty-four hours a day.

Hopkins pioneered an open admissions policy. He hired scientists based solely on their qualifications: there were women, political activists, and people of many different nationalities. After the rise of Hitler it was Hopkins who quietly led the effort to rescue Jewish scientists and find them places in England. Hopkins's own list of publications was much shorter than many other professors, because he never allowed his own name to be put on someone else's paper simply because he was head of the lab. (Szent-Gyorgyi followed the same principle.)

Not surprisingly, Hopkins attracted some of the most brilliant minds to the Dunn. "He had a big laboratory, but he didn't really lead research. He just picked good people and let them do what they liked." He also attracted the most outspoken radicals in science: J. B. S. Haldane, Dorothy and Joseph Needham, and William Pirie—names well-known on the left in the thirties—all came out of his lab.

Yet Hopkins himself seemed above the battle:

He was so kindly that he could never say "No" to any request. One of the great jokes of my day was that the Communist students made a big declaration, a "Communist manifesto" which was published in the local newspaper, and Hopkins was the first signer. They asked him to sign, and he signed it. On the opposite page of the same journal, was a big anti-Communist manifesto, and Hopkins was the first to sign that, too—you know, he just signed everything. He was so good that he could never say "No."

The Dunn laboratory staff also published its own humor magazine, a well-printed annual with a circulation that eventually extended around the world. It was called *Brighter Biochemistry,* and it certainly did make life in Cambridge brighter for its readers. Subtitled "The Illustrated Journal of the Biochemistry Laboratory, Cambridge," *Brighter* contained poems, essays, and pictures, as well as satires on members, developments in science, and life in general.[5]

Albert fit in well in this funny, eccentric atmosphere. Joseph Needham, the great historian of Chinese science, was then a biochemist in Cambridge. He recalled Albert's tendency towards manic-depression:

I was University Demonstrator at the time, and we knew Albert Szent-Gyorgyi rather well. One of my recollections is that it was said that when his work was going well he would come bouncing into the laboratory, but when it was not going so well he would creep in on crutches.[6]

Albert occasionally contributed humorous drawings, notes, and letters to *Brighter Biochemistry*. One, entitled "More Help Wanted," shows his mood at the time:

Dear Sirs,

The great Dutch astronomer, [Jacobus] Kaptijn [1855–1922] was once questioned by a peasant: "I can quite understand how you discovered all those stars, but how did you find out their names?" I am in the same difficulty with biochemistry. I know how to find new compounds. I even feel strong enough to find out their constitution. But how am I to find out their names? I know there are research workers who do this with great ease. They know the name of their substance before they find the substance at all. But, though I have questioned many workers on immunity, blood coagulation, vitamins, and other subjects, they never will tell me how this is done.

I would be most thankful for any advice or reference, for I am in great difficulty on this matter. Until I can find some reliable method for estimating the name of a compound, I must call all my substances by their protocol numbers, and I am afraid, if I go on at my present rate, that the numbers will soon become extremely unwieldy. I might name some substances after the days of their discovery, e.g. Mondin, Tuesdol, etc. but these possibilities are also very limited.

Hoping you can help me in my trouble

I remain,

Yours most faithfully,

A. v. Sz.

It is interesting that Albert was still using the Germanic and "titled" form of his name, "Albert *von* Szent-Gyorgyi." He soon dropped this, calling it "a very stupid business."

His work in biochemistry and his association with Hopkins had made Szent-Gyorgyi well-known among scientists, and not least of all in Hungary. He had published fifty-five papers in addition to his Ph.D. dissertation on "hexuronic acid." In the summer of 1928, Zoltan Magyary, an official of the Hungarian government, visited him in England; he brought greetings and a message from Count Kuno Klebelsberg, Horthy's Minister of Education. Would Dr. Szent-Gyorgyi be interested in returning to his native land?

Klebelsberg's emissary held out to him the possibility of a full professorship, and a chance to do something substantial in helping to rebuild Hungarian science. Albert's prospects at Cambridge at the time seemed limited. A professorship was certainly out of the question, and there were no openings in biochemistry.

Throughout his scientific pilgrimage, Albert had always pictured himself eventually returning to Budapest in triumph. It was, after all, the Lenhossek tradition. He therefore told Magyary what he would really like: to inaugurate the first chair in biochemistry at Budapest University's Medical School. Failing that, he would be willing to step into his "hereditary" position as professor of anatomy and physiology at Budapest.

Magyary explained that this was impossible, on several counts. Mihaly Lenhossek was not due to retire for another five years. The Budapest faculty was too tradition-bound to accept something as newfangled as a "biochemistry department." And Albert's reputation for nonconformism had gotten back to the capital. The conservative senior faculty at Budapest would never confirm his appointment there, despite the fact that he was, by birth, a Lenhossek and had the backing of the Minister of Education.[7]

There was a solution, however. In the southern provincial city of Szeged the professor of medical chemistry, named Reinbold, had just died. Perhaps Szent-Gyorgyi would be willing to assume his seat?

In September 1928 Albert returned to Hungary on a visit—his first such trip since leaving Budapest in 1919. He was the personal guest of Count Klebelsberg, and together the two men traveled to the University of Szeged. They hit it off very well. Albert was always attracted to intelligent men of power, and Klebelsberg was one. An aristocrat who had been financially ruined by the Trianon treaty, he represented the relatively enlightened wing of the Horthy regime. The university was still under construction but Albert was given the grand tour, and shown where his own medical chemistry department could be located: on Cathedral Square, in the heart of the city.

Szent-Gyorgyi listened to Klebelsberg's grandiose dreams for Szeged. The Rockefeller Foundation, he intimated, was interested in supporting a major scientific center in Hungary, and Szeged was the most likely site. Bright young scientists could assist him in steering the university in a progressive direction. And Albert himself would be the linchpin of the whole endeavor. As a Rockefeller fellow, he would wield great influence in Szeged and throughout the country. In fact, said Klebelsberg, his opportunities would be limitless.

It was all very flattering, almost dizzying, for Albert. It was hard to believe that just two years before he had been contemplating suicide in his Groningen basement! Now he was being feted by the Minister of Education and offered a top academic position. With little difficulty, Szent-Gyorgyi accepted the offer and prepared to return to Hungary. In 1929 he wrote to Fletcher:

> My only reason for accepting the offer was that I thought I could be more useful and thus more wanted there than anywhere else, since the

country, getting out now slowly of the postwar misery is very keen to build up again its cultural life, of which they regard science as one of the most important parts. They are in great need of scientists, who are able to teach and encourage young research workers, putting up new schools, providing this way [for] the future with a new young generation of scientists.[8]

He looked forward to quickly assuming his post and moving his family back to Hungary. But the completion of the laboratory was repeatedly delayed, and the Szent-Gyorgyis waited. In the summer of 1929—after another two week visit to Szeged—Albert was presented with an opportunity to visit America for the first time. The physiologists were holding their triennial world Congress in Boston, their first meeting since Albert's fateful encounter with Hopkins in Stockholm. He requested, and received, funds from the Medical Research Council to make the trip.

Their daughter, Nelly, almost eleven, was not with them when they sailed for America; she had been put on a train to Budapest, to stay with Albert's in-laws, the Demenys. This was the first time she had been separated for any time from her parents and it was a difficult experience for both Nellies. Albert, still the physiologist, saw the problem in hormonal terms:

> We are missing our little daughter badly. Naturally Nelly has the worst of this since the motherly gland of internal secretion seems to work much more intensely than father-glands.[9]

In Boston, Szent-Gyorgyi was greeted as an up-and-coming figure by his fellow biochemists, who still had no organization of their own, but formed a coterie among the physiologists as a whole. A flattering amount of attention and discussion was focused on Szent-Gyorgyi's "hexuronic acid."[10]

There was also time for socializing and play. He renewed many old acquaintances. Michaelis, for instance, after teaching in China, was now working in Baltimore. Prof. Mansfeld came from Pecs, Hungary, where he had successfully resettled. Albert also made new friends. Hans Krebs, a protege of the testy Prof. Warburg, had come from Berlin, and they had productive talks. It was the beginning of a long relationship that remained friendly despite periods of intense competition.

As a diversion, some attendees drove out to visit the Marine Biological Laboratory, at the unique scientific colony of Woods Hole, Massachusetts. There, on the beach at Penzance Point, on one of the loveliest spots along the whole Eastern seaboard, the group held a mammoth lobster cookout. Szent-Gyorgyi had never eaten lobster before, and although he did not particularly like the looks or taste of the crustacean, it made the event and place always stick in his mind. This was to turn out to be a very memorable cookout, indeed.

From Boston, Albert and Nelly took the train to Rochester, Minnesota, where he had an invitation to work on "hexuronic acid" at the Mayo Clinic. If "hexuronic acid" could be isolated in quantity anywhere, this would seem to be the place. Here, at his disposal, Albert had lots of money, excellent facilities, and the help of Edward C. "Nick" Kendall, head of the division of biochemistry, and the world's leading expert on the adrenal gland. A critical factor was access to the huge slaughterhouses of South St. Paul, with their nearly limitless supply of fresh adrenals.

As he wrote to Fletcher in November 1929:

> I have here splendid facilities to work with the adrenal and I want to finish this work completely before leaving Rochester, since I am sure I will find nowhere an equally good chance to do this. . . . Rochester on the whole is from a medical point of view quite an intelligent place. They are very keen on research and seem to start it from the good end. They even know, what is yet undiscovered in the rest of the States, that the most important piece of apparatus in research is a good research man.[11]

American living conditions provided quite a contrast with those of old Europe:

> On the whole we are quite happy here. We had a most gorgeous fall with bright sunshine and woods with all colours of the spectrum. It is very interesting to see this petrol[eum-rich?] country for a while from such a close range and to live, after our 500 year old cottage, with its bathtub in the kitchen, in a modern apartment house, where you are lived [sic] by electricity, and get at the same time four different jazz radio concerts from your two horizontal and two vertical neighbors.[12]

As Fletcher had predicted before they left, the Americans would be eager to get their hands on Albert. America had the money and the drive for science, but still lacked outstanding researchers. In the twenties, before the mass exodus of intellectuals from fascism, European scientists were at a premium:

People are very kind to me here. Finding my Rockefeller fellowship inadequate they requested me to resign it, and put me on the staff of the Mayo Foundation, with a more adequate salary. They are almost spoiling me: they also provided me with a secretary and a lab assistant, and as you foretold, tried to induce me to stay here forever, which I however refused.[13]

He had soon purified almost an ounce of "hexuronic acid," a very large amount compared to what he had obtained from oranges or cabbages in Cambridge. In the first week of November he mailed ten grams of these precious crystals—distilled from thousands of pounds of glands—to Prof. Norman Haworth in Birmingham, England. Haworth, the author of *The Constitution of Sugars* and other classics in the field, had agreed to undertake the analysis of Szent-Gyorgyi's mysterious "sugar acid."

Meanwhile, Albert, characteristically, was already on the trail of another adrenal substance.

I was unfortunate enough [sic] to find a new active compound in the adrenal medulla about which I would like to know a bit more . . . the work just begins to be interesting. . . . I think that I am also on the trail of a new active principle of the cortex. . . . If I can really find that other thing in the cortex there will be, together with adrenalin, four active principles in the adrenal, the deficiency of which seems to be related with very interesting pathological conditions such as Addison's [disease] and Myasthenia [Gravis].[14]

He reaffirmed his lack of interest in clinical research:

I myself hate all this hormone-hunting business, and there is no other part of the body which I hate more than adrenals, but still I think, if we will know all about this gland, we will know a great deal more about nervous regulations and oxidations.[15]

Albert had kept about half the "hexuronic acid" and he used his own share to "gain a deeper understanding of the substance's functions." He soon discovered, for instance, that "it could not replace the adrenals," although it "caused a disappearance of pigmentation in patients with Addison's disease."

However, the news coming out of Birmingham was not good. Haworth, for all his expertise, was unable to analyze the "hexuronic acid" that Albert sent him:

Unfortunately, it turned out that the amount of substance was inadequate for finding out its chemical constitution. Through lack of means, the preparation could not be repeated, and no cheaper material was found from which the acid could have been obtained in larger quantities.

And so, the whole trail of discovery, which had stretched from the basement at Groningen to Cambridge to Minnesota, and spanned almost a decade of hard toil, had come to a dead-end. All Albert had to show for his efforts was a tiny vial of off-white crystals, which he took back with him on the ship to England. He did have a suspicion, he later said, of what this "hexuronic acid" really was—a suspicion that would turn out to be correct—but one could not publish, much less live on, suspicions.

When he returned to England, he was informed of yet more delays in completing the Szeged laboratory. He began to suspect that Klebelsberg was not entirely serious, recalling ruefully that in Hungary "yes" meant "perhaps," and "perhaps" meant "no." Magyary was now talking about the winter of 1933 as a target date, and there was a lot of complaining about the effects of the Depression. Albert began to reconsider his decision, toying with the idea of staying in Cambridge:

> You know how people feel who have lived and worked at Cambridge, how they like the place, and how willingly most of them would resign any post to be enabled to stay.[16]

Just at that moment, in fact, a job opened up at Cambridge, in the department of pathology. H. R. Dean, the professor of pathology, wrote Fletcher:

> My own feeling is that Szent-Gyorgyi has a great deal of originality and that he is extremely likely to produce really valuable research work . . . he seems to have a real instinct for new ideas . . . [and] is very popular with all the existing members of our staff.[17]

In June 1929 Albert induced Alan Gregg, the Rockefeller Foundation representative in Paris, to write to the Hungarians urging them to hurry the completion of the lab. Magyary argued that the laboratory simply was not ready and the government needed more time. Gregg let him know that the Rockefeller Foundation would only pay for one more year of Szent-Gyorgyi's sojourn in England. After that, he would have to take up his promised position in Szeged—or find a suitable position elsewhere. Magyary agreed to the demand. After all, the Rockefellers were providing a million pengos ($200,000) to build up

Szeged as a scientific center—an enormous sum under those conditions. So, when the Rockefeller Foundation spoke, the Hungarians listened.[18]

After another visit to England, Magyary and Albert worked out a compromise. The government would refurbish a former hospital on the outskirts of Szeged for Szent-Gyorgyi's use, while the Central Square laboratory was being finished. This could be done by January 1931 at the latest.

On 15 August 1930, therefore, Albert and Cornelia left Cambridge, their "scientific homeland," to reclaim the homeland of their birth. They stopped for a prolonged visit in Paris and Montpelier, where Albert lectured on "hexuronic acid." Wherever he went his talks created excitement; the listeners were attracted as much by his charming, spontaneous style of delivery as by the substance of his talk. From there they proceeded by train to Budapest. After a year, they were reunited with their daughter, Little Nelly, who was still in Budapest with her mother's parents. Albert visited his mother, and made arrangements for her to move to Szeged to live with them.

In January 1931 Albert and his family finally arrived in Szeged, a three-hour train ride south of the capital. It was here that he would live for the next thirteen years. It would be in this sleepy provincial town that Albert would make some of his greatest discoveries and finally unlock the puzzle of "hexuronic acid." This discovery would make him world-famous, but also involve him in the most bitter controversy of his life.

7

A NEW STAR IN THE SKY

Szeged was a poor man's Cambridge. A Hungarian writer has described it in glowing, guidebook terms:

> Parks and lovely squares of an almost Mediterranean air, old buildings, which cast clear-cut shadows in the brilliant sunshine, and bustling streets with a large number of students give Szeged its character. It is a city of students; a mass of university buildings, reminiscent of English colleges, stand at the heart of the town.[1]

In truth, however, Szeged in the thirties was a rather boring place, isolated from European cultural centers and from Budapest which was a few hours away by train. But Albert had not come to Szeged for the excitement. Szeged may have been out of the way, but one could take a positive view of such things; it was also lacking diversions which could take him away from his work.

Szeged was also politically conservative and very Catholic. The Bishop, a man named Glattfelder, cut an imposing figure. Together with two or three other "power brokers" it was said he controlled the town's political life. In fact, in the thirties many of the professors at the University were themselves priests.[2]

Yet Szeged was willing to have Szent-Gyorgyi when more cosmopolitan Budapest refused his appointment there. To understand this, one must understand the "master plan" for Szeged. The Rockefeller Foundation, the most important American institution funding science worldwide, had chosen Szeged as the locale for a major research center. And Count Kuno Klebelsberg was the man chosen to implement this plan. Since Szent-Gyorgyi was a Rockefeller fellow he soon became central to the plan. In fact, Albert would have quickly

63

been overwhelmed by reactionary opposition if he had not had behind him the support of these powerful forces. Throughout the thirties he—and they—kept the major objective in view: to build an American-style scientific center on the banks of the lazy Tisza.[3]

Albert's temporary quarters were in the former hospital on Calvary (now Pioneer) Square, on the outskirts of the city. His new biochemistry department was given a converted World War I hospital in which to work. It was a rococo structure, all knobs and turrets, that looked older and far more grandiose than its original purpose indicated.

On his first day Albert casually asked the old attendant where the bathroom was.

"Herr Professor has a special restroom nobody else may use. It is locked with a special key," the attendant said, reverentially.

"Then give me the key," Albert answered, abruptly.

The man was scandalized. "I cannot give you the key," he replied, "because, as a Professor, you cannot carry it. I must carry it for you." He then took a roll of toilet paper in one hand, the key in the other, and led the new professor on a solemn procession to the executive lavatory.

Albert soon did away with this custom, and with everything else archaic in the department. "Being not bothered too much by conscience," he wrote Alan Gregg in 1931, "I set to work to get research going at all prices, and kicked out all people whom I thought not to be fit for research." For the first time, Albert was in a position of authority. He was the "Prof," as everyone soon called him. And as "Prof," he proved himself capable of being quite ruthless in pursuit of excellence.[4]

The Szent-Gyorgyi family moved into a comfortable apartment in the building, next to the laboratory. His mother (now called "Fini neni" or Aunt Fini, even by the staff) lived with them and was a lively presence. Fini neni was popular with the assistants. Bruno Straub, then a student, remembered her scurrying back and forth from the apartment to the lab, which had one of the few electric refrigerators in all Szeged. She stored her groceries there. In a sense, she now played the same role in the household as her own mother had played when Albert was a boy.

The scientific facilities in the old hospital building were barely adequate, but "Prof" was waiting for his permanent laboratory on Cathedral Square to be finished. There were two large laboratories, an office, and a lecture room. Albert's responsibilities were three-fold: to teach classes on medical and biochemistry; to take some part in the administration of the University itself; and, of course, to carry out his own research.

Albert had had some experience teaching in Holland, but in Szeged he blossomed in a most remarkable way. All those who heard him testified that he was a unique teacher. Fifty years later, his ex-students, now themselves old men, became youthful again describing the electrifying experience of his lectures. Even a brief period in Szent-Gyorgyi's class could change the direction of a student's life forever.

In 1984 the author visited the old anatomy laboratory in Pest and met Prof. Tibor Donat. Like so many scientists in Hungary, he turned out to be a former student of Szent-Gyorgyi's. "In most of the other professors," Prof. Donat said, "something was lacking. Szent-Gyorgyi looked like an athlete. He was very impressive and masculine. His brain function and ideas were really enthusiastic." Although Donat had no special interest in biochemistry, Albert Szent-Gyorgyi became his personal idol. It was because of his lectures, in fact, that Donat went into science, eventually becoming Professor of Anatomy at Budapest, occupying Mihaly Lenhossek's position.[5]

Koloman Laki, later a prominent Hungarian-American biologist, was a second-year medical student in Szeged when Albert Szent-Gyorgyi arrived:

> We waited with great expectations to hear the new professor. After a few minutes of his first lecture, all of us were fascinated listening to him. His presentation was vigorous; complex phenomena seemed simple in his interpretation, and all was explained in an attractive Hungarian. Students are usually good judges of professors and we all felt a new star had appeared in the Hungarian sky. Like a hundred years before when a young Hungarian mathematician, Bolyai, revolutionized geometry, we felt that at this time biochemistry had gained such a genius in Szent-Gyorgyi.[6]

Albert prized, in fact *demanded*, originality from his students. Laki recalled going before Szent-Gyorgyi for his end-of-year exams:

> My turn came on an early June afternoon. The examinations at that time were all oral and conducted in the lecture room open to the public. . . . All of a sudden, I really forgot I was making an examination. I was having a discussion. Only afterward it dawned on me, for heaven's sake, what have I done? I am talking with a professor, not some other student. That will be the end of it.
>
> When it was over, he went into his office with our books into which he would write the results of the examination and he came out and said that he had given me the best mark. He said he liked the way I handled the test and that he would like me to work in his laboratory. You can imagine my elation. I couldn't imagine anything more exciting at the time.

When Laki almost dropped out of school for lack of funds (the Depression had hit agricultural Szeged particularly hard) Szent-Gyorgyi came to his rescue. He told him he "had a friend who lived in Prague—they were assistants previously in some institute—but he married a rich woman and he gave up doing research work." To ease his conscience, this friend had sent some money, to be given to a deserving young person who wanted to be a researcher.

Years later Laki was still trying to figure out if this story were true. There is no evidence of any such mysterious "friend." Laki concluded that Szent-Gyorgyi had invented this providential angel and provided the money out of his own pocket. To give the money openly would have smacked of humiliating "charity," and so he made up this tall tale to spare young Laki's feelings.

Albert's personal relations with his students were relaxed and familiar, scandalously so to Hungary's rigidly proper academic community. He routinely gave parties for his students—an unheard-of occurrence in Hungary. "It was something quite new," said Laki, "that a professor would do this in his own home."

Every week he went to the local movie theater with a troop of students, cheering loudly for the hero of the American westerns. He took frequent trips with them in the rather extravagant Buick he had brought back from America. One day, he, Laki and Ilona "Ilushka" Banga, one of his closest collaborators and the only woman in the lab, set off for the capital. It was a warm day and the Tisza, which ran alongside the road, beckoned invitingly. Laki recalled:

> We decided, ah, we should stop and have a swim, which we did. But we didn't plan for this occasion and we had no swimming suits with us. But the solution was that we went one after the other, finished and got back in the car. So, you could do it without swimsuits.

Sports of every kind were obligatory in Szent-Gyorgyi's circle. In the courtyard was a grassy area, which Albert converted into a volleyball, tennis, and soccer field.[7] Laszlo Lorand, who became a professor at Northwestern University, recalled: "If I hadn't qualified for the department volleyball team, I might have missed all the fun of the research."

Bruno Straub used to play tennis with "Prof" in the park across the river. Although Albert was twenty years his senior he beat Straub almost every time. Albert was also the first one out of the shower, ready to resume the day's activities.

There was seemingly no sport which Albert would not at least attempt to master. His motorbike became his trademark. In the spring of 1936, just after the final examinations, he jumped on his bike and took off for parts unknown. He wound up in the hospital in Spain, luckily not too badly injured. He also became a glider pilot, which was a prerequisite for piloting a motor plane. This was done at a time of national war preparedness. According to Straub, however, "Prof" simply wanted the thrill of flying; he was still a pacifist.

It is difficult to convey just how radical and outlandish all this was at the time. Sports were not a part of the curriculum or the daily life of students, as they were in the United States. Not even instructors, much less full professors, fraternized with their students. They were a class apart, and the job of the teacher was to put as much social distance as possible between himself and his students. "Skinny dipping" with attractive young students, male and female, was not just fraternizing. To the proper people of Szeged who caught wind of these activities, they smacked of wild immorality and outrageous scandal. On the other hand, Albert disarmed much of this opposition with his charming candor and forthright honesty.

This anti-authoritarian behavior could also be used to score political points. In 1932, for instance, a representative of the new radical right Gombos ministry decided to make an inspection tour of Szeged's medical biology department. He found "Prof" not in lab coat and tie, but covered with sweat and grime from a volleyball game with his students; in fact, Albert had deliberately scheduled the game to coincide with the right-wing minister's visit. Then Albert refused to interrupt his game in order to receive his official guests, who were left waiting on the edge of the field.[8]

When Albert was appointed Professor he was required by tradition to pay a formal visit to the homes of his distinguished colleagues. He and his family simply got on their bicycles and rode over to the various houses. Such behavior might pass on Tennis Court Road in Cambridge but was unacceptable in Hungary.

The physicist Zoltan Bay remembered public sentiment at the time:

> He was a young man, even looking too young for his age, but very well advanced in his research work. He was open-minded and frank in telling his opinions and that was when the troubles first began. It was even soon suggested that that childish-looking young guy had better keep his mouth shut.

Szent-Gyorgyi proved himself an educational reformer as well. He had many theories of education, usually based on his own bitter experiences as a student:

People think that education means stuffing your head with facts from a book. In my opinion, we have heads to enable us to think, and books are for reference, to aid the memory. It is much simpler to keep information in libraries, not in our heads. Besides thinking, you should be able to appreciate the grandeur of intellectual life and enjoy the immense pleasure it can give.

Albert put the emphasis in education on freedom and spontaneity, not externally applied discipline:

Personally, I live with my experiments. Shakespeare should be experienced, not learned by heart. . . . Music need not be learned either, only experienced. You have to enter into the spirit of things, become absorbed, so to speak, by science, then you will be able to love it truly.

He reflected on his own upbringing:

In the secondary school I was made to hate literature. Instead of teaching me to see the beauty of it and of intellectual and creative work in general, my head was stuffed with a lot of facts. This is the way to paralyze the human brain and cause it great damage. The load of rubbish stuffed into your head vanishes anyhow. Nothing remains of it. You forget it all. What can persist is the love of science and art, the love of beautiful things. A desire to solve problems, a readiness to act—these are the important qualities to possess.

Albert would have ample opportunities to put his educational theories to the test in Szeged.

His second realm of activity in Szeged was research. One part of this was his work on "hexuronic acid." But many other projects were going on as well. Bruno Straub says there were twenty-five different projects underway at one time. Even Albert's wife, Nelly, was pressed into service as a research assistant.

"It was a busy place, with everyone doing exciting experiments and Dr. Szent-Gyorgyi seemed to be everywhere," Laki recalled.

Dr. Banga was measuring oxygen uptake by tissues. . . . Mrs. Szent-Gyorgyi was injecting various compounds into tumor-bearing mice. A little later, Straub, my fellow student, joined the laboratory and soon was busy determining fumarate in pigeon breast muscle. To me as a young student, being led into one of the world's most advanced biochemistry laboratories, all this seemed like Alice being in Wonderland.

One of the most valuable members of the research team was a mechanic, "Uncle Rozsa," who was said to be the descendant of a famous nineteenth-century highwayman. He was a mechanical genius, said Laki. He could fix not only complicated centrifuges and ultrasound machines but "Prof's" motorbike and Buick as well.

Six months after his arrival, Albert had already established a small but important research center in southern Hungary. He wrote to his sponsors at the Rockefeller Foundation:

> I am working at top speed. In this short time I have spent in Szeged a small school of biochemistry has crystallized out and I have, or will have in the fall, eight research workers under my hand, which is about the highest number any man can deal with. We have set out on great problems, on cancer, respiration, growth, and on the principles of the transfer of chemical energy into other forms of energy within the body. It will be a long way till we get there, but as by-products we have got some quite nice results which justify this year's work.[9]

Six months later he was equally optimistic:

> My first year in Szeged was a rather difficult one though my reception was the most favorable, and I met with utter benevolence everywhere. The great difficulty lay in the general character of a continental university chair, which makes it rather difficult to be professor and scientist at the same time. I think, that for a really conscientious person it must be almost impossible to get both ends at the same time. . . .

Within one year, Albert had initiated the first degree program in biochemistry in Hungary. Previously, when biochemistry was taught it was treated as "medical chemistry," i.e., how to do lab tests. His idea was to take biochemistry out of the hands of physicians "who missed, to a great deal, scientific training."

Then, Szent-Gyorgyi made some unguarded personal remarks to Gregg:

> It is extremely interesting for me not only to test my general research administration theories but also to test myself. I really have no idea, whether I am any good as a scientist. What one feels towards science is to be attracted by the problems, sort of love for the thing, which naturally does not mean that one is a good scientist. One can know a tree only by its fruits. Given all the means at my disposal I can definitely state, that if within a few years I will not produce any results I am a great ass and good for nothing.[10]

This was a remarkably honest way to address one's patrons. But then, remembering his audience, Albert had to put in a few words of complaint about his finances:

> I do not want to pet myself on the shoulders, but perhaps it will interest you to know that from a personal point of view it is a great sacrifice to live out here. . . . Owing to the bad state of finances our salaries have been reduced again. My present pay is $80 a month. The extra income does not make more than $30–40 a month. This way I get the same as my lab girl two years ago at Rochester [Minnesota]. On this pay I have to support my family consisting of mother, wife, and child. It is extremely difficult to manage this, no provisions can be made for the future, and the number of children has to be kept down very carefully. It is true we are said to get pensions in our old days, but these are very, very low and the whole economical outlook so bad that it give you little hold for the future.[11]

He hastened to add, however, that he is "very happy and find my job very fascinating."

Albert now had the freedom to pursue whatever interested him. When he heard about the discovery of ultrasound, he immediately wanted to have a generator. He hired a young physicist, A. Szalay, to build such a machine. Szalay, then twenty-two, built one with a large piezo electric quartz crystal, which vibrated at the then astronomical rate of one million times a second.[12] Szalay, now a senior physicist at the Institute of Nuclear Research, Debrecen, recalls that Szent-Gyorgyi's real purpose was "to irradiate and perhaps to destroy cancerous cells of tumors in rats by high intensity supersonic sound waves."

> We started to irradiate white rats with cancerous tumors implanted in the abdomen. The supersonic waves probably destroyed many of the cancerous cells but some of them survived and the tumors grew again. In the end, it came out that this time the idea did not work, like many other attempts before and since then, to influence the growth of cancer.[13]

In 1931 Szent-Gyorgyi was appointed chairman of the Natural Science Research Council in Szeged. The main function of this council was to administer the $200,000 RF grant. His position now seemed secure, at least as long as the Rockefeller Foundation was. He wrote to Gregg:

> The minister [Klebelsberg] has taken me fully in his confidence and I am a sort of referee who tells in a few words what to do, after the

committees have wasted hours in discussion. I am also glad to say that I
have got the confidence of my colleagues, and I hope that this way I will be
able to fulfill the very unpleasant and difficult duties of the chairman of
the Research Committee to everyone's satisfaction.[14]

". . . . to my great surprise, my colleagues do not hate me as much
as I expected they would," he wrote.[15]

The political life of Hungary was very unstable, however. In some of
his social policies, Horthy anticipated Hitler by years. There were
frequent changes of governments under his regency but the general
drift was to the right. In October 1931 the more liberal Klebelsberg
was forced to resign his post. "Had our moral and material position
not been strengthened by the gift of the Rockefeller Foundation,"
Albert wrote, ruefully, "our University had been in serious danger of
being closed."[16]

In the fall, another Rockefeller fellow was appointed to a pro-
fessorship, making eight such fellows on the relatively small faculty.
Szeged was becoming an island of American influence in a sea of pro-
German sentiment.

Albert naturally had theories on the organization of research, and
Szeged offered him a laboratory to test them, "more or less on the skin
of others, especially in the medical faculty. . . . The baby seems to be
most healthy and vigorous and there are some very fine results in
other departments."[17]

Although Albert emphasized how he wanted "to see every penny
spent as wisely as possible" in 1931–32 the RF began to turn down
his requests for additional funds. In June 1931, for example, they
rejected his request for a salary grant to Professor Miskolczy, a friend
and colleague, whose life would shortly become intertwined with
Szent-Gyorgyi's own in a most painful way. They also rejected his
request, in February 1932, for a grant "to cover expenses of a short
trip to England for consulting physiologists there regarding some
recent developments in S-G's research on adrenal function and vitamin C." It was a modest request, and quite appropriate. The RF's
reasons for this rejection seemed bureaucratic.

[They] agreed that such aid would establish a troublesome precedent and that
a declination had best be made on this ground. It is recalled that S-G was
in England only some 18 months ago and that since Szeged is less than
three hours from Budapest and a few hours more from Vienna—two
important centers of medical research—his plea of isolation is hardly
convincing.[18]

One can imagine Albert's frustrations at this: as if he could find Hopkins, Dale, and Haworth in Vienna! He now felt his isolation in Szeged most painfully. It is amazing to us, that in the era before jet travel, satellite communications and the like, a visit to England eighteen months before was considered "recent."

From this point, in fact, the history of Szent-Gyorgyi's relationship to the RF seems marked by growing frustration and disillusionment on both sides, but especially for the Foundation. The RF could be an exemplary fund-giver (look how quickly they processed Albert's first request for a grant); they could also be obtuse. Albert by nature despised and flaunted bureaucracy; with the onset of the Depression, however, all questions involving money became very complicated.

For instance, after meeting Szent-Gyorgyi in Paris in April 1933, an RF official wrote disapprovingly in his diary:

> Another American foundation [probably the Josiah Macy Foundation—ed.] gave S-G a substantial grant, not long ago, without any conditions whatever as to its use, and since he felt he needed, at the time, a vacation more than anything else, part of the fund was used for that purpose. S-G argues that foundations should have such confidence in the men aided that grants should be unrestricted—an opinion we have heard before—but I doubt if RF officers would find S-G's use of the other foundation's fund a strong argument for greater latitude in our appropriations.[19]

Albert had also evolved a habit of making exaggerated claims for his research, mingling solid accomplishments with wild expectations—dreams, really. In describing his truly impressive work of 1932, for instance, Albert was not content to simply describe the important achievements of that year. He had to "gild the lily":

> We have not played out all our cards yet. We have made some quite intensive work in cancer with the main result, that we begin to know all the tricks of this dirty business and feel strong enough to make a real start.[20]

He was still making such claims, in almost identical language, fifty years later.

For in truth, not all of Albert's experiments ended in success. Some were impulsively started, or were beyond his means at the moment, and there were some maddeningly frustrating failures. For example, he isolated an unknown yellow dyestuff from food, but had no spectroscope with which to analyze it properly. It turned out to be riboflavin, or vitamin B_2, and was "officially" discovered and analyzed in the following year by three scientists including—by coincidence—a fellow Hungarian named P. Gyorgy.

On another occasion a shortage of chemicals in Hungary prevented him from finishing the discovery of pyridine nucleotides, which he had begun. Otto Warburg made the final discovery—a major find with broad implications for the pharmaceutical industry.

Some of these failures undoubtedly resulted from Albert's relative isolation and primitive conditions. But some of them were also the result of his erratic work style. As always, he was much better at intuitively finding a substance than following through with a painstaking analysis. There seemed to be a grain of truth in Fletcher's otherwise one-sided complaint:

> In research, his chief function seems to be that of detonator or catalyst. He has a flair without maintained industry.

By the mid-thirties, however, Albert's reputation had grown and he received numerous speaking engagements all over the world. He no longer had to beg anyone for traveling money. "The very increasing number of invitations from European countries and from America which Prof. Szent-Gyorgyi receives indicates that his work arouses international interest and recognition," an RF official wrote.[21]

On a visit back to Cambridge he was offered a permanent position. Other offers came from abroad, including America. In Stockholm he lectured on vitamins at the world-famous Karolinska Institute, the same institution which awarded the Nobel Prizes. During his stay in Paris he spoke before the Societé de Biologie. Scientists, as much as they sometimes deny it, are also human; part of Albert's appeal was that he was a good entertainer. Everywhere he went he was greeted warmly, and one suspects he was cherished as much for his spontaneous wit, stage presence, and even sex appeal as for his exciting scientific results.

Meanwhile, with the Depression, conditions at home were worsening. A train trip to Budapest, he said, cost him one fourth of his monthly salary.[22] In 1934, because of staff cutbacks, he was compelled to become professor of organic, as well as medical, chemistry. Organic chemistry was a subject he always detested, and the responsibility for it he quickly pawned off on his assistants. And, of course, the political situation was becoming increasingly difficult for him after Hitler's seizure of power in Germany.

Why then did he stay in Szeged, when he had so many attractive offers elsewhere?

There were, of course, practical considerations—his mother, his wife, his daughter. To uproot them after a decade of wandering, would be difficult and cruel. And Hungary was good for his ego. In Szeged, as he himself often said, he was a big frog in a small pond. It was natural that he liked the kind of power and prestige and perhaps even the notoriety that he found at Szeged. No American professorship could have given him the importance he had in this sleepy town. His work in biochemistry was beginning to hit its stride, and he would have to give up a trained group of coworkers, almost a dozen, in fact, who were now thoroughly devoted to their "Prof."

But over and above these practical considerations, there was something else which tied Albert to Hungary. He confessed to an RF official:

> In a small country like Hungary scientists of some renown should be patriotic enough not to expatriate themselves, otherwise the country would be rapidly depleted.

This attitude, a quiet patriotism quite different than Admiral Horthy's pompous pronouncements, greatly puzzled the RF man. "Prof. Szent-Gyorgyi has something of a dreamy idealist about him," he wrote home, "and this remark of his only corroborated the impression he makes."

"Dreamy idealist" or not, Albert Szent-Gyorgyi had returned to Hungary and was not about to leave so quickly. He had come to make his mark on the country of his birth—and the world—and to prove himself not just the greatest of the Lenhosseks, but one of the greatest Hungarian scientists of all time.

8

THE BATTLE OVER VITAMIN C

In the fall of 1931 "a very nice young man" walked into Szent-Gyorgyi's laboratory on Calvary Square (Kalvary Ter). He introduced himself as Joseph Svirbely of Pittsburgh and explained that "he was in Hungary to study for a year or so, and would like to work" with Szent-Gyorgyi.

Joe Svirbely had just received his Ph.D. from the University of Pittsburgh, under Professor C. G. King. At the urging of his family, immigrant steelworkers, Svirbely had decided to do his postdoctoral work in their homeland. He came to Hungary on an Institute of International Education fellowship, wanting to study biochemistry. That could only mean Albert Szent-Gyorgyi, as there was still no biochemistry department in Budapest.

"He talked a little broken Hungarian," said Albert, with amusement, "and so I asked him, 'What can you do?'"

Svirbely replied, "I worked with Dr. King in America. . . . I can tell you whether something contains vitamin C or not."

Albert took a tiny vial of cream-colored crystals down from the shelf and said, rather matter-of-factly, "Here, test this. I think this is vitamin C." It was all that remained of the "hexuronic acid" he had isolated at the Mayo Clinic.

This was not as far-fetched an idea as it may have seemed. In fact, Albert himself had compared the two substances in print a few years before:

> The reducing properties of plant juice have repeatedly attracted attention, especially from students of vitamin C. . . . The reducing substances of lemon juice have been made the object of a thorough study. . . . Indophenol blue is readily reduced by the hexuronic acid, so that it is probable that it was this substance which has been studied. . . .[1]

75

Yet until the day Svirbely walked into his lab, Szent-Gyorgyi had expressed no intention of following up on this lead. In fact, he disliked vitamins and everything to do with them. The popular press was filled with fantastic stories about their miraculous properties, and as a self-respecting pure researcher Albert was repelled by the whole scene.

In fact, he (and many other scientists) tended to spurn nutrition. The historical reasons for this neglect are complex, but one of them might be its association with "women's work." "For some inexplicable, childish reason," he later said, "I felt that vitamins were a problem for the cook."

Even after he became involved in the problem, Albert maintained his intellectual distance. "I was somewhat startled to learn that S-G has no longer an interest in vitamins," a Rockefeller Foundation officer wrote a few years later. "In fact, he stated most emphatically that vitamins per se are of relatively little fundamental scientific interest. . . ."[2]

In this simple, off-handed way Albert became involved in the vitamin C business, which was to play such an important part in his subsequent career and life.

This controversy over "C" had actually begun in the sixteenth century, when Jacques Cartier, the French explorer, reported that his men had been cured of scurvy by an infusion of boiled pine needles. Almost nobody in the medical profession believed in such Indian remedies, or that the disease could be controlled by "miracle" foods, such as the then-exotic citrus fruits.

It took a hundred years for this folk remedy to make any headway. In 1721, one Dr. Kramer compiled a long list of anti-scurvy foods, and citruses headed the list. In 1753 Dr. James Lind finally made a scientific test of this controversial treatment. As physician aboard the H.M.S. Salisbury, he divided the sailors into two groups—one got oranges, the others did not. (This is said to have been the first use of a "control group" in medical history.)

The group with scurvy who did not receive oranges suffered untold tortures, as did millions of other people at that time: their legs became swollen and infected; their teeth fell out; eventually they went into convulsions and comas. Death came as a relief. The group that received the oranges were totally scurvy-free. One could not have asked for more dramatic and convincing proof. Yet many of Lind's fellow physicians reacted with scorn. "There are certain persons," he wrote four years later, "who just will not let themselves be convinced that a terrible disease can be cured easily; yes, that it even can be prevented."[3]

The rest is well-known. English sailors became "limies" and the

British navy ruled the waves. After all, it had a cure for scurvy which others continued to scorn.

From a strictly scientific point of view, however, Lind's experiments added little to human knowledge. For the *nature* of the curative substance in citruses remained a mystery. In 1841 a Dr. G. Budd predicted that chemists would soon be able to isolate the "essential element" from citrus. Budd was an optimist. Although Szent-Gyorgyi's teacher, Hopkins, explained the nature of "accessory food factors" in 1912, the anti-scurvy factor, now called vitamin C, still eluded all searchers.

After World War I, drug companies threw their resources behind the search. In the 1920s the Eli Lilly company requisitioned an entire railroad carload of powdered lemon juice in an attempt to extract just a few pure vitamin C crystals. All they got was a mess of boiled-down citrus.

On both sides of the Atlantic, scientists raced for fame, fortune, and—it was assumed—a Nobel Prize. The leading European group was that of Prof. S. S. Zilva of London's famous Lister Institute. Zilva had laboriously precipitated, fractionated, and fermented various batches of fruit juice. The end product was potent and effective, but it still was not the pure crystal.

In the United States there was a frantic competition. (No native-born American had yet won a Nobel Prize for Physiology or Medicine.) But researchers often found themselves swamped by unexpected difficulties. The vitamin itself was sugar-like and easily lost amid the many other sugars in citrus concentrates. It was also unstable: just as scientists were about to put their hands on it, the active fraction would suddenly disappear. There was no cheap chemical test. The only animal other than man which did not manufacture its own vitamin C was the guinea pig. This rodent's voracious appetite took a big bite out of any researcher's budget. In other words, the whole procedure was messy, laborious, and prohibitively expensive for most scientists.[4]

Some investigators got tantalizingly close to a solution, only to be turned back at the last minute. At the University of Wisconsin, Karl Link prepared several grams of crude calcium ascorbate from oat sprouts. His dean then denied him a research grant of a few hundred dollars to test the substance in guinea pigs. In the Army Surgeon General's office, another scientist managed to obtain crude crystals, but before he could finish the test his "superiors" transferred him to a distant post. End of experiment.

In the United States the leading group was that of young Charles Glen King at the University of Pittsburgh. King had learned his testing techniques from the eminent Prof. Sherman of Columbia University.[5]

C. G. King was an ambitious Westerner with a clear view of the goal. Although he was just barely out of graduate school himself, the University of Pittsburgh had given him six graduate students of his own and a generous amount of laboratory space to purify the elusive vitamin.

King's laboratory wafted the pleasant odor of cooking citrus over the downtown campus. He and his graduate students formed a close-knit team, fighters in the battle for vitamin C. They were almost industrial in their discipline and division of labor; one would expect nothing less from Pittsburgh. A crucial part of the job, that of preparing the concentrates, was given to King's young Hungarian-American assistant, Joe Svirbely.

And now fate, it seemed, had dropped young Svirbely in Szent-Gyorgyi's lap. It was fortunate, because searching for vitamins was not just difficult, but messy and boring. There were all sorts of technical problems involved. Without Svirbely it is doubtful that Szent-Gyorgyi ever would have undertaken such a test. First of all, he hated working with animals. He was a modern biochemist, after all, who worked with test tubes, and had left anatomy and physiology far behind. "I am plenty nervous when I have to touch an animal," he once wrote a British colleague, "which is much too complicated [a] system for me."[6]

He could certainly have overcome these scruples, had he been sufficiently motivated. But he simply was not. When Svirbely appeared at his doorstep, however, testing "hexuronic acid" to see if it were vitamin C suddenly became "relatively easy and convenient."

A vitamin, as Albert quipped, was "a substance you get sick from if you don't eat it," and there was a standard, logical test for identifying one.

By feeding a group of animals a diet known *not* to contain a particular vitamin, scientists could bring on the deficiency disease associated with a lack of that substance. They then could re-introduce various substances, one by one, into the animal's diet. If the animal recovered from the disease—or if a control group given the substance did not develop the disease in the first place—one could be sure that this substance was (or contained) the vitamin. (In 1907, A. Holst and T. Fröhlich had produced scurvy experimentally in guinea pigs.)

Of course, the gap between *containing* a specific vitamin and *being* a specific vitamin was great. To know that one had the actual vitamin in hand meant being able to crystallize the substance, dissolve it, and then repeatedly recrystallize it without any loss of potency. Such a process would eliminate the dross and leave one with the pure, unalloyed vitamin. This, in turn, would allow chemists to identify the vitamin's nature and eventually mass produce it for the market. It was this which no one had yet been able to do with vitamin C.

And so Joe Svirbely put on his apron and set to work. First he autoclaved (i.e., heated with steam) the guinea pigs' food to destroy any stray source of the vitamin. (It was known that vitamin C was destroyed by intense heat.) On that overcooked diet the animals predictably began to die of scurvy. He then added a very minute amount (about 1 mg. per day) of Szent-Gyorgyi's "hexuronic acid" crystals to the feed of half the animals. After a month the guinea pigs who simply received autoclaved food were losing weight, visibly dying of scurvy. The ones who received the crystals as a supplement were growing normally; perfectly healthy, no scurvy, no disease. By ordinary scientific criteria there seemed little doubt.

Early that winter a euphoric Svirbely went to "Prof" and proudly announced, "I now know what your crystals are. They're pure vitamin C." It was a moment of great excitement in the Szeged laboratory.

Albert Szent-Gyorgyi finally understood what "hexuronic acid" was all about. He had not been chasing an adrenal hormone, as he had once thought, but a plant substance which, through ingestion, was also present in the human body. The fact that this substance had been isolated from adrenals was serendipity, a lucky chance. Although the amounts involved were tiny, the lack of competing sugar acids made it somewhat easier to isolate this substance from the adrenal gland than from lemons or oranges.

This all happened quickly; this first test was completed before the end of 1931. Meanwhile, in Pittsburgh, King was still hunting frantically for the vitamin. He too, he says, was aware of a possible link between "hexuronic acid" and vitamin C. "Nick" Kendall suggested it to him at the spring 1929 meeting of the American Chemical Society. Also, King had studied at the Dunn laboratory in Cambridge for a few months in the fall of 1929. (He was the visitor who heard Hopkins ruminating in the library stacks.) Hopkins, he later claimed, shared the idea with him that "hexuronic acid" might be the vitamin.[7]

King thought he was making excellent progress and, in a sense, he was. The test period for vitamin C had been shortened to eight weeks. Its approximate molecular weight had been determined. But, as it turned out, the Pittsburgh researcher was approaching the problem from the wrong end, trying to first refine and isolate the vitamin and then find out what it was. By comparison, Szent-Gyorgyi had the easier route. He already, quite fortuitously, had the chemical in hand. He also had one of King's best researchers to perform the test for him. All he had to do was confirm his own suspicions about its identity.

Svirbely now told "Prof," "I need another month to be sure, to finish the experiment." By the end of 1931, the control group of animals in Szeged had died of scurvy. Just to be sure, Albert told him to repeat the test two more times: he did not want to go public with this claim without being absolutely certain. Yet each time the experiment came out the same, since even tiny amounts of "hexuronic acid" saved the animals from death by scurvy. There simply could be no question about it: they had isolated and identified vitamin C.

Albert had not been trained in vitamin research, had not spent years studying the techniques, and was not part of the worldwide fraternity (some would say "clique") of vitamin C researchers. What he knew about vitamin testing was mainly brought to him by Svirbely. Perhaps it was unfair, but Albert Szent-Gyorgyi of Szeged, Hungary, had almost by accident done what no one else in the world had been able to do: isolate the most elusive vitamin.

For Svirbely, amid the jubilation, there was a difficult problem. "What is my position towards King?" he asked Albert. "He was my teacher, and he's worked all his life to find out what vitamin C is."

"If you were my student and went away and found out what I was looking for and did not tell me, I would say—" he paused for effect— "you were a lousy, lousy fellow." "Lousy, lousy fellow" was always Albert's most damning imprecation. Hitler, for instance, who was taking power in Germany just at this time, was a "lousy, lousy fellow" and one could have no dealings with that sort. "You'd better write to King and tell him what you've found."

And so, in March 1932, Svirbely wrote to King, telling him excitedly that vitamin C and "hexuronic acid" were now proven to be one and the same substance.

At the same moment, King had gone off on a tangent. In late 1931, a report by Norwegian scientists had appeared in the literature claiming that vitamin C was a well-known alkaloid, a derivative of nornarcotine. Szent-Gyorgyi and Svirbely laughed at this report and agreed it was "a pile of crap."[8] But the methodical, ever-correct Dr. King had insisted on closely examining the Scandinavian data, losing, as it turned out, valuable time:

> Their technical journal was not available in Pittsburgh and a search for it caused a delay in our reply. On careful examination of the original papers, however, it was apparent that every one of the test groups of guinea pigs that did not develop scurvy had been fed a basal ration that contained vitamin C, as illustrated by a product called "dried sprouts."[9]

It was at this point in time that King received Svirbely's letter exulting in his victory, or so said Szent-Gyorgyi, for now the discrepancies begin. King did not remember it happening this way. According to him, once the confusion over the false Norwegian report had been cleared up, "we then submitted our paper for the spring meeting of the American Society of Biological Chemists and sent another manuscript to *Science*." These papers, he emphasized, had been submitted *before* word arrived from Szeged:

> A few weeks later in March, I received a letter from Dr. Svirbely . . . in which he mentioned that they were just finishing their first assay in which animals grew satisfactorily and were protected from scurvy when given 1 mg/day of their crystalline "hexuronic acid." They were sending a report of the assay to *Nature*.[10]

On 1 April 1932 a letter from King appeared in *Science* announcing his own discovery of vitamin C. The substance, he said, was identical to "hexuronic acid." No credit for the discovery was given to Szent-Gyorgyi or Svirbely. The letter received wide publicity and four days later the *New York Times* carried a front-page story on the discovery, "Pittsburgh Professor Isolates Vitamin C":

> A young Professor of Chemistry at the University of Pittsburgh announced casually tonight: "We have isolated and identified vitamin C."
> For five years, Dr. C. G. King, not quite 35, and his associates, have labored for a solution long sought by research scientists.
> The importance of his work, the exacting calculations, the arduous research and the patient tests found no place in Dr. King's simple announcement. But he leaned back in his laboratory chair and explained that he had concentrated the vitamin from lemon juice.

In Szeged, Szent-Gyorgyi was astounded, then saddened, then infuriated, by the announcement of King's claim. Ironically, it was at *his* insistence that Joe Svirbely had sent word of the "secret" of vitamin C to his ex-teacher. Now here was King publishing these findings under his own name and prestigious American publications were backing him to the hilt.

But how could Szent-Gyorgyi be sure that King had not simply made the discovery independently? By this: a few days before the announcement, Svirbely had received a letter from Pittsburgh in which King had admitted that he was still confused about the nature of vitamin C and its relationship to "hexuronic acid."

This letter, and Svirbely's own note to King, had apparently crossed in the transatlantic mail. And then, a week or so later, King had suddenly burst into print with news of "his" discovery. To Szent-Gyorgyi it was a case of scientific plagiarism, of theft pure and simple.

King, it seemed to Szent-Gyorgyi, was another "lousy, lousy fellow" who had betrayed not just a student's confidences, but science itself.

But the damage was done. The report had already appeared in *Science,* received the imprimatur of the *New York Times,* and was about to be published in a major biochemical journal.[11] Albert suddenly realized just how isolated he was—stuck away in a half-built university in a provincial town in a defeated East European country. His mood alternated between anger and depression. King was walking away with all the honors. The fruit of eight years' work on "hexuronic acid" had been stolen right out from under him.

"There's not a single experiment—nothing," he cried out in dismay, rereading King's letter to *Science.*

> King had just published our letter, with all the consequences of the discovery. This was a shock to me, but I didn't mind very much because I thought, "It's immaterial for science who discovers it."

A noble sentiment, and no doubt what Albert *wanted* to believe. Part of him probably felt that way; the other part, however, was fighting mad and intended to claim the credit that was due. A few days later Albert sent off his own letter to *Nature,* the British counterpart of *Science,* announcing his own discovery of the vitamin.[12]

In those days priority battles in science were rare. Scientists were supposed to be gentlemen (or occasionally gentlewomen), disinterested in fame or fortune. When Szent-Gyorgyi's conflicting claim appeared in *Nature* it raised eyebrows—and tempers—on both sides of the Atlantic. This dispute had the makings of a European-American rivalry: behind King stood Sherman and the upward-striving American establishment; behind Albert, his staid, but still very influential British mentors.

Both sides could not be right. The solution to the dispute obviously rested on what actually happened in a few weeks in March 1932. There was no doubt over who published first: that was King—sixteen days earlier, in fact. Yet priority was not simply a matter of first *publication.* Science did not give laurels for plagiarism. But to establish such a charge was very difficult, especially since scientists were loathe to pin labels on their colleagues. A scientist's word was supposed to be his bond.

The critical question therefore, of who actually first identified "hexuronic acid" as vitamin C through his own experimental work, was not settled but continued to smoulder.

King's own chronology of the events should have made any impartial arbiter suspicious, however. "We then submitted our paper for the spring meeting of the American Society of Biological Chemists," he had written (in one of his later *apologias*) ". . . and sent another manuscript to *Science. A few weeks later in March,* I received a letter from Dr. Svirbely, in which he mentioned that they were just finishing their first assay"[13] [emphasis added].

But the date of the article received by the Society could not be talked away: it was given in the printed version of the paper as *9 May 1932.* (It was not published until July of that year). Such dates are routinely printed in scientific publications precisely in order to clear up priority questions, and to defend authors' claims against delays in publication on the part of the journal's editors.

The ninth of May was well past the point that King had received Svirbely's letter, and almost a month after Szent-Gyorgyi's own letter had appeared in *Nature.* King's supporters therefore fell back on the argument that at least his letter to *Science* was submitted well before 9 May—in the last weeks of March. But this fact can hardly be used as proof of prior *discovery:* for, as Albert was quick to point out, the *Science* letter contained no details which could not have easily been inferred from Svirbely's correspondence to him.

The crucial fact, the critical piece of evidence, thus became the letter which King was said to have written to Svirbely in mid-March, in which he allegedly admitted that he still did not know what vitamin C was.

Albert wanted some neutral party to arbitrate the dispute. The ideal person was "Nick" Kendall who himself was working on "hexuronic acid," knew both Szent-Gyorgyi and King, and was respected by them both. Albert wrote to Kendall in care of the American Chemical Society, asking him to appoint a committee to investigate the charges and counter-charges. Albert heard nothing, but when he ran into Kendall in Zurich in 1934 he pressed the point.

"Nick, do you remember my letter?" he inquired. "I asked you to look into the facts. Did you do that? What did you do about it?"

According to Albert, Kendall replied, "I looked into it, and it was plain that the only thing I could do was to wring King's neck, and I didn't feel like doing it." Kendall was clearly in a most uncomfortable situation. Not only was King a fellow American, but both of them had been students of the influential Professor Sherman at Columbia.

Joe Svirbely studied with Kendall when he returned to the United States in the following year. Kendall strongly advised him to avoid the entire controversy as potentially damaging to his career. Svirbely followed this prudent course and for years shied away from the controversy. In time, he dropped from sight, taking with him the most important letters and documents relating to the affair.

Fifty years later, researching this question, the author managed to locate Svirbely in a Washington, D.C., suburb. The erstwhile graduate student was now a white-haired man in his seventies, retired after an undistinguished government career. He was clearly of two minds about talking: eager to set the record straight and yet afraid of some unnamed forces which could still somehow harm him. After much hesitation, he allowed the author to read his file on the case, but to photocopy only a single document. The obvious choice was the handwritten letter King had, indeed, sent to Svirbely in mid-March:

March 15, 1932

Dear Svirbely:

It's a great life! We've been holding up a note to *Science,* calling attention to the similarity or identity of Sz-G's hexuronic acid & vitamin C until further word might come from you, & also until a second run of recrystallized material had been assayed. The product appears to be identical with S-G's product, but further chemical work will have to be done before one can be sure. I don't want to "make haste too fast" but it certainly looks like we are on the right trail. Waugh is plugging away as usual, but you know by experience what a slow job it is. It's a good stroke on your part to get the relationship shown there. In the note which should appear in *Science* in a few weeks, I cite your last J.B.C. [Journal of Biological Chemistry] paper as leading up close to where we are now, and took occasion to state that we (it is a joint note by Waugh and myself) thought Rygh had misinterpreted his experimental results. The two notes (i.e. yours and ours) to be followed by detailed reports should cover Rygh's claims (i.e. point out the fallacies in his conclusions) . . . and—I hope—demonstrate that it is not vitamin C. C—will probably start the test in a couple of weeks if all goes well.

We have two groups of [guinea] pigs finishing up the second run, & they have given such fine results that if the "hexuronic acid" is an individual, single, pure compound, it is very unlikely that an adhering material would have reached a maximum activity with recryst[alization].

I'm mightly glad that the . . . results of our own and another laboratory were accomplished in both cases by "our gang", too.

The next thing is "what more has Kendall got up his sleeve?" He hasn't written a word since a year ago when he said that only a few details remained to be ironed out before he would send a pre-print copy of his paper on his "improved" method for isolating large quantitites of hexuronic acid.

It's to your credit too that you persuaded S-G to let you assay his crystals for "c" activity. I think you probably were "using your head" on the 1 mg. level too in view of the age of the prep. and the level you had used in your last run here. Some of these days, when a few more years have rolled around, you, Waugh, McKinnis, Sipple, Grettie, myself and perhaps some new ones, will have to get together & hold a reunion of the "veterans of the Battle of Vitamin C."

Congratulations on the good work. The two notes should come out about the same time in the natural course of events—in a month perhaps, & can be followed by details about the same time too, although that will take considerably longer here at least, on account of the J.B.C. being slow.

With best regards & wishes for continuing success,

Sincerely yours,

Glen King.

This letter contains a number of revealing statements.

First, by his own admission, as of 15 March King was still "holding up a note to *Science* calling attention to the similarity or identity of Sz-G's hexuronic acid and vitamin C. . . ." In other words, King's own research had not yet proven the identity of the two substances. He did not know what vitamin C was, but still had "a second run of re-crystallized material" to do. He still thought of hexuronic acid and vitamin C as two separate substances: "the different kinds of crystals in both interest me considerably," he said. Contrast all this with King's *published* statement that his paper was submitted to *Science* and then "*a few weeks later in March,* I received a letter from Dr. Svirbely . . . They were sending a report of the assay to *Nature.*"[14]

This is clearly wrong. By 15 March, King had still had a great deal of work to do on it. At about the same time, Svirbely wrote announcing his and Szent-Gyorgyi's discovery. Next, King's letter appears in *Science.* It is hard to avoid the conclusion that King received Svirbely's letter, realized that the time for hesitation had passed, and quickly sent off his own contribution to *Science.*

There seemed to have been some informal understanding between the two groups about sharing credit. (Svirbely hinted that this was so, but would not elaborate.) But all talk of simultaneous publication was now forgotten. King was after sole recognition.

Aside from the chronology, however, there is another reason for questioning King's account. In a 1953 article he claimed that "E. C. Kendall . . . sent us a sample of hexuronic acid which he had prepared by a new and very different procedure, from adrenal glands. This product being identical with ours in chemical and biological tests, there seemed to be no room for doubt of the identity of the vitamin."[15]

The doubt, however, was about the nature of the substance Kendall had sent him. He may have had something called "hexuronic acid."

But it is questionable whether this was the *pure crystal* with which Szent-Gyorgyi had started. Whatever it was, King had recrystallized it, and yet was still in doubt about its purity.

Kendall had gone on working with "hexuronic acid" after Szent-Gyorgyi's departure. But it seems doubtful that he had developed a method of large-scale, purified production by this time. Albert said he never heard of such a development. And Svirbely, who worked with Kendall in 1934, said that all Kendall had in his possession were some bottles of dark liquid labelled "hexuronic acid," not pure crystals.

There is also a letter in Svirbely's possession from Frederick L. Smith, a former colleague at Pittsburgh, dated 5 February 1938. In it, Smith recalled that King "certainly tried to get some of Szent-Gyorgyi's material from someone in the Middle West for me but was unsuccessful." Kendall was the only person in the Midwest working on this problem.[16]

Part of King's difficulty, therefore, was that he had an uncertain supply of "hexuronic acid," and had to spend a great deal of time trying to come up with a thoroughly reliable product. Albert, as we have noted, started with that crystalline product in his possession.

On the other hand, Albert had a number of proofs that he himself discovered the nature of vitamin C before reading King's letter to *Science*. On 18 March 1932, for instance, several days before the letter could have arrived from Pittsburgh, Szent-Gyorgyi spoke about the identity of "hexuronic acid" and the vitamin before the Hungarian Medical Association. A report of this talk was given in a German medical journal. In addition, the author found an entry in a Rockefeller Foundation official's diary that on 24 March 1932 (a week before King's letter appeared in *Science*) Szent-Gyorgyi had told him, "we identified vitamin[e] C."[17]

In 1933 King and his coworker Waugh applied for a patent on both vitamin C and its process of manufacture from lemons. A valid patent on the vitamin would have probably been worth a great deal of money. (Even without a patent, drug manufacturers have made a fortune out of it over the years.) For more than a decade King fought a hard and long struggle to obtain a commercial claim. But in a landmark case, *In re King et al.*, the examiner and the board of appeals rejected both process and product claims relating to vitamin C. The court ruled:

> Appellants were not the first to discover or produce hexuronic acid in its pure form which is vitamin C. They did not discover that vitamin C is a specific [cure] for scurvy. Appellants contend it was invention to have discovered that hexuronic acid is vitamin C. Had the substance not been known before it was isolated by appellants there would be force to the

contention. All they did, however, was to produce a compound that was old in the art as is shown by the publications of Szent-Gyorgyi.[18]

Read carefully, this might not give clear precedence of discovery to Szent-Gyorgyi, but it was certainly no comfort to Prof. King and his supporters.

Although in time it was generally accepted that Szent-Gyorgyi had discovered the vitamin, he paid a price for this. King became Albert's *bête noire* and seemed to dog his career. Everything that went wrong seemed to Albert to stem from Prof. King. When Albert would visit America, he felt that people were looking at him as "that lousy Hungarian" who stole credit for vitamin C away from a "good American." He recalled every insult:

> The Academic Press gave a big dinner in the United States at the International Chemical Congress, and I was asked to be an after-dinner speaker. A pupil of mine was sitting there next to an American. In a speech you give away your character, more or less, and after my speech, this American said, "I think, after this speech, that this Szent-Gyorgyi is not such a dirty skunk as I thought he was."

Even in victory there was bitterness. He and Svirbely, not King and his coworkers, were the true veterans of the battle over vitamin C, with scars to prove it. The Hungarians are a proud people, and in Albert's youth such an affront to his honor might have ended in a duel. Albert scorned such feudalistic traditions, of course, but the insult remained to rankle. Even decades after the affair had died down for the rest of the world, it continued to trouble and pain him. His faith had been betrayed, his best intentions doubted, his good name besmirched. Even today, when Szent-Gyorgyi's claim seems undeniable, some American texts continue to credit King. As just one example, the prestigious *McGraw-Hill Modern Scientists and Engineers* says that it was C. G. King who "succeeded in isolating the crystalline vitamin in the fall of 1931."

When things went wrong it became difficult to distinguish factual from imagined persecution. For instance, Albert claimed that King tried to bribe and, when that did not work, to threaten Svirbely into silence. Svirbely flatly denied this.

When Albert discovered the bioflavinoids in 1933 he wanted them recognized as a vitamin; he even gave them a letter, "P." But although these substances gained favor within the health food world as a supplement, the international scientific community would not agree that they constituted a true class of vitamins. The bioflavinoids were nearly ubiquitous in foods, scientists argued, and it was impossible to demonstrate any particular *disease* caused by a lack of them. Albert could not accept this: he was sure that the machinations of King, who headed a crucial nutrition committee in the United States, had decided the matter.

Even in 1985, at the age of ninety-two, Albert hesitated to submit a paper to a prestigious scientific journal where one of King's students was the editor. He was certain the paper would be rejected for this reason alone. It did little good to point out that King himself was beyond caring, quietly living out his remaining days in a Pennsylvania retirement colony.

The feud revealed something about Albert's character. These open and whispered accusations seemed to tap a submerged lake of self-doubt in Albert's mind. If the child is father to the man, we must remember that this child had been rejected by an absentee father, mistrusted by his famous uncle and, worst of all, disfavored by a beloved mother. Beneath the surface of Albert's bounding self-confidence there was still a reservoir of insecurity.

In some ways the King affair also heralded a change in science itself. People like Albert Szent-Gyorgyi, who came of age in Europe before the First World War, had gone into research with the highest ideals and expectations. That war had shattered their faith in everything—except science. "I was convinced that everybody who was in science must be an honest man," he wrote.

Yet science itself was in the process of changing from the gentlemanly pursuit of truth to a business proposition, whose coordinates were profit and power.

"The savants and artists of all Europe were so closely united by the bond of a common ideal that cooperation between them was scarcely affected by political events," Albert Einstein once wrote. Under the impact of greed and nationalism, however, that noble idealism of science began to break down. "Today," Einstein continued, in the thirties, "we look back at this state of affairs as a lost paradise. The passions of nationalism have destroyed this community of the intellect."[19]

It was high-minded and youthful idealism that brought young men such as Albert Einstein or Albert Szent-Gyorgyi to science. It was their generous, unselfish desire to add to the store of human knowledge which made them into not just good scientists, but outstanding intellectual figures. But by the 1930s, any good-natured belief in ideals was strained to the limit by the harsh realities of cut-throat competition.

9

THE ROAD TO STOCKHOLM

Albert, in the summer of 1932, found himself in an embarrassing position: he had staked his claim to the isolation of vitamin C, but could not repeat the experiment. In discovering the nature of the vitamin, he had used up the last supply of crystals. In Birmingham, the chemist Norman Haworth waited for Szent-Gyorgyi to send him some more "hexuronic acid" crystals. He had exhausted the samples Albert had sent him from the Mayo Clinic.

With no large-scale supply of adrenal glands on hand, Albert tried to isolate some from citrus fruits and cabbages, but with no more luck than in previous years. By September, the isolator of vitamin C had by necessity given up research on the topic.

Szeged, it so happens, is the paprika capital of Hungary, if not the world. In Hungary, paprika—dried and ground sweet pepper—is not just a spice but a great national tradition. (Restaurant tables there sport matching salt and paprika shakers.) In Szeged peppers are also served fresh in the harvest season as a popular side dish.[1]

Albert did not share the local enthusiasm for this food:

> One evening my wife, Nelly, gave me paprika for supper, but though I did not feel like eating it, I had not the courage to tell her so. I looked at the paprika and it occurred to me that I had never tested it. I told my wife I would not eat it but take it to the laboratory with me.

That evening the Szent-Gyorgyis had a particularly boring guest for dinner at the Calvary Square apartment. Albert excused himself and, pushing open the screen door of the dining room, ran down the narrow back steps, through the walled-in garden, and into a door halfway down the path. This was his private entrance to the lab. It was late now, but "Prof," always a very light sleeper, often haunted the laboratory at night.

"A husband's cowardice" now impelled him to test fresh paprika for vitamin C content. The plant quickly yielded a positive reaction for the presence of the acid.

A. Szalay, the young physicist on his staff, gave a slightly different version of this event. He was at the laboratory himself one summer Sunday, having just returned from a boat trip on the Maros and Tisza Rivers. He was eating a snack in the kitchen, when "Prof" appeared in the doorway:

> A Bulgarian vegetable gardener followed him with a big basket of green paprika on his back. Szent-Gyorgyi called me soon: "Come on, Szalay, help a little." "With pleasure," I answered and wondered what should we do with green paprika and supersonic waves? But this time my task was just that of a dishwasher or kitchen aide.
>
> We cut out the cobs with seeds and discarded them. The juicy husks were crushed by means of a meat-grinder and the juice was separated from the plant fibres by a centrifuge. . . . It came out within half an hour by titration analysis that it contains a much higher concentration of vitamin C than cabbage juice does.[2]

According to Szalay, Szent-Gyorgyi first thought of testing paprika when "he noticed on his evening walk the street vendor, trying to sell his green paprika; and it occurred to him to investigate it." It is difficult to reconcile these two accounts: perhaps Albert sought out the grocer after he had already tested his wife's paprika. "Prof" further surprised his young colleague by predicting, quite confidently, that paprika juice would "conserve its vitamin C content better" than other sources:

> He started to investigate this immediately. He poured out the paprika juice into a flat open dish and shook it for about a quarter of an hour and the vitamin C content was determined again with the result that nothing of it was oxidized by its contact with air.
>
> He noticed on my face that I was astonished by his successful intuitive expectation and instructed me immediately. A freshly cut apple surface or peeled-off potato turn rapidly yellow or brown under the oxidizing effect of oxygen of air. Plants contain more or less oxidase enzymes which accelerate oxidation. The freshly cut surface of paprika does not get a brown stain, it is defended from oxidation.
>
> It is the exceptional ability of an outstanding scientist to notice such an insignificant phenomenon and immediately draw the proper conclusions from it.[3]

Albert's intuition was right on target, for further tests revealed the pepper to be "a regular mine of vitamin C." And since paprika was not a particularly sweet fruit, like oranges, there was less difficulty in separating vitamin C from the other extraneous sugars which gummed up the works in the Sherman-King experiments. The very next day, in fact, a large-scale attempt to produce ascorbic acid began in Szent-Gyorgyi's laboratory.

Although there were more than a dozen other projects underway, everything else now ceased. The entire staff was mobilized, infected by "Prof's" enthusiasm. One large room of the laboratory was emptied; students fanned out to the local markets where they startled the local vegetable dealers by buying up all the paprika in sight. On "Prof's" instructions, they demanded the tomato paprika (named for its globular shape), which tests had shown contained five or six times the vitamin C content of orange juice. And so, by a strange quirk of fate, it turned out that one of the most abundant natural sources of the vitamin was growing almost in Albert's very backyard.

When news leaked out of what was happening, Szeged was elated but hardly surprised. For local folklore had always insisted that paprika was good for whatever ailed you—from malaria to vampires.[4]

For a man who disdained his father's business interests, Albert proved himself a regular paprika magnate. Szalay recalled:

> During the next days the whole atmosphere of the little institute changed. It became similar to an industrious, enterprising farm family, trying to produce paprika juice for the market. Horse-pulled carts arrived with huge heaps of green paprika. Everybody in the institute, including Szent-Gyorgyi's wife and daughter, were busy processing green paprika. Big 50-liter balloon flasks were filled up with the juice and closed tightly in order to exclude the oxygen of air [until] the vitamin C content would be extracted from them.

Local peasant women were employed to turn peppers into paprika powder and powder into vitamin C. The biggest problem were the red-hot seeds, which now and then would jump up into the womens' eyes. At last, Albert even found a use for his medical training: he became the workshop's impromptu medic, soothing the women's eyes, and hurrying them back to work.

In Minnesota, he had labored for a year to produce an ounce of this substance. Now, in one glorious week, he and his co-workers produced over three *pounds* (one and a half kilograms) of pure, crystalline vitamin C!

It is difficult today, when vitamin C is almost as common as salt, to understand what this meant or recreate the excitement. This "clean, concentrated, miraculous substance" (said Szalay) had unknown, but certainly wonderful properties. And this was the first time that it, or for that matter any vitamin, had been produced on such a large scale anywhere in the world. It was a great breakthrough.

Nor did it escape anyone's notice that there was a potential for enormous financial gain in this situation. Here, after all, was the beginning of what was soon to become the whole multi-billion dollar vitamin industry. And at this juncture Albert did something which, to this day, brings him as much credit as the actual discovery. Without a moment's hesitation, he decided to give away both the vitamin and the secret of its production to those who needed it. According to Szalay:

> The possession of this huge amount was a world monopoly since this was the only place in the world having it. The situation was very similar to that of Mme. Curie with her first radium preparations. Many people, even some outstanding scientists, would have preferred to preserve this monopoly for themselves or their collaborators at least for some time. This would have the advantage of further priorities, e.g. determination of its chemical structure, synthesis from cheaper substances for a cheap industrial production with its business advantages, patent rights, etc.
>
> But Szent-Gyorgyi acted similarly to Mme. Curie, but in a different way. He distributed his vitamin C immediately among the most able, competent scientists in the world, so that these tasks could be solved as quickly as possible. He was more interested in the rapid, general progress of human science than in some group interests. Preserving a monopoly would have retarded progress, at least for some time.[5]

Some of it was sent, of course, to Norman Haworth in Birmingham, who quicky established its chemical nature. It was obvious now that these crystals were not "hexuronic acid" at all. Prof. Harden had been wrong about this; in fact "Ignose" or even "Godnose" would have been more accurate! Nor had Albert found a mysterious new hormone specific to the adrenals. Rather, the adrenal glands stored and possibly used, but did not manufacture, vitamin C.

The first thing to do was to give "hexuronic acid" a new name. It was Szent-Gyorgyi and Haworth who decided to call it the "a-scorbic acid," meaning that it prevented the scorbutic disease, scurvy. The name "ascorbic acid" is so familiar today that it is surprising to realize it was coined in such relatively recent times.

Batches were next sent to scientists around the world who were working on this, or collateral, problems, even before they requested it.[6] A whole pound, for instance, was sent to the Health Organization of the League of Nations (predecessor of the World Health Organization) for distribution to those areas of the world still plagued by scurvy. One such country was Norway, where in the winter schoolchildren often suffered health problems from a lack of fresh fruit and vegetables.

After the method of manufacturing vitamin C became widely known, Szent-Gyorgyi did obtain a patent on a product called "Pritamin," a tinned preparation of seasoned paprika. According to a Hungarian account, "This pleasantly piquant concentrated paprika spread, which can be used for sandwiches, for meat dishes, etc. . . . is exported to all parts of the world." (Originally Albert had called the product "Vita-prik," but was mystified when the spread did not sell well in English-speaking lands. His mastery of English slang was not yet complete! Eventually, says Professor Straub, the problem was pointed out to him and the name was changed.[7]) Profits from Pritamin were used to fund further research in the laboratory.

Albert's personal attitude towards vitamin C remained contradictory, however. The discovery which made him famous had come about as a sideline, a by-product of his main activity, which was to understand intracellular metabolism. Vitamins were still "a problem for the cook." Yet once the discovery had been made, Albert was swept up by the excitement and an almost-childish pride in his finding. He toured Europe, in his own words "preaching vitamin C." Every week, it seemed, he was touting some wonderful new properties for what he unabashedly called his "baby." These claims predated and often anticipated those made for vitamin C fifty years later.

But what exactly did this wonderful ascorbic acid actually do? It prevented scurvy, of course, but that could be done with an orange or a few milligrams of powder. Using his intuition, Albert quickly put forward a central idea of what later was dubbed "megavitamin" or "orthomolecular therapy," that there is a wide margin between the absence of disease and complete health:

A partial lack of this vitamin manifests itself in a decreased resistance of the body. The many colds in this time of the year [winter] may be due, in part at least, to this decreased resistance. Since the vitamin is available now in crystalline form in quantity this question is more than of theoretical importance.[8]

Years later, Koloman Laki recalled:

I myself often came down with colds in the winters and on Dr. Szent-Gyorgyi's suggestion I took large quantities of his vitamin C daily. From that experience I am convinced that Professor [Linus] Pauling is right when he advocates taking large quantities of vitamin C in the winter months.[9]

In 1933 Albert tried to arrange large-scale clinical trials to test this theory. He wrote to Sir Walter Fletcher in England:

> I wonder, dear Sir Walter, whether it was not possible for you, to have a big test put on this line. There is no danger in the experiment and I could offer you 50 grams of the crystalline vitamin prepared by the Chinoin Works Ltd, Ujpest, for this purpose. The material is enough to have a test done really properly on [a] big scale.[10]

Szent-Gyorgyi's proposal was to give thirty babies 5 mg. per day of pure vitamin C. Another group would not get the vitamin, and "the incidence of colds, otitis, etc. would be observed."

Some preliminary tests along these lines had been done in Hungary, first on rabbits, then on a few babies, but without conclusive results. Hungarian facilities were not set up for major clinical trials, nor did Albert himself have the patients (or patience) to carry out such experiments.

Fletcher, obviously nonplussed, turned the proposal over to a Miss E. M. M. Hume, a bureaucrat on the "Vitamins Committee" of the National Research Council. It was a poor choice, for Miss Hume was not amused by this Hungarian's wild theories. At the end of a chilly memo, she voiced an opinion that would become quite common in the years to come:

> I do not personally think that there is any indication that the commonly-observed liability of infants to common colds has anything to do with a partial deficiency of anti-scorbutic. . . .[11]

Getting this reply, Fletcher simply neglected to write back to Hungary, perhaps not realizing how seriously Szent-Gyorgyi took this issue. "Prof" therefore turned to his fatherly friend, H. H. Dale. Dale diplomatically wrote to Fletcher, "I expect that you got his letter and found it difficult to improvise, on the spur of the moment, a clinical trial of the kind which he suggests." But he warned Fletcher that if the British did not respond to the offer someone else would—in America or on the Continent.[12] It was, in essence, the same strategy Dale had used on Fletcher ten years earlier when Albert had approached them with the first hints of "hexuronic acid." Dale was always protective of Albert and his interests. Fletcher, on the other hand, seemed temperamentally ill-disposed, and critical of what he called Albert's "flair without maintained industry."

A third scientific administrator, Edward Mellanby, was brought in. "Tell Szent-Gyorgyi," he said, in his no-nonsense way, "first to carry out the animal experiments on infection and, after that, if he got positive results with the hexuronic acid, it might be advisable to do a clinical trial."[13]

The British committee woman wrote this, and graciously agreed to *accept* some of his vitamin C! But Albert unexpectedly withdrew the offer. "I have become a bit doubtful myself whether I was quite logical," he wrote Fletcher. "It needs no ascorbic acid to prove on a big scale whether vitamin C has any effect or not, since lemons or orange juice can be used just as well as the crystalline preparation." More likely, he was miffed by the cool reception he had received from his British colleagues. No one seemed to realize the great importance of what he had done.

Part of the problem, however, was that he himself was not sure exactly what he wanted tested.

> I am very keen, that this baby of mine, this ascorbic acid, should grow up in time into a good thing, and anything you can do for it will meet my very deep and sincere gratitude,

he told Fletcher. In the spring of 1933, he made a "delightful trip" through Scandinavia, England, France, and Holland, where news of his conquest was spreading. He made a dramatic appearance at the 1934 meeting of the British Association for the Advancement of Science held in Aberdeen, Scotland. Everywhere he was greeted as a conquering hero. His story of the discovery of ascorbic acid, including the famous "cowardly husband" incident, was told and retold till it was polished smooth, and it grew with the telling. He charmed audiences everywhere. "I was preaching vitamin C," he informed Fletcher on 10 May 1933, " and have found much interest."

Instead of a friendly reply from Fletcher, however, this time Szent-Gyorgyi received a frigid memo from a total stranger, Dr. E. A. Thomson of the Medical Research Council. Thomson wrote:

> (1)The antiscorbutic properties of ascorbic acid can best be tested in animal experiments, and should be proved in this manner at least in the first instance.
>
> (2)The value of administering vitamin C to very young babies is a separate question which it would in the meantime be better to investigate by use of a preparation of recognized potency.
>
> If there is anything which you think we might usefully do within the limits of these propositions, we should be glad to hear from you.[14]

Dr. Thomson clearly did not know who Szent-Gyorgyi was, but he knew how to get rid of a crank! He had, of course, missed the whole point. That Fletcher would let such a letter be written in his absence may have reflected his own ambivalence toward Albert. Perhaps it also reflected a suspicious attitude towards what he privately called "clever foreigners."

Albert, barely able to contain his anger, replied to Thomson:

> I must have been very unclear in my writing and given you an entirely wrong impression about the problem. The ascorbic acid, isolated by myself, is already entirely tested as to its anti-scorbutic property and is definitely identified with vitamin C. . . . The problem is whether the Vitamin is of any use in Medicine or not.[15]

But Thomson was not to be persuaded. He never replied, and that was the end of Szent-Gyorgyi's attempt to arrange clinical trials for the effect of vitamin C on colds. The whole incident was a chilling reminder that Szent-Gyorgyi, for all his British manners, was not in the end British.

Closer to home, a Hungarian colleague, suffering from a rare disease known as Henoch-Schonlein's purpura, was brought to Albert's attention. One of the clinical signs of scurvy is the rupture of the tiny capillaries under the skin, or purpura. A doctor thought there might be a connection here. Henoch-Schonlein's purpura involved not just skin hemorrhages, but internal bleeding, joint pain, and swelling. There was no known cure.

In early 1932 Szent-Gyorgyi suggested the man eat raw paprika, since there was no purified vitamin C yet available. The man did so and his condition dramatically improved, despite the fact that there is still no known cure for Henoch-Schonlein's purpura.

"When I had crystalline ascorbic acid," he recalled, "we tried it again, expecting a still stronger action. It did nothing. Evidently my impure extract contained an additional substance responsible for the action," i.e., something in the paprika which was missing in the purified crystals. (The idea of other therapeutic elements in paprika certainly came as no surprise to the loyal citizens of Szeged.)

The patient continued to eat paprika, but Albert went back to the raw fruit and eventually isolated a yellow substance which was not vitamin C, but which was biologically active. Gabor Fodor was a student in Szent-Gyorgyi's lab at the time:

> He asked me, a young graduate student, what the yellow stuff was that he had just isolated. When I told him "that's carotene" he said, "Nonsense. It's something else," and I said, "It's a flavinoid." And as a matter of fact, I was right, by accident. He said, "Yes, that's a flavinoid."[16]

"I isolated the flavones from paprika and they cured purpura," Albert recalled. He dubbed this substance, or rather group of substances, vitamin P. The "P" did not stand for purpura or even paprika, as most people supposed. "I used the letter," he said, "because I was not quite sure that it was a vitamin. The alphabet was occupied only up to F so there was ample time to eliminate "P" without causing trouble if its vitamin nature became disproved."

In fact, vitamin P, as we have indicated, is now more commonly called the bioflavinoids. Although its status as a vitamin was later called into question, newspaper reports about Szent-Gyorgyi's scientific acumen multiplied. He was "known the world over for his work in trying to find out of what vitamins are composed," the *New York Times* informed its readers as early as 1933.[17]

In 1935, while on a speaking tour of Belgium, he was asked to treat the Prince of Liège, second son of the King. The young man was running a persistent fever and his physicians were baffled. Dr. Szent-Gyorgyi prescribed (what else?) ascorbic acid crystals, and the young man recovered. This was either a testimony to vitamin C or to Albert's formidable powers of persuasion. In either case, it added to his fame as a medical genius. This was an unexpected outcome for someone who hated anything clinical.

In fact, Szent-Gyorgyi started to prescribe vitamin C quite freely. "Later I met an almost identical case in Sweden," he wrote, "where the son of the Hungarian cultural attaché had similar troubles. I prescribed vitamin C and D and the trouble disappeared."

But despite this initial enthusiasm, vitamin C proved disappointing as a miracle cure. After a few years, his own interest in the vitamin waned, and he wanted to return to basic research. In fact, when Mellanby wrote to "Saint George" in 1936 and asked, pointedly, "Will you please tell me what you consider to be some of the practical uses of ascorbic acid, apart from the prevention or treatment of scurvy?" Albert modestly replied:

> You have asked me a very unpleasant question: what is ascorbic acid good for. I think I am the last man to ask such a question from. My interest got diverted long ago from this substance and I do not know more about it than I heard from my friends at the dining table. As far as I gather it is good for nothing and everything. There is no special therapeutic application, apart from scurvy.[18]

He still believed that a lack of vitamin C seemed to contribute to many other illnesses:

> I do not mean to say that ascorbic acid is no use at all. On the contrary, I think it is one of the most useful substances, since a lack of this vitamin has a hand in very many pathological conditions, . . . in their incidence [as well] as in their course.[19]

By 1937, however, the discovery of vitamin C was history and Albert was on to other things. The controversy with Prof. King had quieted down. It thus came as a total surprise when, on 2 October 1937, Albert received an excited telephone call, quickly followed by a telegram, from Stockholm, Sweden. The medical faculty of the Royal Karolinska Institute, he was informed, had chosen him to be that year's recipient of the Nobel Prize for Physiology or Medicine.

The award, consisting of a scroll, a gold medal, and the equivalent of $40,000 in cash, would be presented to him for his work on vitamin C and the nature of cellular metabolism.

There had been two other candidates for the award: his Birmingham collaborator Norman Haworth and Paul Karrer, another vitamin pioneer. The debate within the chambers of the Karolinska had been long and heated. It was so acrimonious that when the chairman of the nominating committee, Hans Christian Jacobaeus, came out to make the announcement he dropped dead of a heart attack on the spot.[20]

The committee had decided that Szent-Gyorgyi would receive the medical prize unshared. Shortly afterwards, however, it was announced that Profs. Haworth and Karrer would share the 1937 prize for *chemistry*. Thus, in a sense, the discovery of ascorbic acid was honored by *two* Nobel Prizes that year—Szent-Gyorgyi's and Haworth's.

Albert had no inkling that the prize was coming and no one had contacted him before the announcement. While there is no "secret" to winning a Nobel Prize, it is clear that a disproportionate number of laureates are themselves the students of laureates. Szent-Gyorgyi was no exception. To his fellow scientists he was known as the disciple of Hopkins (Medicine, 1927) and Dale (Medicine, 1936). Hans Krebs, who won the prize several decades after his own teacher, Warburg, explained one reason this might be so:

> What, then, is it in particular that can be learned from teachers of special distinction? Above all, what they teach is high standards. We measure everything, including ourselves, by comparisons; and in the absence of someone with outstanding ability there is a risk that we easily come to believe that we are excellent and much better than the next man. Mediocre people may appear big to themselves (and to others) if they are surrounded by small circumstances. By the same token, big people feel dwarfed in the company of giants, and this is a most useful feeling. So what the giants of science teach us is to see ourselves modestly and not to overrate ourselves.[21]

Hopkins was just such a giant to Szent-Gyorgyi. He had received a Nobel Prize ten years before, and upon returning to Cambridge had jocularly instructed his own students to go out and win some more.[22] Szent-Gyorgyi had never consciously set out to win anything, but by following Hopkins's example he had achieved what many other scientists were unsuccessfully striving for.

In Hungary, when the award was announced, there was wild jubilation. Szent-Gyorgyi was the fourth person of Hungarian descent to win the prize, but the first to win it while actually residing on native soil.[23] The "Paprika Prize," as *Time* called it, was the whole nation's triumph, and seemed to restore Hungary's tarnished reputation in the eyes of the world. It was particularly important that here was one outstanding Hungarian intellectual who had emigrated but had chosen to *come home.*

In Szeged, the night of the announcement there was a spontaneous torchlight parade; then the new laureate greeted a huge, cheering crowd from the balcony of Cathedral Square. In his long white lab coat, he looked like a kind of scientific pope. "There wasn't a shepherd in the hills that hadn't heard the news," Koloman Laki enthused. "I doubt that we could have found a person in Hungary who did not know who Szent-Gyorgyi was."

In Szeged, fifty years later, the author and Professor Bruno Straub stopped one old man at random in the New Szeged park and asked him if he remembered Albert Szent-Gyorgyi. The old fellow's eyes lit up, and he cried out, delighted. Of course he remembered Szent-Gyorgyi! He had been the caretaker of the tennis courts on which "Prof" used to play. Then, surprisingly, he broke into song.

"Paprika," he sang, "you are hotter than gin. Paprika, you are vitamin C!" This was the song, he said, that the throngs of people had sung on that memorable night in Cathedral Square. Whether it was a folk song or—less romantically, as Straub suggested—a jingle for "Pritamin," could not be determined. But in any case, the memory of that great night flared for a moment on the banks of the Tisza.

The actual presentation of the award occurred in December 1937. Szent-Gyorgyi and his fellow recipients were treated to a week of parties, ceremonies, carolling, and lectures—a whirlwind itinerary. Finally, on 10 December, the recipients received their heavy gold medals from King Gustavus V of Sweden. The presentation speech for Szent-Gyorgyi's award was given by Professor E. Hammarsten, speaking for the staff of professors at Karolinska, "pursuant to the task devolving upon them by the terms of the will of Alfred Nobel."[24]

Technically, Albert's award was given in recognition of his "discoveries concerning the biological combustion process with especial reference to vitamin C and to the fumaric acid catalyst." However, Hammarsten also dealt at great length with Albert's unique personality. Referring to him as "the new conquistador from Szeged," he compared him to the great biochemists, Otto Warburg and Heinrich Wieland, whose opinions, as a young student, Albert had helped reconcile.

"Each of the three," he said, "has conquered new ground by intuitive daring and skill." Addressing Albert directly, he said, "You never swerved from your unyielding purpose to study the primary and fundamental processes of biological oxidation . . . . You are the discoverer and idealist to the mind of Alfred Nobel."[25]

Szent-Gyorgyi responded with a speech entitled "Oxidation, Energy Transfer, and Vitamins." In it, in addition to giving a clear presentation of his research, he discussed the unusual circumstances in which his discoveries were made. He recalled the first excitment "in my little basement room in Groningen" when he found "hexuronic acid" in adrenal glands, as well as his work in Cambridge, at the Mayo Clinic, and in Szeged. The speech was thoughtful and beautifully phrased, in some ways more like a kind of fable than a scientific paper. He concluded eloquently with this impassioned plea:

> From the moment I seized my staff, a novice in search of knowledge, and left my devastated fatherland to tread the wanderer's path—which has not been without its privations—as an unknown and penniless novice, from that moment to the present one, I always felt myself to belong to a great, international, spiritual family. Always and everywhere I found helping hands, friendship, cooperation and international solidarity.
>
> I owe it solely to this spirit of our science that I did not succumb, and that my endeavours are now crowned with the highest human recognition, the award of the Nobel Prize. This Nobel Prize, too, is but a fruit of this spirit, of this pan-human solidarity. I can but hope, my heart filled with gratitude, that this spirit may be preserved and that it may spread its bounteous rays beyond the limits of our knowledge, over the whole of humanity.

Here was an affirmation of science and of humanity itself, at a time when the world was about to be plunged into an orgy of bloodshed and darkness.

Albert Szent-Gyorgyi was only forty-four years old when he received the award.

> When I received the Nobel Prize, the only big lump sum of money I have ever seen, I had to do something with it. The easiest way to drop this hot potato was to invest it, to buy shares. I knew World War II was coming and I was afraid that if I had shares which rise in case of war, I would wish for war. So I asked my broker to buy shares which go down in the event of war. This he did. I lost my money but saved my soul.

The presentation of the 1937 award had its detractors as well. One Budapest savant loudly insisted that the Karolinska professors had made a terrible mistake: he himself had been meant to receive their Prize, not this upstart Szent-Gyorgyi. "He forgot that his name was never known outside of Hungary," Zoltan Bay recalled.

In America, also, there was a more serious protest. The award stirred up the old animosity with Prof. King and his supporters and furious voices were raised. "I got the reputation to be a dirty scoundrel in this country, one who stole," said Albert. "This appealed to people that America lost one Nobel Prize, lost a piece of glory through the dirty trick of a dirty Hungarian and a faithless assistant who gave away the secret of this great King."

This may sound like hyperbole. Yet old newspapers clipping (preserved by Svirbely) show that the Pittsburgh press, at least, was practically rabid over the award. The steel city's laboratories, readers were told, "seethed with talk of what to many of them seemed an amazing miscarriage of scientific justice."[26]

King, after all, was a local hero, described as if he were the new Pirates' batting champion:

> As every informed Pittsburgher knows, Pittsburgh itself has a researcher who for years has been tracking down elusive vitamin C—dark, little, indefatigable Biochemist Charles Glen King, a shining-light of the University of Pittsburgh's ace Department of Chemistry.[27]

The Pittsburgh *Post-Gazette* jumped into the fray. "Pitt Savant Real Finder of Vitamin C," it announced. "Nobel Prize Winner Not Discoverer, Papers Show." In reference to Dr. Svirbely, the papers were uniformly uncomplimentary.

"Secret is Betrayed," one screamed. "Former Pupil of Dr. King Reveals Find to Scientist in Europe." His humble origins were suddenly rediscovered: it was pointed out that he was the "son of a Hungarian immigrant steel-mill worker."[28] He was all but accused of scientific theft:

> The records prove that not until a student of King's, Dr. J. L. Svirbely, carried the knowledge gained in King's laboratory across the ocean to Gyorgyi's [sic] laboratory did Gyorgyi discover Vitamin C and go on to win the 1937 Nobel prize in medicine.[29]

What the newspapers were alluding to was the manner in which Svirbely had arrived in Szeged. Both he and Albert said this was entirely by accident: he just happened to be in Hungary for personal reasons. Yet King's supporters suggested another explanation: Svirbely, they said, suspected that "hexuronic acid" was vitamin C. Leaving King, he deliberately went to Szent-Gyorgyi's lab, because he also knew that "Prof" had the only supply of pure "hexuronic acid" in the world. His testing of "hexuronic acid" for vitaminicity thus was not a matter of chance, but of calculation.

Svirbely defended himself as best he could from such charges:

> Dr. J. L. Svirbely, of Carnegie Tech, yesterday said that he worked with Dr. Albert Szent-Gyorgyi, Nobel prize winner, in vitamin C research after learning the technique under Pitt's Dr. Charles Glen King, the man who first isolated the elusive substance [sic].
>
> But he denied that he revealed King's secrets to the Hungarian scientist. He said that he simply followed out Gyorgyi's instructions in isolating the vitamin from peppers. Svirbely said that when he left King's laboratories in the summer of 1931 King's research had not progressed far enough to enable Svirbely to carry important clues to Gyorgyi even had he wanted to do so.[30]

In the newspapers, King came out blameless. "The protesting, bashful chemist," readers were told, "would not speak in his own behalf and would voice no criticism of his former pupil, of the man who won the laurels that are his by right, or of the Nobel committee which made the award."

Someone in King's corner, however, *was* speaking to the press. On 10 December 1937 *Science* published an article by Dr. G. J. Cox, a colleague of King, entitled "Crystallized Vitamin C and Hexuronic Acid." The article began by calling the Nobel prize to Szent-Gyorgyi "well-merited" and then spent five pages ripping into Szent-Gyorgyi's claims and achievements. Reduced to its elements, Cox's argument mainly rested on the fact that King's letter to *Science* predated Szent-Gyorgyi's letter to *Nature* [see chapter 8].[31]

Albert was quite weary of the struggle, and with the Nobel Prize behind him, could afford to be generous. His only public response was a letter of his own to *Science*, in which he suggested that questions of priority should most justly be dealt with by posterity.

At least "posterity" was what he meant to say, but he wrote "posteriority" instead, and this is how it was printed. His English friends suggested that perhaps this Freudian slip was his way of calling his opponent an ass.

For all intents and purposes, however, the controversy was over. It has been settled in Stockholm. For most people, Albert Szent-Gyorgyi would go down in history as the discoverer of vitamin C.

10

THE NAZI WAVE

In 1933 Hitler came to power and the official persecution of Jews in Germany began in earnest. One of the Nazis' first acts was to dismiss all Jewish professors from their posts, including Albert's brilliant friend Hans Krebs, the student of Otto Warburg.[1] When he learned of the firing, Albert immediately wrote to Krebs:

> I very much regret to hear that you have personal difficulties in Germany. I was in Cambridge during the last few days where people talked of doing something for you. I have of course encouraged them as far as possible and I hope my words will have contributed something towards the realization of the plans.

The language—Krebs's difficulties were anything but "personal"—was cryptic and guarded, because it was assumed the mail was being opened. As a footnote, Albert added:

> P.S. If you really like to go to Cambridge it would be best if you wrote to Hopkins and assured him that you would be contented with a modest livelihood. There are no big jobs and people might hesitate to offer you a small one. So if you like to go to Cambridge ask Hopkins for facilities to work. If you wish you may mention that I have encouraged you to write.[2]

Krebs did in fact write to Hopkins the same day:

> I have heard today from Prof. Szent-Gyorgyi that your great kindness might make it possible for me to work at Cambridge. Prof. Szent-Gyorgyi encourages me to ask whether you can accept me in your laboratory.
> As a Jew I am about to lose not only my present position, but any possibility of working at all in Germany.[3]

103

Hopkins responded immediately, "I admire your work so much that I am very anxious to help you."[4] Krebs was successfully resettled in Sheffield, England, and resumed the work on biological oxidation which he had begun in Warburg's laboratory.

Helping Krebs was the first of Albert's anti-Nazi acts. At first, his political activities did not stem from political ideology. They were an attempt to uphold the highest values of science and culture at a time when, to quote the poet W. H. Auden, "intellectual disgrace stared from every human face." He soon found himself being drawn into politics, while at the same time trying to maintain his own scientific momentum.

> The Nazis became worse and worse, and I got into deeper and deeper trouble and became more and more against them. You see, they started to burn books and kill Jews, take my Jewish friends away. I just cannot keep neutral. I say "No," and they sent me word that if I go on, I will live very short. . . . I went to visit my Jewish friends who were already shut up, locked up, and that was an awful crime in those days. I didn't make a secret of my great resentment of Nazism.

Szeged presented its own peculiarities. Since the faculty at Budapest was notoriously pro-fascist, Jewish students in the thirties found it easier to get admitted to the provincial colleges, working their way around the hated "numerus clausus." Thus, each September, Szeged's university inevitably had more than its five percent quota of Jews. This, in turn, served as the pretext for riots by right-wing students, mainly members of the Turul student organization.[5]

Prof. N.A. Biro remembers those days well. Of Jewish origin and from a liberal family to boot, he was accepted into Szeged with the help of a Gentile family friend. In the fall of each year, anti-Semitic rioting broke out in Szeged. Forewarned, Biro and other Jewish students hid across the river in New Szeged until the fighting was over.[6]

It was not long before "Prof" himself was caught up in the campus turmoil. He gave an examination and was generally disappointed with the results, but pointed out the fact that the Jewish students had done well:

> The Jewish students were really well educated, but most Christians were very ignorant. This just annoyed me, and I said, "You'd better learn a little intelligence and interest from the Jews."
> This was then awful to say, so you see, the next day, the law students came to my lecture with sticks to beat me up. I went to the lecture and saw all these new faces. I knew, or felt what it was all about so before they

could start throwing apples and bricks, I said, "I see there are many people here who didn't come for science, so I will give no lecture today."

I turned around and before they could do something I went out. My colleague went down to ask them to leave the building, and they thought it was me and almost beat him up. I got in trouble. It was not very simple to say such a thing then, given the Nazi wave.[7]

These attacks became increasingly frequent. Straub recalled one occasion on which he and Szent-Gyorgyi confronted a mob trying to enter the chemistry department through the basement. It was at this point that he became aware of Albert's almost-reckless physical courage, for "Prof" faced down this angry crowd, and by his unyielding presence made it turn away.[8]

On one occasion, because of his unconventional behavior, Albert was challenged to a duel by a right-wing officer. The precipitating event was itself trivial. Bored by all formal social occasions, Albert sneaked out of a debutante-style ball on his daughter's eighteenth birthday in the autumn of 1936. It was a thoughtless thing to have done, and one can imagine Little Nelly's chagrin. Albert's self-justification was that he had made his appearance and needed the extra sleep. (He was always a light sleeper and when the family moved to an apartment on Rudolph Square, he found himself continually awakened by the heavy early-morning traffic.) The officer in question, whose own daughter was also "coming out" at this ball, was deeply offended by Albert's actions. He therefore demanded the "Prof" choose his weapons:

> In my youth, in Hungary, dueling was the only way to settle a personal dispute. I can still remember asking myself in vain: what other way is there? There seemed to be none, a duel seemed the only logical one.

But Albert, like most liberal intellectuals, soon came to regard dueling as a "childhood disease of our history." Not so the old-fashioned military. The incident at the ball, however, was becoming a pretext to murder a well-known political maverick. Albert may have been brave, but he was not in a suicidal mood. He disarmed the officer with a sincere-seeming apology, and that was the end of the matter.

This small event was indicative, however, of how dismal life in Szeged was becoming; dismal and dangerous. After about five years, Albert was ready to move on. By chance, Pal Hary, the professor of physiology at Budapest, died and his Chair was left vacant. Szent-Gyorgyi, by now internationally celebrated, made all the proper moves to obtain the post, but the Budapest faculty was still adamant.

No Szent-Gyorgyi! To discredit him, rumors were spread that the "whole vitamin C story was a humbug and Szent-Gyorgyi was not an appropriate person for the post," said Straub. Prof. Gabor Fodor, one of "Prof's" graduate students at the time, remembered:

> All his enemies tried to spread the word that vitamin C was just a public relations stunt, that he was a Freemason, that he was this and that. All lies, but unfortunately, Hungary is a small country, and if somebody grows too tall they chop his head off.[9]

And so, Szent-Gyorgyi did not get his long-coveted Budapest position.

In February 1935 he was invited to give a series of lectures at Harvard University Medical School. Professor Otto Folin had died the previous year and Harvard was looking for a replacement. Albert Szent-Gyorgyi was a leading contender.

Albert made a startling impression on the starched-collared Harvard faculty. His physical appearance was a bit strange perhaps: British tweeds and pipe and rather wild hair, now growing grey. He also seemed, somehow, too irreverent. As usual, he was brimming with jokes and a small boy's mischievousness. This was innocent enough but an American might wonder if this humor were not edged with too much irony. All the same, Albert managed to work his personal charm on most of the faculty, and to some of them at least his visit was a breath of fresh air. George Wald, who later himself won a Nobel Prize, reflected the opinion of many younger members of the faculty:

> I realized from the beginning that Albert Szent-Gyorgyi was a very special person, with a tremendous capacity for life in his voice, gesture and speech.
>
> He deeply offended the power figures at the medical school by being perfectly frank about wanting the appointment, about needing the money, and by altogether being himself. The Professors at that time all felt the utmost self-importance and the deepest dignity. They were offended by Szent-Gyorgyi's freedom of expression.[10]

What finally undid Szent-Gyorgyi at Harvard was a disastrous encounter with Prof. Edwin Cohn (1892–1953), professor of biological chemistry and head of the Department of Physical Chemistry at Harvard Medical School. Cohn has been largely forgotten by all but a few specialists, but at the time he was an important man and clearly the person to please. It was Cohn who assumed the job of judging Albert's suitability.

Albert's reaction to this formidable figure was characteristically visceral. "I had no objection to Prof. Cohn," he said, "but his work seemed very dull to me, and the way he talked from behind his nose somewhere—funny noises came out from behind his nose which I couldn't understand very well."

Finally, the day of decision came:

> They gave me a big dinner. I knew that the festive occasion of this dinner was the decision, and at the dinner I had wine and good food, lots of it. After the dinner, Professor Cohn took me up to his laboratory to test my intelligence, and he set me in a big easy chair and began to talk about his own research which was very dull and uninteresting. He wanted to see my reaction, and my reaction was that I fell asleep. When I woke up, I knew that I would never be a Harvard Professor.

Thus ended Albert's best chance of leaving Szeged. After lecturing at other American universities, he booked passage home.[11] He had to pass through Germany on his way back. His reaction to this (and other) brief visits was peculiar. Writing to Edward Mellanby of the Medical Research Council in early 1937, Szent-Gyorgyi said:

> After having been to Germany I want to correct a statement of our last chat. I agreed too well with you, that there will be war within a few months. Now I think, there will be no war for the next ten years or so to come. I accept any bet on this point.
>
> I agreed with you as nicely, because I had all my information from the English press—*Manchester Guardian*. We were in the same boat. Now I feel I have been misled rather badly.
>
> Do not suspect me of having been converted to fascism. I hate it. But I think I understand the underlying psychology of recent events better than you do, because I know not only your point of view, but have fought the war on the other/wrong side and shared the misery of Germany after the war, living there for several years. Germany is a psychological problem and I am amazed by the inability of your politicians to grasp the underlying psychological factors. The entire failure of your continental policy amply proves this.
>
> I am not going to annoy you with a treatise on European politics. I just want to correct my statement and tell you, that I think *there will be no war in the next [i.e., near] future.*[12]

Perhaps the most surprising thing in this surprising letter is the way in which Albert refers to "your point of view," "your politicians," "your continental policy," in referring to the British. Technically that was true, of course, but six years in Hungary had obviously had their effect, and he no longer looked at Britain as his "intellectual home."

These naive ruminations on fascism ("peace in our time" was already in the air) were not the only utopian notion in which Albert indulged. In September 1936 he wrote in all seriousness to the Rockefeller Foundation proposing that they pull their resources out of the rest of Europe and concentrate their efforts in Switzerland. Why Switzerland? Because Albert had just visited it for the first time and liked it. After explaining the "political lunacy" in Germany, he reflected:

> The idea came to me that perhaps it would be worthwhile to shift our science towards that country [i.e., Switzerland] and to try to concentrate what is still good in European (continental) science and to try to make a center of international science there.
>
> I would very gladly collaborate on these lines. Switzerland is, quite apart from politics, an ideal place for scientific research. It is not only a quiet and cultured country, but at the same time the only country in the world where you can do research, walking, climbing, skiing and sailing almost on the same spot.[13]

One can only imagine the reaction to this letter, with its reference to Switzerland's famous sports facilities! (RF officials had already complained about Albert's tendency to use foundation funds to pay for staff vacations.) Needless to say, the offer was politely refused. In a broader sense, however, there was something far-sighted here. It was difficult for anyone to imagine that within just a few years the Rockefeller Foundation would in fact have to shut down all its continental operations because of the war.

Albert's approach may have been naive, but any sign of toadyism is happily missing. He was a scientist and they, after all, were merely bureaucrats. Not that he felt superior to the Rockefeller men; he was democratic enough to extend equality to them. He could hardly have imagined how little his advice in long-term planning was appreciated or desired.

The general turmoil of these times found its reflection in Albert's personal life as well. In the mid-thirties his twenty-year marriage to Cornelia began to unravel. This came as a shock and a surprise to their friends (Straub, for instance, had no prior intimation of their troubles) and initially to Albert as well.

One day Albert came home, unexpected, from the university and surprised his wife in bed with a woman: the family's maid. Albert was outraged. Not only was his wife being unfaithful, but the idea that she would desire another woman seemed abominable to him.

Glider pilot, late 1930s. *Geoffrey Pollitt.*

With favorite Buick, late
1930s. *Albert Szent-Gyorgi's
personal collection.*

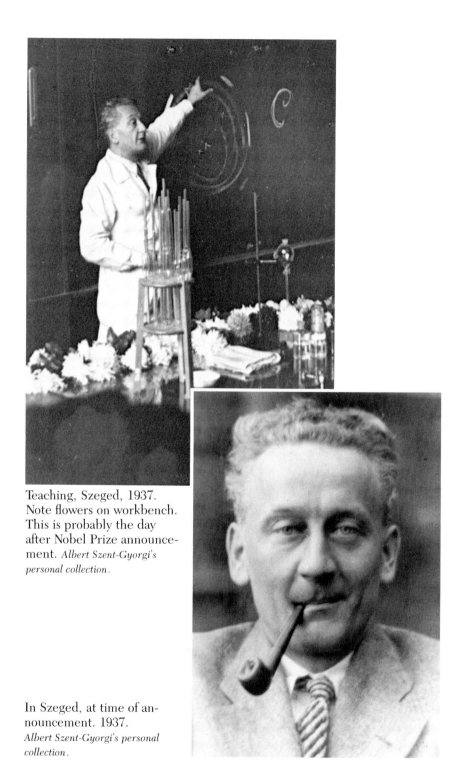

Teaching, Szeged, 1937.
Note flowers on workbench.
This is probably the day
after Nobel Prize announcement. *Albert Szent-Gyorgi's
personal collection.*

In Szeged, at time of an-
nouncement. 1937.
*Albert Szent-Gyorgi's personal
collection.*

Albert with three famous Hungarian beauties: Ella Gonibahogi, Tevi Fejes and Elenna Bulla. 1937. *Photo by Bela Liebmann.*

At work, time of an-
nouncement, 1937.
Photo by Bela Liebmann.

Presentation of the Nobel Prize, Stockholm, 1937. With other prize winners, from left to right: Roger Martin du Gard, Albert Szent-Gyorgyi, Paul Karrer, Sir Walter Haworth, and Clinton J. Davisson. *National Library of Medicine.*

With daughter Nelly, probably 1939. *Geoffrey Pollitt.*

The rebuilding of the
University in Budapest
with workers' help.
1945.
Library of Congress.

At time of NIH appointment, 1948. *Photo by J. W. McGuire, NIH Photo Services.*

In Woods Hole. Afternoon tea, Marta Szent-Gyorgyi foreground. In rear, Albert (left) entertains his co-workers. January, 1952. *Saturday Evening Post*.

At work in Woods Hole with his cousin, Andrew, January, 1952.
Saturday Evening Post.

With Mary Lasker, holding the Lasker Award. 1954. *Photo by Arthur Avedon.*

She drifted to the other side—she became more and more masculine until it ended up in a very serious hormonal disturbance. She became completely masculine, dropped me out of her whole sentimental life, had affairs with girls, and I don't know what until our marriage went to pieces with a great deal of misery—a very great deal of misery.

In an attempt to patch things up, Albert and Nelly went off by themselves to a cabin in the woods. That night there was a pounding at the door. When Albert answered he was confronted by "the other woman," who brandished a gun at him. He was not sure if she wanted to kill him or Nelly, and he was not about to find out. Instead, he slammed the door in her face and made a dash out the back exit of the house.

There is no doubt that the breakup was distressing to him. "We lived together twenty years. That's an enormously strong link which cannot be broken without very much pain." Nevertheless, he managed to come out of it blaming Nelly and her "hormonal disturbance" for everything that happened.

There are those who believe that the underlying problem was Albert's male chauvinism. He was proud of Nelly in a sense: she was good-looking, stylish and athletic. But in his mad dash to do science, he had done nothing to develop her potential. He had solemnly promised Nelly's mother, Mrs. Demeny, that he would see that she got a good education if she married him. Once married, however, he conveniently forgot all about that promise.

In addition, the Nobel Prize had exacerbated their differences. After World War I, he had lost everything and had to live in great poverty. "So I had to have a very good companion, and my wife was very good at that." Despite their poverty, "my wife was pretty and chic, and we had a very interesting life. My rich friends always envied me." When Albert won the Nobel Prize, however, he refused to give Nelly any of the money for her own or for household use. Instead he used part for research and invested the rest. Nelly realized that Albert had no intention of sharing his good fortune with her.

In his Cathedral Square laboratory, where she sometimes helped out, Nelly had her own ideas on how things should be run, a situation Albert found intolerable. (Science was still very much a man's preserve, and women like Ilona Banga were rare exceptions.)

In 1938 the Szent-Gyorgyis travelled to the United States, where he had a lecture engagement at Vanderbilt University.[14] After the lectures, Albert left Nelly in America and returned to Budapest. As it turned out, they were never to meet again.

Albert was not at a loss for women, however. A newspaper photograph of the time shows him explaining the workings of a microscope to three of Hungary's leading actresses. He was now, in effect, a bachelor and it is said he put as much energy and ingenuity into his love life as he did into his scientific work. He could be seen nearly every night in the clubs and cabarets of Budapest or Szeged, although reports of his profligacy grew with the telling and became positively mythical among his students.[15]

Many years later, past ninety, he was asked what he would have done differently in his long life. The questioner expected an answer in the realm of scientific discourse. Albert looked at his interlocutor and replied, rather sadly, "I would have devoted as much attention to my love relationships as I did to my scientific work."

On 6 September 1941 the Szent-Gyorgyis were formally divorced. This was bad enough, in Catholic Szeged, but soon he announced his intention of remarrying and this created an even greater scandal; for his intended was Marta Borbiro Miskolczy, wife of his friend, Professor of Psychiatry Reyse Miskolczy. Marta intended to leave her husband and, if necessary, her family to marry Albert.

Marta was thirty-one, an aristocratically good-looking woman, and the mother of two children, Ursula and Gabor. She came from a locally prominent family, originally from Szabadka, an area which became part of Yugoslavia after World War I. Her father was a local official of the Horthy regime. Albert and Marta had met at an academic function and fallen passionately in love. For Albert, it was his first experience with an all-consuming romantic affair. Picasso, it is said, needed the stimulus of a new companion to enter a new period in his career. Szent-Gyorgyi may have felt similar stirrings within himself: a new woman for a new era.

In August 1941 Marta finally obtained her divorce and she and Albert were married on 18 October of that year; it seems likely that a clandestine affair had been going on between them for some time. Miskolczy was heartbroken. (Luckily for Albert, he did not believe in duels.) He had originally taught at the Hungarian University of Transylvania in Kolosvar, and when the Hungarians reoccupied that Romanian city during World War II, he seized the chance to return. Albert and Marta moved from his apartment in downtown Szeged to a comfortable two-story house at 38 Gyupjas Pal Street in suburban New Szeged.

The whole divorce and remarriage were a wrenching period, and the repercussions reverberated for many years. Albert was tortured, torn between his passionate desire for Marta and his guilt over hurting the other parties involved, including the children on both sides. "It was a terrible thing," he reflected sadly, years later. "But what could I do? I was madly in love with her."[16]

In 1930–40 (just before this marriage scandal rocked Szeged), Albert was made Rector of the "Royal Nicholas Horthy University" as the school was then known. The Rectorship was rotated among the chairpersons of the various departments, and that year was Chemistry's turn. Szent-Gyorgyi used his one-year tenure to institute some very radical reforms in university life—and naturally to get into trouble as well.

On the occasion of a big university celebration, for instance, he deliberately snubbed a German official: "I invited everybody but the German consul. . . . That was a very bad point with the Nazis for me, and I was astonished that they [i.e., the local authorities] didn't arrest me then."

He also reformed the student organizations. Under Horthy, these were strictly divided along religious and ethnic lines. The one thing they all had in common was that they excluded Jews. Szent-Gyorgyi created a non-discriminatory student organization at Szeged. In a daily newspaper of the time, *Hungarian Nation (Magyar Nemzet)*, he put forward his vision of the role of a University Rector such as himself.

As the head of the university, the Rector, he wrote, is the "father" of the students. His main task is to create an atmosphere in which students can feel that the university is their home. In this ideal university they can freely develop their talents and fill their mind with the love of science and fine arts for the rest of their life.

The university, he continued, collaborates in all forms of scientific cooperation without regard to language, national boundaries, or frontiers. The university has to be inspired by a love of truth and maintain an atmosphere of complete liberty, the lack of which causes a decline of all culture.[17]

Today this seems mild enough, but such talk of "cooperation" sounded quite subversive to right-wing nationalists. What it meant, in practice, was cooperation of Jews and Gentiles, leftists and conservatives, foreigners and Hungarians. The majority of students, Szent-Gyorgyi believed, were themselves anti-fascist, as were most of the professors. But they were all afraid. The existing organizations did not really serve their interests. The obvious conclusion was that a new group was needed. At that moment there was still enough maneuvering room left in Hungary, because of Horthy's need for a facade of democracy, to build such an organization above ground. That did not mean it would be easy—or safe.

Characteristically, it was Albert who volunteered for the job of "belling the cat" of fascism on the Szeged campus. He started off by constructing an American-style student center in the basement of one of the buildings on Cathedral Square:

> I built a bar where the students could have milk, not alcohol, but they sat on bar chairs. Of course, at once people came down and said that I was making a drinking hall of the university—all this Nazi stuff, and there was all sorts of picketing against me.

Prof. Straub remembers articles in the newspapers of the time saying that under Szent-Gyorgyi's rectorate one could see "all sorts of curly-headed, hook-nosed people" drinking in the University. The fact that they were drinking *milk* was not mentioned. It was true that the new organization attracted Jewish students, but how could it not when for nearly two decades the Jews had been denied basic rights in the Hungarian universities?

Word of the experiment at Szeged quickly spread. Prof. Daniel Bagdy, now a Hungarian pharmacologist, was then a self-described "cultural leader of the students of Debrecen." He took the next train to Szeged, he says, to find out if the newspaper reports were true. Together with other "cultural leaders" Bagdy formed a "Liberty Front of the Hungarian Students," under Szent-Gyorgyi's aegis.

This new organization soon became the dominant one on campus. "The nationalist and clerical organization of students in Szeged rapidly collapsed and the unified organization of students in Szeged was founded," Bagdy said. Others did not recall that the old organizations collapsed, but the new organization certainly made a dent.

The right wing assailed the new organization as a "Communist front group." This was unlikely. The Communist Party at the time was illegal, and only had a few hundred members throughout the country. None appears to have been in Szent-Gyorgyi's group. At afternoon tea, however, all sorts of dissident literature were read, and some of it, Prof. Straub recalls, was of Communist origin. This was part of Albert's openness towards all points of view.[18]

Albert also helped form a theater group at Szeged. "As Rector, my ambition was that literature and art should not only be taught, but lived at the university," he said.

Among his chemistry students was one named Istvan (Steven) Horvath, "a remarkably talented boy with a passion for directing plays." Horvath was the son of a Budapest theater director, and although still a teenager, had already studied with the Shakespearean company in Stratford, England. It was logical for Szent-Gyorgyi to ask him to stage *Hamlet*. Horvath himself chose fellow student, Kata Toth to portray Hamlet's mother. The production was a great success. The National Theater in Budapest even invited the student troupe to give a performance in the capital—an unprecedented honor. "It was so good that we had to repeat it three times," said Szent-Gyorgyi, who was godfather of the entire enterprise and even wrote the program notes.

This enterprise became controversial, however, because Horvath was a Jew, and was in love with his leading lady. Kata Toth came from a right-wing family in Szeged, which opposed the young couple's marriage plans. In 1940 a law was passed making intermarriages between Jews and Gentiles illegal. Frustrated at every turn, the two students finally went to Budapest and committed suicide together. Istvan was nineteen, Kata eighteen years old.

This modern-day "Romeo and Juliet" tale shook all of Hungary. Albert was devastated. To him, and many other people, the incident, with its brilliant promise ending in untimely death, was a symbol of the whole tragedy of modern Hungary. Such intermarriages had been common and unremarkable before Horthy. To the fascists, however, it was proof of the need to further segregate "degenerate" Jews such as Horvath from the rest of society. The right-wing newspapers laid ultimate responsibility for the tragedy on Albert. He had thought up the outlandish idea of a student theater, and of student activities in general. He had to be held accountable, they screamed.[19]

In the autumn of 1941, Szent-Gyorgyi's tenure as Rector of the University came to an end. Prof. Karoly Kogutowicz, a right-wing sympathizer, succeeded him and quickly undid most of the changes "Prof" had instituted. But some things could not be undone. Albert's charismatic personality had affected thousands of students, and his spirit had become a rallying point for the opposition. His personal integrity and courage were rarely doubted, even by his enemies; in addition, he commanded international respect. In effect, a breach had been made in the walls of bigotry that surrounded Hungary. The independent student movement, although it was soon dissolved, was a herald of the very active anti-fascist underground which was to develop within a few years.

11

MUSCLE MAN

It may seem amazing that Szent-Gyorgyi had any time left for research in these turbulent years. Yet it was during the Fascist period that Albert made several of his greatest discoveries.

Albert did most of the spadework on the famous citric acid cycle, one of the fundamental discoveries in biology. This schema is the linchpin for understanding the internal respiration of the cell. Most of the credit for this discovery (and eventually a Nobel Prize) went to the man who finally put all the pieces in place: Albert's friend, Hans Krebs.

Krebs himself conceded "that the pieces of information on which the concept of the cycle rests became gradually available through the efforts of several investigators." And of these, he said, "Szent-Gyorgyi made the most important discovery." It was, in fact, by a single misstep in a chain of otherwise brilliant deductions, that Albert was deprived of what could have been his greatest single achievement.[1] The citric acid cycle helps explain in detail how almost all cells, from protozoa to man, derive their energy. The very idea of such a cycle, in which metabolites follow a predetermined sequence of synthesis and degradation, seems elementary to us now, but was unknown half a century ago. It was Szent-Gyorgyi who first broke this ground and did much to introduce the concept of a self-regulating cycle into biology.

To understand his contribution to this question it is necessary to go back ten years to the time of the twelfth International Physiological Congress in Stockholm in 1926—the one at which Albert had his fateful meeting with Hopkins. At that meeting, the latter proposed that "in certain cases of oxidation hydrogen is transported not directly from primary donator to oxygen, but by stages." It was for elucidat-

114

ing this basic concept that Hopkins had cited and praised Albert's early work.

Referring to Szent-Gyorgyi's work, Hopkins pointed out that there are certain substances in cells which seem to play a contradictory role; they can act alternately as intermediate hydrogen *acceptors* or *donators*. Hopkins viewed this as applying to "certain cases." But, as Albert intuitively realized, this step-wise marriage of hydrogen to oxygen in the cell applied "to most cases of biological oxidation."[2]

In science, major conceptual breakthroughs often go hand-in-hand with new tools or techniques. It was at this critical juncture that Szent-Gyorgyi introduced an important new tool into the study of cellular respiration: *minced pigeon breast.*

To the non-biologist, this might seem a bizarre kind of tool. But Albert was looking for some readily-available living system in which respiration would take place at a very rapid rate. He reasoned that, ounce for ounce, the flight muscle of the pigeon was one of the most powerful muscles found in nature. He therefore "developed a tissue preparation in which the key structure for oxidations—the mitochondrion—stayed intact," Krebs later wrote. This particular muscle burned foodstuffs at a very high rate, since "flight can only be maintained by a very rapid energy supply." Albert coarsely minced the muscle from freshly-killed pigeons and then suspended that mince in a saline medium.[3] What we today know about aerobic metabolism, another scientist has said, is ultimately founded on what Szent-Gyorgyi discovered with his minced pigeon muscles back in the 1930s.[4]

Fifty years ago it was known that plant acids, such as fumaric, malic, and succinic acid, played some role in respiration, but it was thought they were consumed in the course of combustion. When Albert minced pigeon muscle and then added small amounts of these three acids, collectively called the dicarboxylic acids, it caused an uptake of far more oxygen, however, than would normally have been required to oxidize the added substances. Szent-Gyorgyi realized that "the plant acids were not consumed by combustion, were not ordinary nutrient substances, but were on the contrary themselves active groups of catalysts which served to maintain the combustion without themselves suffering any diminution thereby."[5]

It was then that Szent-Gyorgyi made what one popular textbook calls an "extremely important discovery." He concluded that

each of these acids greatly stimulates the oxidation of some endogenous carbohydrate substrate in the tissue, presumably glycogen, and that this effect is catalytic, one molecule of succinate being able to promote the oxidation of many molecules of the endogenous substrate."[6]

"For the first time," his student Bruno Straub wrote, "it was shown that some metabolites are not simply fuels, but rather play a catalytic role."[7]

The rate of respiration in minced pigeon breast, initially very fast, did decrease with time, but could be restored to its original level by adding small amounts of succinic or fumaric acid. "This is no doubt a catalytic process. . . . This was indeed a new idea. The catalyst was not an enzyme but an enzyme-metabolite pair. In the proposed scheme the hydrogen from a donor, for example a carbohyrate, reduced a first dicarboxylic acid, the oxaloacetic acid; the resulting malic acid reduced fumaric acid, the succinic acid thus produced transferred in its turn its hydrogen to cytochromes."[8]

By 1937, Szent-Gyorgyi had identified the process as a cycle, pinpointed many of the elements in this cycle (including the three named acids), and seemed poised to elucidate the whole process. In fact, this was one of the main reasons he received the Nobel Prize. The award citation read "for his discoveries in connection with the biological combustion processes, with especial reference to vitamin C and the catalysis of fumaric acid."

"The magnificent series of Szent-Gyorgyi's discoveries commenced in 1933," Prof. Hammarsten said in his presentation speech. "They were carried out and pursued at Szeged with extraordinary rapidity and precision. The flaws are numerous," Hammarsten admitted, "but not of a character to constitute any essential breach in the highway of the oxidation-chain." It seemed to everyone that the final pieces of the cycle were within Szent-Gyorgyi's grasp.

One of these seemingly-minor flaws, however, was to be Szent-Gyorgyi's undoing. His preoccupation had been with how hydrogen was transported, not with the intermediary metabolism. He expressed the view, therefore, that the functions of malic and oxaloacetic acids were *not* to serve as fuel but as catalysts in the system. But then Szent-Gyorgyi suggested that this malate/oxaloacetate system might act as one of the *hydrogen carriers* between the fuels of respiration and molecular oxygen. This was erroneous, and it was this error, as Krebs himself said, "which was responsible, at least in part, for the fact that people today talk of the Krebs cycle and not of the Szent-Gyorgyi cycle."

Krebs, on the other hand, learned from Albert's errors. He had followed the scientific debate very carefully from Sheffield University, where he had reestablished himself as a professor. In the very year Szent-Gyorgyi received his Nobel Prize, Krebs (and a coworker, Johnson) published a brilliant paper in which they postulated that it was *citric acid* which was the key link in the cycle. They redubbed

Szent-Gyorgyi's cycle the "citric acid cycle." Krebs later called it the "tricarboxylic acid cycle." Everyone else called it "the Krebs cycle" and so it remained.

It was an epochal find.

It is now certain that the cycle is virtually universal; it represents the major if not sole pathway for oxidation of acetic acid residues in all tissues of higher animals, in most aerobic microorganisms, and in many plant tissues.[9]

There was to be no priority struggle here. The glory, rightfully, went to Krebs, who then generously granted Szent-Gyorgyi his secondary role in the discovery. If Albert felt jealous or disappointed, he never let these feelings show. His relations with Krebs were always on a high plane, never marred by the kind of scandal associated with vitamin C. Working on the cycle, Albert said, "gave me the greatest mental satisfaction which I have ever experienced in my life as a scientific worker."[10]

In retrospect, it seems that the non-scientific aspects of vitamin C may have distracted Albert from the far more important problem of the cycle. At the Nobel ceremony, Prof. Hammarsten praised him for handing over to others "the tempting pursuit of the further development of that discovery [vitamin C] . . . to devote the whole of his energy to the problem of combustion."

This does not seem to have been the case however. Albert always had a tendency to divide his attention in fifteen different directions. He lectured far and wide—from Stockholm to Nashville—about his discovery of the vitamin and spent a good deal of time trying to arrange ill-thought-out clinical trials. He similarly spent, in fact, wasted, precious time trying to get his British colleagues to set up a clinical trial of succinic acid as a treatment for diabetes. It was a wild hunch and he met with no more success in this than he had with his proposed vitamin C trials.[11]

In mid-1938, Szent-Gyorgyi travelled to the Alps for a skiing holiday. (The Seventeenth International Congress of Physiological Sciences was being held in Zurich that year.) Bruno Straub came to join him from Cambridge, where he was studying for the year. Straub was surprised to find his teacher, the reigning Nobel laureate, as it were, plunged into a deep depression. He seemed to Straub like a man without a purpose in life.

Geoffrey Pollitt, his future son-in-law, had a similar impression. He accompanied Little Nelly in a visit to her father, who was lecturing in Belgium shortly afterwards. At the time they were both students at

Cambridge University. Geoffrey remembers how cold and distant Albert seemed, visibly upset at the idea of Nelly having a boyfriend; he treated him more as a rival for his daughter's affection than as a potential family member.

This depression could not have been helped by Krebs's recent triumph, nor by Szent-Gyorgyi's own marital problems—still a secret from even his closest associates. But ironically, the main source of his depression seems to have come from the Nobel Prize itself.

Most scientists who receive the Prize do so near the end of a distinguished career. But Szent-Gyorgyi was still in his early forties and had no intention of retiring from active research. With the solution of both the "hexuronic acid" and the citric acid cycle puzzles behind him, however, there did not seem to be anything very challenging left for him to do.

He could, of course, have continued to fill in the details on both these topics. But he felt the need for something much bigger with which to wrestle, yet also something capable of being solved with the limited means available to him in Szeged. He toyed with the idea of emigrating. In a word, in the late thirties Albert was a famous, but unhappy, man who no longer knew what he wanted.

Out of this deep discontent with his life and career, in the following year, came what many consider to be his most brilliant inspiration. His field, he suddenly decided, would be muscle, and the driving question would be *how muscle moves*.

Once again it was a relatively simple, almost childlike, question that motivated him; he proceeded not through a series of logical steps, as scientists are *supposed* to do, but in leaps of intuition that seemed to grasp the solution and the problem all in one illuminating flash. It was more akin to the way an artist would conceive of and execute a painting than to any rational textbookish scheme of attack.[12] Perhaps one could also link it to the musical inspiration which motivated his brother Pal, who had become a concert artist, or even that of his younger brother, with his mysterious talent for detecting underground water.

In an immediate sense, Albert's source of inspiration was a 1939 letter to *Nature* by the well-known Soviet scientist V.A. Engelhardt and his colleague, M.N. Ljubimowa. In this short communication the Russians reported that threads of the muscle extract myosin could interact with and split the chemical ATP.[13]

Szent-Gyorgyi quickly grasped the wider significance of this finding. ATP had been discovered in 1929, but its importance as the principal source of energy in the cell was not yet known. As Szent-Gyorgyi later wrote:

The discovery of this substance is one of the most important achievements of biochemistry. ATP is one of the main axes about which life revolves. The ATP molecule bears three phosphate groups linked by oxygen atoms. The manufacture of each such link requires 11,000 calories of free energy. When the links are broken, the energy is released. Their splitting is a source of all muscular energy.[14]

The other key element in the Russian experiment was myosin. Myosin had been discovered in the 1860s. It was observed that if one soaked a piece of muscle meat in salt solution, within an hour or so it released a viscous protein. That was myosin.[15]

In the early 1930s, it was generally supposed that myosin had something to do with contraction and with *rigor mortis*. Several scientists had begun to investigate myosin's composition. They prepared threads of myosin fiber by shooting them out of a hypodermic needle into a salt solution. It was just these sorts of myosin threads, in fact, with which Engelhardt had experimented in his Moscow laboratory.

What Szent-Gyorgyi realized in a flash was that the interaction between myosin and ATP might explain the movement of muscle; and that, in turn, might provide some fundamental answers about life itself, because movement is so integral to animal life.

Muscle was also attractive because its effects were so visible, and more open to experimentation in Szeged's relatively backward conditions. "The functioning of muscle may be seen by the naked eye, and may be indicated by simple means," he said.

> Muscle is a classical material. Since the beginning of physiology it has been the most classical material for study, because there are such enormous changes which you can measure.
>
> The work of the scientist is essentially to measure, and the rapid changes in muscle can be measured much more easily than the slow changes in liver or in kidney. The functioning of muscle may be seen by the naked eye, and may be indicated by simple means. The electrical change of nerve, on the other hand, may be observed only with involved and subtle devices. The great motility of muscle demands that it be built of small units, arranged with great regularity and bound together by relatively weak forces. This means that we may disentangle and isolate these small units without destroying them, and that they may be studied ouside the body.[16]

Szent-Gyorgyi maintained his distaste for doing animal, much less human, clinical experiments. He would much rather deal with test tubes.

Needless to say, this new absorption in muscle physiology quickly cured Albert of his depression. "As often happened," Straub recalled, "he became very enthusiastic. 'This is how we will understand life!' " He now lectured his students in ebullient terms, such as these:

> Muscular contraction is one of the most wonderful phenomena of the biological kingdom. That a soft jelly should suddenly become hard, change its shape and lift a thousand times its own weight, and that it should be able to do so several hundred times a second, is little short of miraculous. Undoubtedly, muscle is one of the most remarkable items in nature's curiosity shop.[17]

His plan of attack was two-fold: first to study the contractile material which accounted for the dramatic changes in muscle's shape and size; then to investigate the chemical nature of those substances. His main tool in the first stage of these studies was the psoas (or internal loin) muscle of the rabbit. Like the pigeon breast, the rabbit psoas was a powerful engine in a small space.

Discovery of this "tool" was another major advance for the science of physiology. Of course, for those familiar with modern biochemistry, this all may seem to be science on a rather primitive level. But one tends to forget just how simple biology still was in the 1930s, especially in a place like Szeged. Szent-Gyorgyi had few of the modern instruments at his disposal with which to accomplish the ambitious tasks he set himself. According to Straub:

> We did not have such tools of research as spectrophotometry, for example. Ion-exchange was not in use; the ultracentrifuge had just been evolved; electron microscopy did not exist; gel electrophoresis was unknown; chromatography was applied only to dyes; trace methods had not yet been worked out; there were no cold rooms or refrigerated centrifuges; there were no commercially available biochemicals; and there were practically no trained technicians.[18]

Looked at in retrospect, the Szeged laboratory was engaged in "scientific craftsmanship, instead of science provided with advanced technology," Prof. Biro has said. Nevertheless, it was with this "fingertip science" that Szent-Gyorgyi proceeded to make what is probably the most fundamental breakthrough in twentieth century muscle physiology. He began at the beginning: repeating the classical muscle experiments of the nineteenth and early twentieth century. This was always his method when he started in a new field:

If you go into a new field, the question is what will you do with yourself? How do you start it? There is one thing which you can always do, and that is to repeat old work, classical old work. The old scientists—they didn't have many machines, but they were very good observers and watched the material very closely. So you can repeat these old experiments, repeat them and see whether you can find something new for yourself. My work is composed of enormous philosophical ideas and what is at my fingertips, smelling it, watching all the small details.

Following the old experiments, threads of myosin were prepared in the usual way. In 1940 he placed some of these threads of myosin on a slide and looked at them under the microscope. Building on the Russians' experiment, he decided to add ATP to see what would happen. The threads, freely suspended in a saline bath, suddenly began to contract—to shrink—down to one-third their original size.

In effect, they were behaving like tiny, microscopic "muscles" themselves, although they had long since been separated from any living matrix. Sometimes these contractions were so violent and spectacular that the interiors could not keep pace with the exteriors and they split apart "like a crocodile's skin," he said.

What excitement this caused in the Szeged laboratory! It seemed as if the very secret of life itself was being unlocked. Life, or at least life-like motion, had been re-created in the test tube. Bruno Straub, a man not given to hyperbole, called it "the most beautiful experiment I ever witnessed." Szent-Gyorgyi described it as "perhaps the greatest excitement of my life, to see motion in the bottle of more or less known substances for the first time. That was a great, a very great experience."

"People expected then in a short-time project of a year or so to discover new wonders," said Straub. And Albert Szent-Gyorgyi was not about to disappoint them.

In retrospect, one can see that Albert was studying muscle but also pursuing "life" itself, and not just the details. A deeply-held philosophical idea lay behind the particularities of his scientific work:

All living organisms are but leaves on the same tree of life. The various functions of plants and animals and their specialized organs are manifestations of the same living matter. This adapts itself to different jobs and circumstances, but operates on the same basic principles. Muscle contraction is only one of these adaptations. In principle, it would not matter whether we studied nerve, kidney, or muscle to understand the basic principles of life.[19]

Yet Szent-Gyorgyi's "life in a bottle" would have only been a curiosity, a scientific conjurer's trick, if it had not been accompanied by fundamental discoveries about the chemical nature of myosin.

On "Prof's" instructions, his close associate Ilona Banga repeatedly minced muscle, put it in salt solution, and then an hour or so later extracted myosin, repeating the classic experiment. One evening, however, quite by chance, she did not have time to finish the extraction and so left the muscle to soak overnight at room temperature. When she entered the lab in the morning, she found the dish filled not with the usual, thin myosin, but with something quite different—a thick and syrupy liquid.

Analysis showed that this also was myosin, but of a quite different kind. To distinguish the two, they called the old or thin extract "myosin A" and the new, more viscous substance "myosin B." When ATP was added to this new "myosin B" the reaction was stronger than with "myosin A." They knew they were onto something important. Here was Szent-Gyorgyi's intuitive "method" at its most productive; do little experiments until something jumps out—some little anomaly. The fact that it was found serendipitously made it all the more attractive. He would then track the hidden secret back to its lair. It was the same method he had used to find ascorbic acid and the first traces of the citric acid cycle.

He now devised a way to quantify the activity of *any* given solution of muscle. When ATP was added to myosin B there was a dramatic fall in viscosity; it became like myosin A again. This, he realized, could be the benchmark for myosin's potency. The maximum activity obtainable with myosin B was defined as "one hundred percent activity."

"Thus," he wrote, "by comparing it with myosin B, the activity of any preparation could be expressed numerically."[20] The other side of his romantic obsession with "life itself" was the hard scientist's compulsion to reduce his observations to *numbers*.

The way was now open to a quantitative comparison of the two myosins and their transformations, back and forth, into one another. The key question yet to be answered was, what actually caused this dramatic difference between them?

Szent-Gyorgyi decided to turn this question over to his student, F. Bruno Straub. Straub had just returned from David Keilen's laboratory in Cambridge, where he had gained considerable attention for his isolation of the muscle flavoprotein, diaphorase. Returning to Szeged from England, he began to work on enzyme isolation. Szent-Gyorgyi asked him instead to study the difference between myosin A and B. Straub reluctantly agreed.

Straub soon discovered that in myosin B there was *another protein* present which was not found in myosin A. This protein was dubbed "actin" (from its ability to "act") and myosin B was renamed actomyosin, because it was now understood to be a combination of actin and myosin. (It contained 16.7 percent actin.) In fact, Straub soon found that *all* forms of myosin were actually actomyosins; even myosin A was an actomyosin, but with a very low actin content.

Straub also discovered that there were two basic forms of actin. It started out in the form of tiny globules, but then combined with myosin to form fibers. The first form was called "G" (for globular) actin; the second "F" (for fibrous.) The change from one to another was called the "G-F transformation of actin."

As a sideline, these discoveries cleared up one of the most puzzling phenomena in physiology: rigor mortis. This, of course, is the stiffening that comes just after death; it is a temporary phenomenon which disappears, usually in a day or two.

In 1943 Szent-Gyorgyi and his coworkers finally explained the nature of this age-old mystery. They showed that if a rabbit were killed and its psoas muscle excised immediately, it shortened by about twenty percent. Thus even when technically at rest a muscle is still under a strain, and not really in perfect equilibrium. If they waited about four hours after death before cutting it out, however, they saw an entirely different picture. When excised at that time, the muscle did not shorten. When stretched it was not rubbery, but offered maximum resistance at once. And if stretched by force and released, it did not snap back, like fresh muscle, but was entirely inelastic. Its consistency had changed from a supple softness to rigidity. Simply put, it was in a state of rigor mortis.

When these changes were measured in the laboratory, they were found to set in immediately after death, to increase gradually, reaching a maximum in only a few hours. Sometimes there was a short lag after death. Parallel to this increasing stiffness, the muscle's myosin became less and less soluble. Seeking to find the biochemical cause of these changes, Szent-Gyorgyi's student Tamas Erdos measured this increasing stiffness and, at the same time, the concentration of ATP in the muscle. The less ATP that was present, Erdos found, the stiffer the muscle became. But how did he know that the loss of ATP was the *cause* and not simply a side-effect of the rigor mortis? Because, when he added ATP to the muscle he could render the myosin soluble again. Thus ATP actually *reversed* rigor mortis. Of course, if the muscle were left alone, the rigor also disappeared spontaneously in a day or two. But this was not due to the resynthesis of ATP but simply to the breakdown of the tissue itself.

"These observations leave no doubt," Szent-Gyorgyi later wrote, "that the whole physical state and function of muscle depends on its ATP and that ATP, in resting muscle, is present in an active state and is in contact with the contractile matter."

It was through studies like this that the importance of ATP—"the master substance of muscle"—was first realized. Szent-Gyorgyi was not only an early pioneer of ATP research, but he devised the first method for its large-scale production. Proceeds from this discovery are said to have paid for much of his subsequent research in Szeged.

Perhaps his very isolation contributed to Albert's ability to give a fresh interpretation of the subject, unhampered by the moderating effect of other people's scholarly doubts.

Szent-Gyorgyi's work on muscle is usually considered his greatest contribution to science. Yet after this rapid series of accomplishments, he once again became fundamentally dissatisfied with his career. The investigation of muscle had only confirmed what he had suspected all along. If one could talk about some essential quality of life, it had to exist on an even more fundamental level than one could find in traditional muscle studies. It was more fundamental than proteins such as actin, more fundamental than ATP itself.

But what could that be? Albert's entire career had led him to deal with smaller and smaller units. He had started life as an anatomist in the Lenhossek tradition. He had become a physiologist, a pharmacologist, a bacteriologist, then a biochemist, and finally an early pioneer of molecular biology. Now he felt himself being drawn toward something even more minute than molecules. That could only be the electronic dimension.

His experimental studies now merged with speculations about ultimate questions, about the nature and origin of life on earth. He concluded the first volume of the Szeged *Studies* with these remarks:

> I was always led in research by my conviction that the primitive, basic functions of living matter are brought about by ions, ions being the only powerful tools which life found in the sea water where it originated. Contraction is one of the basic primitive functions and the results reported in this volume corroborate me in my conviction.

Some years later, he summed up his muscle work in this way:

> The reader may ask: When we know all this, will we understand muscle and life itself? The author can only give his personal opinion: We will not, because the fundamental changes in muscle cannot be expressed in terms of orthodox chemistry. We will very likely have to explain them in terms of

how electrons are distributed over the entire molecular structure, an explanation that belongs to the realm of quantum mechanics.

Such a study, he cautioned, would be "one of the most urgent and difficult tasks of biology." Nevertheless, by leading to a full understanding of the protein molecule, it "will mark the beginning of a new era in biology and medicine."

For Szent-Gyorgyi this was to be his new direction, and where he could make his greatest contribution. While other biologists pursued the fields he had helped open up, delving deeper into the *molecular* level, Albert himself gradually abandoned this field and decided to pursue life amid the dance of electrons. Few followed him. But he had finally found a stage for his own restless energy. It was a problem on which he was prepared to spend the rest of his scientific life.

12

THE ADVENTURES OF
MR. SWENSEN

Whether World War II broke out on 1 September 1939 Albert's life was already in disarray. His beloved mother had died the year before. His marriage of twenty years was collapsing. Even his science was in transition. Politically, revanchism, the art of getting even, was the order of the day. In 1940 Hungary seized back from Romania part of Transylvania which it had lost in 1919. Many of the refugees from the old Hungarian University in Koloszvar flocked back, including Prof. Reyse Miskolczy. This cleared the way for Marta's divorce.

Hungary, technically independent, was being led into increasing connivance with the Nazis. In the summer of 1938, Hitler had entertained Admiral Horthy aboard the liner, *Patria,* in Kiel Bay. Hitler had just seized Austria, putting his troops on Hungary's border. He was about to dismember Czechoslovakia. If the Hungarians wanted to be in on the kill, Hitler had told him, they must be prepared to act. "He who wants to sit at the table must at least help out in the kitchen."

From that point, Hungary became Germany's junior partner, coordinating its moves with those of the Nazis.[1] There were still, however, no swastikas flying in Budapest nor jackboots or brown shirts. Horthy managed to maintain a semblance of freedom. A U.S. government document of the time reported:

> There are a lot of institutions in Hungary which . . . no longer exist in Axis countries. . . . In addition to a very efficient dictatorship, there is also "democracy" in Hungary, and a "thousand year old constitution." There is a "parliament," there are political parties, there is even a Social Democratic Party. . . . There is a relatively mild press censorship, since newspapers do not dare to write anything that would not please the censor, anyway.[2]

126

Things could be pleasant. Even Hitler expressed his jealous admiration: "At the moment Budapest is the most beautiful town in the world," he said in 1942, "and there is no town in the whole German Reich that can even compare with it."[3] A few years later he would help destroy it.

In April 1941 Hungary attacked its neighbor Yugoslavia. In Szeged, Albert watched as troops, en route to the front, were blessed outside his Cathedral Square window. "I knew that on the other side of the front, another priest blessed the Yugoslavian guns, wishing good carnage," he recalled. "This made me disgusted."[4]

Sights like this kindled Albert's political impulses. "It was not I who went into politics," he later said. "Politics came into our lives and when books were burned and my Jewish friends were persecuted, I had to say 'yes' or 'no.' I said 'no.' "

This is a simplification. In fact, in the early thirties, Albert had already half jokingly expressed to his friends an interest in going into politics. In his laboratory, at afternoon tea, political discussions predominated, and the sentiment was openly anti-government. As the country's only resident Nobel laureate, Szent-Gyorgyi was asked for his opinion on many topics. And like many people who become highly successful in one specialized field, he had the unshakable belief that he could excel in other fields equally well. Especially politics.

The situation was becoming very complicated, however, even for professional politicians. In 1942 Miklos Kallay became premier. The very name of his party, the Conservative-Liberals, seems a bit like a joke, but it indicates the confusion of Hungarian politics. Kallay himself was officially pro-German but secretly tried to curry favor with the Allies. The Hungarian upper classes, as a whole, hated the Bolshevism on their eastern border but were less than enthusiastic about the Nazis to the West. One writer has commented:

> What the Hungarians as a rule liked about fascism was that it restored the lost territories. But Hungarians were not very sanguine about Mr. Hitler. In the old days of the Empire, they would almost certainly never have taken notice of such an Austrian lowlife. Horthy found him to be lacking in "humor and tact". Not a gentleman. His hysterical outpouring of anti-Semitism embarrassed the Hungarian gentry. Their own brand of anti-Semitism was much more refined.[5]

Hungarian distaste for Hitlerism broke to the surface with the catastrophic defeat of the Hungarian Army on the Eastern front in 1942–43. Fascism, by the beginning of 1943, looked like a lost cause. There was widescale unrest in Budapest and other cities, as bread rations were cut to six ounces a day.[6]

There was still some room for "loyal" (i.e., non-Communist) dissent, however. On Christmas 1942, Albert joined other intellectuals in forming a new "Hungarian Front of National Independence."

Contributors to the group's eloquent manifesto included Endre Bajcsi-Zsilinsky, leader of the Small Holders Party and head of the pro-Western opposition in Parliament; the seven Social Democratic deputies; various trade union leaders, artists, and musicians; and Albert Szent-Gyorgyi.

The manifesto was a courageous document. It called for an end to Hungarian participation in the war, a recall of the remaining Magyar troops, severance of relations with the Axis, and punishment of those responsible for the deteriorating military situation in the Ukraine. At home, it called for free speech and a secret ballot, the final breakup of the feudal estates, and a general improvement in the conditions of the working class. To have adopted this program might have meant, quite simply, war with Germany, but even so it would have been no worse than what was to come.

Albert played a major role in the manifesto's formulation. He provided a leading article for the special issue of the Social Democratic paper, *Nepszava,* in which it appeared, and much of the documentation for the text.

When twenty-four leading Hungarians were asked in a poll to choose the year's most inspiring message, the majority named two: the Pope's annual message and the *Nepszava* manifesto. The right-wing paper, *Magyarsag,* denounced the dissidents as tools of the "Popular Front" strategy and complained, "We smell a rat when anyone enjoys the Pope's message and the Social Democratic paper at the same time." The "rat" presumably was communism, which had little practical influence in Hungary at the time.

This manifesto, and especially Albert's participation in it, had a significant effect abroad. Churchill took an almost proprietary interest in the Balkans, and British intelligence followed Hungarian developments very closely. It called Szent-Gyorgyi's anti-Nazi public statements "almost unprecedented." One report stated:

> It is of remarkable significance that Professor Szent-Gyorgyi has consistently and relentlessly proclaimed the superiority of Anglo-Saxon ways of life.

Another report added:

> His political views show strong liberal and humanitarian tendencies, with decidedly and openly professed pro-British and pro-American sympathies.[7]

Through his new contacts, Albert was increasingly drawn into politics. In 1943 he and some other intellectuals formed a new group, the Citizens Democratic Party. He also began to get involved with underground, clandestine activities, which were beginning at that time.

> I had my own group. We organized resistance against Hitler, all sorts of resistance. I had to be very careful because the whole country was infiltrated with spies. Every second man was a Nazi spy. They forced even decent people into their secret service by threatening them with death if they didn't cooperate.

In early 1943, after the shockwaves of the manifesto had died down, Albert was approached by some prominent members of the opposition, led by Count Istvan Bethlen. Bethlen was an unlikely rebel. He had been the architect of Horthy's right-wing policies in the 1920s. But he and his friends could see the writing on the wall: follow Hitler, and follow the Axis to its doom. The Russians were now starting their counteroffensive, and that could mean the end of all private property in Hungary. Bethlen was widely regarded "as their leader by all forces antagonistic to the new right-wing radicalism."[8]

Bethlen came to Albert with a daring proposal to open secret negotiations with the Allies. Other such attempts had been made and failed. Bethlen would provide the money and a ticket to Istanbul for this new approach. Albert should contact British and American intelligence agents there and attempt to arrange a separate peace.

Albert was flattered by the attentions of this enormously wealthy and powerful man. But why me?, he asked. It was explained that the British trusted him as they trusted almost no other Hungarian. Since he still travelled frequently to give scientific lectures, he could use that as his "cover" to travel to neutral Turkey.

The whole plan, in retrospect, seems dangerous and naive; nevertheless, Albert agreed to do it. He thought he could possibly shorten the war by a year, since without Hungary the Axis would collapse even sooner. Of course, he might very well be killed by the Gestapo, but that thought only seemed to exhilarate him. He was one of those rare individuals who feel immune from danger, and sometimes showed a reckless disregard for his personal safety. Ironically, that very attitude seemed to protect him like a shield.

If he were going, however, he wanted to raise the stakes. Bethlen wanted him to contact the Allies in the name of the opposition. But nobody took this feeble opposition seriously. As the head of a dissedent party himself, Albert knew how limited was its influence. The only way this particular offer would mean anything would be if it came from *the government itself*. And so, in a move of quixotic courage, Albert made an appointment to see the Prime Minister.

He was risking his life by doing so because what he wanted to suggest was tantamount to treason. But Albert chose to trust his intuition. For all his right-wing ranting, underneath Kallay seemed like "a good fellow." Albert laid his cards on the table:

> I told him about my plans to go to Istanbul. Outwardly, Mr. Kallay was a Nazi but I suspected that he was a good Hungarian, waiting for his chance to bring his country over to the other side. My guess was right. Instead of having me arrested, he asked me to represent him and convey certain messages to the Allies.[9]

Szent-Gyorgyi may have credited his "intuition" but Kallay had already made some decidedly pro-Allied moves. For instance, suspicious that the Nazi "resettlement" program was a cover for genocide, he had pointedly disbanded the Hungarian agency charged with the solution of the "Jewish Problem."

In early February 1943 Albert took the train, across pro-fascist Romania and Bulgaria, to Istanbul. His contact there was one Andreas Frey, a foreign affairs editor for the opposition *Magyar Nemzet*, who had arrived in Istanbul only a short time before. German intelligence was suspicious of Frey; "a very intelligent half-Jew" is how Nazi documents described him.[10]

"I looked that fellow up," related Albert, "and I told him what I was about. He said, 'All right, you come tomorrow to some club, and there I will introduce you to diplomats.'" The scene itself, in spy-ridden Istanbul, with its minarets and dark alleyways, was like something out of an Eric Ambler thriller:

> At this club I met two people who didn't talk much, and they said, "Tomorrow at six o'clock, at dusk, go to this-and-this street in the district of Istanbul and before house number so-and-so there will be a blue Buick standing. Now ask no questions, just jump in."
>
> For me, it was all very funny because I am a biochemist—not a spy.
>
> So I jumped in. It was evening, and we went many miles. They took me in the night somewhere, way out. I don't know where because I could see nothing. Then they stopped and took me to a house where I met a gentleman who said he was the head of the British Secret Service.

The British intelligence chief was then operating undercover as a representative of the Socony-Vacuum Oil Co.[11] Albert handed him a memorandum concerning his meeting with Kallay. Verbatim, it read:

Before leaving my country, I visited the Prime Minister, told him [I would try] to come out this way and try to talk to Mr. Steinhardt [the American ambassador in Ankara] and asked him whether I could do any favor to him. He asked me to tell Mr. Steinhardt that 1) he is not giving one soldier or one gun any more to Germany, 2) he has to shout now and then against the Jews but is doing practically nothing and is hiding 70,000 Jewish refugees in the country, 3) he could not follow till now a different policy because in that case Hungary would have been occupied by the Germans and mobilized totally against the Allies and the Jews exterminated.[12]

Albert claimed he had been given definite terms for an armistice, and that he himself had sufficient influence to move "the policy of the government at the right time any way desired." This was sheer exaggeration, born out of the excitement of the moment and Albert's sense of his own importance.

Albert was informed that his proposals would be forwarded by radio to London, and plans were made for another meeting on the following day. He was then driven back to his hotel. "Prof" was understandably nervous, yet excited by this high-stakes game of Byzantine intrigue. It was certainly a long way from the biochemistry bench in Szeged. "What made these dealings exciting," he said, "was that, till the end, I could not know for certain whether I was dealing with the British or the German Secret Service."

Luckily for him, these were genuine Allied agents. According to an understated British Foreign Service aide-memoire, the Professor "appears to enjoy a certain independence and in many respects he seems to be a person with whom discreet contact might usefully be maintained through suitable underground channels."[13]

Albert was then instructed to return to Hungary and set up a clandestine radio station to maintain contact with England. He was also given a message to take back to Kallay: prepare to make a transition to the Allied side. This was heady stuff, and Albert had a correspondingly grandiose vision of his own importance:

> I had the whole fate of the war in my hands. I was to be a connecting link between the Prime Minister and the English government, waiting for a chance to bring Hungary over to the right side. It was a very good idea.

But setting up a secret radio station in the midst of pro-fascist Hungary was easier said than done. Albert's best bet was his old friend, Prof. Zoltan Bay, a prominent Hungarian physicist who had just made history by bouncing the first radio beams off the moon. Without hesitation, Bay agreed to join him. There were endless tech-

nical and political difficulties, however. It was turning out to be easier
to reach the moon by radio than wartime London.

Nor could Albert have imagined the rivalries and jealousies which
his trip would stir up among the Allies themselves. The dispatch of
the American ambassador, dated 13 February, did not even reach
Washington until a month later, on 16 March. "The memorandum
does not appear to have been taken seriously by the Department of
State," one historian has commented.[14]

The Soviet Union reacted even more negatively when they heard of
Kallay's feeler. The Hungarians had nothing to negotiate except their
unconditional surrender, they said. The Russians were suspicious of
Churchill's dream of British hegemony in the Balkans. The Hungarians would simply have to surrender, and since the Red Army was
already moving west, it was clear *to whom* that would be. These last-
minute maneuvers were, the Russians suggested, transparently aimed
at keeping Soviet influence out of Hungary.

Even within British intelligence circles, opinion was divided about
the Szent-Gyorgyi initiative. Eventually the issue was put to Winston
Churchill himself. A "Most Secret Memorandum" of the Foreign
Office, approved by Churchill, put it this way:

> It was fully realized at the time that it was unlikely that the Hungarians
> would risk any open action to implement their offer of unconditional
> surrender until the Allied forces were a good deal nearer to the Hungarian
> frontier and in a better position to afford protection against German
> reprisals.
>
> While therefore stipulating for the earliest possible announcement of
> unconditional surrender, we indicated to the Hungarian government that
> in the interval we expected them to give proof of their goodwill by
> organizing obstruction, delaying actions and minor sabotage against Ger-
> man communications.

The British hoped that Szent-Gyorgyi's secret radio station might at
least give them accurate reports on war production and German
casualties. Before it could even be set up, however, the plan was
betrayed.

"Not being arrested on my return," Albert said, "I was finally sure
that it was the British to whom I had talked." Somewhere along the
line he had talked to someone else as well—someone who worked for
the German Reich.

It is not known exactly how the Nazis found them out, but the
opposition's security was like a sieve. Some historians believe one of
the "Allied agents" Szent-Gyorgyi talked to in Istanbul was in fact a

Gestapo informer.[15] Or the information might have leaked through "Cicero," the British ambassador's valet, who later proved to be a Nazi spy.[16] Most disturbing is the possibility that the informant was one of Szent-Gyorgyi's "anti-fascist" colleagues, a Prof. Meszaros. "It appears Meszaros was active on behalf of the Vienna office of the German Abwehr," it has been said, "and receives 300 Turkish pounds every month for his services."[17]

"Szent-Gyorgyi's activities were also taken seriously by the Reich leaders who came to know about it [sic]."[18] Shortly after Szent-Gyorgyi's return to Hungary, Hitler summoned Horthy to his hideaway at Klessheim Castle, near Salzburg. The ostensible purpose of the meeting was to discuss the miserable military situation: the German counteroffensive on the Dneper was petering out in the spring slush. Hitler, as usual, wanted more Hungarian cannon fodder.

The two leaders presented quite a contrast. The regent was now seventy-five, but "the ramrod-straight Hungarian towered over the Fuhrer."[19] We also know Hitler's opinion of Horthy: "The old man is animated by a fanatical desire to conserve his own health," Hitler had said. "He is a bull of a man, and was, without doubt, the bravest man in the Austrian Navy."[20] Horthy, for his part, found Hitler "embarrassingly stooped, pale and awkward."

No sooner had they shaken hands, than Horthy was confronted with a series of loudly enunciated accusations. Hitler lectured Horthy on the "Jewish question." "The presence of one million Jews, in Hungary," it has been said, "in the very heart of a nearly *judenfrei* Reich, began to rankle."[21]

"I have taken their jobs, I have taken their property," said Horthy. "I cannot, after all, just murder them. Or let them die. Can I?" He was asking the wrong person.

Horthy struggled as best he could. According to a U.S. intelligence report:

> The last conversation between Hitler and Horthy . . . was very stormy. Horthy, in a loud voice, accused Hitler of destruction of the Hungarian army, and he definitely refused to send Hungarian troops to the eastern, or any other front. He said that should Germany endeavour to occupy Hungary, the whole nation will rise against the invaders.[22]

But Hitler directed his greatest fury at the activities of one Albert Szent-Gyorgyi. He called on his foreign minister, Joachim von Ribbentrop, to read out various intercepted and decoded telegrams concerning "Prof's" mission to Istanbul. They were embarrassingly complete and explicit. Hitler informed the regent that, although he retained confidence in him personally, he had lost all trust in Prime Minister Kallay.[23]

Partially-charred transcripts of this meeting were recovered after the fall of Berlin. The expletives were, understandably, deleted. But according to reports which later circulated in Budapest, Hitler literally demanded Szent-Gyorgyi's head:

> I think the peak of my political career was that Hitler shouted my name at the top of his voice. He ordered the governor of Hungary to come to him, and he shouted that he wanted me delivered to Germany, so that the world should be shown how such a *Schweinhund*—a mixture of a dog and a pig—should be dealt with.[24]

Horthy replied evasively that he would investigate the matter. (He had deliberately come to the meeting alone, as a stalling technique, so that he could refer all controversial matters back to his cabinet.)

> He admitted that Professor Szent-Gyorgyi had visited Kallay, but he added that he would vouch his head on it that Kallay gave no political instruction of the kind mentioned by the Reich Minister of Foreign Affairs.[25]

Interrogated by American authorities after the war, Horthy said he told Hitler to

> ask a boy of ten years if it is possible, when a Prime Minister wished to make such a thing, [that] he chooses a professor that he never saw in his life to go to Turkey to speak to the American and English Ambassador for us. It was really ridiculous.[26]

All through the following year, the situation continued to deteriorate for the Germans. German troops finally invaded Hungary on 19 March 1944 when it became apparent Hungary was about to desert the Axis. (At a second meeting at Klessheim, Horthy fingered a hidden revolver, debating whether or not to shoot Der Fuhrer.) The SS came armed with long-prepared lists of prominent left-wing and liberal figures. A puppet government, under an opportunist politician, Dome Sztojay, was soon installed.

"The next day the Gestapo started its activities," a conservative deputy recalled. "It arrested hundreds of people, among them members of Parliament, and held them in custody in the cellars of the Hotel Astoria."[27] When the Gestapo came for the opposition leader, Endre Bajcsi-Zsilinksy, he bravely opened fire on them with a pistol and was himself wounded in the process. He became a national hero.

Albert, being one of the most prominent opposition figures, quickly
went into hiding, concealing himself in a shack in the vineyards that
belonged to Marta's family. One night, while he was sleeping, there
was a knock on the door. "Here they are, the Nazis," he said to
himself. He grabbed his own pistol—his constant companion—and
prepared for a shoot-out in the manner of the celebrated Bajcsi-
Zsilinksy. Instead, at the door stood a handsome Yugoslavian partisan:

> He said he is an envoy of Joseph Tito and Tito wants me to join him. He
> has arranged the whole way—hand-to-hand across the German lines. I
> would have gone, too, but I was not in good health. It would have been
> very rough. A very fine fellow. I said, "You came from Tito. How did you
> get through the lines? And aren't you afraid you'll be arrested here?"
> He said, "No. I will never be arrested," and he opened his jacket. There
> were hand grenades on his belt. The Serbians were like that. Their tiny
> country resisted the enormous power of Hitler.

Eventually, Albert believed the situation had quieted down enough
for him to come out of hiding. Not long after, however, he was arrested
as a "dangerous individual." His influential father-in-law secured his
release. "He talked the police chief into letting me go and not turning
me over to the central Nazis."
He spent the summer of 1944 under house arrest. He was free to
live at home, but had to inform the local officials of his whereabouts
and if he intended to leave the city.

> I was honest, so I held to my promise, but I didn't know how scanda-
> lous the Nazis were. It was difficult to imagine. They wouldn't keep their
> promise that they would leave me in peace.

In early September Albert suddenly disappeared from Szeged. His
friends feared the worst. People—especially Jews—were disappearing
by the tens of thousands and it was plausible that "Prof" had simply
been seized by the Gestapo. Albert's friends were elated when word
reached them a few days later that he was safe in the Budapest
"underground."
Ironically, Albert had not been planning this escape from house
arrest. In fact, in taking a trip to Budapest, he had dutifully informed
the government of his intentions. The Nazis were afraid, however, that
once he was in the capital, he could slip out of their grasp. They
decided to arrest him and sent agents to the Szeged train station to
grab him.
His daughter, Nelly, had returned from Cambridge just before the

outbreak of the war. On 6 May 1944 she married a wealthy industrialist, a man by the name of George Libik. Libik was a "strange
fellow," it was said, a "daredevil" and adventurer. (It was a marriage of
convenience, engendered by the war. For Nelly, it was a chance to
escape from the limelight of being always identified as Albert Szent-
Gyorgyi's daughter.[28]) This son-in-law "talked a lot and did foolish
things" according to Andrew Szent-Gyorgyi, but he was fiercely anti-
Nazi and rescued many people. "He would occasionally go with a
tommy gun in his briefcase into the Jewish compound and bring
some Jews out," Koloman Laki recalled. "That was a very adventurous boy!" Nelly, an artist and (like her mother) an excellent athlete,
shared his daredevil spirit.

The morning of his departure for the capital Libik suddenly showed
up at "Prof's" comfortable house in New Szeged and said, "Don't go
to Budapest by train. I'll take you there in my car."

When Szent-Gyorgyi failed to appear at the Szeged train station at
the appointed time the Gestapo rushed to his house. They knew he
was armed so they devised a bizarre scheme to capture him without
gunfire. The head of the patrol, "a rather big man with big hands,"
appeared at the front door, dressed as a woman. "They thought I
would let a woman into the house and then he would disarm me. If
just a patrol came, then there would be shooting."

Enraged at his disappearance, the fascists viciously beat up the
married couple who served as Albert's housekeepers. Luckily, this
couple did not know where he was staying in Budapest. The patrol
then proceeded to Albert's father-in-law's house, where they thought
he might be hiding. Thinking the father-in-law was in fact Albert
himself, they arrested him instead. (He was soon released.)

When "Prof" arrived in Budapest by car, he received a hurried
telephone call from his wife Marta's sister in Szeged. "You must
disappear immediately and never come to the surface again because
they are out to arrest you," she told him. In Budapest, she continued,
"the Gestapo already is waiting at the station to take you to a
concentration camp—probably to execute you."

For the next half year or so, Albert lived the crazy existence of a
wartime fugitive. Many times he narrowly avoided capture. Consider-
ing his amateurish ploys at escaping detection, it was only his extraordinary good luck which saved him:

> I was very well-known in Hungary. I grew a big beard and had my hair
> combed in a different way, but all that wouldn't have helped me, if they
> had gotten me. It was very difficult for me to hide, and they were really
> searching every corner for me—the whole Gestapo was breathing down
> my neck, and it was really a small wonder that they didn't find me.

Part of the time he hid with his student, Kolomon Laki, in the countryside, moving from village to village. After a while, they returned to Budapest, which had swollen to double its prewar size with refugees.[29]

One of the stranger schemes of this time was for Albert—himself a registered pilot—to seize a Hungarian army plane and fly it to the Russians, who now occupied the eastern half of the country. There he could negotiate an *ad hoc* peace treaty and spare the country total devastation. The idea was for the plane to dip its wings as a signal of peaceful intent once it reached the Russian zone. In reality, the only question seemed to be who would shoot the plane down first, the Germans or the Red Army. Albert volunteered to go, however, knowing that if he made it the Russians might be more willing to listen to him than to anyone else inside Hungary.

A radio connection was actually established between Albert and the indefatigable Dr. Bay. Two days before his departure, the entire resistance movement was betrayed by informers. Bay was arrested and the main organizers were executed. Szent-Gyorgyi escaped at the last minute. Bay was freed through the intervention of two members of the German Industry Commission in Hungary who "wanted to acquire 'good points' for an anticipated trial after the war." Had it not been for these circumstances, "Bay and I would have finished our friendship hanging side by side," Szent-Gyorgyi later quipped.

Eventually, Bay managed to reestablish contact with his old friend "Albi." They rendezvoused at the house of a lawyer near the technical university. Albert arrived sporting a beard and dark sunglasses. Bay laughed and told him:

> You are crazy, Albi, if you think you can't be recognized with that disguise. Your face, even the shape of your head, are too distinctive and well-known to be hidden by such childish maneuvers. Please be more careful.

This was the time, in 1944–1945, that the famous Raoul Wallenberg was working in the Swedish mission, saving the lives of thousands of Hungarian Jews. Marta had joined Albert in his underground exile, and together they too found refuge in the Swedish legation. Since only Swedes were legally allowed to live there, however, King Gustavus V, the same man who had presented Szent-Gyorgyi with his Nobel Prize just a few years before, proclaimed Albert and his wife Swedish citizens. Their names were officially changed to "Mr. and Mrs. Swensen." On 10 October 1944 the Swensens were issued Swedish passports, valid for five years.

It was hoped that perhaps the Germans might respect these if and when the Szent-Gyorgyis were captured. They might have remained hidden among the Swedes in relative safety if Albert had not made a careless mistake.

Until the time he went underground, Albert had continued to work on muscle research, even when his group was reduced to only himself, Ilona Banga, and a single young student, Ferenc Guba (now himself the professor of biochemistry at Szeged).

Strangely, Szent-Gyorgyi almost seemed to thrive amid this adversity:

> If one is a real research man, which I think I am—a full-blooded research man—anything that happens promotes your research. Under Hitler when I had only a few months to work and then everything would be wiped out, then I thought, "I must work double hard to get there."

During the war, communication between Hungary and the non-Axis world had broken down. Until 1939 or so, the Szeged scientists continued to publish in German journals. After that they did not, because these periodicals had become so thoroughly Nazified that they were repugnant and useless from a scientific point of view. (The mood at the laboratory's afternoon teas was becoming increasingly anti-German and anti-Horthy.) When the great muscle discoveries were made, Szent-Gyorgyi decided that the proper course would be to self-publish the results in English. It was the Allies' world which held the future of science, he felt, and he hoped this gesture would be taken as a deliberate affront to Horthy's German puppetmasters.

From the West, as the war raged, some attempts were made to contact Szeged, and to find out what was happening to Szent-Gyorgyi. This was impossible, and everyone feared the worst, since his utter frankness in politics was well-known.

Harvard Professor George Wald recalled:

> None of us knew what had happened to him. Imagine our surprise when [after the war] we discovered that not only was he alive, but he had put the whole field of muscle physiology on an entirely new basis, in effect totally wiping away everything that had gone before.

A series of monographs, *Studies from Szeged,* was written and three hundred copies were printed at a small press in town. Although attempts were made to circulate these in the West, few of the copies reached their destination. He also wrote to his friend, Hugo Theorell, in Stockholm and asked him to publish them in a Swedish journal, "wishing to save these results from being lost and not expecting to survive himself," as he later wrote.

Theorell, a biochemist who would win the Nobel Prize in 1955, not knowing Szent-Gyorgyi's address, cabled his acknowledgment care of the Swedish legation. The Nazis intercepted this polite missive and surmised that Szent-Gyorgyi was hiding among the Swedes. The Germans now made elaborate plans to capture their chief Hungarian enemy. They surrounded the legation and began searching all the neighboring houses, to seal off possible escape tunnels. Since the embassy was officially Swedish national territory, however, it was not a simple matter to break in and take "Prof" even in the midst of wartime.

That evening, as the trap was being laid, a German diplomat summoned the Swedish consul, Per Anger, to dinner. As they ate, the German suddenly and unexpectedly leaned over the table and asked, "Where is Szent-Gyorgyi?"

The Swede, poker-faced, said he did not know, but from the significant way the German stared at him across the table, he could tell that the Nazis were now fully informed about Szent-Gyorgyi's whereabouts. It was in fact a "tip off"; many Germans, like Bay's colleagues, were piling up "good conduct points" for themselves as the Nazi side collapsed. Excusing himself, Anger rushed back to the embassy and told the "Swensens" of this strange encounter. Thinking quickly, he had his limousine brought to the rear of the legation, opened the trunk, and helped "Prof" and his wife in! Covering them with a blanket, he sped off into the night, Swedish flags flying.

At dawn a mob of "irate patriotic Hungarians" (in other words, S.S. men in plainclothes) ransacked the Swedish Embassy, looking for "that traitor Szent-Gyorgyi." But "Prof" was long gone, and the mob vented its anger on the beautiful building and the art works the Swedes were safeguarding.

After this embassy incident, there was a massive manhunt for Szent-Gyorgyi. He was pursued from house to house. He took to hiding in the out of the way "safe houses" of the underground. One day, unable to stand the isolation of this underground existence, he decided to risk a visit to the Vigado Café, a famous spot overlooking the Danube. Sporting a full beard, he sat in a dark corner with a hat over his eyes. No sooner had he ordered his drink, however, than an enthusiastic admirer rushed over and cried, "You're the honorable Professor Szent-Gyorgyi, aren't you?"

"No, I am Mr. Dunai," he mumbled, giving his latest alias—"Mr. Danube"—and hurried out of the restaurant.

Desperate for a place to hide, Albert even tried to have himself put in a total-body cast in a private hospital. However, the head of the hospital, a colleague, had to refuse:

He was a decent fellow. I thought that if I would use plaster of Paris, nobody would recognize me. He said, "No, that is impossible. The hospital was searched yesterday by the Gestapo because they expected Szent-Gyorgyi to be here."

Undeterred, he had himself wrapped in gauze bandages, like a mummy. Marta dressed up as a nurse and the neighbors were told that he was a very sick man, with some communicable disease, who must not be so much as spoken to. This underground existence definitely had its moments of surrealistic humor. Through all of it, Albert remained strangely untouched by fear or despair. In fact, he seemed invigorated by it, approaching it as a game of hide-and-seek, and was virtually unconcerned about the personal consequences of being caught.

In the winter of 1944–1945, the Russians began their encircling siege of Budapest. The Nazis wanted all the intellectuals to retreat to Germany. If they could say that Szent-Gyorgyi was leaving, too, this would influence the others. Albert was invited to a secret resistance meeting in Obuda, an ancient suburb on the western side of the city. Just as he reached the restaurant, where the meeting was to be held, he turned back. There was no particular reason to be afraid, but his intuition warned against it. And, indeed, the whole thing was a trap set by his personal enemy, the fascist education minister, Rajniss. The cafe was packed with S.S. men, ready to pounce on him.[30] In frustration, the Nazis simply made believe they had captured him.

The Secretary of Education made a radio broadcast saying, "Szent-Gyorgyi is here at my side. He went to the Russians, but the Russians burned a big stamp in his forehead, knocked out all his teeth, and tore out his tongue so that he cannot talk to you, otherwise he would talk to you and tell you how bad the Russians are, that you must flee before them."

I know what would have happened to me. They would have torn out my tongue, knocked out my teeth, burned something in my forehead and put me in a shop window for people to see.

"There were daily broadcasts on the radio that Albert Szent-Gyorgyi had been captured," his cousin, Andrew, recalled, "that he would confess his errors, and so forth." (Andrew, then a medical student, continued to receive accurate news about "Prof" from his cousin Nelly, who remained in touch with her father.)

Szent-Gyorgyi also arranged a meeting at this time with Admiral Horthy, who had himself been sidelined by the Nazis:

From my hiding place I contacted Governor Horthy, who was still the master of the situation. We met in secret, and I offered my services as an envoy to the Allies to prepare Hungary's joining them. He seemed to accept but when he noticed my friendly disposition toward the Soviets he edged out of the room and I never saw him again. I can reproach only myself for this failure. I should have taken Horthy's mentality into account. He hated Russia and feared it.

Around this time, Albert and Marta, although still deeply in love, decided to separate for safety's sake. Her family was staying on Vorosmarty Street, in an area controlled by German troops. Albert himself moved into the "no man's land," further east in Budapest, between the German and the Russian lines. Here the dangers of war were greater, but the chances of being captured by the Nazis concomitantly less.

One of the buildings in which he took refuge was the Esterhazy palace on Esterhazy (now Pushkin) Street. This was his old home territory, a few blocks from that cosmopolitan neighborhood in which he had grown up. The whole area lay in ruins, his family apartment destroyed, fires burning out of control, everything else cold and wet in the oncoming winter. The stately mansion of the richest family of Hungary was now a hollowed-out shell.

Albert thought he would be alone in the deserted, freezing building (there was no heating fuel to be had all that winter), but when he walked in he was greeted by many voices with "Hello, Szent-Gyorgyi!" So much for disguises. Taking refuge there he found the Countess Esterhazy, her lover, a governess for her little boy, and a dog.

At one point they glanced up to see a machine gun pointing at them through the window. A Nazi patrol had ventured into the no-man's-land, and was debating whether to wipe out these useless civilians. The Countess spoke perfect German. She explained that they were all "good Germans" who had gotten trapped in their flight from the Communists. The soldier was dubious, but her excellent German made him hesitate. He told them he was continuing on his patrol, but if he found them still in the building upon his return he would pour on gasoline and burn them all inside. They decided to retreat to the basement and all of them slept in one bed. "We six spent the night there," Albert said. "The Countess was very nice." The soldier never returned, or if he did, failed to carry out his threat.

Over that Christmas, the Russians made their long-anticipated thrust into central Budapest. House to house fighting wrecked most of what was left of the city. The Germans retreated to the Buda Citadel and castle redoubts and blew up the Danube bridges. From Buda, the Nazi "Death's Head" brigade resisted General Malinovski's troops.

The Russians eventually pushed their way through the city. "As soon as her street was cleared of Nazis, and we were occupied by the Russians, I went to visit my wife," Albert recalled. In early February 1945 a Russian patrol, led by an English-speaking captain, appeared at the door. "Where is Albert Szent-Gyorgyi?" he demanded.

"I thought they had come to arrest me," Albert remembered. "I escaped the Nazis, and now the Russians are down on me." He had reason to fear. In 1939 he had publicly denounced their war with Finland. In January 1940 Szent-Gyorgyi, stirred by the stubborn resistance, sent his golden Nobel Prize medal to the Finnish Red Cross, as a material contribution to the war effort and "as a demonstration against Russia."[31]

Actually, the Russian patrol had come to rescue Albert and his family from the war zone:

> Foreign Minister [Vyacheslav] Molotov personally ordered the army to send a group of soldiers to find me, to bring me to safety. What moved Molotov I don't know—certainly partly my scientific reputation. He thought a scientist shouldn't get killed there in that trouble, but probably they had halfway the idea that I would be a useful tool in politics for them.

Straub believes that Szent-Gyorgyi's Russian scientific colleagues, especially Engelhardt, intervened with the Soviet government to find and save Szent-Gyorgyi.

Despite other people's tales of abuses at the hands of the Russians, for Albert in 1945 they were truly liberators. "They wanted to bring me to safety," he recalled. "They were excessively kind." Gen. Malinovski wanted to take the Professor to Debrecen, which was already out of the war zone. But Marta refused to leave her family in Budapest and Albert, in turn, refused to leave his wife, with whom he had so recently been reunited. And so the Russians agreed to take Marta's rather extensive family to safety as well:

> Although they were very short on transportation, they removed all thirteen people down to the south of the country.[32] They had a whole motorcade—three trucks and cars. They took me then to the Russian headquarters of Gen. Malinovski, and there we lived for three months with a special nice house, a servant and good food. Then after that, they let me go back to Szeged.

"I was very pro-Russian," Albert recalled. "I talked in their favor just simply with the idea that we had to live together, for heaven's sake, let's understand each other." The war was over, and the swastika no longer flew over the stately Parliament. The Red Army swept on to Berlin, and met their American allies in tears and embraces at the Elbe.

Most of Budapest was destroyed or damaged. In the last year of the war hundreds of thousands of Hungarian Jews had been sent to their death by Eichmann's efficient squads or by the murderous "Arrow Cross" gangs. Albert's cousin, Andrew Szent-Gyorgyi, recalled walking from his home in Buda to the Danube and having to step over dead bodies the entire way. The wealth of Hungary, including the thousand-year-old crown and scepter of St. Stephen and Szent-Gyorgyi's own donated Nobel Prize medal, were looted, vanished, gone.[33]

Yet, in some strange way, it was an exciting, even a hopeful time. The grip of Horthy-style conservatism had been wrenched from the country. The semi-feudal relations of the countryside had vanished with the wealthy landlords who fled the Red Army. The Communist anthem, now broadcast everywhere, promised that after the "final conflict" the "earth would rise on new foundations." In Budapest that is precisely what it *had* to do, for the old foundations were now lying in the streets.

Albert Szent-Gyorgyi emerged from the war not just alive, but a leading political figure of the country. He looked forward to an era of peace and cooperation with both East and West, in which Hungarian science and art could be built to towering new heights. Deeply political, yet in a sense above partisan politics, he readied himself for great new achievements.

13

CAVIAR FOR BREAKFAST

Albert was in an unusual, almost unique, position in 1945. He was a national hero, famous as much for his escapades underground as for his scientific accomplishments. It seemed as if he could, if he reached out his hand, have anything he wanted. A secret Office of Strategic Services report (the OSS was predecessor of the CIA) stated:

> Professor Szent-Gyorgyi enjoys great popularity in Moscow as well as in London and Washington. It is the general opinion . . . that Szent-Gyorgyi will be the first President of democratic Hungary.[1]

After the liberation of Hungary from fascism, Albert was informally offered the presidency of the Hungarian Republic. As he himself knew, however, the postwar situation was as shaky as one of Budapest's bombed out monuments. The ruling classes, whose fear of the Russians had been aggravated by their own hysterical propaganda, had fled to Germany in an enormous caravan, taking with them much of the country's tangible wealth. The Soviets were now masters of the situation, but their intentions were unknown.

Some people were optimistic, however, that the Russians would permit a liberal democracy to evolve. If that were the case, then Albert might prove to have a role. There was a precedent of a kind for this. In 1940 the famous pianist, Jan Paderewski, had been appointed president of Poland by the government-in-exile. There were hopes that Szent-Gyorgyi could play a similar role in Hungary.

Albert's feelings about this were mixed. He wanted to get his laboratory going again, and there were tremendous opportunities in muscle research and "bioelectronics," if he could only get to work.

144

But politics beckoned, and it was heady stuff. Although he continually expressed reluctance about getting drawn into political activity, he also relished the excitement. He especially loved to be praised by those in high positions. What is more, he felt at ease with the kind of democratic socialism that seemed possible in the postwar period. As Zoltan Bay observed:

> Probably the only time in the life of Szent-Gyorgyi when he was not forced to be in opposition to society was a short span of a few years after World War II. On the contrary: in those few years, he attempted to form a society based on advanced democratic principles.[2]

Although his power was primarily based on his reputation, he was also the head of an actual political group, the Citizens Democratic Party (CDP). This may have had only a few hundred members, but in that near political vacuum any coherent grouping was a force with which to be reckoned. Most of the CDP members were well-placed intellectuals like himself. A British intelligence report of the time referred to the CDP as a movement of "the bourgeoisie which was willing to cooperate with the peasants and workers and [was] acceptable to them."[3]

When the Provisional National Assembly was established in Debrecen in December 1944, under Russian tutelage, it recognized the existence of five "legitimate," non-fascist parties in Hungary: Communist, Social-Democratic, National Peasants, Small Holders, and Citizens Democratic Party.

The CDP was asked by the Russians, in early 1945, to make a fusion of all its factions "from Legitimists to Republicans, from Catholics to Radicals, and from exponents of the old Horthy regime to the Octobrists of Count Karolyi."[4] (One can imagine the ideological hubbub within this group of individualists.) According to American intelligence, the Russians further stated that any democratic activity *outside* of this arrangement would be considered anti-Russian and would be held to account by the NKVD."[5]

Szent-Gyorgyi's organization became a catch-all group for the "patriotic bourgeois intellectuals," those who could not comfortably find a home in the other parties. The party made its fusion, but perhaps too well from the Russian point of view. "For two weeks now," the OSS secretly reported, "its official recognition has been delayed by every possible means. The obvious aim of this delay is to compel the mass of the citizens to join one of the Leftist parties."

In retrospect, it may seem strange that Albert cooperated so willingly—at times enthusiastically—with the Russians and their "united front" followers in Hungary. Under the circumstances, however, it was not so strange. Revulsion with fascism made the Russians seem like genuine liberators. Albert later reflected:

> The profound disgust we felt for Nazism made us guilty of a fatal sin in politics—wishful thinking. It made us believe that after Hitler was finished all we had to do to bring on the great golden age of peace was to show goodwill towards the Soviets. It is true that in the short Communist period of Hungary, after World War I, the Communists behaved very badly, but that was long ago. A new world was to come.

In the summer of 1945 Albert was escorted by train to Moscow for two months, to regain his health and to attend the centennial celebration of the Soviet Academy of Sciences. Scores of top scientists were present, including large delegations from the United States and Great Britain. For weeks scientists toured the Soviet Union, visiting laboratories, attending concerts, and feasting at official banquets, including one given by Stalin himself in the Kremlin.[6]

It was a time for the reunion of scientists, East and West. One of those to whom Albert spoke in Moscow was Eric Ashby, who represented the Australian Research Council in Moscow and doubled as his country's Acting Minister. Szent-Gyorgyi held a private meeting with Ashby and asked him to contact the Rockefeller Foundation for him. Ashby promptly wrote them:

> Szent-Gyorgyi is here. Brought here (this is very confidential) by the Soviet Government to "cement cultural relations" between USSR and Hungary. You may read what you like into that expression. He very badly wants to visit Britain or the USA, but he will probably not be allowed to: Russia controls all visas from Hungary. Szent-Gyorgyi is even uncertain whether letters he might write to you or to the Royal Society would get through. He is not allowed to visit British people here in Moscow, and we have more or less clandestine talks now and again. He leaves this week for Hungary.
>
> I have undertaken to send [British scientist L.J.F.] Brimble an account of Szent-Gyorgyi's new work for *Nature,* and to get over tactfully that he is still very pro-English-speaking-scientific-world and badly wants to regain contact with us.[7]

Ashby also conveyed Szent-Gyorgyi's request for more Rockefeller funds. He wanted the RF to initiate this contact because, said Ashby, "if he takes the initiative and writes to you, the Russians will probably say they can supply all this equipment, and Szent-Gyorgyi needn't bother to ask the Western countries. It is this isolation from the West which he is rather fearful of, and wants to prevent, if possible."

Ashby also took note of the excellent treatment which Szent-Gyorgyi was receiving in Moscow, which included caviar at every meal and a luxury tour of sunny Armenia. He added, "Russia is treating him very nicely, but there may be a price for this nice treatment, in loss of his intellectual liberty."

A month later, Albert was still in Moscow. He sent his own letter to Alan Gregg of the RF, his first communication with America since the outbreak of the war:

> I am glad I can write to you again, not being separated from your life any more, which is in fact "our" life.
>
> Till March 1944, when the Germans occupied Hungary—I could work quietly and we worked very hard. I think my laboratory has opened a new chapter in *muscular* physiology—we have opened up exciting new ways of approach and if I will be enabled to carry on I think that in a year's time or so it will come very close to the bottom of the problem. Needless to say that muscle does not interest me as such—but just as an example of life.
>
> Conditions are very indeterminable but if I would have some financial help I would go on. Please, do help me. My fingertips are itching to work. I am full of lovely ideas, I have now 30 years of research experience and my brains are not calcified yet. It would be really a bad waste to have me burnt up by my desire to work in inactivity and have my fine share of biochemistry go to pieces.
>
> It would be a good investment and coffee money would carry me long ways. Of course, I do not know what your policy will be but if possible, help me. I so much want to work and finish off my problem that as I see, I am begging—overcoming all my inhibitions. And who does not love his work sufficiently to make even somersaults for it, if it must be—is not worth you helping.[8]

Gregg's reply was prompt, but surprisingly formal. He sent back a list of nine questions: "In what capacity would you be working? For what would the money be used?," etc. There was nothing terribly wrong with this reply, except for the changed tone. The war was proving to have been a great divide and any dealing with Hungary now impinged on a delicate area of American foreign policy. To receive financial help from the West would clearly not be a simple matter for Szent-Gyorgyi anymore.

At the end of that summer Albert returned to Budapest. What he saw and heard of Russian behavior in Hungary astounded him:

> The Soviet Army in Hungary behaved very badly. Near my home town a Hungarian regiment laid down its arms, not wanting to fight for Hitler.

The whole regiment was crowded into a small prison where it was soon exterminated by typhus fever. In Budapest, the ends of streets were suddenly closed by Soviet soldiers and all the younger men were herded together. Their documents were taken away, which wiped out their identity.

About 30–40,000 men were arrested this way and then herded to Cegled, a nearby camp where there was no food and poor sanitation. Dysentery and typhoid began to decimate them. The screams could be heard from long distances. Those who were left were herded into trains, the doors of which were sealed; nobody knew where they went. We could not guess, at that time, that these people were simply taken to Russia as slaves, the whole transaction recalling the darkest days of the African slave trade.[9]

He witnessed, he said, other atrocities on the streets of Budapest:

They made all sorts of abuses. They were a barbaric band of people who behaved in the most disgusting fashion—you know, they violated children, little girls, and on the street one could see little girls forced down on the ground and the soldiers lined up to "make love" to them—so—just like animals. They destroyed and robbed everything. Really, it was an awful thing.

Albert himself continued to receive excellent treatment, however. Supplies were found to feed him and his many associates, and they even began to do some scientific research. Disillusionment with the regime came slowly and was very painful for him to accept:

With our wishful thinking we tried to find excuses for the Soviet atrocities. We even tried to find excuses for the individual misbehavior of Soviet soldiers; war is a beastly business, and it makes beasts of men.

When the Parliament was reconstituted, Szent-Gyorgyi was appointed a member, as a spokesperson for the intellectuals. In June 1946 he took a controversial step that was to come back and haunt him. At the request of the Communist leader Matyas Rakosi, he agreed to address the first postwar Congress of the Hungarian Communist Party. His presence was greeted enthusiastically:

As a worker of science [he said] I would only wish to greet this mass meeting with a word or two, because every real scientific worker must greet all real popular movements with the greatest joy. This is because science can only flower where it rests on a wide popular basis, a very wide stratum. But our place, the place of scientists, is above all on the side of democracy [extended applause] and I am pleased to state that not one real scientist wavered in these past years.

For us who also search for the improvement of human life, brightness and knowledge, our place is undoubtedly on the side of democracy. This is not empty rhetoric, this is something which is now beginning to come to be realized. . . .

For me, throughout my long career and scientific lifetime here at home, my only ray of hope, my beacon, my encouragement through the entire fascist period was the understanding of the wide strata of workers. I saw this understanding in their eyes everywhere and this gave me strength to fight this long fight through. With these words I wish to express my great joy that the workers, democracy and science are coming together. If science will support the democracy in the work of construction—because great means of construction are in the hands of the scientist—and if democracy will support science and will not allow it to die of poverty, then on these ruins here, soon such flowers will grow which this country has never seen, not even at the time of plenty.[10]

It was the perfect "united front" speech for the occasion, greeted by what the official text described as "extended, thundering applause." Albert's words and presence were a major coup for the Party.

At the same time, he began to feel a creeping dissatisfaction with his position in the new Hungary. He was grateful for the good treatment he had personally received, but felt a heavy responsibility to speak out against the abuses inflicted on others. It was a complicated dilemma. To simply stand up and denounce the Russians would not solve anything. "I knew that the Soviet rule would stay," he said, "and my country's culture could not be rebuilt fighting with the occupying forces."

For quite some time, in fact, Albert believed that these abuses were caused by "the zeal of local commanders." He therefore returned to Moscow, he said, and attempted to make an appointment with Joseph Stalin himself to "tell him that this behavior made friendship between our peoples difficult."[11]

"We Hungarians wanted to be friends with the Soviets, but couldn't be if he did not end this rule," he said. In Moscow he wrote the General Secretary a letter, "which is very funny because if you write to Stalin, you write like 'Dear Joseph,'" according to Communist protocol.

I asked for an interview and was taken into the Foreign Office before Mr. Decanozov, who had to find out what I wanted from Stalin. Mr.

Decanozov must have been a very high official, because he was later executed along with Beria. He asked me what I wanted. I told him. His reaction was unexpected: he began to shout. At this moment I realized that what I thought to be the overzeal of local commanders was all planned in Moscow.

Decanozov yelled that the behavior of Russian troops was nothing when compared to the atrocities committed by Hungarians in the Ukraine in 1941–42:

> I instinctively understood that the treatment of Hungary was planned in Moscow, by Stalin, with the idea of bringing the Hungarian level of life down below that of the Soviets.[12]

In this way, Albert became disillusioned with Soviet rule. He slowly withdrew from national politics, but still had some hopes of making himself useful in the new Hungary. There was certainly a tremendous amount of hard work to be done, and he threw himself into the task of rebuilding the country's cultural life.

A biochemistry department was finally established in Budapest, and Albert assumed the position of Professor. He also founded a Biochemistry Institute at 9 Pushkin [formerly Esterhazy] Street, in the rear of the University complex. How strange it was to be back on this spot where he had once been an awkward medical student. Now he was the leader of a whole new institute. In a sense, this appointment fulfilled a dream that dated back to his days as a youngster, poring over his uncle's physiology texts. It had taken a roundabout series of cataclysmic events, but here he was, the fourth generation of his family to hold a professorship at the Budapest Medical School.

At first, he and Marta lived in the shattered Institute building itself. Conditions were primitive:

> I am sleeping with my wife on a couch in the Institute. She does the kitchen, I do the laboratory and 25 people eat at my table. We eat very simple food, somewhat deficient in protein, but otherwise satisfactory. Meat we do not see for weeks on end, neither cheese or eggs, but we have beans, potatoes, flour and vegetables.[13]

In mid-1945, the Szent-Gyorgyis rented an apartment at 15 Museum Street, where they lived with Marta's mother and father. This street was also familiar territory to Albert: a few short blocks from Calvin Square, where he had grown up, around the corner from the University, and just across from the Esterhazy palace where he had hidden from the Nazis. It was hard to believe that had been only a year before. Hungary was changing very rapidly, valiantly trying to put the war behind it.

His daughter Nelly was a frequent visitor to the apartment. She was now twenty-eight years old and her marriage to the eccentric Mr. Libik was breaking up. She was dissatisfied with her life in Hungary and longed for a chance to migrate to the West.

It was under these difficult conditions that the autumn 1945 term began at the University, and Albert delivered his first biochemistry lectures there. The atmosphere was electric. George Weber, M.D., a professor at Indiana University School of Medicine, was a Budapest medical student at the time. He has drawn a word portrait of Albert at that time, worth quoting at length:

I first saw Professor Szent-Gyorgyi in action in 1945, just after he had taken over the newly-created chair of biochemistry at the medical school in Budapest.

We medical students sat waiting for the first biochemistry lecture of the semester by Hungary's famous son and Nobel Prize winner. Suddenly a side door was flung open, and a young, vigorous man quickly strode to center stage. "If I wanted to create a human being, a homunculus, how would I proceed as a biochemist?" he asked.

With swift chalk strokes, he outlined the basic structures on the blackboard. From time to time he swung around to face us, stepped to center stage and delivered an epigram: "The only difference between medical students and cabbages is that one is greener"—he didn't say which; "The Creator must have known a great deal of wave mechanics and solid-state physics and must have applied them. Certainly he did not limit himself to the molecular level when shaping life just to make it simpler for the biochemist."

The chalk grated on the slate as the chemical structure and bones appeared in white, nerves in yellow, veins in blue, arteries in red. Again he stepped to center stage: "Life as such does not exist; nobody has seen it. What we call life is the sum of certain reactions of systems of matter, as the smile is a quality of reaction of lips." With the consummate skill of a born actor, he paused. And then, full-faced to his delighted students, he said, "I cannot take the girl in my right arm and her smile in my left hand and study the two independently. Similarly, we cannot separate life from matter, but if we study this matter and its reactions, we study life itself."

At the blackboard, a few more swift strokes—and the form of a human being appeared from the chaos. I glanced behind me and saw that the enormous lecture room was jammed with people, sitting on the stairs, in window nooks, standing in the aisles. Professors, students from other classes and from the nearby chemical engineering university, the cleaning ladies, the policeman from the corner—all were mesmerized. When the lecture ended the applause shook the chandeliers. A quick smile and the professor disappeared with his magic. We medical students, awed by the recent presence of genius and convinced that biochemistry was the queen of sciences, staggered out into the bright sunlight.[14]

It is a vivid description, and one repeated, if less poetically, by scores of people who were touched by Szent-Gyorgyi's charisma. Dr. George Haydu of La Jolla, California, was another such student:

What struck me (and others) most forcibly was his fantastic presence, the immediacy of his person. You could sense a tremendously vital being right underneath the words and sentences he spoke.[15]

And Dr. Daniel Bagdy, the Hungarian pharmacologist:

The personality of Albert Szent-Gyorgyi is for me, after 40 years, so remarkable and made such a profound impression that I can only compare him to Albert Schweitzer for his humanity and his devotion to scientific truth.[16]

On 30 September 1945 Szent-Gyorgyi wrote again to Alan Gregg of the RF:

Most of us have lost *everything* and are running about in one shirt, borrowed from some friend who was more fortunate. Food is scarce and is difficult to find. Its price is very high. . . . It follows that anyone who wants to put up a laboratory and wants to have collaborators must provide food, shelter and clothes for them.

Nevertheless, he reported that fresh research had already begun at the new Biochemistry Institute:

I have stamped a very fine and big laboratory out of the ruins. I transferred my quarters to Budapest. I have taken my equipment from Szeged with me. I had some loss but the bulk of the equipment is saved. I have 14 very fine, keen collaborators, 12 postgraduates, 2 undergraduates. My government supports my laboratory very generously so I can buy anything that can be bought with money in this country and the purchase of which is permitted by law. . . . So I have fine research ideas, I have fine collaborators, and a fine laboratory.

Most of "Prof's" students from Szeged had joined him in Budapest. Koloman Laki reached the capital early, travelling on the top of a freight train. Bruno Straub, who as a Hungarian soldier had been taken prisoner in Austria, escaped and walked all the way to Budapest. N. A. Biro, who had survived a work team for Jews in Transylvania, was there as was Ilona Banga, who had saved most of the scientific instruments in Szeged from marauders by posting quarantine notices on the laboratory door.[17]

Szent-Gyorgyi requested RF funds to finance his "soup kitchen," but he bravely assured Gregg that even if American funds were not forthcoming,

we will go on. I am decided to go on at any price. I have charged my banking account to the limit of my credit. If all this money has gone I will think out something else, maybe I will be able to mobilise the rest of my Nobel prize [money],

the residue of which was frozen in two British banks. Conditions in Hungary continued to be very disadvantageous:

Science in this country is in a rather bad shape. Laboratories have no windows, no gas, scientists have no food and clothes. Our salary is equivalent to about $3 a month, if we take the exchange value. So there was danger our scientists would get discouraged and give up the ghost.

Some help was provided by the workers from Csepel Island, the city's largest industrial district. Manual laborers were being encouraged to get involved in cultural affairs. "Perhaps all of us have heard of the new movement: 'Science for the Workers, Workers for Science,'" Albert enthused at the 1946 Party Congress. "It was the workers who came to the assistance of the fallen Hungarian science and it is the workers who, through their volunteer work, put the laboratory once again in order in return for what we are able to give in return for this self-sacrificing effort." Specifically, the workers had agreed to exchange 40,000 hours of volunteered labor to rebuild Szent-Gyorgyi's Institute in exchange for lectures from the professors.

To help the country's starving intellectuals, Albert and his friend, the novelist Lajos Zilahy (1891–1974), decided to start a new Hungarian Academy. Hungary, of course, already had a National Academy of Sciences, housed in a stately old building at the foot of Budapest's Chain Bridge. Szent-Gyorgyi had been a member of this Academy since 1936—although his first application had been denied because he was considered too unconventional. (The composer Bela Bartok had been turned down for the same reason.)

For many reasons, the old Academy could not adjust to the postwar situation. First, it was primarily devoted, despite its name, to literature and the arts. In 1945 Albert proposed that the Academy begin to admit more physical scientists, including young people, as well as those innovative writers and artists who had been excluded by the old guard.

In addition, Albert felt that, under the conditions, the Academy should do more materially to support and organize the research of its members. It should be an activist organization. These changes were resisted by older members who saw this as a power grab and accused Szent-Gyorgyi of applying pressure tactics. Harsh words were exchanged and eventually members of the old Academy initiated a law suit for slander against Szent-Gyorgyi.

The issue never came to trial (there was a non-monetary out-of-court settlement), but the experience convinced Albert that even more drastic measures were necessary. He came up with the idea of starting a new National Academy of Natural Sciences, which would take as its first task the physical *survival* of its members:

> I have founded an "academy of sciences" which is working rather well. We are providing food, money, glass[ware], and issuing international journals for all basic sciences, we provide chemicals, are soon putting up a mechanical workshop, etc. I think I succeeded in helping them out of the gutter. Naturally, I cannot provide for all, but only for the best ones, 40 in number and I am providing stipends for a great number of junior people.[18]

To raise funds, "Prof" also went into the "travel business," with Russian help:

> We got from Gen. Voroshilov three trucks and we transported people to the countryside for very much money. Everybody wanted to get away from the capital, which was very dangerous with epidemics and fire. There was no train and no cars, so they paid exorbitant prices. With the money they paid we bought food right in the country and brought it back to fill the grocery shop at the Academy.

It is amusing to realize that this was the same gray-market scheme which Albert's brother, Pal, had attempted to engineer after World War I. Pal, however, did not have General Voroshilov to provide him with Red Army trucks.

In March 1946 Szent-Gyorgyi's Academy published the first number of its international journal, "Acta Hungarica Physiologica."

There were six papers from Szent-Gyorgyi's laboratory. He also had ambitious plans to issue five separate scientific journals, to be published in a "congress language," such as English. With the journal, not only did Albert spread word of his laboratory's muscle discoveries, but he earned exchange credit for Western scientific publications.

In the lab itself, Szent-Gyorgyi was still the friendly "Prof," but he could also be a stern disciplinarian. The war had hardened everyone. A young student who persistently kept a messy workbench was summarily fired one day. "Prof" expected his young associates to share his enthusiasm for the work but to abide by the collective discipline.

In late 1946 the government disbanded the old Academy of Sciences "as both antiquated and inadequate to the present situation." In effect, it had sided with Szent-Gyorgyi in this academic dispute. A new Supreme Educational Council, or "Council of Six," was formed.[19] This was the high point of Albert's academic influence in Hungary. He now helped carry out a dismissal of some of the most reactionary scientists in Budapest, the academic deadwood. This was part of the same clique that had blocked Albert's appointment to the medical faculty and the Academy in 1936, and had ostentatiously walked out on his speech to the Academy in the early forties.[20]

In the struggle over the Academy, another side of Albert's personality came to the fore: he could be quite ruthless against "lousy, lousy fellows" when he had a chance. The "dreamy idealist" was surprisingly adept at the Leninist-style in-fighting that characterized postwar Hungary.

Although he had spurned all suggestions that he become leader of the country, it was assumed that he would at least become president of the newly-reconstituted Academy. He demurred, however, and instead nominated the famed composer Zoltan Kodaly. This was done to smooth the ruffled feathers of the old academicians and to indicate that he was not motivated by a desire for personal power. Nevertheless, "Prof" himself was elected first vice president, in line for the presidency the following year. Kodaly and Szent-Gyorgyi became friends at this time, and it has been said that "the cooperation of the two great men was of great benefit to Hungarian culture."[21]

Underneath, however, Albert was increasingly uncomfortable in his role as "united front" politician. He was having second thoughts about the Russians and about the growing isolation of Hungary from the West. Letters in the files of the Rockefeller Foundation show that in 1946, in the midst of these battles, he quietly negotiated for a temporary position at the Massachusetts Institute of Technology (MIT) to lecture there for the following academic year. The salary offered, $1,000, would have been an insult before the war; but Albert was eager, almost desperate, to spend some time in England or America. As a scientist, his greatest fear was to be cut off from the mainstream. The RF refused to augment this pittance, not wanting to accept what it felt were MIT's responsibilities. Finally, the Josiah Macy Foundation, which had supported Albert's vitamin C work in Szeged, agreed to supplement the salary.[22]

In mid-November 1946 Albert arrived in Paris en route to Cambridge, Massachusetts. In his pocket he had airplane tickets, secured through UNESCO. What he did not have, however, was an American visa, which had "not yet been granted despite several requests for such a visa from the Budapest [U.S.] Legation." In fact, obtaining the valuable U.S. visa was one of Albert's goals in seeking the MIT appointment.[23] There were unaccountable delays and Karl Compton, president of MIT, urgently wrote to US Secretary of State, James F. Byrne:

> May I urge that this visa be granted as soon as possible. He is well and most favorably known to members of our MIT staff, so we believe that his visit to the United States would be distinctly to the advantage of American scientists.[24]

It was not granted, however. The hold-up, as it turned out, was not in the State Department, but in the Department of Justice. "Apparently the fact that he is an Hungarian citizen and that he had spent some time recently in Russia" was the crux of the problem, MIT's Compton said.[25] At this point, Compton himself backed off: "We have no basis of knowledge on which to argue with the Department of Justice, except we know Szent-Gyorgyi personally and favorably."

Other American friends also tried to intervene on his behalf, but with no greater success. On 5 December a severely disappointed Szent-Gyorgyi was back on the train to Budapest, turned back by "red tape or ill-will."[26]

A few days later there was more bad news. The RF had decided not to support Albert any more "till the peace-treaties are signed."

"So that's that," he replied. "I am sorry we could not discuss the whole situation . . . and regret that Gods on that Olympus/Washington/State Dept. decided differently."[27]

By 1947 Albert's attempts to remain friendly to both East and West were foundering on the sharp rocks of the Cold War. He was also running into increasing difficulties at home. In Parliament he made a speech in which he declared that Hungary did not need an army and should remain neutral. The purpose of the police, he asserted, was simply to direct traffic. The speech was widely quoted. The secretary of defense, a professional military man, took umbrage and challenged Albert to a duel. Shades of prewar Szeged! The general was reprimanded, however, and reminded that duelling was a relic of Hungary's bourgeois past.

On another occasion, "Prof" lectured to the workers in Csepel, Budapest's smoggy industrial island, to fulfill his half of the labor exchange. His lectures on the nature of life were witty and irreverent and delighted most of the listeners, who literally hung from the rafters of a cavernous steel mill to hear him. To his amazement, some leading left-wing politicians disapproved of the lectures. They were trying to hold together their tenuous alliance with the conservative parties and were afraid such speeches would alienate the clergy.[28]

Through experiences like these, Albert began to feel that there was really no place for him in the political life of the new Hungary. "He was a sort of left-liberal," says Biro, "who fitted badly into this 1945–1949 coalition."[29]

Especially disillusioning were Albert's contacts with the leaders of the new regime. With Matyas Rakosi, who proclaimed himself "Hungary's Stalin," he claimed to have had a strange encounter:

> During the short democratic period of Hungary, I sat once on the dais with some government officials during the celebration of a national holiday. My neighbor was Rakosi. . . . Shortly before, he had been to the United States. He was shown all that is really worth seeing.
>
> During the President's speech, I felt a tap on my shoulder. It was Rakosi. He wanted to say something to me, so I bent back to listen to him. "I was in America," he whispered, "and I have seen a lean horse and a man in torn trousers. Not everything is as good there as they say." It was this that he wanted to tell me, and I quote him verbatim. I was dumbfounded. Rakosi, in a way, was an honest man. He was a criminal by all standards, but in a way he also was an honest man who would not lie when lying was not needed. I believed him, that all he saw was a lean horse and a man in torn trousers. . . . We see only what we want to see.

Sometime in late 1946 or early 1947, "Prof" received a letter from a colleague in South America. He offered Szent-Gyorgyi a research position there and volunteered to take his assistants as well. Albert read this letter at the afternoon tea, a custom which had been re-instituted in Budapest. "Who would like to go with me?" he asked in a half-joking way.

Only three of his young colleagues declined. One was a devoted Communist; one had a family he could not leave; while Biro, who was Jewish, felt relatively good about the new situation. All the others, however, said they were ready to follow "Prof" abroad. Nothing ever came of this, but Biro is convinced that "Prof" was already testing the waters for an eventual departure.[30]

What brought about the final break between Szent-Gyorgyi and the regime was not some cataclysmic change in policy, but the case of a single man, his friend Istvan Rath.

Rath had suddenly appeared on the scene in 1945, offering to finance the new Biochemistry Institute. It was an offer that could hardly be refused. Rath was a very wealthy man with widespread interests in coal mines, chemical factories, and—more to the point— drug companies. The Communists called him a "shady character," and alleged that he had been sentenced to death in Istanbul during the war. To Albert, however, he was simply "a very funny fellow, a great industrialist, with great influence and lots of money." He gave "enormous sums" of money to Szent-Gyorgyi's lab and was not afraid to act the part of the flamboyant millionaire right under the noses of the Russians. In other words, he was a cartoon capitalist come to life.

Albert was beholden to him, and his personal code of honor did not include betraying his benefactors. But it should have been obvious that this particular friend would mean trouble.

In March 1947 Szent-Gyorgyi finally succeeded in getting an American visa and keeping his lecture appointment at MIT. On the way, he stopped off in New York to see Rockefeller officials. He was pessimistic about the political situation in Hungary. He told them:

> When Russia retires from Hungary there will be left behind Hungarian Communists under orders from Moscow and in complete control of the police, the army, the courts, the radio, and the press.

But mostly, Albert wanted to talk about science and the science he wanted to talk about was his new theory of "quantum biology." This, he explained, was the application of the "quantum theory of the solid state to biological phenomena." Although he occasionally irritated RF officials by the tenacity with which he held his unorthodox views, "everyone present was much impressed by the charm and stimulation" of his personality, according to one such official.

In June (1947) he returned to Budapest, exhausted from the trip. He decided to take a few weeks vacation at the Swiss resort of Arosa, to ski and do some amateur mountain climbing. No one in Hungary objected. He was still in the good graces of the Russians, and had, in fact, just been elected to the Soviet Academy of Sciences. Albert left Marta behind. A more serious problem was posed by Rath. As 1947 progressed, there was increasing tension between the Communists and the remaining capitalists in Hungary.

Before I left, I agreed with this fellow that he would make no sudden move without my knowledge. My idea was that if he disappears I must be sure that he is in a Russian prison. The Russians didn't arrest people. They kidnapped them and always secretly. If I am sure, I may have a chance to get him out, but if I have a hesitation, then I will have no chance. If I ask the Russians, "Is he a prisoner?" they would say, "No."

And this is precisely what happened. No sooner had Albert arrived in Switzerland than a telegram arrived from Marta saying that Rath had disappeared. Szent-Gyorgyi then fired back a "fairly stiff" telegram to Rakosi, asking for the immediate release of Rath and "guaranteeing that he had done nothing against the Russians."

Of course, they just laughed and did nothing. A week later he was still absent. The next day after he disappeared, all the Communist newspapers had big articles saying he had stolen money and run away. But I knew, of course, that that was bunk.

And so Szent-Gyorgyi sent an even more emphatic telegram to the Prime Minister Lajos Dinnyes, "to make it now really official." He also cabled Soviet Foreign Minister Molotov through the Soviet Academy of Sciences, trying to use his influence as a member. This time, he backed up his demand for Rath's release with a threat:

I left no doubt that if they didn't let this fellow go, then I would make an international scandal and tell the world what was going on in Hungary. Nobody knew what was going on, but *they* knew and they thought I knew, and they were afraid.

Unexpectedly, the Russians and/or the regime decided to let Rath leave the country. It turned out, Albert said, that his friend had been tortured "in the most beastly fashion for a fortnight. He was half dead when they decided to let him go," he said. He could not leave for two weeks because he was in such pain.[31]

Marta Szent-Gyorgyi bravely decided to accompany Rath out of Hungary. She was afraid he would be kidnapped in transit, and drove with him to Austria, and then Switzerland, to insure his safe passage. "My wife hoped that they wouldn't dare to kidnap her," Albert recalled.

When Albert heard the details of Rath's story, he knew that he could not return to Hungary. "He was never a Communist," an RF official noted in his diary, "though he was sympathetic to them. Now they make him sick to his stomach. He does not want to go back there because he knows they will read that on his features."[32]

Once out, Albert became vehemently, even violently anti-Soviet. In part, this was revulsion over what he had seen. He may also have been trying to justify his own two-year involvement with the regime. He went overboard the other way. For example, he was convinced that global war was coming within the following ten years. According to a Rockefeller Foundation official:

> He believes the only possible way for America to avoid destruction is to pursue at the highest capacity level the support of basic and military research, so that when it comes to a showdown, when Russia has enough atomic bombs, we can destroy more on Russian soil than they will be able to do in our own land. . . . He thinks there are no alternatives to conflict and does not believe that Russians can be educated or that the people will revolt against their leaders.[33]

His friends in the West discounted some of his views as "self-justification" for "abandoning his country and the allegiance he has had with the East . . . but it is nevertheless not a pretty picture when painted by one of the world's great thinkers."[34]

For years, Albert had been torn between East and West, between socialism and capitalism. Culturally, he was strongly inclined toward the Anglo-American way of life, and towards such virtues as democracy, decency, and fair play. That very belief also fed a belief in *economic* equality. He was against the "unequal distribution of wealth," a belief fed by his experiences as a child, in the Army, and by the intellectual atmosphere at Cambridge. Since he had few material ambitions himself, and had grown up in relative prosperity, it was easy for him to embrace a vision of a society freed from cutthroat competition for scarce goods. This view was represented for him by the political left. As he said at the Communist Party Congress:

> I often ask myself what is democracy, and I have asked others, too, but I have not been able to receive or give myself a uniform answer. But one thing is clear to me, i.e. that democracy is goodwill, knowledge and bright light and is directly opposed to what is known as reaction, fascism, which is bad will, ignorance and violence.

His trip to the Soviet Union after the war had not been entirely disillusioning. He found Moscow to be very poor, but also "one of the most cultured places in the world." The government put a great deal of effort into raising the cultural level of the masses. Russians in general feel, he said at the time, a confidence in the doctrines of Communism, and also each man feels he is an important part in a very large enterprise and one that is thoroughly worthwhile.

At the same time, it was these same "semi-Oriental" Russians who were oppressing his own compatriots, stamping out the opposition, and torturing his friends.

In balance, his involvement with the Russians was not that different from his involvement with the Rockefellers or with Mr. Rath. He was "used" by all of them. He used them, too: to establish his laboratory, to finance his projects, even to work his will on the Academy. His aims were generally unimpeachable, but the means he used could be ruthless. Albert's relationship with the Soviet-backed government, as with the others, was a kind of Faustian arrangement. Albert, quite simply, would deal with anyone to continue to do his science. On the other hand, Albert did have a conscience, and sometimes a compulsion to speak honestly. This led to very contradictory situations. While the "united front" persisted in Hungary it was still possible to adhere to two sets of values. If capitalists and Communists could still lie down like lions and lambs, why could not their ideas coexist in one brain? With the onset of the Cold War, however, it became increasingly difficult to reconcile these opposites. The capitalists would no longer accept a Szent-Gyorgyi who delivered friendly speeches at Communist Party congresses, or breakfasted on beluga caviar in Moscow. The Communists, in turn, could hardly accept a Szent-Gyorgyi who sought money from the Rockefellers and hobnobbed with the likes of Istvan Rath. Something would have to give.

For Albert the overriding consideration, in the end, was not abstract political freedom, but his own freedom to do state-of-the-art scientific work. Despite his complaints, the Russian-backed regime did everything it could to facilitate his work, but it was clearly the Raths, Macys, and Rockefellers who could provide the cyclotrons, electron microscopes, and centrifuges without which modern science could no longer be practiced.

Rath's case provided the impetus, and Szent-Gyorgyi, on both idealistic and practical grounds, chose the West. One would think that anti-Communists would have lionized him for choosing democracy. Yet, ironically, just at that moment harsh voices were being raised to keep "that Communist Szent-Gyorgyi" out of the United States.

14

IN SEARCH OF DR. SAYGYGI

And so, once again, Albert Szent-Gyorgyi was thrust into exile. In September 1947 he was fifty-four years old, and whether he realized it or not, this time he was going to have to rebuild his career almost from scratch.

There were three main reasons for this. Ironically, the Nobel Prize itself was in some ways a handicap. People hesitated to offer him positions they thought would be beneath him. Second, having been the head of a large institute, he was unwilling to become just another professor in a biochemistry department somewhere. Finally, there were scores of distinguished refugees flooding the academic market and not all of them could be accommodated in the style to which they had become accustomed. The treatment Albert had just received from MIT and the Rockefeller Foundation should have been a warning of what he could expect.

This emigration was especially wrenching for Marta, who had spent almost her entire life in the area around Szeged. She left behind friends and family, including her two children who stayed with relatives. Since it was becoming more difficult, day by day, to cross the "Iron Curtain," it was not at all certain when—or if—she would see them again. The fact that she chose to go with Albert is a testimony to her devotion.

Nevertheless, Albert was in a buoyant mood. He told his Hungarian colleagues, shortly before leaving, that in America he would have a large, well-equipped laboratory, should they wish to join him.[1] Of what was he thinking? Perhaps of the Rockefeller and Macy Foundations, which had supported him so generously in the thirties. But more likely, he and Istvan Rath had been making plans, feeding each other's dreams of success in the New World.

162

When Szent-Gyorgyi applied for entry to the United States in July 1947, however, his application was promptly rejected. He still had his visa, from the lecture series at MIT. But through friends he now learned that he was secretly being denounced by an anti-Communist doctor at the American Embassy, who thought Albert was "tainted" with Bolshevik ideas. It was not an entirely preposterous charge. Albert had sincerely tried to cooperate with the Russians, mostly on pragmatic grounds, but also because of sympathy with some of communism's egalitarian ideals. But the era of "McCarthyism" was beginning. A few years later, Szent-Gyorgyi probably would not have been able either to leave Hungary or be admitted to the United States.

He and Marta spent July in England, where he lectured at various universities. Finally, they received the welcome news that they were going to be allowed entry to the United States. A group of American scientists, led by the biochemist Michael Heidelberger, had appealed to Attorney General Tom Clark for help. An investigation showed that Szent-Gyorgyi was leaving Hungary because of his *disagreements* with the Russians, not in order to spy on the West. On 2 August he and Marta arrived, via Pan American Airways, at New York's LaGuardia Airport as "displaced persons." When an immigration official routinely asked if he could read and write, he quipped (quite accurately), "I don't read much, but I write a lot." Their entry papers listed them as "of Swedish nationality," since they were still travelling under their Swedish passports. Albert was afraid to travel as a Hungarian, since he was not even sure if he were still a Hungarian citizen.

The Szent-Gyorgyis had no place to stay in the United States, and no one in particular to see. After a few days in New York, he and Marta therefore decided to take a (now-defunct) ferry from New York to Woods Hole, Massachusetts, and settle there. Woods Hole stuck in his mind from the memorable lobster cookout he had had there, back in 1929:

> Living in a continental country, lobster was a great excitement, and I could never forget that. If it hadn't been for the lobsters, Woods Hole would have dropped out of my memory altogether.
>
> I remembered that there was a laboratory where you could rent a table, and I didn't want to depend on anybody or ask for any favors. I thought, "I have enough money to pay for that table and live here quietly for one or two years, and that's enough for me."

They had very little available money, and the residue of his Nobel award was tied up in two British banks, Barclays and the National Provincial. Mostly they were dependent on the generosity of Istvan, now renamed Stephen, Rath, who had emigrated with them. Rath had financial interests all over the world, and had hardly been ruined by the advent of the Russians in Hungary. He offered Albert $100,000 (then a huge sum) to bring his team of young scientists out of Hungary.

It was early August, the height of the summer season at Woods Hole. The town was buzzing with scientists, working at the Marine Biological Laboratory or the Oceanographic Institute, or simply vacationing in this intellectual playground. It seemed like an ideal place to live. "I intend to stay for some time," he told a local reporter. "It is very beautiful here." At first the Szent-Gyorgyis stayed at the home of Mrs. Edmund B. Wilson on Buzzards Bay Avenue. In the following weeks, Albert travelled back and forth to New York City to visit friends. An RF official noted in his diary:

> He appears in good health and is well clothed, and seems less excited and disturbed than on the occasion of his previous visit [April 1947]. This, however, is a superficial impression, for his outlook on the European situation is far from sanguine.[2]

Together, Rath and Szent-Gyorgyi had decided to start a private foundation to raise money for muscle research. Albert told his Hungarian patron:

> You will be the secretary, and you can have ten percent, for administrative costs and overhead. You will have a position, standing, and a natural salary. I have my Institute. I do the science, and you do the finances of the Institute.

In the fall, they set up the Szent-Gyorgyi Foundation, with a nonprofit charter in New York. The incorporators were four American businessmen, all associates of Stephen Rath.[3]

Many famous refugee scientists had come to the United States, but most of them had eventually taken academic appointments. But that was not to be Albert's way. The scientific world buzzed with word of Szent-Gyorgyi's grandiose plans. These entrepreneurs had pledged $200,000 a year, for an indeterminate number of years, to support Szent-Gyorgyi's work. The idea was to bring seventeen scientists out of Hungary, a plan that was "strictly confidential . . . since he would be unable to get these people out if the facts were generally known."[4]

But eyebrows were being raised. Who were these businessmen? And who exactly was Rath, a man whose physical appearance—slicked-back black hair, portly carriage, shifty eyes—was not likely to generate much confidence. Warren Weaver, a high official of the RF, wrote:

On the basis of rumors from Texas, it is necessary to check up pretty carefully as to the exact nature of S-G's support in this country. Do these men by any chance have an interest in profitable discoveries?

Weaver wrote to the president of Princeton:

I have heard rumors that his financial backing in this country is possibly questionable in character, the implication being that those who furnish the cash have some interest in possible commercial discoveries. There might even be some patent agreement lurking in the background, although I hardly see how that squares with the profitless foundation whose papers he showed me.

Szent-Gyorgyi's options were narrowing. When he came to the United States, he was not even certain he had come to stay. But now he could not go home. In fact, when it was realized in Hungary that he had left for good, there was an uproar. He was denounced as a renegade and traitor in Parliament and the Academy of Sciences.

When Joszef Revai, the minister of Culture, verbally attacked him, many of Szent-Gyorgyi's friends, including Bruno Straub, just sat on their hands. In fact, in the autumn of 1947, Revai called Straub back to Budapest to assume Szent-Gyorgyi's chair. Straub says he accepted reluctantly, thinking that "Prof" would become disillusioned with the United States and return. But the seeds of discord between the teacher and some of his prime Hungarian disciples were now being sown. Albert claimed there was even a play staged in Budapest at this time with himself as the thinly-disguised villain.[5]

Like it or not, Szent-Gyorgyi was now committed to staying in the United States. Perhaps, he now said, he would go to California (he liked the outdoors life there as much as the science) but the treasurer of his new foundation quickly vetoed that idea: "All the people from whom we are expecting money are in the East."[6]

At first, things seemed to be going well. Through Warren Weaver, Albert received a visit from a Mr. McKenzie of the Office of Naval Research. McKenzie was accompanied by George Gamow (1904–1968), the physicist and author who became one of Albert's closest friends in America. After chatting about "quantum mechanical biology," McKenzie said: "That's splendid. Can the Navy help you?"

Szent-Gyorgyi said yes, and asked for money to bring his research group out of Hungary. According to him, McKenzie replied:

All right. The Navy will give you a hundred thousand dollars a year, but we cannot give money for transportation because there is no such fund.

But bring out your people somehow. We don't care how. And then we will give you a hundred thousand dollars a year.

Szent-Gyorgyi wrote Weaver that the Navy was ready to sign "a contract in which care would be taken . . . of the salaries of my physics-mathematics group."[7]

Because of the increasingly-strained relations between Hungary and America, however, the only people who were readily being allowed to enter the United States were priests and professors. Most of Rath's $100,000 was therefore spent in establishing fictitious teaching positions in the United States or Western Europe for Albert's young colleagues. The New School for Social Research, in New York, issued affidavits and titular appointments for many of them.[8]

After Szent-Gyorgyi had brought over at least half a dozen colleagues, he contacted the Navy. In the spring of 1949 he received bad news. The deal had fallen through; there would be no money. Albert at first blamed anti-Communist politicians, but was stunned to learn that the actual source of opposition had been Prof. Detlev Bronk (1897–1975), the highly-regarded president of the National Academy of Sciences.

Why would Bronk oppose him?

I knew Bronk, and he was a very nice, decent fellow. I heard he vetoed this whole thing and probably because he said, "A thief shouldn't be given money"—because he also heard that I was a thief who stole the whole vitamin C business.

It is possible that Bronk was influenced by Szent-Gyorgyi's nemesis, Prof. C. G. King. But it was equally likely that Bronk had heard the same rumors as Warren Weaver and the president of Princeton, and had drawn his own conclusions about Szent-Gyorgyi's American connections. In the late 1940s there was a very strict code among scientists not to exploit their reputations for personal gain. The age of high-flying high tech had not yet dawned.[9]

Following the Navy's rejection, Szent-Gyorgyi's finances became perilous. In February 1948 he had contracted to buy a beautiful house on the tip of Penzance Point in Woods Hole. Built in 1912, this rambling structure was called "Seven Winds," because the eighth, northern wind presumably never blew there. The whole thing was "far too big for my own personal use." Albert's idea was to house a whole summer colony of scientists—"people whom I am really interested in, who will live with me and will, without noticing, start thinking and working on my lines. . . ."[10]

To add to his difficulties, the British banks refused to release his money to a "displaced person." He had to attain "permanent resident" status first and the only way to do that was to leave and then re-enter the United States. This was a risky step. For reasons that will be explained, the FBI was already keeping a vigilant eye on Albert. Secret reports on him were filed four times in the summer of 1948 alone.[11] It was not inconceivable that once Albert and Marta stepped off American soil they would be denied re-entry.

Nevertheless, they had few choices. On 3 December 1948 they went to Canada by train and then applied for reentry at Rouses Point, New York. At the border Albert had to attest that he was not an idiot, an imbecile, or a person "afflicted with a loathsome or contagious disease." He also had to explain why he was seeking permanent status in the United States. He wrote:

> I had to launch a violent attack on the [Hungarian] government in 1947 in order to have an arrested friend released. Then I was in Switzerland. This attack would lead possibly to my re-arrest if I return. Moreover, I am the leading scientist of my country and if wanting to be safe would have to collaborate with the government, which I am unable to do.[12]

"The male alien" alleged he was "engaged in scientific research," the immigration report stated. Luckily, the male alien and his wife were then readmitted to the United States as permanent residents. It is noteworthy that in the above statement, more than a year after leaving, he still referred to Hungary as "my country."

The British banks then released the money. After paying for "Seven Winds," Albert had $2,000 left. He was also in the lamentable position of having assembled a large research team and then being unable to support them. The only thing to do was to look for an ordinary job.

Somewhat earlier, anticipating trouble, he himself had found a position at the National Institute of Health (NIH) in Bethesda, Maryland. In February 1948 he received a Special Stipend—$10,000 a year. Every week or so he and Marta commuted back and forth from an apartment in Bethesda to the big house in Woods Hole. It was some consolation, however, that Marta's two children by her former marriage, Gabor and Ursula, had been allowed to leave Hungary. They came to live with her and Albert at this time.

NIH was not as prestigious in those days as it later became, and for them Szent-Gyorgyi was a major "catch." They had great plans for him. They rebaptized the old Department of Industrial Hygiene the Department of Biophysics:

Their idea is not to make a scientific hotel where anyone can come and go who wants to mess about. They want to have a very small number (2–3) senior research people and give them all the facilities necessary to do good work, give them apparatus, personnel, peace and relieve them of administrative trouble.[13]

Albert brought two associates with him to NIH, one of whom, Koloman Laki, stayed till the end of his life in 1983. It would have been a good home for Szent-Gyorgyi as well, but "Prof" simply could not be happy as the employee of a huge bureaucracy, even one as sympathetic as NIH. He had to be the head of his own outfit.[14]

In the spring of 1950 he accepted an invitation from J. Robert Oppenheimer to come to Princeton's Institute for Advanced Studies. He stayed there till October. This was a stimulating experience, because of daily contact with some of the great minds assembled there. Einstein he only met in passing, but he got to know Nils Bohr somewhat better:

He was one of the greatest human beings who ever lived. He was a fascinating personality and he talked most of the evening, but when he left I had no idea what he was talking about. I could not understand a word of his Danish-English.

The same thing happened when I attended an informal lecture of his, sitting right behind him. I only knew from the program that he was talking about 'complimentarity.' Again I could not understand a word of what he said, but I was thoroughly fascinated by his wonderful personality.[15]

Albert could not stay at Princeton, however. Not only did he have a short assignment there, but the Institute was quite literally a "think tank." Albert needed to do more than just think, however; he needed to act, to get his hands on living material, thumb on test tube. Plus, he had to consider his young Hungarians—six of them still at Woods Hole, three in Bethesda. The "Szent-Gyorgyi Foundation" was paying the married scientists $330 a month, and the unmarried ones $220, or $10 less than the wages of an average factory worker.

The RF reluctantly gave "Prof" $5,000 in March 1949 for equipment, but went out of its way to inform him that times had changed; money was tight. Szent-Gyorgyi, however, was growing desperate, and as he did so his claims became more grandiose. He wrote the RF:

I am approaching the solution of rheumatic fever, hypertension and myasthenia [gravis]. . . . If I would accept money with this flavour it would not be entirely under false pretenses.[16]

There was no response. Six months later he wrote again:

> We have completed the system of thermodynamics of muscle (and probably living matter in general). We have discovered a new electric field in cells which will become most important for nervous conduction, biological function in general and the understanding of the idea of cellular organization. Lately, we discovered a new constituent of blood which promises to be of the greatest theoretical and practical importance.

These exciting claims no longer worked any magic on the RF, however. Times had indeed changed, and scientific funding agencies were more sophisticated and skeptical about such promises. Besides, Albert's words smacked of "cure-mongering," and when added to the suspicions about his American supporters, did not make a good impression. Despite growing irritation, the RF's Warren Weaver still took it on himself to find an academic appointment for Albert. But even he met with steady rebukes. The word seemed to be out that Albert was difficult and unpredictable. The University of Washington, for example, replied that "he is likely to devote his rather overwhelming energies to building himself up . . . rather than to developing the department." At UCLA they felt that "Szent-Gyorgyi is evidently an eccentric, as well as a brilliant person, and it would be difficult to fit him into our small faculty group. . . ."

Albert, for his part, showed little inclination to join someone else's department. He had to be his own boss, an institute head such as he had been in Budapest. Warren Weaver finally exploded and told Szent-Gyorgyi "what has been on his mind all along":

> He has really been attempting the impossible. It is just not very reasonable for a European, however distinguished, to come to this country and hope to set up here an institute after the European pattern, and exclusively populated with the members of the scientist's own personal following from Europe.[17]

Instead, Szent-Gyorgyi should be "absorbed into American academic and scientific life in a somewhat more natural, and, to be very frank, in a somewhat more modest fashion."

Weaver was, of course, being sensible. Although (judging from these letters, at least) a dour man, there is no question he had Albert's best interests at heart. But Albert had convinced himself that his case was unique and that his work *required* an equally unique style of organization. He shrugged off the criticism. Weaver wrote:

He takes all this very well, but bounces back in a somewhat ridiculous fashion by continuing to argue that the character of his work is such that it is absolutely essential to have a minimum group of trained and experienced persons. And thus we end up just about where we started.[18]

To drive home its displeasure, in 1950 the Rockefeller Foundation pointedly turned down Szent-Gyorgyi's next request for a small amount of travel money to attend the International Physiological Congress in Copenhagen, where Albert was scheduled to present a paper on quantum biology.

By the fall of 1950, Albert claimed he was near bankruptcy: practically "in the prison of debtors" and "ruined completely," to use his own melodramatic phrases. Another desperate appeal to the Navy (he would find a way, he promised, to prevent algae from growing on the bottom of ships) also failed. In September he received his last check from NIH and Princeton. There was no more money coming in from Rath.

But the worst blow was that one by one, most of his young Hungarian colleagues now deserted him for decent-paying research jobs elsewhere. Albert was furious. He had suffered "hunger edema" for science in the 1920s; he expected no less from these young scientists whom he had brought over at great expense. But America in 1950 was not Germany in the twenties. Albert had not reckoned with the seductive power of the American dream: these young immigrants wanted to share in the "good life."

While Albert never entirely forgave these fellows for their desertion, one could see their side. Had they come five thousand miles only to sit idle in Woods Hole drawing sub-factory-level pay? They had greater potential in them, and new opportunities beckoned. And, in fact, many of them did very well indeed, some of them even becoming world-famous scientists in their own right.

The British scientist W.T. Astbury visited Albert in autumn 1950 and found a dismal scene:

> I was shocked at discovering to what a low ebb his scientific fortunes had fallen. His group of collaborators, with whom he had so confidently hoped to rebuild in the New World a school of muscle research, was all but dispersed, and as far as I could gather, it was only a matter of time before the whole scheme collapsed completely.
>
> His enthusiastic originality is still so impressive that it simply must not be allowed to lapse—it would be a scientific tragedy. . . . Science cannot afford to throw away such talents. His is a rare spirit that should be cherished.[19]

The RF, once the backbone of his support, was now thoroughly alienated. "I am fed up at being attacked by so many people," Warren Weaver wrote in his diary, "who think that Szent-Gyorgyi is so much of a genius that he should be supported in spite of the ridiculous character of his demands."[20]

In response to Weaver's cold shoulder, Albert wrote passionately, "If I would be a gentleman I would leave it at that. I am not a gentleman but a researchman whose first consideration is not to be dignified but to do his research and accomplish what he was made for."

But he was coming to the end of his rope. He had cut his contacts with Hungary, and now America seemed to be abandoning him as well. He later called this time "in many ways worse than the Nazi struggle."

Relations of twenty-five years standing with the Rockefeller Foundation seemed at the breaking point. But in mid-October the tide suddenly turned. Albert was able to assure the RF that he no longer needed their help. "I do not forget that without a Rockefeller Fellowship I would be no scientist today," he wrote, magnanimously. He had travelled to the Midwest and "brought back a ray of hope to keep alive, stay at Woods Hole and continue my work."

That "ray of hope" was made public at a press conference on 1 November 1950. It was an extraordinary and unexpected solution to his financial problems, and a dramatic reversal of fortune. Armour and Co., the Chicago meatpacker, had agreed to give him $50,000 a year "to conduct fundamental studies in the field of muscle research." The grant was for one year, with proposed renewals until 1954.

"My research is progressing wonderfully well," Szent-Gyorgyi suddenly reported. At the bottom of a letter announcing this news, he scrawled exuberantly "Merry Christmas and Happy New Year!" As Joseph Needham had noticed at Cambridge twenty-five years earlier, Albert either bounded or limped, with no in-betweens. As 1951 started, he was definitely bounding, in fact, walking on air.

But what an odd bargain he had struck in order to keep his independence from academia! On the one side, there was this idealist, a Nobel laureate after Alfred Nobel's own heart, and theorist of the abstruse "quantum mechanical biology." And on the other side was F.W. Specht, president of Armour, explaining to reporters that "muscle is our chief stock in trade," and that this famous scientist would help him understand such pressing questions as "What makes some hams and bacon soak up salt too fast?" and "What causes a 'dark cutter,' or steer with too-dark meat?[21]

One can be sure that Albert did some fast talking on his visit to Chicago that fall. He was willing to take Armour's money—at that point, *anybody's* money—if it would enable him to get back into active research again. He nodded and smiled at the Armour press conference, but one can be sure he had no intention of ever researching "dark cutters" for his new employer.

On official documents he listed "Armour and Co." as his employer. This was fairly accurate: he had agreed to sign over to the meatpacker any inventions or discoveries he made during the period of his grant. In Hungary's Academy of Sciences, however, there were some cynical smiles: had they not predicted that Szent-Gyorgyi would eventually "sell out to the U.S. imperialists"?[22]

Despite Albert's outward enthusiasm, he had learned a bitter lesson about America. No one really cared, he said, about fundamental, undirected research in biology:

> Nobody knew what basic research was. People just looked blank if you said "basic research."
>
> They asked, "What's it good for? A headache or a tummyache?"
>
> You'd say, "It's good for nothing."
>
> Then they'd ask, "what are you going to spend your money on?"
>
> I'd say, "I don't know because in basic research you don't know what you are going to do."
>
> Then they'd say, "You are a lunatic. You don't know why you do it, and you don't know what you do, so why should we spend money on you?"

Building on the Armour connection, Stephen Rath now changed the name of the Szent-Gyorgyi Foundation to the Institute for Muscle Research. It was a recognition of a simple fact: few people in America knew or cared who Albert Szent-Gyorgyi was, or even how to pronounce his name. At times, there seemed to be more interest in curing ham than in curing disease. The renamed Institute, however, was soon able to secure a grant of $25,000 a year from the American Heart Association. The heart, after all, was a muscle, and Albert soon learned to speak about his basic research in terms of concrete, practical gains over heart disease.

At the same time, there was a political drama being played out that almost ruined him. One of the scientists "Prof" most wanted to bring to the United States was Pal (Paul) Gombas. Gombas was a theoretical physicist, the youngest member of the "Council of Six" in Hungary after the war. In July 1948 Albert arranged for Gombas to join him in America. The young physicist got as far as Switzerland and turned back. He had become ill, he said. Some months later, Gombas wrote again and asked Szent-Gyorgyi to send him a one-way airplane ticket out of Hungary.

Deep sea fishing in Mexico in the late 1950s. *Photo: Sotelo, Acapulco.*

Surf fishing off his house, Penzance Point, MA. 1952. *Saturday Evening Post.*

With second wife, Marta, on visit to Canada. 1954. *Varkony Studio, Montreal.*

On motorbike, Woods Hole, 1957. *National Library of Medicine.*

With daughter Nelly, relaxing at Woods Hole. Cousin Andrew is in the background. 1964. *Geoffrey Pollitt.*

The prodigal son returns. Hungary, 1973. *Albert Szent-Gyorgyi's personal collection.*

As Uncle Sam, leading the Woods Hole bicentennial parade. With him is his adopted daughter, Lola. 1976. *Albert Szent-Gyorgyi's personal collection.*

With the Salisburys (foreground) at the Foundation.
National Foundation for Cancer Research.

Relaxing over chess (Andrew was his regular partner), c. 1980.
Albert Szent-Gyorgyi's personal collection.

Grandson David playing
for his grandfather,
Woods Hole, 1970.
Courtesy Csilla Felker Dennis.

With fourth wife, Marcia, at a National Foundation for Cancer Research conference, 1983.
Pacific Street Film Project.

With Peter Gascoyne, at time of film "A Special Gift." 1984.
Pacific Street Film Project.

Think boldly, don't be afraid of making mistakes, don't miss small details, keep your eyes open and be modest in everything except your aims.

Szent-Gyorgyi's words of advice. *Author's collection.*

At desk. 1983. *Pacific Street Film Project*.

On 17 November he and his wife finally arrived in America and joined "Prof" at Woods Hole. But things did not go well from the start. According to Albert's later recollection, Gombas was childishly disappointed with his reception:

> He thought he was a great quantum mechanist, a great physicist. He thought the President of America would receive him on the jetty with the American flag. He came, and suddenly found that he was just simply Mr. Gombas, one of many physicists here.

Although Szent-Gyorgyi later ridiculed Gombas's high self-estimate, at the time he himself fed the young man's ego. Szent-Gyorgyi never had detailed knowledge of the new physics, so he had to rely on experts such as Gombas to help him apply these concepts to biology. In the narrow confines of Hungary, Gombas was certainly a leading expert. In fact, at the time Albert called him "my faithful guide" in quantum mechanics, a "top-notch atomic physicist," and an "expert on the theory of the solid state."[23]

Gombas must have been disappointed with what he found at Woods Hole. Szent-Gyorgyi's inability to reconstitute the Pushkin Street Institute in America was painfully obvious. In America, "Prof" was merely an honorific title; in fact he held no academic appointment, and did not seek one.

No wonder that Gombas, soon after he arrived, began to look for a job outside Woods Hole. Szent-Gyorgyi said, "Paul, I spent $10,000 on you to bring you out. You must at least spend one or two years with me because I didn't bring you out to get a new physicist for the University of Pennsylvania." Gombas reluctantly agreed to stay.

At the same time, the Hungarian government, alarmed at the exodus of scientists, began issuing appeals of this type to emigrés:

> There are many Hungarian scientists who are living abroad. Several of them are progressive and have not returned home because they are influenced by the allegations of Western propaganda. We call upon these scientists to return to Hungary. They should put their knowledge at the disposal of the Hungarian people's democracy which has become the country of progress, of science and peace.[24]

They also sent out "missionaries," Szent-Gyorgyi said, to convince scientists to return. Because he was disgruntled and had held a high position in Hungary after the war, Gombas was an obvious target; Szent-Gyorgyi warned him that if he wanted to return, that would be no problem. He should first inform the U.S. State Department, however.

"If you just disappear," he said, "everybody will think that you are an atomic spy." This was, of course, the era of the Rosenbergs, Alger Hiss, and the Communist "Foley Square" trials. Gombas might have had reason to feel afraid. One Friday in 1949 he casually told Szent-Gyorgyi he was going to use the library in Boston, but would be back that Monday or Tuesday. On Monday morning, however, Szent-Gyorgyi received a postcard which began, "When you get this card, I will already be flying over the Atlantic Ocean. . . ."

It was a terrible shock and Albert panicked. He could imagine the repercussions: he would be denounced as the head of a spy ring—a clever fellow who put the "Reds" in touch with atomic scientists and helped them disappear with secrets. Albert immediately telephoned J. Edgar Hoover, director of the Federal Bureau of Investigation, and a probe of the "Gombas Affair" was promptly launched.

It should have quickly become obvious there was no "ring," and no secrets had been stolen. In those times, however, nothing touching on national security was obvious. At least there was an aspect of black humor to the affair. Once the machinery had been set in motion, various federal agencies, charged with protecting the safety of the Republic, bumbled their way through an investigation of Albert, the "dangerous" Nobel laureate. The FBI, for instance, reported it already had "this man or his uncle under investigation." His uncle? Mihaly Lenhossek? Of course "Prof" (now almost sixty) had no uncle in the United States. He did have a younger cousin, however, Andrew Szent-Gyorgyi, then teaching at Dartmouth. Andrew had been routinely investigated when he entered the country and found to be "clean." But it was probably his existence which added to the confusion.

Not to be left out, the Central Intelligence Agency jumped into the case. CIA agents discovered the important information that Szent-Gyorgyi used aliases, such as "Dr. Szengygi" and "Dr. Saygygi." There was no other mention of these tongue-twisters before or since. Neither Albert nor anyone around him ever heard of them. The most likely explanation is that these were some clever sleuth's interpretation of "Prof's" sprawling signature. About his *real* wartime aliases, such as "Mr. Dunai" and "Mr. Swensen," the CIA discovered nothing.

In April 1954, five years later, the FBI was still investigating Albert, however—a fact revealed through Freedom of Information Act disclosures. They had succeeded in discovering that he was under "deportation proceedings." Szent-Gyorgyi himself never heard about this. Most likely, the investigating agents had misunderstood some reference to the Szent-Gyorgyis' *citizenship application.*

In October 1954, in fact, Albert and Marta were questioned by Immigration Officials as part of this application. The main line of questioning was to find out if Prof. Szent-Gyorgyi harbored any Communist sympathies. That alone could have made him ineligible for U.S. citizenship, under the 1952 McCarren–Walter Immigration Act.

Albert gave a straightforward account of his association with the government and membership in Parliament. He pointed out that Cardinal Mindzenty had also been a member of the postwar legislature, as had the Chief Rabbi of Budapest. In explaining why he had left Hungary, he referred to "Russian imperialism working with criminal methods" in his country. The examiner probed.

"Were you ever a member of the Hungarian Communist Party?" he asked.

"No," Szent-Gyorgyi replied.

"Were you at one time a member of the Hungarian-Soviet Cultural Friendship Society?"

"Yes," "Prof" said, adding with disarming egotism, "I was practically the founder of that Society and was president of it for about two years." Its purpose was "solely to promote cultural relations between Hungary and Russia. Later politics entered into it and this Society was used for propaganda purposes and then I dropped out."

"Isn't it true, Professor," the well-informed examiner pressed (probably briefed by the FBI) "that you headed a delegation of Hungarian officials to an anniversary celebration of the Soviet Academy of Sciences held at Moscow?"

"I would not say that I headed it," Szent-Gyorgyi said, growing uncomfortable. "As a matter of fact, I did not attend with this delegation. I was there when they came, and I mingled. This celebration was an international affair attended by a sizable representation from this country."

Then the interrogator posed his "$64 question":

"Isn't it true, Professor, that you addressed the Third Congress of the Hungarian Communist Party?"

This was a question that Szent-Gyorgyi had rehearsed in his own mind a hundred times. "Yes, it is true," he admitted. "I was asked by the then Communist dictator of Hungary to attend for a few minutes and then I was asked to say a few words. Refusal would have been impossible for me without sacrificing my higher aims of rebuilding my country's cultural life and my address dealt purely with cultural matters. I did not discuss politics."

This was ingenious—and ingenuous. First Secretary Matyas Rakosi was not the "Communist dictator" in 1946, when Szent-Gyorgyi spoke at the party congress: the Communists did not actually take power until August 1949. In the period of the postwar coalition, many decent intellectuals believed it would be possible for non-Communist Hungarians to cooperate with the Communists to rebuild the country. And *that* was the real reason he spoke at the congress—not fear of Rakosi. In fact, Szent-Gyorgyi had already shown himself remarkably unafraid of Rakosi or his Stalinist sponsors.[25]

After once again certifying that he was opposed to Communism, Szent-Gyorgyi was asked if he would be willing to take up arms in defense of his country. It was certainly a bizarre question to ask a sixty-one-year-old Nobel laureate.

Albert, however, had his answer ready. "Yes," he cried, vehemently. "Definitely yes, especially against a Communist country."

Under such pressure, with his long-sought citizenship (and future career) at stake, even a self-professed pacifist was forced to bend. Not that he did not love America. In six years he had become more American than perhaps he himself realized. But there was a practical aspect as well. He and Marta simply *had* to get citizenship. There was nowhere else to go. And shortly afterwards, having given the right replies as their lawyer had coached them, they became United States citizens. The event was heralded, with pictures, as a victory for democracy in newspapers around the country.

In Hungary, at the same time, many of Szent-Gyorgyi's former colleagues became "devoted" Communists in a mirror-image process. Ilona Banga was one who refused, and she says she suffered for it, by a loss of jobs, promotion opportunities, and prestige.

The polarization was now complete. There was almost no communication between East (including Hungary) and West. Each side was cut off from the other, as if they lived on separate planets, ready to destroy one another at the drop of a bomb. The high-minded internationalism which Szent-Gyorgyi had championed so eloquently in Stockholm was dead. It had survived the inferno of World War II, only to freeze to death in the arctic blasts of the Cold War.

15

PORTALS OF DISCOVERY

Armour had saved him, yet in the midst of his euphoria Albert hardly realized that he would never be able to fulfill his dream of a large-scale institute in America. He still was unwilling, indeed constitutionally unable, to accept a normal American academic appointment. His only alternative then was to work alone, with a small and frequently-changing group of young colleagues to help him.

Albert himself was still so given to flights of fancy, however, that for him to do productive work he needed more stable collaborators. Brinkman in Groningen, Dale in England, Banga in Szeged; he always needed someone rock solid off whom to bounce ideas.

From the early fifties, this role in Albert's life was played by Jane McLaughlin. A recent graduate of Trinity College (Vermont), she arrived at Woods Hole in the fall of 1952, and for the next three and a half decades made Albert Szent-Gyorgyi's career the primary focus of her life. Never married, Jane McLaughlin devoted herself to Albert's work as his friend, assistant, coworker and defender. It was a very special relationship, without which the achievements of his later years would have been impossible.

A changing cast of characters, most of them Hungarians, also came to work with "Prof," including his younger cousin Andrew (always "Csuli" to the family) and Andrew's wife, Eva. Marta also played an important role. She not only helped out with experiments, but presided over the afternoon tea, that very European institution which Albert had transplanted onto American soil. In this role, crucial under the circumstances, Marta was graceful, dignified, and more than competent. To the young Hungarians she was always "Profne," or Prof's wife, just as Szent-Gyorgyi himself was "Prof," despite his obvious lack of an academic appointment.[1]

177

Woods Hole proved a peculiar place. Almost dead in winter (skunks meandered unmolested down Water Street), in the summer it swelled to ten times its size. Physicist Michael Kasha described it well:

> In the summer research period it would be difficult to be anywhere in Woods Hole, at the beaches, docks, streets, restaurants, and to not meet with a scientist or a group of scientists, as hundreds make their annual pilgrimage there.[2]

It is said that three dozen Nobel laureates have been associated with this little Cape Cod town, and sometimes it seemed as if all of them were present at once. But Albert enjoyed a special status in this special town because he was a *year-round* resident. One calculation had been correct: his huge house on the promontory became a magnet for some of the world's leading thinkers. This was not entirely because of his personal brilliance, for he could also offer visiting scientists a home-away-from-home in one of the country's most beautiful oceanside spots. In the fifties a visit to the Szent-Gyorgyis was a cherished invitation and a memorable experience in the lives of scores of scientists. Kasha recalled:

> Life with the Szent-Gyorgyis was colorful and gay. Swimming in the cold ocean, fishing for flounder, daring motor boat rides through narrow channels in the nearby islands, night fishing for striped bass in the swift tidal currents around the peninsula, volley ball—all these things were part of the informal life of Albert Szent-Gyorgyi. Mornings of intensive science and late afternoons of intensive recreation became the delicious summer diet at Woods Hole.[3]

Albert himself was now over sixty years old, but had not begun to slow down. The mood at "Seven Winds" was upbeat to the point of silliness. There were frequent parties and costume balls, in which Albert—his self-confidence now restored—would enthusiastically take part. He would dress up as Father Time, Uncle Sam, or his namesake, Saint George, complete with aluminum-foil sword and shield.

> He invented an ocean swimming course around the peninsula where he lives, in which one swims along with the icy current at seven knots, then reverses at the point, and must backswim vigorously against the current in order to enter a side channel. Albert has led many groups of visitors on this swim. The one lady who did not succeed was later rescued by boat from the Point, on her way out to sea![4]

For many local residents, Albert was not famous as the discoverer of ascorbic acid, or the father of muscle physiology, but as that strange old man out on the peninsula who "swam the Hole!"[5]

In particular, his beachside cottage, "The Pebble" as it was called, served as a summer resting place for many stimulating visitors. Leonor Michaelis, his old teacher from the twenties, spent his last summer there, just before his death in October 1949. The composer Zoltan Kodaly came from Hungary with his young wife. George Gamow was a frequent visitor, and later, James Watson wrote part of his famous book *The Double Helix* in that cottage.

One of Szent-Gyorgyi's best friends of this period was John von Neumann (1903–1957), whom Albert always described as "the most splendid human mind I ever knew." "Johnny" von Neumann, a Hungarian-born mathematician, is considered one of the founders of computer science. One summer day he was asked to deliver an informal lecture on his work to Szent-Gyorgyi's guests and coworkers. He began his lecture on the beach, illustrating his talk with a chalk board Albert kept for such occasions. The lecture topic was engrossing, to von Neumann as well as the others, and before anyone realized it, the tide had come in. But von Neumann just kept talking, until the water was up to his knees.

On another occasion, a famous scientist sent out printed invitations in the name of "Mr. Tompkins," a fictional hero of writer/physicist George Gamow, calling practically all of Woods Hole to a gala party at the cottage. Gamow learned of this when he began receiving a deluge of RSVPs. On the appointed day scores of world-famous intellectuals descended on his house expecting and demanding entertainment. He had put in a stock of liquor but Marta saved the day with an impromptu party.

Eventually, these summer get-togethers crystallized into annual summer conferences. After the launching of the Soviet "Sputnik" in 1958, the U.S. government gave some money to organize these conferences—playing catch-up with the Russians. Participants included Hugo Theorell, Szent-Gyorgyi's Swedish friend who had just won the 1954 Nobel Prize; Zoltan Bay, now at the U.S. National Bureau of Standards; the French biophysicists Alberte and Bernard Pullman; Dr. George Weber; and many others. These conferences mainly discussed the relationships of biology to quantum physics. In addition to their scientific importance, many significant friendships were formed here.

After the tortuous period of resettlement, Szent-Gyorgyi seemed to have put down roots in Woods Hole. He indulged himself in good talk, music, art, and sports. "He is forever seeking the fresh intellectual and emotional experience," said Kasha. "He always seems to find a new piece of music about which he is excited." He sometimes splurged on works of art. A replica of a Greek sculptured horse's head took its place on his mantelpiece. It appealed to him, he said, because the sculptor had captured the vitality of its musculature "through a just-credible anatomical distortion."[6]

At the same time, Albert's monetary situation began to improve. He confidently left his finances to Stephen Rath, who had an unquestionable talent for that sort of thing. Whatever misgivings his more cautious colleagues had about Rath were dismissed with the wave of a hand. Money now came in to the Institute for Muscle Research, not just from Armour and the American Heart Association, but from the Association for the Aid of Crippled Children, the Muscular Dystrophy Association, and NIH. With the aid of a Sorvall Company designer named Josef Blum, Szent-Gyorgyi even found time to invent a new kind of centrifuge:

> While it is running at very high speeds, you can feed in material, and it will run out again cleared up, while the sediment is left in the tubes. It is a continuous thing. That was a very difficult problem, how you can put in fluid and get out a very small quantity of sedimenting material.

This centrifuge brought in about $8,000 a year in royalties from Sorvall, its manufacturer. Szent-Gyorgyi left Rath in charge of the disbursement.

He also began to recoup his scientific reputation. Throughout the late forties and early fifties, Albert and his coworkers kept up a remarkable stream of publications.

He wrote a number of small books summarizing his results with muscle. These included *Chemistry of Muscular Contraction* (1947; revised 1951), which was basically an expansion of the *Studies from Szeged* monographs; *The Nature of Life* (1948); and *Chemical Physiology of Contraction in Body and Heart* (1953).

These made him well-known among scientists in America, many of whom were just becoming aware of the breakthroughs made in Szeged, and had a deep impact on the scientific community worldwide. The English biophysicist, H.E. Huxley of Cambridge, wrote:

> These books were extremely influential not only because they described what were clearly important results, but because they were written in a marvelously enthusiastic and invigorating style and were full of stimulating ideas and speculations.[7]

Even for the lay reader, these works can be worthwhile reading, filled as they are with startling ideas and images. Anyone could see that Albert was not only a scholar, but a *scientific raconteur* of the first order, who could involve the reader in uncovering the fascinating secrets of nature. In these thin books Albert also restated and refined *philosophical* ideas he had struggled with for over fifty years:

> We are all but recent leaves on the same old tree of life and even if this life has adapted itself to new functions and conditions, it uses the same old basic principles over and over again. There is no real difference between the grass and he who mows it.

> In principle, it does not matter which material we choose for our study of life, be it grass or muscle, virus or brain. If we only dig deep enough we always arrive at the center, the basic principles on which life was built and due to which it still goes on.[8]

Reading such passages, it is surprising to realize that Szent-Gyorgyi learned English in his twenties, and although he spoke it fluently, still spoke with a heavy accent. Yet he had become a master of English scientific prose. The fusion of hard data and cosmic observations was especially rare at the time, reminiscent perhaps of his old hero, Claude Bernard.

Such poetic ideas, interspersed among the data, charmed most readers, but did not endear him to some hard-nosed scientists. "Metabiology," they scoffed. "Many biologists are tempted to become biological mystics," his friend Michael Kasha conceded, "so overpoweringly mysterious do the ways of living organisms seem, and so inadequate the simple laboratory methods and concepts."[9]

Albert argued back that science needed both empirical data and a theoretical framework. He defended the need for theory, against the plain-and-simple empiricism common in America:

> Facts alone are apt to be dull things and need to be tied together by theories or applied to practical problems if they are to be made reasonably palatable.[10]

One should not imagine that Albert's time was entirely taken up with theorizing, however. A surprising amount of laboratory work was accomplished, even during the worst periods of financial uncertainty. This work tied up many loose ends in muscle research.

Cousin Andrew, with his wife, Eva, discovered "meromyosins," the naturally-occurring subunits of myosin, in his lab and began the sophisticated analysis of muscle proteins.[11] Albert was eager to apply the latest tools to analyzing muscle. With colleagues, G. Rozsa and R.W.G. Wycoff, he analyzed muscle under the electronmicroscope, and with others used that amazing tool to study the human heart. With Jane McLaughlin he studied, among many things, "the quenching of fluorescence by flavinoids and other substances."

In fact, during the course of the fifties, Szent-Gyorgyi and his colleagues produced 120 scientific papers, plus three books. He was still driven by a seemingly unending desire to discover new things. Perhaps he also had to prove, to his old Hungarian colleagues, to his American friends, and to himself, that he was not "over the hill," and that he could still do first-rate investigative work.

And he could. In 1949 he found that a muscle could be extracted from an animal's body and then stored in fifty percent glycerol solution in the cold "without losing contractility, without any damage to the contractile matter of its architecture."

This was another basic "tool box" discovery, similar in its significance to the use of minced pigeon muscle. Until then, muscle had to be studied fresh, in solution, or not at all. Szent-Gyorgyi had discovered a simple and inexpensive model by which full muscles could be stored indefinitely for study in any lab in the world. Even a year or more later a whole rabbit's muscle could be made to "come alive," just with the addition of ATP.

Benjamin Kaminer, then a young associate, asked "Prof" how he had decided on a *fifty percent* solution of glycerol—the optimal concentration for preserving the muscle. Szent-Gyorgyi looked at him in amazement:

> My dear boy, I don't even know why I chose glycerol! It was just a feeling. I know glycerol and I know muscle, and I think they will like each other.[12]

Then in 1954, the same year he became a United States citizen, Albert received the Albert and Mary Lasker Award from the American Heart Association, for his contribution to understanding cardiovascular diseases through basic muscle research. The Lasker Award, with its $1,000 check and statuette of Winged Victory, is often considered the American equivalent of the Nobel. In some ways it was a sweeter victory than the Swedish prize, for it signalled recognition in his adopted homeland. Through his hard work and dint of personality, he had conquered America!

In seven years he had gone from a displaced person, having to answer questions about idiocy and "loathsome diseases," to one of the most honored scholars in the land. Not every emigré scientist had fared as well. And he had done it without the backing of any major research institution. Now he was a hero not just in the "small pond" of Hungary, but in large and prosperous America. For a brief time, in fact, he became a genuine celebrity. His name and picture were in the newspapers, and his opinion was sought on a variety of topics. *Time* lauded him:

> In discussing the scientific aspects of his work, from the beating of a monkey's heart to a new process for combining elements to produce a muscle contraction, he is articulate, witty, and highly convincing. His accent lends color, but never confusion, to a masterly command of the English language. As a "pure" researcher, he follows strange paths with no apparent destination in mind. Yet in almost any field in which he chooses to work, he makes a practical and valuable contribution to medicine.[13]

He became a favorite of the leading science writers—described in glowing terms in *Reader's Digest,* the *Saturday Evening Post,* and the *New York Times.* He was elected to the National Academy of Sciences (U.S.A.) and received hundreds of invitations to speak. He almost never turned these down—whether they came from the Harvard faculty or the Falmouth (Massachusetts) Kiwanis Club. He spoke to all of them with a directness remarkable for its candor and lack of condescension. He also kept up a voluminous correspondence; like Einstein, most of the time he did so without the help of a secretary.

Some of the more bizarre examples of his correspondence got preserved in Marta's scrapbook: Mr. Universe, Mickey Hargitay, a fellow Hungarian who described himself as "the best developed athlete in the world," offered to trade "muscle secrets" with him. A woman wrote asking for medical advice, on gaining "30 lbs. within the next four or five months" and requesting "your courses and the prices of your lessons." He wrote back courteously, if humorously, to all of them.

He claimed to be immune to the lure of publicity, yet sometimes he craved attention in an almost childish way. For instance, after a conference on the bioflavinoids (vitamin P) at the New York Academy of Sciences, Albert was quoted as follows:

> One day soon [bioflavinoids] will be a household remedy for a widespread range of ailments. . .including the common cold, heart disease, diabetes, high blood pressure, polio, tonsilitis, nosebleeds and chicken pox.[14]

Bioflavinoids, readers were informed, were also effective against radiation sickness: "If true," the *Chicago American* enthused in good Cold War style, they "would be of vast importance as a defense measure in the event of an enemy bomb attack."

Soon after, a St. Louis drug company brought out a new medicine called "Citroid Compound." Full-page advertisements appeared in newspapers announcing "Medicine's Newest Weapon for Control of Colds." It was a mixture of bioflavinoids, vitamin C, and aspirin. Albert was quoted as the sole scientific expert for the effectiveness of this mixture. There is no proof, but one suspects the hand of his enterprising business friends in this pharmaceutical venture.

Another area of persistent interest was cancer. This problem had deep roots in his career, dating back to the 1920s. The problem with cancer treatment, as Albert saw it, was that basic science had not progressed far enough to make a cure practicable:

> Cancer research cannot progress any faster than work in the underlying biological sciences. The surest way of progress is to gain more understanding of life processes. A mechanic who thoroughly understands his engine can fix it when something goes wrong. It is the same in biological and human diseases.

In tinkering around with the cancer problem, Albert's intuition told him that the thymus gland was a good place to start. It was not a bad hunch: the thymus was known to be involved in growth processes, and cancer seemed to be a disruption of normal growth patterns. The thymus shrinks as a person gets older, and cancer incidence increases. Szent-Gyorgyi was among the first to propose that this gland produces a growth-controlling hormone. He began a cancer experiment and soon got results that were "equally fascinating and disconcerting."

He began to "fool around" with extracts in his old-fashioned laboratory, much as he had worked with adrenals in Groningen forty years before. Some thymic extracts were found to promote growth; others to inhibit it. In fact, the same batch could be a promoter one day and an inhibitor the next! Any hands-on biologist is familiar with the occasional "insanity" of living materials. Rather than curse his materials, however, Albert proposed an ingenious theory to explain this anomaly: the extracts actually contained two substances, a growth promoter *and* a growth inhibitor. These two substances usually counterbalanced each other, resulting in an apparent absence of activity.

At a 1955 meeting of the New York Academy of Sciences, Albert unveiled a vial of brightly-colored bioflavinoids, derived from animal tissues. They had been extracted from the thymus gland, where he believed they existed in the form of colorless complexes.

It was an important finding, but for Albert, then on a publicity roll, it was also another chance to captivate the public. "Wishing to contribute more than words to this discussion," he said,

I have before me a test tube which contains 1.5 grams of an intensely yellow substance which I extracted from animal tissues, from the thymus gland, in which it is present in an amazingly large quantity.

It seemed to be an important new discovery, from the man who had brought the world vitamin C. His manner of presentation and charismatic appearance added drama to the event. The audience, according to the *New York Times,* was "electrified" and the story was carried around the world. At a press conference after the event, Albert speculated that this yellow powder might even be "the hormone of youth."

"Peter Pan Hormone," the evening editions screamed, and they wondered aloud if the average life span would soon go to 100 or even 130 years. Szent-Gyorgyi's own vitality added credibility to this fantasy. Yet once again his name was linked to some fantastic claim which, if not entirely of his making, he did nothing to suppress.

Albert wanted to try his new flavinoid as a cancer treatment but since there were so many different proteins in the thymus, he and his small team decided to switch to a much simpler tissue source, the aorta of the calf. They managed to isolate two substances from this, which "Prof" dubbed "promine" and "retine." Promine *pro*moted growth, and retine *re*tarded it.

For the next few years, in fact, Albert's scientific work focused on these two substances. Fairly refined preparations of the chemicals were eventually produced and Albert was able to show that retine could make tumors regress in three experimental animal systems.[15] It took a relatively large amount of retine to bring about regressions, though—roughly equal to the amount of the substance normally present in the animal's body, injected daily.

Scientists at Columbia University, working with tissue cultures and animals, obtained similar results. When Szent-Gyorgyi's findings, the fruit of ten years' work, were reported in *Science,* they caused quite a stir. The *New York Times* devoted three major articles to the discovery, calling it the key to "the gyroscope of life."[16]

Because it dealt with a potential cancer cure, however, the topic was handled most gingerly. Even *Science* published it in its "Reports" section, rather than as a refereed scientific paper.[17] This was, after all, the era of Krebiozen, and some people feared that the eccentric Szent-Gyorgyi might become another Prof. Andrew Ivy, the Illinois scientist who was promoting a controversial treatment for cancer.[18]

All sorts of interesting experiments now opened up. For example, retine was found in the urine of normal children. "Possibly urine may reflect the ratio of promine to retine in the body and allow the closer study of this ratio in relation to cancer," Albert wrote. He dubbed these new substances *autobiotics,* comparing them in interest and importance to antibiotics.

But Albert could never isolate the *pure crystals* of retine or promine, recalling the dilemma of "hexuronic acid"! This time, however, there was to be no Hollywood ending to the story. In early 1965 he sent a batch of retine to his old friend, J.D. Bernal, one of the great crystallographers of the day.[19] Bernal was all set to begin work on them when he received an urgent message from Szent-Gyorgyi to stop. In July a puzzled Bernal wrote:

> It is now two months since I received your telegram bidding me to hold my hand on the subject of your crystals of retine. I hope nothing had gone seriously wrong with it. I retain my interest in it.

But everything had gone wrong. The crystals were simply not pure nor was he able to purify them, the way he had with ascorbic acid. This difficulty was one of the most frustrating of his career, for—right or wrong—Albert was convinced that he had in his hand a potential cure for cancer. Yet, unlike the ill-fated Dr. Ivy, he realized it would be futile to try to propose a treatment without first providing a rigorous definition of his substance. Deep down, for all his flights of fancy, Albert was still an old-fashioned rigorous chemist.

Throughout the sixties, in fact, Albert was still trying to purify these elusive substances. By the end of the decade, he admitted sadly:

> After about ten years of such research, I had to give up. It would have taken me ten more years to have gotten even close to isolating these substances. This is a very unsafe way of going about attacking cancer.

The most enduring part of the retine/promine work may have been the philosophical framework it provided. Szent-Gyorgyi formulated his concept of a dynamic balance in nature:

> To regulate something always requires two opposing factors. You cannot regulate by a single factor. To give an example, the traffic in the streets could not be controlled by a green light or a red light alone. It needs a green light and a red light as well. The ratio between retine and promine determines whether there is any motion, any growth, or not. Two different inclinations have to be there in readiness to make the cells proliferate.

In the end this attempt to find a practical handle to the cancer problem ended in failure; but it was an ambitious failure. As Albert phrased it, "When I fish I always use the biggest hook I can find, since I would rather *not* catch a big fish than *not* catch a small one." This was the big fish that got away.

To Michael Kasha, Szent-Gyorgyi's main role in this period was to serve as a stimulus to younger scientists, such as himself:

> Albert Szent-Gyorgyi's role as a scientist in the second half of his career has been generally to make curious new discoveries, and to stimulate others to embark on wholly new directions of research. . . . Even though he himself has made no major discoveries in this period to match his earlier career, his influence has been widely felt.

As early as the twenties, in fact, Sir Walter Fletcher had described Albert as a "detonator" and "catalyst" for other scientists. Albert would have vigorously disputed this idea of himself as elder statesman, a kind of Bernard Baruch of science. At all points in his life, he wanted to do *original* work, and he and his most devoted followers believed he was doing so.

Kasha has sketched this valuable portrait of Szent-Gyorgyi at work:

> He begins with a notion based on some physical idea, gleaned intuitively from reading, or a discussion. He approaches the laboratory bench with enthusiasm. He has an idea to test. His store of chemical experience sets his choices. He fills test tubes, measures out portions by eye, mixes solutions, thumb over test tube. Colors appear. Solutions are frozen. Observations are made. The laboratory is not neat. In fact, the bench is frequently a mess. But new things are seen, experiments no one has thought of are done, and the curiosity is intense. No one has ever worked at the laboratory bench with more joy or more curiosity toward an intuitive goal.[20]

Andrew Szent-Gyorgyi agreed. "There was the prevailing attitude," he wrote, "that to do research was tremendous fun, and the most exciting thing one could do with one's life. Prof's personality, his writings, his speeches, all project in a most vivid and convincing manner the joy of finding out new things about 'life.'"[21]

When Albert Einstein died mid-decade, Szent-Gyorgyi was deeply moved. He kept a photo of Einstein in his bedroom. Their two lives had run parallel in many ways and so he was asked by a Jewish-American newspaper to write an obituary of the great physicist. Albert responded with this:

Nobody represented better th[e] great unity of knowledge, morals and ethics than Einstein. His kind human understanding, his religious fervor in the search of truth and the fearless pursuit and announcement of the truth were the living symbol of this great unity.

His actual work in physics was but part of it. So I regard Einstein as one of the great moral leaders of man and wish that the world would take from him not only what he has contributed to physics, but also what he represented as a humanist. We would all go marching towards a more cloudless future.[22]

This excellent description of Einstein, however, was something more. It was also a self-portrait, as eulogies often are. It was a picture of the kind of person Albert Szent-Gyorgyi himself wanted to be. To Szent-Gyorgyi's legion of friends, no one could have better summarized his own contribution to their lives and work.

16

FAMILY MAN

Albert Szent-Gyorgyi always had mixed feelings about his relatives. His own upbringing had been peculiar. His father had practically deserted him, and his mother and uncle made their love conditional on his intellectual achievement. His experiences in Holland had shown Albert how family responsibilities could hamstring a scientist's career. He was therefore determined never to let his obligations to the two Nellies stand in his way. And after he won the Nobel Prize, he was suspicious of relations who wanted things from him because of ties he considered irrelevant.

Towards Marta's family he could be singularly resentful.

> I didn't like the family very much, and they wanted to have their way. They opposed this marriage and did everything to ruin it. Marta was such a good mother, she couldn't live without the children. The family said, "You must give up the children if you don't give up the man." All the time they made this trouble which made the situation very unhappy. They interfered all the time.

Especially after the Hungarian revolt of 1956, many in-laws arrived on the scene and Marta, with characteristic generosity, took them in. "They all came here and made it very difficult," Albert complained.[1]

Ties of family, which form such a tangled skein in most people's lives, simply had no emotional claim on Albert Szent-Gyorgyi. He insisted on judging all his relatives by their intelligence, sensitivity, and cultural achievements. (It was for this reason that he refused to see his younger brother when he asked to visit.) The net result was that he faced an old age largely ungraced by the presence of loving relations.

For a man who practically worshipped youth, however, it was a particular disappointment that his own grandchildren, Nelly's children, lived thousands of miles away in Africa. By 1960, in fact, he had almost written off these relationships. Yet suddenly, one day in 1961, Nelly, her husband, and their three lively children, Michael, Lesley and David, arrived at Woods Hole. His contact with them was to be a source of unaccustomed joy and, in some ways, of terrible anguish in his final years.

Nelly was an extremely talented and vibrant person, an artist of great perception and honesty. Her postwar career had been almost as adventurous as Szent-Gyorgyi's own. She got out of Hungary as a member of the national ski team, and in the summer of 1946 she settled temporarily with her aunt Sari in The Hague. From there she wrote to Geoffrey Pollitt, her English friend, who was now managing a wealthy uncle's farm in Rhodesia (now Zimbabwe). Would he be interested in seeing her again? He was interested enough to make a special trip from Africa to rendezvous with her in Holland.

On 9 December she divorced Libik and in June 1947 (after a visit to her mother in the United States) took a ship to southern Africa. She and Geoffrey were married the day after she landed at Cape Town and the newlyweds drove across the Kruger National Game Reserve to Geoffrey's plantation in Mazoe, Rhodesia.[2]

In 1961, the Pollitts moved to the United States, joining Big Nelly, who was then living in Arizona. The elder Nelly had also been leading an interesting and exciting life. She had changed her name to "St. George" and teamed up with a wealthy Grand Rapids widow named Lotta Broadbridge, whose passion was building and selling houses. The two women also co-directed a girls' camp at Rhinelander, Wisconsin called "Brynafon." In the wintertime they migrated to Tucson, where Big Nelly had built herself an adobe-style house. There she studied Andean and Mexican art and gave recruiting lectures for the girls' camp. It promised to be an interesting life for the Pollitts, too, but in February 1961 Big Nelly suddenly died of a heart attack. And so the Pollitt family moved *en masse* to the home of their only other American relative, Albert Szent-Gyorgyi.

Luckily, Szent-Gyorgyi had the cottage in which to put them up. To the children, Marta was not the charming hostess described by adult guests, but a strict and crotchety taskmistress: for example, she would not allow them to drink water with their meals because of a tenaciously-held theory that this disrupted their digestion. "There was no love lost between her [Little Nelly] and Marta either," Geoffrey recalled. It took some time for Little Nelly and Albert to warm up to each other. Although Nelly had initially sided with Albert in the divorce, experience had made her more sympathetic to her mother.

Nevertheless, the Pollitts decided to settle in New England. Geoffrey, who had studied at the Dunn Laboratory in Cambridge, got an administrative job at Dartmouth College and eventually became director of the biological laboratories at Harvard University. The Pollitts formed part of Albert's intimate circle—the closest he had come to a "real family" in decades. They stayed at the little cottage every summer and over the major holidays. The Szent-Gyorgyi and Pollitt households in time became completely intermingled.

In late April 1962, Albert and Marta were invited to the White House, as part of what the press called Kennedy's "Easter Egghead Roll." This was a gathering of Nobel laureates of the Western hemisphere and their spouses. Among the attendees were some of Albert's friends from the past: "Nick" Kendall, Carl and Greta Cori, J. Robert Oppenheimer and Linus Pauling. It was satisfying—and remarkable— to see just how many of Albert's friends and acquaintances had won Nobel laurels over the years.[3]

Albert charmed his Hyannisport neighbors, the Kennedys, with his sharp Hungarian wit, but on this occasion it was Linus Pauling and his wife, Ava Helen, who stole the show. They created a sensation by picketing the very party they were due to attend.[4]

A few months later, Pauling won the Nobel Peace Prize, the first person in history to win two unshared Nobel awards. Albert, although he never admitted that he was jealous, often mused that he himself should have won such an award, or that he was about to win it.

After almost a decade of happiness at "Seven Winds," however, Albert's personal life suddenly began to unravel. On a visit to Rome, where Albert was attending a scientific conference, Marta suddenly discovered a suspicious lump in her breast; this turned out to be a malignant tumor. They flew back to the United States and she checked into a hospital in Chicago, where Albert knew a prominent doctor. Marta went through a mastectomy to no avail, as the cancer had already metastasized throughout her body. Albert agonized over his own inability to help this woman he cherished, and learned that a Nobel Prize in medicine was no defense against intractable cancer. Like many "ordinary" people in such situations, when orthodox medicine failed, he desperately went in search of various unorthodox cures. Nothing worked. On 13 July 1963, Marta Szent-Gyorgyi died of cancer. She was fifty-three years old. She was buried in a simple ceremony, without eulogies, in which five or six close friends each placed a little flower on her grave. Albert was devastated by her death. He was totally dependent on his wife to run his everyday affairs. But Marta, to be sure, was more than just a capable administrator. Almost twenty-five years later he confessed, quite poignantly, "I still love her . . . and I don't know what to do about it."

The whole experience left him with pent-up feelings of rage at the medical profession:

> It's the surgeons who destroy you. They operated on her and operated and operated. Eventually she had a metastasis to the brain, and they operated on the brain and irradiated her brain and destroyed her personality. I suffered with her just as much as she did with cancer. The bad thing about cancer, especially if you are a famous man's wife, is that the doctors don't let you die in peace and decency.

Throughout this whole ordeal, Albert marvelled at Marta's exceptional courage, which he attributed in part to her Yugoslavian blood:

> When my wife knew she had cancer, she asked me to help her commit suicide, which I couldn't do. She was a marvelous woman. She said, 'Help me to die because once I am over a certain point, I know that I will cling to life. I will do everything to stay alive when I am past a certain point of weakness.'

And that was precisely what happened.

Marta had been his friend, lover, and coworker. She had been a stabilizing and reassuring presence in his life. Her death left him "suddenly and completely alone and broken." Her partnership in his life had helped to keep him vigorous. Seventy that autumn, he began to age precipitously.

To compound matters, on 12 January 1962, his patron Stephen Rath had suddenly died. Albert was naturally upset at the loss of this long-time friend. He was more upset when he opened the books of the Institute of Muscle Research. Rath had told Albert and other IMR researchers that since the Institute was a non-profit organization, they themselves did not have to pay income taxes. This should have triggered a flashing yellow light in Albert's brain. But Rath was a smooth talker and promised to put the employees' tax payments into an escrow account pending a decision by the Internal Revenue Service. Since they were not paying income tax, Institute employees were given concomitantly lower salaries.

Albert knew little about finances and much less about American tax law. He simply accepted, he said, the word of Rath and of the IMR's New York attorney that all would be well. Little Nelly was the one person who warned him frankly about this association with Rath. When inquiries started after Rath's death, however, it quickly became apparent that no escrow account could be found. The IRS, following its own logic, demanded ten years' worth of back taxes, with six percent accumulated interest. Szent-Gyorgyi's personal debt came to $18,000.

Had Rath embezzled the money or had it been somehow misplaced upon his death? His heirs searched, but the mystery was never cleared up. Albert fulminated against him in terms as extreme as he had once used to praise him.[5]

In the fifties, when his institute was thriving, Albert had bought and then rented out a small house in Woods Hole. His purpose was to provide for his own old age by eventually selling the very valuable "Seven Winds" property and moving into this more modest dwelling. He now had to sell the little house, however, to pay his tax bill from the $20,000 proceeds. Out of his own pocket—and at great personal hardship—he also paid the back taxes of the Institute's other employees, which ranged from $3,000 to $8,000 apiece. This he did without question or regret, according to Jane McLaughlin, who was one of the employees affected.

However, another calamity stuck: $38,000 was found to be missing and unaccounted for from the previous years' National Institutes of Health (NIH) grants. Rath had been good at getting grants. "He was a grand gentleman," Albert said bitterly, "but there were no bills to cover the alleged expenses."

Mishandling (or misappropriating) NIH funds was a very serious charge, which could profoundly affect Szent-Gyorgyi's reputation for probity among scientists and his future research prospects. "I was very worried that some journalist would come and poke that out and make a big fuss about it," he fretted. Albert gave NIH $10,000 in cash, and a promissory note for the rest, to be paid off $2,500 a year.

To round off a less-than-perfect year, a tax inspector arrived from New Bedford and demanded even more back taxes, on the royalties from the Szent-Gyorgyi/Blum centrifuge. Technically, it was true, these royalties had been sent to Albert as personal income. He argued, however, that he personally had never seen a dime of that money (all of it had gone to do research for the Institute) and he had many witnesses to back him up. The government agent was not impressed with this highmindedness, however, and demanded an additional $30,000. With the help of an attorney this bill was knocked down to $12,000. But Albert's total indebtedness to the U.S. government now totalled over $40,000.

"So that's how a scientist who spent all his life on basic research is treated in the United States," he fumed. In Hungary, there was more than a little gloating. Rath had turned out to be bad business, and Albert had run into predictable problems in capitalist America.

In the depths of his depression, Albert searched for a scapegoat and found one in his nemesis, his old *bête noire*, C.G. King. Almost all his problems, he decided, were ultimately caused by the Pittsburgh nutritionist. "I told this King what vitamin C is," he groaned, "and I have been punished for that all my life to the present day." It never entered his head to blame himself for trusting his finances to Stephen Rath. When the money was coming in he ignored his daughter's warnings. Rath provided money for research: beyond that there was no need to look.

With Marta gone, Albert proved incapable of looking after himself, much less taking care of a big house like "Seven Winds." For a while he lived alone. His idea of a homecooked meal (as the author once learned) was a can of baked beans and a beer. Eventually, as he began to emerge from his depression, he decided that what he needed was a woman to take care of him—a young and attractive one.

One day (perhaps through the intercession of his daughter) he received "a desperate letter" from two young women in Hungary, stating, "we want to learn, but being middle class we have no chance to get into any institution. We can only get menial work. Will you please help us?"

The girls, Tunde and Csilla Felker, were distant relations—so distant that no one seemed able to explain the exact relationship. But "Prof" decided to take up their case. He offered to use his influence to get Tunde into a Hungarian university. (He still could pull strings in Hungary, through his many influential students.) "But I cannot do it without knowing you," he wrote, while on a trip to England. "Come to London," he added, impetuously. "I will meet you, and then I can speak for you." He even sent her money and an airplane ticket.

Tunde came to London, but Albert had already gone to lecture in Paris and Greece. He left her money and a message: "Go to America, and wait for me there until I come home, and then we will see what happens."

What happened was predictable: once she had made herself comfortable in Woods Hole, she showed no inclination to leave. Nor did he want her to go. "There was no intimacy between us," he said later. "She just stayed here."

Eventually, when Tunde applied for permanent resident status she was "very rudely refused." Albert finally appealed to some politicians he knew, and Tunde eventually received her immigrant's "green card" and enrolled in a midwestern college.

Whereupon, Csilla wrote: "Now take care of me!"

Albert wrote back, "You come and take care of *me!* It's beautiful here, and you can work in the laboratory and learn, and maybe I'll send you to college." And so the eighteen-year-old Csilla Felker came, too, and stayed with him on and off for almost a decade. It turned out to be a good relationship for both of them. Csilla was awed by her sudden good fortune, he said:

> In Hungary, intellectual, creative work stands very high in many people's minds, and to this little girl, Csilla, I was a demigod who had won the Nobel Prize. She wanted to sacrifice her life for me.

He found the Felkers' presence in the big, old house enchanting:

> They laughed all day long and thought that this life is just wonderful, that this house is wonderful. If we went shopping in a big supermarket and they could choose whatever they wanted, they had the greatest time. For an American girl, that's all nothing.

To Csilla Felker, Albert Szent-Gyorgyi was "the greatest man I have been privileged to know. It was a unique opportunity. His way of seeing the world was much broader, with a much larger perspective than other people's. He had a vision of how things would turn out."

The relationship between Albert and Csilla was, at her insistence, that of father and daughter. She worked in the lab. He enjoyed her youthful enthusiasm. It was especially important that he could speak Hungarian to her. She called him "Uncle" and after a while, he even expressed a desire formally to adopt her. Together with the Pollitts, the Felker girls became part of Albert's intimate family circle.

According to his granddaughter, Lesley, Albert was affected by a peculiar dichotomy in his relationships to women. He could be very chauvinistic in his attitudes. (When a certain disciple showed up, the Hungarian jokes he and Albert enjoyed were so off-color that Csilla was driven to leave the house.) He would tell Lesley that women were only good for their physical charms. On the other hand, he was always greatly influenced, almost slavishly so, by the women with whom he was living. And in this case Csilla had a marvelous influence on Albert's whole personality, making him into a genuinely considerate and gentle person while she was with him.

Csilla was his constant companion, taking care of his needs and travelling around the world with him. At the same time, both Felker girls were intelligent and had ambitions of their own in America. Tunde wanted to be a scientist, and Csilla dreamed of a career in art. As much as he felt attached to these young women, it was clear that the living arrangement was not a permanent one.

It is essential to understand that the idea of "possessing" a young and attractive wife began to exert an almost irresistible pull on Albert in these years. This was to be a determining factor in his behavior after the death of Marta. A young wife, in his mind at least, was proof of his virility, proof to his less-fortunate contemporaries that he was still a potent and powerful figure. "He was combining a lot of things," said Geoffrey Pollitt, with a touch of British irony, "and the combination always ended up to be a young girl."

In Hungary, Albert rationalized, great older men often married attractive younger women. (Bruno Straub and others scoffed at the idea.) He cited the case of the composer Zoltan Kodaly, who had stayed at the cottage with his young bride in the early sixties. But Kodaly had married the young woman out of gratitude to her family for helping him during the war. Their cases were totally incomparable; Albert conveniently overlooked the differences.[6]

That spring, not quite two years after Marta's death, he accepted a lecture engagement at an east coast university. At a banquet afterwards he sat next to a young woman named Susan, the daughter of a professor whose family spent their summers in Woods Hole.

Sue was a sensitive and insecure woman, with an overprotective father. Although already twenty-four and a registered nurse, emotionally, she says, she was more like a twelve or thirteen year old. Albert appeared to be not just "the most exciting man [she] had ever met," but someone desperately in need of care and attention—sad and unkempt.

Albert drove her home that night. They started corresponding and Albert called her frequently. Soon, she says, he asked her to go to England with him. "People—women—just use me," he told her. "I know you're different. You'd never do that." He enthused about his work and the important role she could play in it. "I have the answer to cancer," he told her on another occasion. "But I need someone to help me get it out."

She was strangely attracted to this man fifty years her senior. In August 1965 Sue moved into the big house at Woods Hole. There she was overwhelmed by the panoply of famous scientists who came to visit. She thought she would dedicate herself to helping Albert find the cure for cancer. Emotionally insecure, she had a desperate need to be needed. Albert, of course, enjoyed the presence of this attractive young companion in his house:

> When one gets older, one is more sensitive—one likes youth because one needs youth. It is a wrong idea to have old people around when you are old. You need youth to keep you young and active.

Since Sue was a colleague's daughter, however, he felt he could not just "let her live here as my mistress." And so, he proposed marriage.

Albert and Sue were wed in a small chapel in Falmouth. Only her bemused parents showed up for the ceremony. Albert's family and colleagues all expressed their disapproval by staying away. For two or three months, everything seemed to go well. Albert said he wanted his young bride to see all the beautiful things in the world—things that had made his own life enjoyable. He took her sailing in the Caribbean, and out to Mexico and Arizona for horseback riding. (At this time, he was still deeply in debt to the U.S. government and, technically at least, too poor to pay the money back.)

At first, Sue and Albert appeared to have a good relationship but underneath all was not well. By December, Sue discovered that her own desires and ambitions were being frustrated by this peculiar arrangement. Sue's whole life was dedicated to making sure her elderly husband slept well, ate well, and got to his laboratory on time. She had previously spent summers with her family at Woods Hole, but she could hardly imagine how lonely that town became after Labor Day. She had no one to talk to but Albert. Her relations with the Pollitts and the Felker girls were cool but cordial.

Sue also had a desire to study art; she had, in fact, been accepted to study at an academy of fine arts before she met Albert. Feeling lonely and isolated at "Seven Winds," she finally made contact with a sculptor in Boston. Three days a week she went to work with him and Albert even bought her a car to do so. Slowly, however, he grew suspicious that she was having an affair in Boston. This she denies, saying that sexually, as well as emotionally, she was rather inexperienced at this time.

At the beginning of 1966 the marriage really began to fall apart. Albert needed someone to take care of him; Sue, on the other hand, was realizing that what she wanted was an equitable relationship. Albert, she complained, was always the Nobel laureate, both on and off stage. She pleaded with him to "let go of that."

But the worst blow came when she complained that she wanted to be married to "a real man." Whatever she may have meant by that, Albert (who remained sexually active well into his seventies) took it as an insult to his virility. It was, at the very least, a bad choice of words. The more she tried to explain, the less he understood. How could she say she wanted a "man," he fumed at her parents, when she had Albert Szent-Gyorgyi, the Nobel laureate? There were vast cultural and generational gulfs between them. Finally, in the summer of 1966, Sue suffered a kind of nervous breakdown. She fled Woods Hole, became too depressed to work, and ran out of money. To compound matters, in her depression she became a compulsive eater and gained sixty pounds.

Some months later Albert received an unexpected sign of life from her—a bill for several hundred dollars from Abercrombie and Fitch, the expensive New York sports outfitters. Unable to fit into any of her old clothes, she had gone to New York and used the one credit card in her wallet. Albert paid the bill, cancelled the account, and never heard from her again.

Albert's explanation of the failure was simple:

> Suddenly she turned. She followed that trail of many American girls— just to get somebody, get married, and then turn against him. She became utterly nasty—I should have kicked her out.
>
> But I was so lonely and miserable that I was not in a position to say, 'No, I don't want it.'

Eventually he obtained a divorce, buying his way out of a messy relationship. It was "a real disaster," Geoffrey Pollitt said.

Albert may have been disappointed but Sue was left devastated by the whole experience. He was "cruel" and "bitter" at the end, Sue recalled. Even his lawyer refused to repeat some of the negative things he said about her. Sue was left to pick up the pieces of her life, but not without a residual amazement at Albert's charisma. "He's a child," she reflected many years later. "An idiot savant," totally absorbed by his own work but uninterested in the feelings of those around him.[7]

With Sue gone, the family reverted to normal for several years. In some ways, these times at "Seven Winds" were the happiest in Albert's long life: there were ping-pong championships, swimming contests, cookouts at night on the beach. One time when he was almost eighty "Prof" learned to water ski with the rest of the family—on one ski. (It took him only a day to learn, Lesley recalled proudly.) In the fall they had massive Thanksgiving dinners. In the winter Albert always bought the biggest Christmas tree in Woods Hole. But the brief marriage to Sue was the first warning sign of big trouble on the horizon.

He and his grandson David struck up an especially close relationship. David was one relative who certainly earned Albert's respect. He was sixteen in 1969, a sensitive boy with a definite gift for music, about to go on to Juilliard to study the violin. David bore a striking family resemblance to Albert as a youth. "That's my grandson, David," Albert would say to his friends, almost in awe. "He can play the Kreutzer Sonata."

But Albert's feelings were mixed, even mixed-up, on the topic of his young relatives. He was extremely proud when David gave a concert at Woods Hole and several hundred people showed up. But for the first time in his life, when Albert looked around a room at Woods Hole, all eyes were not focused on him, but on one of his relatives. It was a humbling and discomfiting feeling. David remembers Albert walking out of one of his concerts. On another occasion, David was chosen to play as a soloist with the Boston Pops Orchestra. Albert failed to make the two-hour drive, although he would readily fly to New York or Florida for a scientific meeting or even a vacation.

It seems ironic that this beloved grandson would take up the very instrument that Albert's brother, Pal, also played so expertly. Albert was one of those people who not only loved classical music but *worshipped* the musicians themselves. He passed this attitude on to his daughter, who taught it to her own children.

In a 1980 interview, the author asked Albert what he would have become if he had not decided to be a scientist. Without any hesitation he answered, "conductor of a symphony orchestra." It is certainly not coincidental that at that time, his grandson David was training to become a conductor, as well. (Bruno Straub recalled how brilliantly Szent-Gyorgyi had mimicked the motions of a famous conductor the morning after his appearance in Szeged.)

In the late sixties, the family was struck by another terrible blow. Little Nelly discovered a malignant lump in her breast, which eventually resulted in two mastectomies. Once again, Albert became involved in a life-and-death struggle to save a family member from cancer. As a desperate measure Albert urged his daughter to drink mushroom juice, which he thought had some anti-cancer effect. She drank this concoction until she was sick of it—but to no avail. On 21 September 1969, at the age of fifty-one, Nelly Szent-Gyorgyi Pollitt also died of breast cancer.

Even here, Albert's feelings and behaviors were ambivalent. He did not visit Nelly at Massachusetts General Hospital, when it was clear that she was dying. He was strangely detached and dry-eyed at the funeral. The main result of her tragic death was not the grief it caused him, but the effect it had on the cohesion of the family. For Nelly's had been the one powerful voice of reason and restraint in his life.[8]

It is a well-known phenomenon of public life that great people tend to attract, or to surround themselves with, a coterie of followers—"yes men" (and women). There are considerable benefits to be derived from being associated with a famous and well-respected Nobel laureate. These people, often minor talents in themselves, ride the coattails of the rich or famous and survive by feeding the great ones' egos. This sycophancy can be a powerful corrosive of the powers of discernment that originally made the great person great.

Anyone who met Albert knows that he hated this corrupt system. He was exceptionally honest in his dealings with people, open about his own life and feelings, a simple, down-to-earth man. He got along exceptionally well with children, who had an intuitive feeling of trust in him. Albert himself exhibited no snobbish prejudices and would more happily converse with an intelligent worker than with a pompous laureate. In his dress, speech and manner he never made an attempt to appear superior to anyone.

That is why it is all the more surprising that at this time he managed to attract to himself such followers and hangers-on. David Pollitt was especially contemptous of these false friends. After a while, from David's point of view, his grandfather heard only what he wanted to hear. People used their association with "Prof" to increase their own professional standing.

Nelly, however, was never afraid to tell her father exactly what she thought, even when that led to conflict. And he, by and large, listened to her. With Nelly gone, there was no one who spoke to him with the same authority. This was to have major repercussions for Albert's life. For when, in his eighties, he suddenly decided to cut his moorings and set off into uncharted waters, there was no one to slow his headstrong course.

17

THE 500-TON RAT

John Kennedy's election in 1960 rekindled Albert's interest in politics. He was now an American citizen, and with the passing of McCarthyism, was no longer under FBI surveillance. Consequently, he began to speak out publicly on political topics. For him, as for so many others, the overriding issue of the day was peace.

Albert Szent-Gyorgyi had devoted his life to science, but what possible meaning could that activity have, he wondered, if civilization itself were to be destroyed in a nuclear holocaust? Socially-conscious scientists had a special responsibility, he felt, since ironically it was peace-loving men such as Einstein, Szilard, Oppenheimer, and Bohr who had provided the world with the very means of destroying itself.

Some other prominent scientists joined groups, started movements, signed petitions. Albert did some of those things, too, but his political activity in the sixties remained wonderfully *sui generis*. That he was left-of-center there was never any doubt; his belief in social and economic justice had survived the fifties. But his mind could not be cut to fit the proscrustean bed of any party program.

He did support the political careers of the Kennedys, his famous neighbors down the road in Hyannisport. One suspects that it was more the style than the substance which he endorsed: a worshipper of youth, Albert enjoyed having a young, vigorous, and virile president. He liked Jack—and Jackie even more! In 1962 he invited the President to visit him at Woods Hole and Kennedy accepted but was killed before he had a chance to fulfill that promise. After her husband's assassination he seriously urged Jackie to run for president. She politely declined.

During the sixties and early seventies, Albert issued a steady stream of clever, charming, and occasionally quixotic articles on the question of peace and survival.

Like Benjamin Spock, Linus Pauling, and George Wald, Albert was one of those well-respected father figures who spoke out forcefully against the danger of militarism. But there was a unique quality to Albert's writings. He was generally more broadly philosophical than the other older statesmen of the peace movement, and his acceptance of and *identification* with the youth movement seemed boundless.

In Woods Hole, a town which attracts students from around the world every summer, Albert became an underground hero. Denis Robinson, then chairman of the board of the Marine Biological Laboratory, recalled his public lectures:

> The young people pack that little auditorium every time his lecture is announced. There's nothing except a white sheet of paper that says "Albert Szent-Gyorgyi, 8:00 pm, such and such an evening." And they pack in. And the enthusiasm is just infectious. He wows them. He was turning off the biologists, but not the young ones because they did not have preconceived notions. They weren't part of the biological establishment. And he always put in some political stuff. He was never very extreme, but he was always criticizing the bureaucracy for this, that or the other.
>
> He has always been an anti-militarist. As you can imagine, around this time Berkeley went "on fire," then Columbia and all the rest, and the kids, although they weren't part of the dissident group, already had this fever against Vietnam in them.
>
> Szent-Gyorgyi was very intelligent in his criticism. He never went to the extreme position, but he would make off-hand remarks, throw away lines which were just marvelous and the kids just roared.[1]

Although some of the people at MBL were upset with "Prof's" performance, Robinson always enjoyed the experience:

> I would have come just for the show to watch him wow these young people, because they were a different crowd almost every year. But the word went around, if you're in Woods Hole, go and hear Szent-Gyorgyi. And he just suited them. It was marvelous. Here was a man, already in his seventies, who could talk in a way that young people understood. Not many adults are capable of that.

Much of what was written in the 1960s now seems comically naive. But Albert's writings from that period have in general aged well. His three books and many articles from this period, in their simple, unassuming style, have an enduring value as literature and as the testament of a unique mind.

The first book, *Science, Ethics and Politics,* consisted mainly of articles Albert had written for the *New York Times* and the *Saturday*

Review. (Szent-Gyorgyi was friends with *Saturday Review* editor, Norman Cousins, and once signed a public letter urging him to run for President.) The next two, *The Crazy Ape,* and its sequel, *What Next?*, were directed to young people. They represented a summation of Albert's provocative way of looking at the world.

The idea of struggle was central to his conception of history:

> Erasmus of Rotterdam, the great thinker of the Early Renaissance, distinguished between calm and troubled periods of history. Trouble, *tumultus,* is the sign of transition. History is molded by ideas which create a certain order, and order creates tranquility. The ideas change, and the new ideas have to fight against the partisans of the antiquated order; there is trouble until the new ideas are generally accepted and a corresponding new order is established. The greater the transition, the greater the tumult. We have to burst our skins to grow. The faster the growth, the more painful the process.

Human history, he continued, is divided into three great periods. The first he called (following philosopher Lewis Mumford) the age of "paleotechnics," in which man used "his primitive daily experience to shape primitive tools or weapons." This lasted from the dawn of history until a few hundred years ago.

The second age was the Renaissance, when "man found a new way to approach nature by measuring, calculating, asking questions from her—that is, doing experiments." This lasted well into our own day. The greatest burst of scientific creativity occurred in the ten years 1895–1905. Even Galileo, Newton, and Darwin had only reinterpreted a world we already knew from our senses. But within one decade five discoveries were made which revealed the existence of an unsuspected world: X-rays (1895), the electron (1895), radioactivity (1896), the quantum (1900), and relativity (1905). The world would never be the same.

This appearance of *modern science* at the turn of the twentieth century was *the* pivotal event in all human history. The third, and truly modern, age came suddenly, and was the only one which can be dated with precision. It began on 6 August 1945, at 8:15 A.M. when an atomic bomb pulverized Hiroshima and "in a matter of a few seconds . . . levelled a big city, one that was built over many centuries, and wiped out about 100,000 human lives." Hiroshima was the great divide, separating the generations and causing the much-talked-about generation gap. "Parents belong to the pre-cosmic, their children to the cosmic age," Albert wrote.

The leaders of the world were almost all pre-cosmic thinkers. A great many of Albert's essays were therefore dedicated to interpreting the enormity of nuclear power to conventionally-minded leaders. Albert demonstrated his outstanding gift for explaining science in simple terms for the layperson:

> Hiroshima announced to man that life would never be as it was before. This last period had its roots in discoveries made at the turn of the century, which showed that the ultimate units of our world were not rocks, caves, trees, bears and the like, as man had thought before, but quanta, atoms, atomic nuclei, radioactivity, electrons, and electromagnetic radiation. This new knowledge made man the master of cosmic forces, and at the same time made our terrestial rules obsolete.

Human thought, he said, is basically conservative, and only changes under pressure. Humans were "forced to face this situation with our caveman's brain, a brain that had not changed since it was formed."[2] He viewed the mind and brain in starkly materialistic terms:

> A cow could never lay an egg. Man, too, can do only what his brain allows him to do. In their struggle for life some animals grew fangs, others grew claws or tusks, while still others produced poisons. Man grew a brain.

Verbal arguments, he felt, were mainly rationalizations of hidden desires. The only hope for survival lay in education, since the brain, like a computer, can be programmed. But education was itself a two-edged sword, since education was in the hands of a brutal government apparatus. It could be employed to ennoble people, but instead was generally used to turn them into killers.

Even after Hiroshima most leaders dealt with nuclear weapons as if they were the same as conventional weapons, only larger. But Albert pointed out that this monstrous change in scale had led to a profound change in quality. He used a humorous example:

> If I would make a rat as big as a rabbit, it would still be a rat. However, in extreme cases, quantitative differences become qualitative. If I were to make my rat a million times bigger, make it weigh 500 tons instead of 500 grams, then it would be a terrific new monster, something entirely new—different qualitatively.[3]

The Bomb was that "500 ton rat" which mankind had created and which now confronted us with life-threatening urgency. He returned again and again to the role of the scientist:

As to politics, up till lately, there was no need for the scientist to take cognizance of its existence. However, lately, politics had penetrated not only into science but also into the private lives of individuals, forcing the scientist, too, to take a stand.

"One might think," he wrote, "that the forces released by science can be governed without mortal danger only by the same principle which caused them." Since science obviously did *not* govern political discourse, it could at least explain to laypeople "how formidable these new forces are which threaten to gobble us all up." Yet even scientists themselves had difficulty conceiving the "terrific nature of these cosmic energies."

I am faced here with a very queer problem. Why is it that the suffering of one man moves me, while the suffering of millions makes no impression on me whatsoever? My brain is made to help me to get through the petty problems amid the petty dimensions of my everyday life. Our brain is made to deal with the primitive fire in our caves, but not with the cosmic fires with their 15 million degrees.

He likened himself, in his living room at Woods Hole, to this caveman:

I know that if I am too close to my fireplace, in front I scorch while behind I freeze. If I move away, the heat received falls off very rapidly, with the square of the distance; that is, if I move away from one foot to ten the radiation energy received by my body will fall, not by one-tenth, but to one one-hundredth, and will become negligible. This is a very important experience because I know that the sun is at a distance of 100 million miles from our globe. I can thus conclude that the radiative energy reaching our globe is only an infinitesimally small fraction of the energy emitted by the sun. The sun itself must emit energies the magnitude of which I am entirely unable to imagine.

Nuclear weapons unleashed a bit of that solar power on the earth. "Though I am not a moralist, but a scientist," he wrote in the *Saturday Review* in 1962, "I strongly believe that what decides human history is not gadgetry but morals."

Albert was in the minority in believing that science itself embodied an implicit moral code. He explained it this way:

If you have a problem, meet it as such. Collect data and then try to find the best solution with a neutral mind, with a cool head, unbiased by sentiment, hatred, fear or profit, with an uncompromising, intellectual honesty, with good will and equity.

In a talk entitled "Social Responsibility of Science," delivered at the inaugural meeting of the Society for Social Responsibility at Harvard, he explained this credo:

"Meet your problem as such." This meant that science had changed all the major factors in life, but man's mind, in many ways, had remained back in the caveman era. A new political world structure had to be built. To build it, however, we had to answer what sort of world we wanted to build. This is the basic question.

"With a neutral mind, etc." This is the opposite of how politicians (such as Kennedy and Khrushchev) meet. Are we not meeting our adversaries with sentiments, with fear, hatred, distrust and a narrow national egotism? Instead, we and our antagonists should meet together to search for the best solution with a cool head and a neutral mind as we do in science, where even our adversaries are our allies in the search for truth.

"With an uncompromising intellectual honesty." Four hundred years ago, in the age of Machiavelli, murder was the main instrument of international politics. Today it is untruth and half-truth.

"With good will and equity" is based on Lincoln's precept "with malice toward none; with charity toward all." By "charity" Lincoln meant what we today would call kindness and mutual respect.

I think that scientific thinking shows the way towards the solution of the problems it created. The dangers of the day are so great that ways must be found to catalyze the spread of scientific thought and enlightenment, its spread to the people and its penetration into government. International lawlessness has to be ended, if we want to stay alive. Something has to be done and done fast.[4]

One problem with this philosophy, as Albert realized, was that enlightenment spread very slowly. People are short-sighted and put creature comforts above the common good.

It is only very exceptional brains (you may call them pathological) which can put truth before advantage. Their owners usually end on the stake or in a chair—electric or academic. These people become the great scientists—like Galileo, Newton, Pasteur, and Einstein—who lift human existence to higher levels.

As the sixties wore on, Albert's social concerns became focused, quite naturally, on the Vietnam War. He spoke out—at first moderately, then with growing anger—at the course of escalation and the general direction of the country's policies. In March 1965 he wrote to the *New York Times:*

> I feel disappointed, alienated, if not betrayed. I am sure many of my fellow scientists feel as I do. We are deeply concerned because it was our work which opened the way both to a better future for mankind or its final catastrophe. We are going the wrong way, and it is time for scientists to get together once more, this time to sound a warning.[5]

"The great majority of the American people is opposed to this war," he wrote in a more sanguine mood. But this conflict "also scuttles the UN, on which mankind pinned its hopes and which we promised to support."

The war escalated, and even the massive "March on Washington" in 1967 did not seem able to slow this juggernaut. Szent-Gyorgyi wrote in the *Times* again:

> This senseless, hopeless Vietnam war tarnishes our good name. We escalate endlessly to avoid admitting past and present errors. The end is nowhere in sight and soon we may find ourselves at war with China.
>
> President Johnson has offered unconditional negotiation to everyone except to the people whom we actually fight. The first step toward peace should be for both sides the stating of the principles they are fighting for. Once the principles are clarified, technicalities of their implementation could be most easily settled. The only principles we can stand on are those laid down in our Declaration of Independence. These are often quoted by Ho Chi Minh, so there can be no really basic difference between us, and hostilities could be stopped any minute by calling off our raids and inviting President Ho Chi Minh to a conference. Our friendly gestures, such as the March on Washington, are reciprocated by Vietnam, showing that the Vietnamese people want our friendship.[6]

Nor did Albert limit himself to letters to the *Times.* In March 1966 he joined A.J. Muste, Joan Baez, and other passive resisters in announcing that he would not pay his 1965 income tax to protest U.S. aggression abroad. According to their collective statement, the action of the United States "will go down in history alongside the unforgivable atrocities of Italy in Ethiopia and Russia's criminal intervention in Hungary" in 1956. "The indifference of so many Americans to the crimes being committed in their name reminds us more and more of the indifference of the majority of the German people to the killing of six million Jews."[7]

A cynic might say that Albert had little to lose: he already was tens of thousands of dollars in debt to the IRS. Yet, looked at another way, precisely for this reason he may have been taking a greater risk. And, in fact, documents obtained through the Freedom of Information Act show that within the month his file was being reviewed for action by the IRS. Luckily for him, "no basis for Service investigation or other action" was found.[8]

In October 1970, Szent-Gyorgyi, his fellow Woods Hole resident George Wald, and other self-described "Eastern intellectuals" met with some prominent liberal trade union leaders. Their purpose was to "achieve common social and political objectives" and to counter "reactionary political forces in our country." After the massacre at Kent State and the 1970 student strike, both the power and the limitations of a campus-based antiwar movement had become clear. The meeting, said Wald, was "aimed to counter divisive and repressive tactics [of] President Nixon and Vice President Agnew." Other participants at the meeting included MIT scientist and Nobel laureate, Salvador Luria, Leonard Woods of the United Auto Workers, and Anthony Mazzocchi, a vice president of the Oil, Chemical, and Atomic Workers.

Like his teacher Hopkins, fifty years before, "Prof" signed almost every petition put before him. In 1972 he joined other rebellious scientists in trying to mount a protest at the annual meeting of the American Association for the Advancement of Science (AAAS), the nation's largest scientific organization. Out of 7,000 people attending the meeting, only 250 signed their petition. The statement asked, rhetorically, "Can we scientists meet in Washington and ignore the fact that our national Administration is launching from this city the most massive air attacks in history?" Apparently the answer was yes.[9]

The Vietnam era made Albert, like many people, reconsider his entire political philosophy. "Democracy," he said at Harvard "is inseparably connected with peace. Peace and democracy will have to live or die together. Neither is something ready-made, prefabricated. Both mean a permanent struggle."

As a political refugee, he especially felt his trust in American democracy had been betrayed:

> In a democracy like ours the Government and its foreign and military policy should reflect the basic characteristics of the people. The American people are characterized by clear, simple and honest thinking, straight dealings, a regard for human rights, and a blend of idealism and realism. Our foreign policy and military planning show the opposite characteristics. . . . We have God Almighty on our lips but deny his existence by trusting bombs only.

America's problems, including the war in Vietnam and the ghetto rebellions, had a common root:

> Our policy has departed from the foundations on which this nation was built, those of sincerity, honesty, goodwill and human understanding. It denies to other people the right to pursue happiness in their own way. Once we return to the earlier foundations the solutions will present themselves.[10]

Albert's thinking was changing, although still difficult to classify. From at least the time of World War I he was a visceral leftist, without party affiliations. He was a free radical. His experience with Russian-style Communism, both in 1919 and after World War II, was disillusioning. For fifteen years he had remained essentially apolitical, occasionally making vehemently anti-Communist statements. By the mid-sixties, however, he had evolved a political position in many ways similar to that of the "New Left." Like the New Left, it was difficult to classify because it was deliberately anti-theoretical. To some people, however, Albert seemed like a tool of the Communists, if not one himself. "If you can show definitely that their opinion is wrong," he wrote of such opponents, "they do not change their mind but become angry and call you a Communist, which cuts short discussion."

But he was no Communist. "Stalin had most of his comrades executed," he wrote in *Science* in 1957. "The whole world listened to their confessions of guilt, and it occurred to nobody that all this may be just the result of a new invention, brainwashing." He gave the United States credit for "good will and friendly disposition" after World War II, and blamed the Cold War on "the cold hostility of Stalin, who was intent on making his bid for world rule." He believed that a major change had overtaken Communism since then, however. Hungary was the Communist country he cared most about, and significant economic reforms had begun there in 1968. The political policy was also growing more liberal. In 1970 Albert wrote:

> Stalin is dead and there appears to me to be a sincere desire in the present leaders to live in peace. Communism is there to stay and we cannot wish it away. There is no reason why we should not be friends. Communism has, I think, passed its juvenile, messianic, expansive stage, and a fruitful competition between the two camps could bear many good fruits.

In surveying the world situation, he understood very well the appeal of Marxism-Leninism. He told an audience of young people:

> I visited Cuba under the reign of Batista. He was our friend and ally, our shield against Communism. I was shocked to see children, mostly in ill

health, ill-fed and dirty, all day long in the street. "Have you no schools?" I asked. "We have no schools," was the answer. Batista was our great friend and ally. We liked him. He could be bought cheaply. Supporting Batista only opened the door to Castro.

Many people are simply afraid of any change and want to keep the world as it is or make it as it was. They are afraid that any change, eventually, may lead to destruction, revolution or Communism. They think that it is the road to the left that leads there. You must convince them that it is the road to the right, the rigid adherence to the past, which leads to trouble.

The high point of Albert's political efforts in America was the publication of his short book, *The Crazy Ape*. Alternately provocative and moving, in eighteen short chapters *The Crazy Ape* set forward the philosophy which Albert had distilled over the years.

One can detect in this book, and its sequel, *What's Next?*, an elegiac tone that is absent from some of his previous writings. He seemed to be losing hope that a solution to the nuclear dilemma was even possible, or that mankind could even survive.

The Crazy Ape began with the simple question: "Why does man behave like a perfect idiot?" Because, he answered,

> today is the first time in man's history that he is able to truly enjoy life, free of cold, hunger and disease. It is the first time he is able to satisfy all his basic needs. Conversely, it is also the first time in history that man has the capability of exterminating himself in one blow or making his tragically shrinking little globe uninhabitable by pollution or over-population.

One would expect that even an idiot could make a wise choice between these two alternatives, he wrote, angrily. "It is basically a choice between pleasure and pain." But man—the crazy ape—chose death over life.

He urged young people to question pat solutions: "He who understands the situation is not well informed," he wrote, trenchantly.

In his unhappiness at the direction of society and his own life, Albert, in his mid-seventies, put his faith in youth. The book is subtitled "written by a biologist for the young." It is in fact a paean to youth. He thought back to his own early years in Budapest and reflected:

> If I, at my seventy-six years of age, am still impatiently running every morning to my laboratory, this is because as a child I learned from my family that the only thing worth striving for is the creation of new knowledge and beauty.

Times had changed radically. Now the older people had to look to the youth for guidance:

> I have written that it is the old who teach the young. No longer. The young have broken away; they teach themselves and are creating a world of their own.

Albert's endorsement of youth took some surprising turns. As an experiment, he smoked marijuana with two young friends. They had a hilarious time. He was also enthusiastic about the sexual revolution. In his own day, he recalled, ideas about sex were "in an awful muddle." Girls, he wrote, "were considered the more attractive the less they knew about sex." All of these old customs "had the pretense of morality, and caused no end of suffering, creating unbalanced minds and psychopathic aberrations." Penicillin took care of most venereal diseases and "the Pill" made unwanted pregnancies unnecessary. The generation of the sixties took this one step further:

> In my view the most wonderful achievement of our youth—a sign of their great moral courage—has been their ability to restore the sexual drive, the strongest human feeling, to its purity and dignity. They have made human life much richer and cleaner, and have made me wish I had been born fifty or sixty years later.

In a *New York Times* interview on 20 February 1970 in conjunction with the publication of *The Crazy Ape,* Albert carried this one step further [see Appendix B]. Asked what he would do if he were twenty years old again he replied:

> I would share with my classmates rejection of the whole world as it is— all of it. Is there any point in studying and work? Fornication—at least that is something good. What else is there to do? Fornicate and take drugs against this terrible strain of idiots who govern the world.

Szent-Gyorgyi's remarks were widely quoted and widely misunderstood. He was, in fact, strongly *against* escapism. But such escapism, he felt, grew out of intolerable surroundings—not just physical, but psychological and social as well. The proper response was not to throw pot-smokers into jail, but to create a livable world, with "the restoration of dignity of the individual and the value of endeavor."

But at times Albert was not as liberal as he proclaimed. One of the most distressing experiences in his grandson David's youth was when he brought a girlfriend to stay with him in Szent-Gyorgyi's cottage.

Since it was a very warm summer night, and the "Pebble" was stifling, the two young people went to sleep on the beach.

The next morning Albert cornered his grandson, enraged. "How *dare* you sleep with that girl out in the open, where all the world can see you!" he demanded, angrily. "Go do it behind the house where no one will notice you." David began to protest that he and his friend were doing nothing, and were behind the seawall; it would have been impossible for anyone to see them from the road. He suddenly realized, however, that they *were* visible from one spot—Albert Szent-Gyorgyi's bedroom window! Albert simply could not stand to see his grandson sleeping so unashamedly with a young woman.

Like most adults of the time Albert also failed to see the logic of the violence of much of the student movement. "It is an admission of impotence, lack of clear thought and intelligence, and should be avoided. . . . It is letting off steam in the wrong place." He urged the Vietnam War protestors to be polite and persuasive, and even to cut off their long hair and wear jackets and ties if that would win over people to their point of view. He recalled:

> When I was a young man there was a great boxing champion who, when asked if he didn't feel safe because of his skills, answered that "a polite tongue gives more safety than a strong fist." So does good will.

Szent-Gyorgyi concluded *The Crazy Ape* with his "Psalmus Humanus and Six Prayers" [Appendix C]. This was a series of poems which he had composed in the summer of 1964, after Marta's death. They were subsequently set to music by the Hungarian composer, Agi Jambor, and recorded by Szent-Gyorgyi and Jambor. These poems contained many passages of rough-hewn beauty:

> My Lord, Who are You?
> Are you my stern Father
> Or are You my loving Mother
> In whose womb the Universe was born?

> Are you the Universe itself?
> Or the Law which rules it?

> Have you created life only to wipe it out again?
> Are You my maker, or did I shape You,
> That I may share my loneliness and shun my
>   responsibility?

Since his adolescence, Albert had never been religious in any conventional sense. Quite the opposite; in many ways his views were those of an old-fashioned nineteenth century materialist. In "Psalmus Humanus," however, one hears the prayers of an agnostic. They are, to steal a phrase from Dylan Thomas, "poems in praise of God's world by a man who does not believe in God."[11]

On a talk show some years later, an inquisitive host asked Albert if he were religious. He obviously expected some platitudinous answer, but Albert replied, "I am not a religious [man], but I am a *pious* man." Pressed for the difference, he said, "A religious man says 'God is this,' 'God is there,' 'God is that. Your God is not my God.' But a pious man looks up with awe and says, 'What is God?' and "I'd like to know what this creation really means! A pious man is really touched by the greatness of nature and of the creation."[12]

Approaching his ninth decade, Albert was able to strike this note of awe quite eloquently in his "Psalmus Humanus." Towards evening he would walk on the beach at Penzance Point and think not just about his work but about the long, strange journey of humanity, and of the perils that still surrounded it. Looking up at the magnificent night-time sky over Cape Cod, the Milky Way stretching nearly from horizon to horizon, his thoughts alternated between hope and despair. And then something else would take over, a feeling of wonder towards the whole phenomenon of the universe—what Schopenhauer called "sad astonishment." It was certainly not the comforting dogma of religion, but, in the end, it made of Albert's agnosticism a positive and appealing creed.

18

"DON'T LIE IF YOU DON'T HAVE TO"

To those who met him in 1970, Albert Szent-Gyorgyi seemed a remarkably vibrant and energetic person. He was in excellent shape. From spring to fall, he swam in the ocean every day, riding the currents off Penzance Point. In the winter he remained active, chopping wood or riding the motor scooter which had become his trademark.

Once, wealthy neighbors invited Albert to "drop in sometime." He showed up on their patio several weeks later, sopping wet. He had swum over to their house via the ocean and literally dropped in on them while they were having breakfast.

On another occasion, a massive snowstorm closed the Marine Biological Laboratory. Homer Smith, the laboratory director, struggled in to work, but was the only person there. Looking out the window, at a sea of white, he spotted a tiny figure struggling across the snow. It was "Prof"—fighting his own way to the laboratory on a pair of skis. He was indignant that his own laboratory assistants had not made an equal effort to do the same.

Yet, in fact, his luck had run out. That year he was seventy-seven years old. Was there a role in this country, he wondered, for older scientists who still had something to contribute? In Japan he might have been declared a "living treasure" and given the means to continue research.

"When he started out as a young man," said his friend, Zoltan Bay, "he was too young. Now he was declared to be too old, such that he could not reasonably pursue adequate scientific work."[1]

Without a steady source of funds, no one can be much more than an armchair scientist. Asked once to define research, Albert said it was four things: "Brains with which to think, eyes with which to see, machines with which to measure, and, fourth, money." In the 1950s

214

and 1960s he had received over a million dollars in National Institutes of Health (NIH) grants. Yet by the end of the sixties, all of his sources of funding had dried up. His contacts at Armour were long gone. The reporters who had lauded him in *Time* or the news services had themselves retired or died. As far as the Rockefeller or Macy Foundations were concerned Albert Szent-Gyorgyi was ancient history.

Painfully, his thoughts now turned to Hungary. He had come to America to be free to pursue his research without hindrance. Now he found out what such freedom could sometimes mean: the freedom to starve and be scorned. He was deeply in debt to the Internal Revenue Service. If he had stayed in Hungary, he felt, at least he would have been treated with deference and respect. He even began to toy with the idea of going home.

His most logical source of funding was still the federal government. In late 1971, President Nixon (whom Albert always regarded as a personal nemesis) had launched the "war on cancer" as his "Christmas present to the nation." Almost a billion dollars a year would be allocated to cancer research. Since Szent-Gyorgyi had been doing such research for over forty years he might seem like a natural candidate for cancer funding.

Lab scientists were now expected, however, to spend a considerable amount of their time drafting, writing, and refining grant applications. This sort of paper-pushing seemed almost *designed* to weed out errant geniuses like Albert Szent-Gyorgyi. There was clearly no way he could fit into the government's cookie-cutter schema.

Albert, not coincidentally, was philosophically opposed to the very idea of grant applications. "The reviewer, feeling responsible for the taxpayer's money," he once wrote, "justly hesitates to give money for research, the lines of which are not clear to the applicant himself." He was not always so forgiving, however.

For instance, he maintained that it was pointless for him to describe *what* he was going to do, when the whole point of basic research—and here he always quoted Claude Bernard—was to venture out into the unknown. "You take your gun under your arm,—" he pantomimed the action, momentarily transforming himself into a Hungarian peasant—"and you go out shooting. If something flies up,—" he raised his hands and sighted the target, "you shoot at it. But whether you hit something or not depends on your brain." He tapped the side of his head and smiled. "It requires a gift, a special gift, for understanding nature, for hearing her voice, which is very low."

"If I already know what I'm going to find," he added, quite seriously, "there's no point in doing it." This paradoxical insight seemed merely whimsical and childishly petulant to National Cancer

Institute committees. Using such an excuse, they complained, *anyone* could demand funds without accountability. How did they know that at the end of the grant period Szent-Gyorgyi would not just say, "Sorry, but I didn't find anything?" and walk away with the money. They all put up with this system, so why not Albert Szent-Gyorgyi? What made him think he was better than the rest?

"Albert is constitutionally unable to write a research grant," his cousin, Andrew, himself a successful biochemist, said ruefully. "It is something everybody must do in order to survive," he added shaking his head, "but he cannot do it."

In this way, Albert was becoming a lonely survivor of the Golden Age of Biochemistry. Life was moving on. Young researchers repeatedly expressed amazement to learn that he was still alive. Yet here he was, at age eighty, trying to compete in a system he could not fully understand, much less master. The prevailing attitude seemed to be that Szent-Gyorgyi had earned his place in history, his page or two in the biochemistry textbooks, but now should step aside in favor of younger people.

It should be emphasized that his ideas about cancer seemed strange—almost incomprehensible—to some scientists. They were more physics than biology, and modern biologists already had their hands full, without having to chart the vagaries of quarks. Almost everyone was thinking about cancer in terms of molecular biology. Quantum mechanics seemed bizarrely irrelevant. (see Chapter 20)

"When you are presented with new ideas, you have two choices," said Albert, holding up two fingers. "Learn and study—or reject. But learning is difficult, so most people take the easier way and simply reject." He might as well have been asking for money to build a perpetual motion machine as to apply quantum mechanics to cancer. Four times his requests for government funding were turned down. One such rejection, he later claimed, was signed by a dentist. A dentist passing judgment on a Nobel laureate—the ultimate indignity of American bureaucracy!

Albert also tried to put his personal difficulties into a philosophical framework. Following Frederick Nietszche, he discerned two basic personality types among scientists, the Dionysian and the Apollonian:

> In science, the Apollonian tends to develop established lines to perfection, while the Dionysian rather relies on intuition and is more likely to open new, unexpected alleys for research. Nobody knows what "intuition" really is. My guess is that it is a sort of subconscious reasoning, only the end result of which becomes conscious. . . . The present methods of distributing grants unduly favor the Apollonian.

It was definitely the Apollonians who wrote the rules for grantsmanship.

> The Apollonian clearly sees the future lines of his research and has no difficulty writing a clear project. Not so the Dionysian, who knows only the direction in which he wants to go out into the unknown; he has no idea what he is going to find there or how he is going to find it. Defining the unknown or writing down the subconscious is a contradiction *in absurdum*.

The Dionysian relies on "accidental" discoveries, but these are rarely true accidents, he said, echoing Pasteur, since "a discovery is an accident finding a prepared mind."

But surely Albert was not the only "Dionysian" in science. How did the other intuitive geniuses cope? According to him, they simply faked it. He recalled a conversation with another great Hungarian-American scientist:

> I always tried to live up to Leo Szilard's commandment, "don't lie if you don't have to." I had to. I filled up pages with words and plans I knew I would not follow. When I go home from my laboratory in the late afternoon, I often do not know what I am going to do the next day. I expect to think that up during the night. How could I tell them what I would do a year hence?

Albert's inability to generate grants began to raise questions about his relations with his home base, the Marine Biological Laboratory (MBL). From approximately 1968 to 1972, Albert was supported primarily by MBL's liberality and the generosity of friends. Louise Crane, a wealthy neighbor, donated a sum to help him continue his work, and he dedicated *Electronic Biology* (1976) to her, "without whose support this book could not have been written." The relatively small Christine and Alfred Sonntag Foundation also helped out. But clearly his life as a scientist was imperiled.

And then, in April 1971, something very strange happened. He presented a paper on cancer at a meeting in Washington of the National Academy of Sciences, of which he was a member. In this paper, he reported on some cancer research he had done with Jane McLaughlin and Dr. Laszlo G. Egyud, telling how a substance could be obtained from mouse liver which destroyed implanted tumors in other mice. It was an exciting concept, anticipating, by several years, more publicized work on biological anti-tumor factors. "Prof" readily acknowledged the defects in his earlier work:

Only in the last six months have we really been on solid ground. For years I have been working with intuition and my evidence was very poor. I simply could not answer the really good questions from the good people. Now I think I can. That is why we are reporting here at the Academy.[2]

In the same interview he took a highly combative stance towards his critics. "I don't care what they think, whether I am a senile old man or not," he said. "So long as someone comes up with the money. I cannot run around injecting batches of one hundred mice twice a day and still continue my research. My trouble is that I've always been two steps ahead of everyone and it's hard for them to catch up. It's okay if you're only one step ahead, but two? Never!"

This seemed like shouting into the wind. Yet this particular interview had an unexpected result. One week later, he received the following letter at Woods Hole:

Dear Sir:

I read with interest the article in the *Evening Star* of Thursday, April 29, 1971, indicating that you are seeking further funds for your nonprofit organization to continue cancer research. Could you send me the name and address and a little information about the fund—assuming it is a nonprofit foundation on the "Cumulative List"—so that I may make a small contribution. I am sure others will be similarly interested. Any information that you may have that I could spread around would be appreciated.

The letter was from a well-to-do Washington, D.C. attorney named Franklin C. Salisbury. Albert knew nothing about the "cumulative list" of fund-raising organizations, and all that remained of his Institute for Muscle Research was the engraved stationery. But he wrote back to say that donations could be made directly to the Marine Biological Laboratory. On 19 May Frank Salisbury wrote a check for $25 and sent it to Woods Hole. That was the last he expected to hear of the matter.

A week later, however, he was startled to receive a letter in return from Szent-Gyorgyi:

I am deeply touched by your great generosity and compassion. I have worked very hard all my life with the aim to conquer this terrible disease, and now I see my way clear through to an understanding and cure. I will do my best to spend every penny most carefully to the greatest advantage. What I want to add is that such a donation means much more than its dollar equivalent. It is a great encouragement which, sometimes, is badly needed.[3]

The letter amazed and intrigued Salisbury and his wife, Tamara. As a corporation counsel and businessman, Salisbury was used to dealing in large figures. The gratitude of a Nobel laureate for a twenty-five dollar donation struck him as odd. Something must be terribly wrong with the "war on cancer" for such a man to go begging.

He did nothing about this for a year. In June 1972 the Salisburys were scheduled to drive to New Haven for Frank's Yale University reunion. He wrote to Albert again, proposing that they include a visit to Woods Hole on this trip:

> I have been thinking how I could be of help in the financial side of your work. I have for years been connected with a non-profit organization as house counsel but recently have resigned and am interested in using my accumulated familiarity with the non-profit field.

The two men met for the first time on 19 June 1972. "It was love at first sight," said Koloman Laki. "Salisbury had a feeling for talent, an eye for genius." On the surface, however, one could hardly imagine two more dissimilar individuals. Here was Szent-Gyorgyi, nearly eighty, but still the anti-estabishment maverick. After a lifetime of work he was now convinced, he told Salisbury, that a definitive understanding of cancer was within his grasp. Albert implied that he had the answer to cancer—if only he could find the money. It was a speech that always had a startling effect on lay visitors.

And here was Salisbury, the quintessential American businessman, whose whole life had been spent in practical pursuits. By his own admission, he knew nothing about science. He was a man of few words, outwardly a bit gruff, but disarming by his very bluntness.

Nonetheless, one could find an underlying similarity between the two: all his life Frank Salisbury had considered himself an "idea man," not a stickler for details. His approach to business, and people, was basically intuitive, like Szent-Gyorgyi's. One also sensed hidden depths here, and unfulfilled promises. (He had studied Classics at Yale and still plugged away at his Greek and Latin in spare hours.) Approaching retirement age himself, he seemed to be grappling for something really significant to do with his life. Although outwardly a success, a *pater familias* with an attractive wife and five children, the idea of helping Albert Szent-Gyorgyi find a cure for cancer seemed to provide, in his own words, "the necessary kicker" to motivate him.

This is not to imply that Frank Salisbury was blind to the practical benefits of starting a new foundation. The American Cancer Society was a great success story. Astronomical sums were being pumped into the cancer war, and the public was primed to give freely. Even mavericks such as Linus Pauling were turning to the public to generate support for their projects.

Salisbury explained at that first fateful meeting that some associates with knowledge of direct mail solicitation had already approached him with plans for something called "Project C.U.R.E." This would be a kind of private "war on cancer," soliciting money from the public through snappy direct-mail appeals.

Szent-Gyorgyi himself could provide a much-needed focus. Frank Salisbury, in a flash of insight, saw how "Project C.U.R.E." could be built around the cause of a neglected, persecuted, but lovable old Nobel laureate. His fund-raising friends were interested, although Albert himself remained skeptical. After all, he was still paying off huge debts accumulated during the Stephen Rath period, more than a decade before. But he liked and put his trust in Salisbury. In truth, he had little choice.

Tamara Salisbury, by coincidence, had once worked at NIH and had been a project officer in the Office of Naval Research some years before. She became actively involved in the project as well. If Albert had any qualms about his association with the highly aggressive Salisburys, he quickly stifled them. After all, he convinced himself, he had little to lose at this point. And so he agreed to allow the Salisburys to build an organization around his name and needs.

Frank's idea was to flood America with millions of direct mail appeals. This was 1972 and such appeals still had a scintilla of novelty to them. Although some scientists, more than adequately funded through normal channels, turned up their noses at such methods, Albert could not be so choosy. Frank took the administrative knowledge he had accumulated as a lawyer, board member, and businessman and applied it to the task of supporting Szent-Gyorgyi's research. He and his associates proved to be masters of the art and science of direct mail solicitation.

It would be very easy for a critic to see Frank's involvement in simple pecuniary terms. A "non-profit" organization can be quite profitable to the individuals involved and the Salisburys certainly stood to gain good incomes and "perks" from their leading positions in the foundation. In the fire-engine-red sports jacket he sometimes wore, Frank Salisbury appeared to some people to be simply another American Babbitt making a living from other people's dying. Salisbury, by his own account, was "already rich and ready to retire." His net worth, he says, "went down over the period of our sponsorship of the Foundation from where it could have been if we had continued in the business world."[4]

There was no doubt that Frank was seriously interested in Albert's work and captivated by his charm. At his end, Frank maintained an almost childlike faith that "Prof" would find the cure for cancer within a few short years. And Albert, in turn, was grateful for Frank's support and kept him enthusiastic by frequent allusions to rapid progress and big breakthroughs. These usually took the form of statements that he knew what cancer was or that he was about to discover the cure.[5]

From the start, this peculiar partnership of Salisbury and Szent-Gyorgyi was a combination of high idealism and hard-nosed practicality. Albert's friends worried that he was being "used." If so, then Frank's friends might have worried as well.

Frank spent the rest of 1972 setting up a board of directors and raising money for a "trial balloon" mailing for the following year. Dr. Mary H. Aldridge, a friend and neighbor of the Salisburys and professor of chemistry at American University, agreed to serve as chairperson of the board. Salisbury himself became Executive Director of what was dubbed the Bethesda National Foundation.[6]

Right from the start the new group was controversial. The first reason was the choice of name: its offices were located in a small upstairs office in Bethesda, Maryland. Just by coincidence, of course, the government's massive National Cancer Institute (NCI) was also located in Bethesda. If potential donors mistook the two organizations, that was not the Salisburys' fault.

"I see with great satisfaction that you are working very hard on my project and really doing your best to help me in my fight against cancer," Albert wrote Frank later in the year.[7]

In the following month, Frank Salisbury procured tax-free (501c3) status for the organization and suggested that Albert become its research director. It was a logical choice, but Albert at first demurred, saying, "I would be reproached that I am research director and use all the funds to my own advantage. This would make a very bad impression and would harm my reputation and my integrity."

Salisbury immediately responded, in gingerly fashion, "Since we will always try to conduct our fund-raising in a way which will benefit you and your great work and bring you no embarrassment, we will not burden you with the job of Director of Research."[8]

At this point, their only idea was to raise enough money to fund Szent-Gyorgyi's work. The dynamics of growth, however, were about to create something quite different, which neither man could imagine at the time. One day in December Salisbury opened his mail and found two checks, one for $50, the other for $5. They were addressed to "Project Cure, Bethesda National Foundation." The peculiar thing was that no publicity had yet been done. No one had any idea how these two donors had even heard about the new Foundation. Obviously, in the early seventies, people were beating down the door, eager to contribute money to the fight against cancer. Here was a fund-raiser's dream!

The first direct mail solicitation was sent out in March 1973 to 50,000 subscribers to *Prevention,* the natural-food health magazine. The returns were encouraging, according to the experts on such things. Letters, in fact, started to pour in, seeking information about Szent-Gyorgyi's work and its relationship to various diseases. After some deliberation, Albert decided it might be acceptable, after all, for him to take the position of scientific director, as long as he was insulated from the management of the money. His back against the wall, he had to do everything in his power to help the foundation succeed.[9]

Frank Salisbury's next mailing was to 250,000 potential donors, and was even more successful than the first "trial balloon." He was aware, however, that resistance to his concept might come from the more established fund-raising agencies. He cautioned Albert:

> We plan strictly to adhere to all laws, regulations, etc. that we can find or are brought to our attention. One accumulates "enemies" as one prospers so we have to be doubly careful to comply with all standards of conduct.[10]

In June 1973 Salisbury visited Woods Hole and spoke with an administrator at MBL about the project. The man was far from encouraging and denigrated Albert's work and ability. In guarded terms, Salisbury wrote "Prof" about this and he replied:

> I was not astonished at what you tell me. Good will and human understanding are none of his virtues. He is a rather unpleasant fellow, though he may be a good administrator. He made various calamities for me. I think that he cannot forbid you to mention in your publications that I am working and have my labs at the MBL, Woods Hole. This is a fact, not a secret. . . . I am not astonished about your difficulties with bureaucracy. That is what bureaucracy is for, to prevent people doing something decent.[11]

With the first year's modest proceeds, the Foundation was able to supply Albert with some modern equipment he badly needed for his research, such as a high-performance liquid chromatograph, a device pioneered by his friend and student, Csaba Horvath of Yale. By 1974 the Salisburys had set up a parallel Massachusetts foundation to pay the salaries, rent, and other costs of the Woods Hole lab. For Albert, this money was a godsend, freeing him from a decade of anxiety about his finances. But Frank's support was more important to him than mere money. For, as he wrote his new patron in a Christmas greeting:

> Without my knowing you are behind my back I would be now in a desperate mood, knowing that my reserves will give out after New Year. I have no application pending and nothing to expect. I have no way of paying back except by working hard for our common goal, to solve cancer.

In a most extraordinary way, then, Albert had once again been rescued from the brink of economic disaster. His debts had been paid off, he had new equipment in place, and money for his coworkers. There was no doubt that the new foundation had saved his career, even his life. It was a providential thing, he thought—something simply too good to be true.

19

THE BALLET OF ALBERT SZENT-GYORGYI

In 1973, Albert was also busy reestablishing ties with his homeland. In the back of his mind was the thought that if this new cancer foundation did not pan out he might decide to return to Hungary to pursue his research. In October 1973, at the age of eighty, he returned to Hungary for the first time in over twenty-five years, as a guest of the government. The occasion of his visit was the inauguration of an impressive biochemistry institute in Szeged, headed by Bruno Straub. Despite all that had happened in the intervening years, the scientific saplings Albert had planted in Szeged forty years before still flourished.[1]

Visiting Budapest, Albert spoke about his work before the Hungarian Academy of Sciences, of which he was now a "rehabilitated" member, and visited old friends in various parts of the country. It was an emotional homecoming; wherever he went large crowds turned out to greet the prodigal son.

As much as possible, both Albert and his Hungarian hosts put the disputes of the past behind them. Albert was genuinely impressed by the material progress and the relatively liberal climate of his homeland; the Hungarians conveniently forgot the bitter things he had said about the regime in the intervening years.

And, in fact, much had changed. With the reforms of 1968, Hungary had turned away from Stalinism. There was a spirit of excitement in the country. Yet, ironically, these very changes made Hungary seem unfamiliar to him. It was, he said with a touch of fatalism, a different country than the one he had left. Twenty-five years had also made him into an American, in ways difficult to define. But this visit also confirmed that Albert was still profoundly Hungarian.

His speech to the Academy, on 15 October, dealt with his work on "electrons, molecules, biology and cancer." It was well-received. Since this trip came in the midst of Albert's well-publicized financial difficulties, the idea of resettling in Hungary was broached a number of times. He later claimed that someone from the government even offered to return his ancestral farm in Nograd county if he would return to the homeland.[2]

One nervous moment for the regime came when "Prof" visited Szeged, as Bruno Straub's guest, for the opening ceremonies of the new laboratory. Albert remembered that there had been a plaque at the entrance to the university memorializing his old friend Count Kuno Klebelsberg. It had read simply but eloquently in Latin "these stones remember you." But the plaque was gone (Klebelsberg was, after all, one of Horthy's bureaucrats) and in its place was a memorial to Greek partisans killed fighting "Yankee imperialism" in the late 1940s. Undeterred, Albert journeyed to the local cemetery and there placed flowers on his old patron's simple grave.

After this incident, Albert asked to address the local young people. Party officials sweated, but in the end allowed him to do so. His speech was brilliant, iconoclastic, and non-political, at least in the conventional sense.

The high point of the visit came when Albert was interviewed on Hungarian television by Istvan Kardos, a much-respected science correspondent. They spoke for two hours, and the program was widely broadcast. Albert kept the country enthralled. Although his Hungarian was a bit rusty and old-fashioned, he never was more charming, effusive, and persuasive. For the older Hungarians it was a chance to see this popular figure again after so many years. For the younger people Albert Szent-Gyorgyi was a legend come-to-life. He concluded his television interview with this moving appeal to his countrymen:

> I live very, very far from here and many a frontier separates us; but in intellectual life there are no frontiers. I try to be a useful subject of another country, namely the United States, but also of a larger unit: humanity, for I try to work towards our common human goals.
>
> This does not change the fact that I am a Hungarian, as I was in the past. . . . The great affection you have shown me, the attentive care I have received and all your manifestations of loyalty show me also that the country has not disowned me as her son. Fearful that these ties might wither, I came home to strengthen them.
>
> As a Hungarian I wish Hungary to belong to the 'great powers,' to be great in every way possible to a small country. The possibilities are there,

all you have to do is to sustain intellectual life and retain the knowledge that you are Hungarians. I am the most peace-loving person, yet I would like Hungary to conquer the whole world. The political boundaries of a country cannot be extended without suppressing or hurting others. In intellectual life, however, growth is limited only by the capacity of one's brain. It is in this sense that I wish Hungary to become one of the great nations of the world.[3]

It was a beautiful note on which to end his visit and created a mood of harmony among his many friends. Yet immediately following this trip to Hungary, Albert, for reasons still hard to fathom, chose to embroil himself in a battle which quickly destroyed that unity. For upon his return to America he suddenly and radically revised his view on the important question of who discovered actin and actomyosin. He announced that it had been Ilona Banga, working of course under his supervision, who had actually discovered these important substances. They had then generously *given* them to Bruno Straub for analysis. Straub had been in the army for two or three years. To help him make up for lost time, Albert said, he had presented him with this important "gift." Straub, he acknowledged, had done an excellent job of analysis, but credit for the original discovery now had to be assigned to Banga. These remarks caused turmoil and consternation among Hungarian and Hungarian-American biochemists—almost all of them old students of "Prof."

For many years, there had never been a question about who discovered actin and actomyosin. "This work was undertaken by F. B. Straub," Albert himself had repeatedly said, "who made the discovery that the transformation of myosin A into myosin B was due to a second protein which is brought into solution on prolonged extraction. He called the new protein 'actin.'" Naturally, the world gave overall credit to Albert himself, because he was the senior scientist, he made the initial findings, and all the work took place under his personal direction.

Straub, for his part, always acknowledged Albert's role as "god-father' of the discovery, with himself as "happy parent."

In effect, this sudden announcement, by forcing people to take sides, split a fairly cohesive group of scientists into two hostile camps. Banga publicly agreed with Albert, although both of them claimed that the impetus for this attack came from "Prof" alone. On Albert's ninetieth birthday she published an article in a Hungarian publication pressing her own claim to the discovery of actin.

Straub was reluctant to rehash an old question that had long been settled in his favor. Albert wrote him a letter demanding that he acknowledge Banga's claims. He did not answer, nor did Prof. Janos Szentagothai, the highly-respected president of the Hungarian Academy of Sciences, who received a similar request. Albert became very agitated by all this. He felt that he personally had been responsible for a gross injustice to his loyal coworker, Ilona Banga.[4]

Straub denied that either Banga or Szent-Gyorgyi knew, at the time, that a new protein was responsible for the difference between myosin A and myosin B. He had brought his own interest in proteins back from David Keilen's laboratory in Cambridge. When he arrived in Szeged, Albert and Banga were still thinking in terms of colloids, which Straub considered a "fad" of the 1930s:

> Albert had the idea that something must cause a colloidal change in myosin. My low opinion of colloid chemistry . . . let me start on a different line: I thought that myosin B might contain another protein component.[5]

About one thing Albert certainly was wrong: Straub had not returned to his laboratory from the army, nor had he lost several years. He had come directly from his highly successful stay in England. Albert had no reason to pity him. What caused Albert, then, to reopen this long-settled question?

In part, he certainly felt guilty about having poorly treated a faithful friend. Banga's career never progressed as far as Straub's. She subsequently did make some important discoveries, but most of these (e.g., elastin) were made jointly with her husband, Prof. Josef Balo. Banga may have suffered from some of the same discrimination that affected women in science in the West.[6]

But there was more to it. When "Prof" left Hungary most of his associates were youngsters in their twenties. When he returned in 1973 these students had matured and established important positions for themselves. A few of them held the positions Albert himself had held in the thirties and forties. For instance, Guba held "Prof's" old post in Szeged and Biro was now the biochemistry professor in Budapest. But the most successful of all had been Straub.

Straub had risen far but, by his own admission, had never fulfilled his brilliant promise. He had gotten caught up in the administrative affairs of the socialist state. Albert resented this apostasy from the religion of pure research, and he also may have resented the credit he saw being heaped on Straub for his role in establishing the new institute. Albert insisted that he was not jealous of anyone's genuine achievements, but simply indignant at ill-gotten power and prestige.

His attitude was compounded by deep-seated political differences which surfaced with the visit. Banga was often on the outs with the regime because of her refusal to join the Communist Party. Straub, by his own account, had joined for several years and had prospered; and Albert resented what he saw as his political road to success.[7]

Perhaps, too, as his life drew to a close, Albert began to worry about his own place in history. While most American texts credited him with the discovery of actin, it rankled that the Hungarian *Uj Magyar Lexicon* credited Straub.[8] One thing no encyclopedia did was give Ilona Banga credit for the discovery of actin.

The whole question was especially important since in the intervening years scientists had realized that actin was an extremely interesting biological substance, responsible for movement in almost every kind of cell, not just muscle. It was even considered possible that a Nobel Prize would be given to its discoverer—if the Committee could decide exactly who discovered it. (Albert himself would have been ineligible, since one cannot win two Nobel Prizes in the same category.)

Banga claimed that she knew from the start that myosin B contained two substances, and that Albert himself had given it the name "actin." In America, Dr. Koloman Laki agreed with her. On his deathbed in October 1982 Laki wrote a statement saying that the priority question should be settled in this way: "Banga as the discoverer of actin and Straub the discoverer of the G-F transformation of actin. . . . It is unfortunate that things turned out [to] Banga's disadvantage." In Hungary, Profs. Guba, Biro, and other former members of Szent-Gyorgyi's coterie emphatically denied this and supported Straub.[9]

There was to be no easy solution to this tangle. Despite Szent-Gyorgyi and Banga, Straub continued to be credited by most people as the discoverer of actin. In fact, Albert's inexplicable silence on the question for thirty years became the most important piece of evidence in Straub's favor. The time to have pushed Banga's claim, if at all, was in the 1940s when the events were still fresh. Albert seemed to realize this, which made his pleas on his faithful assistant's behalf all the more poignant and quixotic.

Some time after his return from Hungary, Albert's friend Benjamin Kaminer, professor of physiology at Boston University Medical Center, organized a "Search and Discovery" conference in honor of his eighty-second birthday (October 1975). It was an extraordinary event, which elicited contributions from such colleagues and admirers as Hans Krebs, Linus Pauling, and Charles B. Huggins, winner of the 1966 Nobel Prize for his discoveries in chemotherapy.[10]

Pauling's talk on vitamin C was especially interesting. He recalled this quote from a 1939 Szent-Gyorgyi paper, and talked about its effect on his own work:

I have a strong faith in the perfection of the human body, and I think that vitamins are an important factor in its coordination with its surroundings. Vitamins, if properly understood and applied, will help us to reduce human suffering to an extent which the most fantastic mind would fail to imagine.

When Pauling first became interested in vitamin C, in 1966, he wrote to Szent-Gyorgyi for his opinion. Albert wrote back:

As to ascorbic acid, right from the beginning I felt that the medical profession misled the public. If you don't take ascorbic acid with your food you get scurvy, so the medical profession said that if you don't get scurvy then you are all right. I think that this is a very grave error.

Michael Kasha has given an evocative portrait of this conference:

The build-up of warmth of personal response toward Albert Szent-Gyorgyi was steady, with each lecturer's recounting of his career experiences. The build-up of esteem for Albert grew hourly . . .

After two days, the stage was set for Albert himself.

There was a certain tension and excitement. What would our great friend do? Would he, too, reminisce? Would he falter? The only person not looking backward, not even casting a glance over his shoulder that day was Albert Szent-Gyorgyi.

"Prof" started his talk a little hesitantly, in a slightly hushed voice. He was feeling enormous pressure to make an unusually dynamic presentation. "He started to build up his case with physiochemical caution and solidity"—block by block. "It went well, and a physical chemist's ears heard music," said Kasha.
Like a magician, Albert suddenly produced his props:

Holding giant test tubes in his hands, first one above his head, then the other, gesturing with each to make his point, his face vividly animated, a brilliant red color sparkled as the liquids mixed. . . . Albert danced about the platform, alternating his attention on the audience and on his test tubes. It was a ballet, the "Ballet of Albert Szent-Gyorgyi," flushed with energy and scientific drama. The physical chemistry and biochemistry were too tightly knit, too convincingly demonstrated, to be taken lightly. It was an hour of triumph.

Kasha compared Albert's phenomenal energy to a magnetic monopole, which, "if captured, would represent a field strength, an energy, unmatched in the physical world":

> That afternoon in Boston, October 17, 1975, at 5 P.M. the magnetic monopole seemed captured within the heart and soul of Albert Szent-Gyorgyi. The intense magnetism, the pulsating energy, the sheer radiance, were felt by all.[11]

The conference brought together Albert's friends from the past thirty years in America—"the old guard." It was a fitting tribute to a distinguished colleague, the reprise of a lifetime's achievement. But he had no intention of quitting center stage. At a social after this Boston meeting Albert made an announcement that startled many of his oldest friends. He proudly introduced his beautiful bride, Marcia Houston Szent-Gyorgyi.

The first thing everyone noticed about Marcia, of course, was her age or, rather, her youth. Like his third wife, Sue, Marcia was a good fifty years younger than "Prof." She was a strikingly good-looking divorcée, rather petite and delicate-featured, with a shy smile—in all, a "femalish woman," to use Albert's evocative phrase. Like so many of the women in Albert's life, she was also an artist.

In the spring of 1975 Csilla Felker had been accepted as an art student at the University of Massachusetts, Amherst, for the coming term. Amherst is almost 200 miles from Woods Hole and it was clear that he could no longer rely on Csilla for day-to-day support. Csilla had been with him for almost ten years, and even Albert recognized that it was time for her to go out on her own. But according to his granddaughter Lesley this decision left him almost desperate for someone to take care of him.

Undeterred by his experience with Sue, Albert still wanted a young woman with whom to share his life. Marcia was a graduate student and teaching assistant in art at Washington University, in St. Louis. She also happened to be a friend of Arpad I. Csapo, a professor at the University's medical school, and one of "Prof's" far-flung disciples. Eventually it was Csapo who arranged a liaison between Marcia and "Prof."

To Marcia, the peace and stability of "Seven Winds" was attractive, since it would enable her to paint and raise her daughter, without economic hardships. Marcia visited Albert at Woods Hole and they took a liking to each other. The relationship was both mutually convenient and mutually agreeable.

To all appearances, genuine affection developed between them, despite their wide difference in age. In 1976, he was asked how he bridged this gap of half a century:

> We are all human beings, and all the human qualities are the same, regardless of age. You do it with a certain understanding, and accommodation, and appreciation of each other's qualities, and [by] not trying to impose your ways on them. Freedom. It is very easy. There is no problem.

Nevertheless, for Albert's family Marcia's arrival was devastating. Marcia turned out to be an intensely private person, with a very strong will of her own.

"We initially made serious efforts to accept Marcia," said Geoffrey Pollitt. "In fact, I believe that even David had a special talk with her to try and make her feel that she was welcome."[12]

"I made a very concerted effort," David said, "to welcome her genuinely. In fact, in consultation with Grandfather, we decided that to really allay any problems I should have a nice chat with Marcia. . . . In no uncertain terms I reassured her, saying how pleased I was that Grandfather had 'someone to take care of him.' It was only a year or so later that such efforts became idiotic in the face of her clearly pre-conceived course of action having little to do with familial integrity."[13]

"We were rebuffed," Geoffrey added, "and I can only surmise that she felt threatened by us. . . . Later on, the acceptance of her became so difficult as we saw the wall being built around Albert."[14]

In 1975–76, the grandchildren were still living in the cottage, which Albert had promised to them at their mother's death. But, David noted,

> all physical activities such as swimming, water skiing, boating, etc., which had played such an important part in my grandfather's life, rapidly came to a halt. During this time visits from Grandfather were more and more infrequent and we started to notice that it was only when Marcia would leave for shopping, etc. (she had to drive right by the cottage) that Grandfather would in effect sneak down to see us.[15]

Albert was in a bind. He was in need of someone to offer him companionship and to attend to the daily chores (housekeeping, meals) which his obsession with his work led him to neglect. Marcia was in general a good wife who worked hard to keep him happy. Nevertheless, he also loved and needed his family.

Life at Woods Hole became very uncomfortable for the family. "Marcia made it very clear by her attitude to any overtures we tried to make that we were not welcome," said Geoffrey Pollitt. On one occasion, for instance, Geoffrey arranged to visit Albert at the house. He found "Prof" sitting down by the cottage, about a hundred yards from the big house. At first Geoffrey thought that Albert was just using the opportunity to take in the sun and tried to make some small talk to that effect. But, he says, he soon realized what had happened: Marcia no longer wanted Geoffrey in the house itself.

These sorts of family problems—and especially the bitter rupture with his outspoken grandson David—were to be a source of grief for Albert for the remainder of his life. Every attempt at reconciliation foundered.

"Within a couple of years," said David, "all family [celebrations of] holidays, i.e. Christmas [and] Thanksgiving came to an end and upon inquiries as to the reason Grandfather explained that the retribution [from Marcia] was very difficult to stand. . . ."[16]

In November 1978, Geoffrey made another attempt at reconciliation by inviting "Prof" and his wife to Thanksgiving Day dinner in Concord. Albert replied:

> It is terribly nice of you to invite Marcia and myself for Thanksgiving dinner and I can guess all good intentions which made you do so. I would love to attend, but the psychological situation is such still that it would achieve nothing and cause a great deal of trouble. It is terribly nice of you to leave me all options open without resentment. It is impossible to argue with psychotic factors. So please excuse me without bearing me a grudge. The pleasure would be great but the trouble still bigger.
>
> By the way Marcia is a good wife for me only that patch in her mind which made things difficult still exists.[17]

Marcia, say the Pollitts, went so far as to mail them back pictures from the family album, torn to remove their portraits. The whole topic of his family relations was so painful for Albert that at times he tried to blot out its existence. When the author first interviewed Albert, he evasively brushed aside all questions about grandchildren, leaving the impression that he had none.[18]

The other big change in his life was no less controversial to his old friends and family. On 1 January 1974 the Bethesda National Foundation had been renamed the National Foundation for Cancer Research (NFCR) and incorporated as a non-profit charity in the state of Massachusetts. An even more aggressive fund-raising drive was begun and those who donated as little as a dollar were enrolled as "members" of the Foundation. By the end of 1976, there were 35,000 such members, each giving an average contribution of $10. NFCR moved to larger quarters at 7315 Wisconsin Avenue, in the heart of Bethesda's rapidly expanding business district.

Suddenly Albert's foundation had a most unaccustomed problem: *too much* money. Szent-Gyorgyi's lab could use about $300,000 in support a year, but the Foundation was raising more than that and Frank Salisbury was not a man to discourage donations. With this sudden largesse, Albert saw an opportunity to support his long-time colleagues as well—the Pullmans, Csaba Horvath, Michael Kasha, and Gabor Fodor. Albert had no intention of gathering them all in one place. Rather, he proposed a "laboratory without walls," an innovative institution in which scientists would loosely collaborate, under his intellectual leadership, in finding a cure for cancer.

If Albert saw this in intellectual and moral terms, Salisbury gave the "laboratory without walls" a practical twist. Most charitable foundations put money in bricks and mortar because large donors like to see their names on buildings. NFCR, however, had few large donors, and therefore no pressure to erect expensive tabernacles of science. Besides, the "war on cancer" had built lots of new laboratories, such as the magnificent government structures right down Wisconsin Avenue. No one needed yet another high-rise laboratory.

And so NFCR established a "project director" approach to funding. Basically, an already-established researcher at a major institution would have his laboratory redesignated an "NFCR regional laboratory." In effect, NFCR would *rent* those facilities from the universities or industrial research labs in which they were located. Albert also was very anxious that the red tape be kept to a minimum:

> The public understands that all this blah, blah about federally-funded research is just a sham. NIH gets 10,000 applications a year. What can you do? So they set standards, but the standards don't fit every individual and become stupid in themselves.

One thing was certain: Albert Szent-Gyorgyi would never again submit to so-called peer review. Nor did it appear he would ever have to. He could never forget the treatment he himself had received at the hands of the big, established cancer institutions. The last time he had been turned down by the National Cancer Institute; in 1975, the director, he said, had refused to see him. Another time, at the age of eighty-two, he had been asked by an executive of a major cancer center to present his ideas to the staff, and made a long trip to do so. When he got there, he said, the man had forgotten he had made the appointment.

And so he got on the phone to one of his friends. "Joe," he said, "I've got a problem. Can you help me? I've got this guy in the office who thinks he's got the cure for cancer. His name is Szent-Gyorgyi. Could you come up here for fifteen minutes or so?"

Although the story was basically sad, it became hilarious in the telling, as Albert tried to imitate American speech patterns in his own Hungarian-flavored accent.

Any organization he had a hand in building, therefore, would have to be quite different: responsive to creative thinkers, and following a policy of *basic* research first. This "laboratory without walls" would support the work of scientists on the frontiers of biophysics. From the start, it was clear that Albert conceived of these scientists as an *auxiliary force* to his own thrust. In a sense, he had finally found that big institute he had wanted since he left Hungary, although it was taking an unpredictable form.

The first regional NFCR laboratory was that of Dr. Ronald Pethig at the Electronic Engineering School of the University College of North Wales. Pethig, and his graduate student, Peter Gascoyne, were to become two of Albert's closest collaborators and most ardent disciples. Both were remarkable young men. Pethig was trained in electronics and had risen quickly in his field. One of his interests was in the relationship of electronics to biology. One day he happened to read a paper by Szent-Gyorgyi and found it truly electrifying. It was, he said, as if this man had peered into Pethig's own mind and put down his very own thoughts. It was an old paper, however, and Pethig, like many others, assumed that Szent-Gyorgyi was long dead.

By a string of coincidences, Pethig found out that Szent-Gyorgyi was very much alive. A visit to Woods Hole and he was like a convert; his enthusiasm for Albert sometimes seemed tinged with religious-like zeal. He in turn "converted" his student, Peter Gascoyne, a bearded but boyish Englishman who soon moved to Woods Hole to work full-time with "Prof."

It had been observed that living tissues gave off strong signals in an electron spin resonance (ESR) machine. Dead material did not. To Albert, this ESR signal provided an important clue about the electronic dimensions of life, as well as of cancer, which he considered a distorted form of life. One of Gascoyne's many jobs was to maintain and run this complicated machinery for "Prof." Gascoyne, Pethig and a young colleague, Stephen Bone, began the long-neglected job of *quantifying* what, until then, had been mainly intuitive theories about electrons and cancer.

Three more NFCR laboratories were added in 1976: those of

Alberte and Bernard Pullman, of the Institut de Biologie Physico-Chimique in Paris; Trevor Slater, a biochemist at Brunel University, Uxbridge, England; and Sidney Fox, an origin-of-life investigator at the University of Miami.

This was the beginning of a remarkable expansion. Salisbury was equally busy on his end. In the mid-seventies, NFCR began running a national sweepstakes. That fall, brown envelopes started arriving, by the millions, in mailboxes across the country. Snippets of information about cancer mingled with headlines such as, "Which one of these grand prizes will *you* choose?" Sensitive portraits of Albert at work were juxtaposed with pictures of alluring "Credit Suisse" gold bars. "$5,000 in Gold" was the first prize, announced in huge blue and yellow letters.

Of course, it was not necessary to make a donation in order to enter the sweepstakes and win the gold or the Lynx or the Sony home viewing center. But in his enclosed letter, Frank Salisbury warned participants that failure to do so would be "a setback for cancer research." Guilt and greed were thus skillfully mingled. What disturbed some observers (especially scientists) were statements that Albert's work was "very possibly the key to cancer's cure" and that "a donation now can be a timely investment in your family's continued freedom from this terrible disease."

Was this true? Only if you believed that Albert Szent-Gyorgyi and his colleagues held the key to cancer. The danger here was that people were so desperate for a cure that they would uncritically support *any* theory that offered hope. In practice, the fund-raising seemed to do little harm; most of the money went to support established laboratories that were doing innovative work. The approach was down-home Americana: hokey to some, an example of Yankee ingenuity at work to others. But no one could say that Frank Salisbury's methods were not effective. With the inauguration of the sweepstakes, in fact, contributions to quantum biology took a quantum leap. By the organization's eighth year the yearly take was almost fifteen million dollars.

This was still only about one percent of the total spent on cancer research in the United States, but NFCR was growing as fast as any component of the "war on cancer," and seemed to be developing a momentum of its own. It had suddenly become a force to be reckoned with.

With its new wealth, NFCR proved equally skillful at recruiting outstanding scientists to join the organization as regional directors. These included Ilya Prigogine of the Free University of Brussels and the University of Texas, a brilliant theoretical chemist and philosopher of science, who won the Nobel Prize in 1977; fellow Nobelist Ivar

Giaever of General Electric; Bruce Ames (famous for "the Ames test" for carcinogens) and Lester Packer of the University of California, Berkeley; Harold Dvorak, chief of pathology at Beth Israel, Boston, and Mallinckrodt Professor at Harvard; and Per-Olov Lowdin, a well-known Swedish quantum chemist who served on one of the Nobel Prize selection committees.

NFCR was also remarkable for its internationalism. It even funded a laboratory in Debrecen, Hungary—an unusual bit of East-West cooperation at a time of growing strains. By 1984, there were laboratories at sixty different institutions in over a dozen countries, from Japan to Israel.

There were some who objected to NFCR's growth, however. These objections included honest doubts about Albert's far-out ideas; questions about the Salisburys' methods and motives; distaste for the foundation's populist approach; as well as some jealous backbiting, inspired by the Foundation's nervous competitors. Some old friends, such as Prof. Benjamin Kaminer of Boston University's medical school, felt that Albert's association with the Foundation was demeaning and damaging to his reputation in the scientific community. They held out another, more traditional academic appointment as a substitute source of funding. In fact, in 1975 "Prof" accepted such an offer, which would have brought him a prestigious title and a baseline grant of $100,000 a year. But the offer fell apart when he refused to break his ties with the Foundation. Quoting an old Hungarian proverb he told his would-be benefactors, "You cannot ride on two horses with one bottom." And NFCR was the horse he intended to ride.

Many of these questions finally surfaced in a 9 February 1979 article in *Science*. In a piece entitled "Albert Szent-Gyorgyi, Electrons, and Cancer," Constance Holden commented on the growing controversy.

Szent-Gyorgyi, she granted, had not only won a Nobel Prize, but his contributions over the years "could easily have added up to a couple of more Nobels." Many people, she added, "now don't know whether Szent-Gyorgyi is alive or dead. He is in fact quite alive at 85, and working . . . on a little known and less understood 'bioelectronic theory of cancer' that he has been developing for decades."

What saved him from being "forced out to pasture" was "the enthusiasm of a retired lawyer and businessman who took a shine to his ideas." Frank Salisbury, she wrote, was attracted to Albert "for reasons not entirely clear." He "knows next to nothing about science, but like many other citizens wants cancer cured—and fast."

Contrary to the rumors that NFCR was "an organization committed to supporting a group of maverick scientists intent on proving an unorthodox theory of cancer," she wrote:

Most of the investigators are interested in, but skeptical of, Szent-Gyorgyi's hypothesis. Some have little interest in it but are working in related fields. They are willing to associate themselves with Szent-Gyorgyi because of his record of accomplishments and his extraordinary scientific intuition which has long been acknowledged even by his detractors.

In other words, they were "by no means an eccentric brotherhood" devoted to a guru, but appeared to be "investigators of good repute whose work has varying degrees of relevance to the bioelectronic hypothesis."

Why, then, she asked, was Albert having such difficulty in gaining acceptance for his theory? There seemed to be a difference in scientific *style,* as much as anything. At the crux of the matter were geography and culture. Albert was of East European origin. "Americans are probably the world's most cautious and data-oriented scientists. As you move farther East," she opined, "there is more sympathy with fantastic ideas." And at the time it was true that Europeans, and especially Hungarians, played a major role in the Foundation.

The most unintentionally revealing quotation in the article came from Congdon Wood, an official of the American Cancer Society (ACS). "They are competing with us in fund-raising," he said bluntly, "and they're creating a good deal of confusion."

What confusion? Obviously Americans were giving $15 million to NFCR that might have gone elsewhere if NFCR did not exist. This was the kind of "confusion" upstart competitors always create for established organizations.

"The unfortunate thing about people like Szent-Gyorgyi and Linus Pauling," the ACS official continued, "is that when they start to taper off there is the danger that people will start to use them." There was no substantiation for the charge that Albert (or Pauling) *was* in fact tapering off, or that people *were* using them.

In her investigation, Holden found that "no one connected with NFCR appeared to feel that age had dimmed the man's judgment or dampened his legendary ability." Much of the suspicion of NFCR, then, came down to Frank and Tamara Salisbury's methods and motives. "The personal Salisbury presentation is not particularly reassuring," said *Science,* drily. Frank scoffed at government red tape, while failing to mention that Albert's own grant applications had been turned down. "He told *Science* that Sloan-Kettering Institute for Cancer Research was interested in the theory, although several calls to Sloan-Kettering did not uncover any interest."[19]

Despite these negatives, Holden concluded her article in a rather upbeat fashion. "Were it not for a gung-ho American businessman, a

scientist of monumental achievement might have found himself be-
calmed in his later years for lack of money."

On the whole, NFCR could not have helped but be pleased by the
Science piece. At least they were now on the map. Soon, however, the
organization began to face a barrage of criticism in the media, which,
Salisbury was quick to charge, emanated from the larger fund-
raising organizations. He unsuccessfully urged reporters to investigate
this "smear campaign."

First there was a series of syndicated newspaper articles which
portrayed NFCR in a rather negative light. Then, on 22 December
1980—a fateful day for NFCR—Jane Bryan Quinn published an
article on the Foundation in the pre-Christmas issue of *Newsweek*.
The date was significant; it coincided with the last two weeks of the
NFCR Sweepstakes, the most critical time in the foundation's yearly
fund-raising effort.

Entitled "Look Before Giving," it carried the provocative subtitle:
"Modern Fagins pay children to ring doorbells, selling Christmas
candy for bogus charities."

This second headline as it turned out, was not connected with
NFCR or the Salisburys, but with *another* alleged charity rip-off cited
in the article. The article began with a description of NFCR, but to
NFCR it seemed as if the Salisburys, by a subterfuge of juxtaposition,
were being called "modern Fagins." No epithet could have hit them
harder, personally.

In two succinct paragraphs, Quinn managed to encapsulate almost
every charge and innuendo made about NFCR since its founding:

> "I am given to exaggerate," Franklin C. Salisbury jokes. He and his
> wife, Tamara, manage the National Foundation for Cancer Research in
> Bethesda, Md.—no connection to the American Cancer Society or to any
> government agency. As part of its latest fund-raiser, a sweepstakes, Salis-
> bury tells potential contributors that he needs money for an "unexpected
> reason"—namely, that his researchers are developing a control for cancer
> "faster than we anticipated." Spurred by this hope, donors gave the foun-
> dation $7.7 million in the year ending March 1980.

Nothing in this paragraph was particularly untrue. But the facts
were put together in a way that made NFCR appear to be a boiler-
plate operation instead of a legitimate cancer foundation. Nothing, for
instance, was even mentioned about Albert or the eminent scientists
discussed in the *Science* article. Instead *Newsweek* readers heard only
about "his," meaning Salisbury's, researchers, as if such eminent
scientists as Ilya Prigogine, Bernard Pullman, or Csaba Horvath were
part of Frank and Tamara's "stable."

The phrase "no connection to the American Cancer Society" would have been amusing, if it didn't carry such weight with the donating public. The ACS has worked for over forty years to have itself recognized as the preeminent cancer fund-raising agency in the United States. To Salisbury, attacking him on these grounds was like criticizing Lee Iacocca for being unconnected to General Motors. For Quinn, apparently, only ACS, NCI, and organizations they approved of, had legitimacy in the cancer field.[20]

In her second paragraph, Quinn was even more damaging. She claimed that nearly half of the foundation's contributions were spent on fund-raising costs and that only twenty-six cents on the dollar went to research projects, "which is a very low percentage."

According to the Foundation's reckoning, however, in the year ending 31 March 1980, with in-kind contributions included, program costs were sixty-two percent, while fund-raising expenses were only twenty-eight percent. Administrative costs totalled six percent. Without in-kind contributions included (and some critics claimed it was wrong to include them), the figures were not as good, but not as bad as Quinn claimed. Program costs then came to forty-eight percent, while fund-raising costs were thirty-eight percent.

Did this indicate that NFCR was a rip-off? On a percentage basis, small foundations have higher operating costs than large ones. This is due mainly to the economies of scale in fund-raising costs available to the larger groups. Also, most donations come from a stable base of prior donors. To develop such a base costs a great deal of time and money. Quinn appeared to be comparing NFCR to its big competitors, such as the American Cancer Society, rather than other relatively small operations.

Nevertheless, Quinn's criticism, and similar charges from the National Information Bureau and the Philanthropic Advisory Service of the Council of Better Business Bureaus (CBBB) were highly damaging to NFCR and devastating to the Salisburys personally. Mrs. Salisbury was a fashionable, status-conscious woman, who for years had lived in Potomac, Maryland, one of the wealthiest communities in the country. Some of her neighbors, she said, ostentatiously snubbed her after this article appeared; who in Potomac would want to associate with "modern Fagins"?

Franklin Salisbury, a graduate of Hotchkiss School and Yale, saw himself as a pillar of the Washington establishment. He had, he said, altruistically given himself to a noble task, the support of a great scientist in his quest for a cancer cure. Now he was being thrown to the dogs. Being himself a lawyer, and a bit litigious, he sought justice, if not retribution, in the courts. In 1981 he sued the powerful *Newsweek* organization for libel, asking $86 million in damages.

Albert was made aware of these developments, but did not directly involve himself in them. Having been through financial problems with Stephen Rath he must have had his moments of doubt. How well, after all, did he know the Salisburys? But, for him, the important thing was that he was working again, with resources he had not had in twenty years. History would never care, he said, *how* he raised his funds. Achievement was everything. Who remembered where Ehrlich, Koch, or Pasteur got their funds? Who cared? What was remembered were their earth-shaking accomplishments.

And so Albert's public posture was that of solidarity with Salisbury. NFCR would be vindicated by its successes in the cancer field, much as the efforts of the National Foundation for Infantile Paralysis— another upstart criticized in its time—were vindicated by the Salk vaccine.

He wrote consoling words to Salisbury:

> I am not unduly worried about it not only because I trust your ability, but also because our work is going so well that if we will have the time to come out with it, we will have such strong support in public opinion that nobody can harm us. It will be the old story of a dog biting a man, and dying from the bite (the dog dying and not the man.)

In June 1984 District Court Judge Walter E. Black, Jr. turned down the magazine's request for a summary judgment and stated that the genuine issues of fact should be decided by a jury. The preparations for trial stretched on for months and then years. Suing a national news organization turned out to be no simple matter. The Salisburys' case received little sympathy in the media. The press was simultaneously under attack in the Ariel Sharon and William Westmoreland trials. This NFCR suit seemed to raise the spectre of censorship at a time when writers and editors were under siege.[21]

The preparation of the suit exhausted, exasperated, and thoroughly distracted the NFCR staff, including the Salisburys themselves. They persisted because they felt that a great injustice had been done to them as citizens and to the scientists in the Foundation. One unforeseen consequence, however, was that the suit created strains in the relationship between Albert and the Foundation that would have been impossible to believe just a few years before.

20

FREE RADICALS

"One of Albert Szent-Gyorgyi's greatest gifts to science," according to Prof. Barry Commoner, "has been his long and persuasive campaign to relate the phenomena of life to the behavior of molecules, atoms, and subatomic particles which comprise the substance of living things."[1] For more than four decades Albert was in fact preoccupied with developing a fundamental theory about the nature of life, a new field which he called "submolecular biology."[2]

Some scientists agreed with Commoner that Albert's arguments were "persuasive." Others were skeptical, exasperated, or—worst of all—disinterested. To many, it seemed as if Szent-Gyorgyi was simply working on some far-out treatment for cancer. But those who took the trouble to investigate, quickly saw that Albert was doing far more than touting just another unorthodox cancer cure. His theory of submolecular biology was something very big—a whole new way of looking at the essential elements of biology. It was a sweeping and daring reformulation of essentials, a revolution in the sense proposed by philosopher Thomas Kuhn, in that it posed a new "paradigm" for science and opened up promising avenues for future experimentation.[3]

What everyone wants to know, of course, is whether or not this theory is "correct." Even more, people want to know if it will cure cancer. Given adequate research, these questions will be answered in time. But because it is such a fundamental proposition and covers so much new ground, one should not expect quick answers. This is not to offer special pleading on Szent-Gyorgyi's behalf. His theories, obviously, must conform to the same rules of evidence as anyone else's. But with "submolecular biology," it must be emphasized, we are not looking at a simple proposition or even a set of facts, but at a

241

world view. The man struggled to create a new way of looking at biology. If his view is ultimately accepted, it could change the face of modern science as profoundly as the work of Pasteur, Curie, or Watson and Crick. But even if it is eventually discounted, it will undoubtedly go down as one of science's more glorious failures, similar to that of Einstein's later years—one which, at least, has stimulated others to do very fruitful work.[4]

In this chapter we can only hope to touch on some of the most salient points. A major difficulty in understanding this theory is that Albert did not formulate it in linear fashion. As the reader has gathered, he never was a good compartmentalizer, but rather chafed at the very idea of specialization. "It is difficult to know whether one should call him a biochemist, or a physiologist, or a biophysicist," said an exasperated Warren Weaver, of the Rockefeller Foundation, in 1947.

His scientific work was never neatly divided into vitamin C, muscle, cancer. For the sake of the exposition it has sometimes been necessary to present it that way, but now is the time to correct that impression. In fact, while he was working on these disparate elements he was always in truth working on the same thing: the question of *life*.

What is life? How did it get that way? What's the difference between "alive" and "not-alive," animate and inanimate? These were the things that truly bothered him; time and again his own dissatisfaction with conventional answers pushed him forward and motivated his work. He returned again and again to the same puzzle, and often to the same materials—the internal respiration mechanism of the cells, the role of ascorbic acid, the movement of muscle—with new tools and insights. In his nineties, he expressed amazement that somehow without his knowing how or why his research had worked its way full circle back to the topic of vitamin C, which he had "abandoned" in the 1930s. Somehow everything seemed connected. Streams of thought did not really disappear, but simply went underground to merge and then reemerge at some future juncture. This process of constantly puzzling, of working and reworking the same material, of obsessively trying to answer a passionately disturbing puzzle reminds us not so much of a dry researcher as of a great artist at work.

The comparison in Szent-Gyorgyi's case was inevitable. Some (such as his former student W. Mommaerts) compared him to Picasso, with whom he shared a Dionysian love of pleasure, a spontaneity and a masculine charisma. To Peter Gascoyne, who was among his closest collaborators, Albert was "the Monet of modern science":

> His research is a great canvas upon which he casts a speck of light here, a reflection there. He is free to lay down a shadow, then to jump large

stretches of blank canvas to augment it with a highlight. Slowly but surely the whole picture emerges from the fog of scattered fragments, though like Monet, the details of each segment are blurred.[5]

If the following account of Albert's later work also occasionally seems "blurred" that may be because it is part of a great canvas, left unfinished at the artist's death. In discussing submolecular biology we find ourselves in the artist's workshop, looking around at the often incomplete results of half a century's restless seeking.

Life is such a common phenomenon that we tend to forget how strange it really is. Its very degree of organization makes it a "very improbable state." "No other contrast," wrote the naturalist Joseph Wood Krutch, "is so tremendous as this contrast between what lives and what does not."

"What is life?" is a meaningless question, however, if we are looking for some vitalistic principle, something we can isolate in a test tube and call "life itself." As Albert often said:

> Many have asked this question, but nobody has answered it. Science is based on the experience that nature answers intelligent questions intelligently, so if she is silent there may be something wrong with the question. The question is wrong because life, as such, does not exist.

What we can see, however, are *material systems* which have the "wonderful quality of being alive." What then is this quality? It must be something very fundamental, said Albert, because it allows us to divide the whole world into two parts, which we call "animate" and "inanimate," alive and not-alive. This division is quite sharp and unequivocal.

To Albert the difference between these two realms lay in the "wonderfully subtle reactivity and flexibility of the animate." The flicker of a serpent's tongue, the spring of a jaguar, or the workings of a human brain trying to fathom a new theory are all examples of nature's highly subtle reactivity. If the extreme speed and subtlety of living reactions is the essential characteristic of what we are looking for, then the next question has to be "where do we look for the *physical basis* of this reactivity?"

The body contains many different kinds of cells and tissues, but ultimately the two most important components are *nucleic acids* and *proteins*. But how reactive can nucleic acids be? After all, nucleic acids contain the blueprints of the body's structure, its hereditary legacy. To carry out its function it must remain relatively secure from change, coiled in the nucleus of the cell or carrying out some specific messenger function.

That leaves proteins.

Proteins are macromolecules, built of simpler constructional units called amino acids. Sometimes proteins contain chains of hundreds or even thousands of such amino acids, put together like a tinker toy. "I could never believe that the wonderful subtlety of biological reactions could be brought about by clumsy, relatively unreactive macromolecules," said Albert.

"Even the most involved protein structural formula," he said in 1941, "looks 'stupid,' if I may say so."

Which seems to leave us with—nothing. Not so, said Albert. The answer *does* lie in proteins. But proteins need something added to them in order to become reactive: smaller and more mobile units. What is smaller than a molecule? An atom. And an atom is composed of particles, a small, dense nucleus and the light electrons that swirl around it in a large, diffuse cloud. In a living system the relevant mobile particles could be nothing other than these outer electrons, because the enormous energy liberated by *nuclear* reactions would destroy any biological structure.

But electrons are only reactive on a conductor. And so, in his well-publicized 1941 Koranyi lecture, Albert proposed that proteins may be conductors and that this might prove to be the basis of the phenomenon of life. It was a startling idea, so provocative that it was greeted with simultaneous publication in both *Science* and *Nature*. Yet the theory was instantaneously and unanimously rejected by almost all the experts who looked at it at the time. "The more lenient critics called it a 'lame duck.'" Albert recalled, with amusement, "and the more severe ones called it a 'dead duck.'"

The main reason for this rejection was that many proteins had been studied and none had ever shown a sign of being a conductor of electricity.

"This was a powerful argument," Albert conceded, "And nothing could be said against it." As time went by, however, he reflected on the nature of proteins: they are the most versatile of substances, capable of performing many different functions. In thinking about proteins, then, one had to distinguish between two very different kinds of reactions. The first were the simple tasks which were performed by single protein molecules floating in solution (i.e., molecular dispersions); the second required complicated, highly integrated *systems* of molecules.

It was the latter complex systems, Albert suggested, which performed the great biological functions by which we know life, such as motion, secretion, and nervous activity. But such integrated systems are, by definition, rigid structures, insoluble.

The simple functions, such as maintaining osmotic pressure, or enzymatic activity, which could be performed by single molecules in solution, demanded no electronic mobility. But it was *only these* molecules in solution that were readily available for study. For their analysis, protein chemists needed solutions. So what the chemist did was, in effect, to take the juice out of the tissue, call this juice "the essence," and flush what they called "the residue" down the drain. In so doing, Albert said, they were "throwing out the baby with the bathwater," flushing away those very *systems* which were responsible for the higher biological functions.

Albert presented a humorous analogy:

> If I would be put into a hydraulic press which would press out all my juices, then I would be decomposed into two fractions, the "press juice" containing all my soluble molecules, and the "residue" containing all my structures. If it were possible to put the two fractions together again, then the exchange of my *juices* with those of a young girl would make no difference. But if the two *residues* were exchanged, then I would become a young girl and she an old man.

Individuality, he concluded, is linked to structure.

To repeat: when Albert spoke of the reactivity of life taking place in protein, he was not speaking of the kinds of proteins which can be shaken in a test tube or extracted, precipitated, purified, or crystallized. "I doubt whether they would still have the subtle qualities which characterize life and could tell us the difference between 'animate' and 'inanimate' " in that condition, he said.

He was speaking of the structures, the throwaway part of protein science.

By carrying his search for life to the level of electrons Albert had wandered into another dimension of biology. Few were willing or able to follow him, for modern-day biology is above all a *molecular* biology, and proud of it; it searches for answers at this level and has done remarkably well in this search. This approach seems logical because the body is built of molecules. But remember, cautioned Albert, that these molecules themselves are built of nuclei and electrons. Thus, there has to be "another dimension below the molecules which has been disregarded by biology."

Here is where some knowledge of physics was necessary and useful. (Albert himself only started learning physics in the 1940s.) The electrons which surround an atomic nucleus are in "orbitals," which, in a way, can be looked upon as boxes containing pairs of electrons. The two electrons of this pair spin in opposite directions. In this way they compensate each other's magnetism (magnetic moments), which makes them coupled and highly stable. "An electron placed on such a molecule would find no place to go to."

One can also think of a closed-shell molecule (to use William Shockley's analogy) as a completely filled parking lot, to which no car can be added and in which no cars have any mobility at all. Such "self-satisfied" molecules could hardly be the basis of life. Could something possibly transform an unreactive macromolecule into a highly reactive unit with a measure of electronic mobility?

Using the parking lot analogy, if one were to take a single car out of the lot, it would make shuffling possible and make all the other cars theoretically mobile. By taking a single electron out of a closed shell system you do the same thing, opening the way to the shuffling of electrons. But this leaves the former partner of the removed electron with a "desire" to couple with another electron (this is what physicists call an uncompensated magnetic moment). A molecule containing such uncoupled electrons is called a "free radical." And free radicals are known to be very important, reactive, and unstable entities.[6]

By removing the electron we have, in effect, upset the balance of the whole molecule. The more electrons we take out, the more mobile and reactive the molecule becomes. By removing molecules, according to research by two of Albert's associates (Janos Ladik and Koloman Laki) we also accomplish something else of great importance: we greatly increase the possibility of *interaction* among molecules.

Thus this very simple act—removing electrons—actually paves the way for all the higher and complex structures, which are capable of increasingly subtle reactions. "We have opened the way to development and differentiation," said Albert. "We have opened the way to evolution."

All of this work (and bear in mind that this is a quick summary of many years of reasoning and experiments) led Albert to formulate what he called the first rule of electrobiology: *the living state is the electronically desaturated state of molecules. The degree of development and differentiation is a function of the degree of electronic desaturation.*

CHARGE TRANSFER AND PERMITIVITY

"Charge transfer" is the method by which electrons are taken out of molecules by other molecules. Sometimes, however, two molecules can form a single electronic system in which the electrons rearrange themselves. Since electrons are negatively charged particles, when an electron leaves a molecule it leaves its former host with a positive charge. This positively charged molecule is called the "donor" and the one which receives the negative charge is called the "acceptor."

But this situation, in which an electron definitively leaves its own molecule, and permanently cleaves to another, is a relatively rare event. More commonly, the electron is shared between several molecules and only a *percentage* of its total charge is passed along to another molecule.

"Such a partial transfer of electrons," said Albert, "may play a very important part in biology and contribute to the subtle adjustment of biological reactions. It may have also a major importance for the mechanism of evolution."

Here, however, we meet with another difficulty: by transferring an electron we create two electrically-charged free radicals. But such free radicals are exceedingly reactive, so reactive in fact that "it is doubtful whether this reactivity is compatible with life." There is a way out of this difficulty as well. The two molecules in question can incorporate themselves into a single unit before this transfer occurs. In that case, free radicals might be formed as before, but no net charge would be generated, since the change would take place within the complex. It is a case of robbing Peter to pay Paul.

There is a common name for such incorporation, accompanied by intramolecular charge transfer. It is called "doping" and it forms the basis of the entire electronic industry, which is aptly named "Silicon Valley." Through doping with electron donors and acceptors, substances like silicon, which are very poor electron conductors when pure, can be made into extremely good conductors.

Thus the creation of life, said Albert, demanded both electron donors and acceptors. It is this activity which got the ball rolling. From a theoretical point of view, the best electron donor is hydrogen and the best acceptor fluorine (and the other halogens). In reality, however, the halogens are acceptors *too strong* to be used by life. All of their electron-accepting activity is consumed when they are chemically incorporated into a molecule. On the other hand, oxygen (and sulfur) still retains one of its electron-accepting bonds after incorporation. So for a good biological acceptor nature turned to oxygen and sulfur. Oxygen in particular became the universal biological acceptor. "The energy driving life is derived from the transfer of an electron from hydrogen to oxygen."

METHYLGLYOXAL

When life originated, about three and a half billion years ago, this planet must have been a very unpleasant place, hot, steamy, and dark.

There was no light or free oxygen, and the earth was covered by a dense layer of water vapor. The oxygen that was present was bound in the form of water, carbon dioxide, etc., which were of no use as electron acceptors. Yet according to Szent-Gyorgyi's theory, there could be no life without desaturation, and oxygen is the universal acceptor.

The protein molecules that formed in that primordial era had to have been rather stable things, with no loose ends or unbalanced forces. They had to be essentially "closed-shell molecules," with their electrons arranged in pairs. There must have been a strong reducing atmosphere, containing electron donors, such as hydrogen, but no suitable electron acceptors. Whether we could even call these early combinations of amino acids "life" is debatable.

Under those conditions, only the simplest forms of life could evolve; to make this a continuous process, these primitive "cells" had to proliferate as fast as conditions permitted. At some point, however (we know from the end result), life must have found a way of using some *bound* oxygen as an acceptor.

Nature achieved this, Albert suggested, by utilizing a very simple chemical, a mixture of hydrogen, carbon, and oxygen called *methylglyoxal* (MG) — very simple, but very subtle, for methylglyoxal is a unique substance with special characteristics. In a sense we can think of it as "primitive oxygen," i.e., the kind of oxygen life used before there was free oxygen floating in the atmosphere.

"That I have not lost myself in meaningless speculation," Albert wrote, "and am still close to the central problems of biology is indicated by the fact that more than sixty years ago [in 1912, ed.] a most reactive and apparently ubiquitous biological enzymic system was discovered, 'glyoxalase,' which . . . can transform, at an extreme speed, methylglyoxal into D-lactic acid."

The existence of a widespread system for *breaking down* methylglyoxal is a major clue that we are looking at a biologically-important substance. "Nature does not indulge in luxuries," said Albert. If it preserved such a widespread and active enzyme system it probably did so for a good reason. Until Szent-Gyorgyi, nobody had been able to suggest a use for this ubiquitous enzyme, however, since neither methylglyoxal nor D-lactic acid was known to have any major biological function (except as a waste product).

Szent-Gyorgyi postulated an important biological role for methylglyoxal, and its various "cousins" which are called, as a class, the quinones. If we think of a chain of protein as a straight line, one finds a lysine (amino acid) side chain attached to it which "can be looked upon as a fishing rod, fishing for methylglyoxal." By some bending of the chain, which has been calculated, methylglyoxal can be brought into contact with the protein, enabling the two to enter into a charge transfer reaction, the giving and taking of electrons.

In many proteins, in fact, there is a lysine "fishing pole" at every eighth amino acid. This, said Szent-Gyorgyi, is the kernel of the mechanism proteins carry with them for their own desaturation (i.e., removal of electrons).

To support this theory, Szent-Gyorgyi performed the following experiment. If casein (the principal protein of cow's milk) is treated with methylglyoxal, it turns "the color of Swiss chocolate"—a color, Albert noted, very similar to that of liver. Albert always tried to remain sensitive to the colors, smells, and faint hints produced in his experiments. To him, this color was more than incidental. It was due to a more intimate complexing of the protein and the other chemical. "This makes it seem likely that the liver actually owes at least part of its color to its electronic desaturation by methylglyoxal," he concluded.

Gabor Fodor, a professor at the University of West Virginia in Morgantown (and a student from Szeged days) performed some experiments which in fact isolated and identified a methylglyoxal compound linked to the liver protein.[7]

One way of identifying free radicals is through an electron spin resonance, or e.s.r. machine. This device, which looks rather like an advanced washing machine, gives a signal when it spots uncoupled electrons. Different free radicals give distinctive signatures. Living materials in general give off e.s.r. signals. Why is that? According to Albert, these signals are actually due to the free radicals in the protein *structures,* and not entirely to some undefined free radicals in solution, as most scientists supposed. In some experiments, the structural proteins in liver gave off a much stronger signal than the soluble proteins—another support for Szent-Gyorgyi's theory that protein structures are veritable beehives of free radical activity.

FROM ALPHA TO BETA

The appearance of light was the cardinal event in the history of life on this planet. As we have stated, in the planet's first epoch, the entire globe was covered by a thick blanket of dark water vapor. There was no free oxygen and therefore no stable electron acceptors. Life, under these conditions, could only reach a very low degree of development, which has left practically no traces behind. The source of oxygen during this period was methylglyoxal, a poor acceptor compared to the free atmospheric oxygen we now enjoy. Proliferation in this period was everything, a mad scramble of simple life forms to survive on the earth's inhospitable surface.

All the energy of these primitive organisms had to go into this one task, constant reproduction. Very little, if any, went into keeping these cells together (cohesion) or into allowing specialized functions among the cells (differentiation). Cohesion and differentiation, hallmarks of life's evolution, were luxuries which such simple organisms could not afford. Szent-Gyorgyi called this first dark proliferative period the alpha period.

As the planet cooled and the dense water vapor fell as rain, light was able to reach the surface of the earth. What the primitive life forms did with this light was to use its energy for the separation of the elements of water, producing hydrogen and free oxygen. With an oxygen atmosphere, strong acceptors were literally in the air, and development and differentiation became possible. "The end result of which is us," said Albert.

This second, light, oxidative part of life's history he called the beta period. Proteins were able to give up their electrons (i.e., cars were taken out of the full parking lot), and they started to adhere to one another and organize. This in turn led to increasingly complex and subtle reactions between them. They stuck together; they specialized; they grew.

But cohesion and structure have a drawback: they interfere with proliferation. The result is that when a cell divides it still has to lower its cohesive forces and dismount part of its structure—something readily seen under the microscope in any beginning biology class. Szent-Gyorgyi identified this process as a partial return of the advanced cell to the alpha state, the ground state of life.

After the cell had completed its division, it had to build up its more complex beta state once again. In some cases, however, the cell, after completing its division, might find the way back to the beta state blocked. Here was a serious malfunction. The cell had no choice at this point but to persist in its proliferative alpha state and continue to divide, even when no division was called for. It was like a broken record, stuck in a groove.

And we know all too well where this winds up: in an oncologist's waiting room. A tumor, in fact, is an accumulation of thousands or millions of such proliferating cells, which have not found their way back to the beta state. It is in this sense that Szent-Gyorgyi's theory of life is also a theory of cancer.

The classic characteristics of cancer are the abnormality and primitiveness of its cells, its uncontrolled growth and lack of cohesion. The lack of cohesion can be seen in the tendency of cancer to metastasize, or break away from the primary tumor and spread to other parts of the body.[8]

The more complete the return to the primitive alpha state, the faster the proliferation and the lower the cohesive forces; such tumors are highly malignant. This may also explain, said Albert, why all types of very rapidly dividing cells resemble one another, be they embryonic, cancerous, or simply very rapidly dividing normal cells.

ASCORBIC ACID

Free oxygen, O_2, as we have said, is a strong electron acceptor. Its appearance opened the way to evolution. But once free oxygen had appeared, what happened to the old methylglyoxal machinery in the cell? Was it simply junked, like a molecular dinosaur? Albert's basic philosophy and intuition told him no. "If nature develops a new method, as a rule," he said, "she does not throw the old one out, but simply adds the new one to it, improving it." ("Natura nihil agit frustra," Sir Thomas Browne had written in the seventeenth century, "is the only indispensible Axiome in Philosophy.") Thus methylglyoxal could continue to play a biological role.

This would not be primarily to produce energy for the cell, however. We know how this is done, and Albert himself helped explain much of this question between 1925 and 1945. Activated oxygen is combined with a biologically active form of hydrogen called NADH, which is, in turn, derived from glucose. This energy is not used at once but is shaped into little packets of energy called ATP in specialized cell "power stations" called mitochondria. ATP fuels the necessary life functions of the cell and carbon dioxide is given off as a waste product of this "burning" process. This gas leaves the cell through its encasing membranes to be carried off in the blood.

But there is one function which received very little attention before Szent-Gyorgyi's latest work. That is the crucial *balance* between oxygen and hydrogen in the cell. Something has to regulate their combination, so that the cell does not have too much of one or the other. Such a malfunction could take place, for instance, in the course of cell division and lead to the cell's inability to get back from the primitive alpha state.

Szent-Gyorgyi called this "oxygen/hydrogen balancer" the cell's *protometabolism*. It is a kind of pacemaker of the cell, so important that it must have existed very early in evolution, even before nature developed the sophisticated energy-producing machinery of the mitochondria.

How does the protometabolism work? According to Peter Gascoyne, who helped Albert work out the details of this theory:

> This protometabolism takes some of the NADH produced from glucose and combines it with oxygen. This seems to be no different from what goes on in the mitochondria at first sight, but it differs because its function is to *balance* the active oxygen and NADH supplies in the cell rather than to provide chemical energy in the form of ATP.[9]

According to Szent-Gyorgyi, methylglyoxal is crucial to this protometabolism.

But oxygen cannot interact directly with methylglyoxal. In order for oxygen to be used as an acceptor for protein, a substance had to be found, a link by which oxygen could hitch up to methylglyoxal. This substance had to be able to link up with *both* substances and to have an electronic mobility by which it could transfer the acceptor strength of the free oxygen.

It so happens that such a substance exists: none other than ascorbic acid. Remember that he discovered this substance in the course of his studies of cellular metabolism. It was only later that it was found to have *anti-scurvy* activity, "and to be identical with the then unknown antiscorbutic component of fresh vegetables called 'vitamin C.'"

In a remarkably short time the chemical nature of ascorbic acid was cleared up and it became available in every corner drugstore. "But while we have learned everything worth knowing about its chemistry," he said, "its biological function remained unknown, preventing medicine from making full use of its remarkable activity."

Anti-scurvy may have been the acid's most visible, dramatic, and marketable property but its role was far more important than merely preventing a single disease. Ascorbic acid was—and is—the basic intermediary, the middle man of all advanced life on the planet.

"We can control only what we understand," Albert reiterated. "Even a simple question, such as the magnitude of the recommended daily dose, has remained unsettled, oscillating between megadoses and a few milligrams."

The development of ascorbic acid in past millennia was one of the landmarks of evolution, comparable in importance, he said, to the appearance of light and oxygen on the earth's surface. That ascorbic acid readily interacts with oxygen is apparent from e.s.r. experiments. And Gabor Fodor showed that it could interact with methylglyoxal as well.[10]

Thus, it was theoretically quite capable of playing the kind of role that Albert assigned it. Other studies showed that ascorbic acid did increase charge transfer in methylglyoxal-containing compounds, as measured by e.s.r. activity. Peter Gascoyne found that when the protein casein was treated with methylglyoxal in the presence of vitamin C a new signal appears, which seemed to indicate that ascorbate was actually "built into the charge transfer complex." This observation, Albert said, "may have far-reaching biological consequences and introduces new viewpoints into the medical use of the acid."

To sum up, "oxygen brings the life-giving light into the living system. Ascorbic acid catalyses this reaction. It is involved in bringing matter to life."

A THEORY OF CANCER

A cell, although microscopic, is a very complex little machine, in which all the reactions are neatly connected to one another. In normal cells, the reactions are coupled to one another in such a way that "activity improves activity." (We observe this phenomenon when our capacity for exercise increases *through* exercise.) On the other hand, things that inhibit normal interactions can cause further inhibition. We call that a "vicious circle."

If the desaturation of proteins is indeed necessary to life, then inadequate desaturation could inhibit further such desaturation. This can push the cell into such a circle, which the cell is unable to break, and lead it to a state of disorganization. A cell in trouble may try to divide and suddenly find itself stuck in the alpha state. If the situation is not corrected in time it may become an irreversible characteristic of the cell itself.

The public understandably wants—even demands—a cure for cancer, one of humanity's most dreaded diseases. But to the end of his life Szent-Gyorgyi held to the belief that in order to cure something we must understand it. Assuming his theory is on the right track, there is still not enough known about the various steps of this process to devise a cure. "The blindfold search for a cure for cancer," he said often, "seems a hopeless waste."

Until the time that our knowledge of submolecular biology allows for a really precise intervention in the cell, prevention is the best medicine. We should try to keep the machine in perfect working order.

In summing up his view of human health and disease Albert wrote: "More than sixty years of research on living systems have convinced me that our body is much more nearly perfect than the endless list of ailments suggests." Its shortcomings, he suggested, "are due less to its inborn imperfections than to our abusing it."

One factor which he felt deserved special attention in any preventive program was vitamin C. Research indicated that ascorbic acid was built into the very heart of life's machinery. Since we are constantly building and rebuilding this machinery all the time, Albert thought that a continuous supply of ascorbic acid was very important. But he was also averse to quick fixes. A machinery built without ascorbic acid cannot be corrected by suddenly administering megadoses. Correction of defects may take the better part of a year, he suggested.

He also believed that wheat germ was a very important dietary component. Characteristically, he had gotten the original suggestion for wheat germ's curative ability not from a scientific text but from a persuasive man he met on a cruise in the Caribbean. He himself took wheat germ rather religiously with his breakfast every morning and urged all his friends to do so. But there turned out to be a scientific basis for this belief, as well. The kernel of wheat, a 1952 report had shown, contained small amounts of two of methylglyoxal's close chemical cousins.[11]

Despite all the practical obstacles that cluttered his path, to the end of his career Albert maintained an optimistic faith in the ultimate wisdom of the human body to right itself. He believed that not only a cure for cancer, but the conquest of ill-health in general, was possible.

> The ideal of medicine is the curing of all diseases. The ideal should be full health, which leaves no room for any shortcomings. In the U.S.A. we are still losing the battle against cancer: every day there are nine hundred casualties. I strongly believe that cancer is accessible to a complete analysis on the basic level, and that understanding it means also the ability to control it.

Albert Szent-Gyorgyi believed in the human body. He believed, almost as an article of faith, that science could show us the way to almost complete health. In this he was still the same "dreamy idealist" a visitor to Szeged would have described fifty years before.

21

A NATURAL ENDING

In September 1983 relations between NFCR and Albert Szent-Gyorgyi still appeared harmonious. The Foundation even hosted a gala celebration in honor of Albert's ninetieth birthday at the Harvard Club in Boston. His old friend, Studs Terkel, was the eloquent and humorous keynote speaker. Albert was presented the Order of the Flag with Rubies of the Hungarian People's Republic by the Consul General, Miklos Kocziha. Ronald and Nancy Reagan sent congratulations. However, Albert had been quite ill just days before the ceremony and attended with great difficulty. He hated the whole idea of a formal ceremony honoring his birthday. But he was a relaxed and smiling guest of honor gussied up in an unaccustomed tuxedo but still wearing tennis shoes. (In addition, August 5 had been declared "Albert Szent-Gyorgyi Day" in Woods Hole and a day-long symposium had been organized on his behalf.)

In 1984 NFCR entered its second decade, celebrated in September with another ambitious program, a Washington, D.C. symposium highlighted by the premiere of the author's documentary film, *A Special Gift*.[1] This was the first time that many in the audience realized the full scope of Albert's life and accomplishments. The warm feeling surrounding this screening was compounded of nostalgia and hope. There was little indication then of the explosion to come.

In the course of the *Newsweek* litigation, however, major changes had overtaken the Foundation. The Salisburys realized that they would have to stand up in court and defend the basic respectability of their organization. As they got deeper into the preparation for the trial, the Salisburys sought to protect and defend their personal integrity. Mrs. Salisbury even attended the trial of William P. Tavoulareas vs. the *Washington Post* in the District of Columbia. But in

255

tackling *Newsweek* the Salisburys had a tiger by the tail. Although they themselves were the plaintiffs, they seemed to labor under a constant need to prove themselves innocent of Jane Bryan Quinn's accusations. Through NFCR activities abroad, the Salisburys now received various honors including the Belgian Order of Leopold II "for support of worldwide basic science research"; an honorary law degree for Frank from the University of Wales, presented by no less than his Royal Highness Prince Charles for "dedication to the support of cancer research"; an award from the University of Debrecen School of Medicine, Hungary, "to honor great services of outstanding persons in the cause of progress of medical science"; an award from the International Society of Quantum Biology for "outstanding contributions to the development of Quantum Biology"; and a Medal of Merit (given only five times in the past century) from the University of Turin, Italy.[2]

But the high point of all this activity was the day the Salisburys were included in an audience of cancer scientists given by Pope John Paul II. Frank received a special citation for the promotion of an interdisciplinary approach to cancer research.

These awards, and the pictures accompanying them, became part of NFCR's public relations armamentarium. More substantial were the basic revisions in the administrative structure of the Foundation. The "old" NFCR had been rather nonchalant and unconventional in its structure. This reflected Albert's unique, individualistic approach to research.

In the beginning, the choice of scientists to be funded was largely in the hands of Albert, with Tamara Salisbury providing the actual day-by-day decision making. Tamara did a very competent job at this, but she was not a scientist and could command little scientific authority among researchers. Albert, on the other hand, had little idea how times had changed. The "younger scientists" he chose for the Foundation were in fact almost all middle-aged European men, few of them working in the latest fields.

In the early 1980s, after many complaints, two review committees were set up to oversee grant applications. The composition of these committees was kept secret, in order to avoid outside influence on their choices, although it was generally known that one was headed by a distinguished Johns Hopkins professor. Shortly afterwards, Charles C. Pixley, M.D., a former Surgeon General of the U.S. Army, was brought in as vice president for scientific administration of NFCR. Pixley is a patient, gentle, and experienced man. By training and temperament, however, he is a pragmatist who was uncomfortable with Albert's unconventional flights of fancy.

The tenor of NFCR quickly changed. The new people who received NFCR contracts were almost uniformly young, aggressive, and bright. Except for the presence of Albert and his dwindling "old guard," an NFCR conference was soon indistinguishable from similar gatherings of scientists at the National Cancer Institute or the American Cancer Society. In fact, almost all these scientists were also affiliated in some way with "the cancer establishment." NFCR, which had begun as a maverick attempt to do things differently, was in danger of becoming just another source of funding for hungry scientists.

Albert and his unusual ideas were tolerated by these aggressive young scientists, but sometimes just barely. For some, he had become little more than a front for their own fund-raising needs. The topics they dealt with were, as the publicity brochures proclaimed, "on the cutting edge" of basic science. They were virologists, immunologists, molecular biologists. Very up-to-date and respectable, in other words. But the more respectable they became, the further NFCR seemed to drift from Frank and Albert's original vision.

After one such seminar, Albert was asked if he thought the meeting was going well. "Too well," he commented, with a touch of bitterness. Things had become smooth and polite. No one would argue with him, out of deference to his age, or because they did not want to rock the boat. In such a struggle-free atmosphere, he seemed to be saying, one could not create anything really original and new.

One might think that this sudden turn towards credibility would increase NFCR's fund-raising appeal. Quite the opposite. For reasons difficult to fathom, the more conventional NFCR became, the less money it seemed to take in. After reaching $15 million or so in 1983, yearly donations began to fall, precipitating a crisis within the organization. When its original fund-raiser, John Swain, died of cancer in 1985, the Foundation hired the sophisticated "database marketing company," Epsilon, to handle its direct mail solicitations. Yet the decline continued and no one knew exactly why. (It has since begun to stabilize.)

One theory was that there was more competition than there was in 1974 and the public had become jaded by too many strident appeals from too many causes. If people remembered NFCR at all it was for *Newsweek's* "modern Fagin" charge. Or perhaps NFCR was by nature a fringe organization, appealing to the small percent of donors who were discontented with the establishment and liked the idea of a feisty, unorthodox "St. George" engaging in single combat with the cancer dragon.

Along with what might be called this "crisis of acceptability" came some across-the-board demotion of the NFCR "old guard." Some had their funding cut, others were encouraged to build their own satellite organizations, others were simply dropped. Tensions were highest at the September 1984 Annual Meeting when arguing broke into the open at a plenary session in the Marine Biological Laboratory's Swope Hall. At that moment NFCR seemed to be two foundations. The first was the efficient, new, modern NFCR, carving a little niche for itself in the research establishment. But there was also the original NFCR, made up of Albert and his friends, centered around his Hungarian colleagues and the Woods Hole group. And this faction had their one staunch supporter in Bethesda—Frank Salisbury.

The goal of the newly-arisen faction was modest and reasonable: to raise money to fund established scientists in many areas of cancer research. The goal of Albert's group remained grandiose and romantic, in fact positively Dionysian: nothing less than the conquest of cancer based on the most advanced concepts of electronic biology.

The one substantial practical upshot of Albert's work had been the formulation of two chemical substances, Nafocare A and B (named for the National Foundation for Cancer Research), which helped to stimulate the body's immune system. In 1986 NFCR received Patent No. 4,620,014 for these compounds.[3]

Frank Salisbury was pushing for a clinical test of the effect of these compounds on cancer. Fired up by Albert's claims, Frank truly seemed to believe that the cure for cancer was at hand. He even helped set up a spin-off company, the American Biotechnology Company (ABC), of Rockville, Maryland, headed by Robert Veltri, Ph.D., an NFCR researcher, to test these compounds in the laboratory. Frank and Albert also began to contact prominent Mexican doctors to do experiments on dogs. Albert himself even flew to Mexico in the summer of 1984 to pursue these contacts. He tried to encourage the Mexicans to perform these tests immediately on patients. It was a move, he said, necessitated by the slowness of the U.S. Food and Drug Administration (FDA) in approving clinical trials of new drugs. For many, however, it raised disturbing memories of such drugs as Krebiozen or laetrile, the favorite unconventional cancer treatments of prior decades.[4]

"From the standpoint of theory the Professor was right," Veltri concluded. "In the test tube the mixture of quinones and ascorbic acid was very active. In the reduction to practice, however, there were problems."[5] By 1985 Veltri's tests had shown only limited activity in animal models for Albert's compounds. (Albert's own tests had shown more definite results, but these were now reinterpreted as poorly constructed.) Since Albert was really interested in *basic* scientific concepts, Veltri's animal results were not devastating to "Prof's" scientific supporters. They hardly expected him to come up with a cancer treatment on demand. In fact, such all-or-nothing tests seemed premature by years.

Frank Salisbury did not see it that way. His expectations had been unreasonably raised, and now he was just as unreasonably disappointed by the failure. It was not just Albert's failure, but his own, and there were those close to him who were not adverse to pointing this out. Frank had spent over ten years of his own life on this quest and it had all seemingly come to naught.

At the same time, Prof's health was declining. This sad change was visible from meeting to meeting. As the decade began he was a vigorous eighty-seven-year-old, still ocean swimming, riding his motorbike, telling anecdotes, and trading witticisms. Even as late as the winter of 1984, he, Marcia, and the Gascoynes hired a boat and crew in the Caribbean and went sailing together for two weeks. Peter recalled how "Prof," unattended, lifted himself from the water into the dinghy—something Peter himself, fifty years younger, found difficult to do. "Prof" also responded vigorously to challenge. When a senior member of the Foundation had the temerity to question his ability to lead, it was this fellow—not Albert—who was squeezed out of the leadership. He was like an aging, but unvanquished, lion.

By 1985, however, old age was finally overtaking a man who had sometimes seemed immune from its effects. When he was lucid he was very lucid—his charming, funny, and powerful self. But his afternoon naps became longer, and his bouts of illness (with the debilitating side-effects of medication) more frequent. At times he seemed to be withdrawing into a pleasant twilight world, in which the most he could do was sit and smile.

He was also prone to sudden fits of anger and ill-humor. He agreed to receive a medal from the Hungarian government at the time of the fortieth anniversary of Hungary's liberation from fascism. He was aware that some Hungarians regarded this anniversary with chagrin, because it marked the entry of Soviet troops onto native soil. Albert agreed to accept this award from the Hungarians as a gesture of friendship to Hungary, although he himself was uneasy about the political implications. He therefore did not want any publicity in the United States in connection with this presentation.

Frank Salisbury flew up to Woods Hole at this time to ask a favor of Szent-Gyorgyi. He wanted "Prof" to nominate a scientific acquaintance of theirs for a Nobel Prize. Albert chafed at this request, however, which he considered highly inappropriate. "He was terribly disagreeable about it," said Frank. "Far beyond what was required." Neither of them saw any reason for him to stay for the presentation. Frank left two of his aides at the meeting with the Hungarians and went home to Bethesda, upset at the undignified way he had been treated. To Albert, it seemed that Frank was asking him to trade the prestige of his own Prize to promote someone he considered unworthy of a Nobel.

Ironically, it was primarily Frank Salisbury who was protecting Albert from his detractors both inside and outside the Foundation. "Frank was the only person who was defending 'Prof' from the rigmarole," Peter Gascoyne later said.

There followed a series of angry exchanges with hasty reconciliations. In the summer of 1985, the Foundation sent Albert a contract to sign. This was supposed to be a formalization of his previous mainly verbal agreements, differing only in the manner in which he would receive his funds. Albert, quite uncharacteristically, asked his wife Marcia to take this contract to their lawyer. According to this counsellor the new contract would have resulted in a net loss of $17,000 a year in income.

As the September 1985 annual meeting loomed, "Prof" suddenly decided that he would communicate with Frank Salisbury only through this attorney. Frank says he was happy at this rather unexpected move. "I can get along with lawyers very well," Frank quipped. "I am one myself." In addition, communicating with Albert had become very difficult because of his progressive deafness.

At the annual meeting itself, Albert began to complain that he was not being paid enough. "He kicked up a big stink about not getting enough money," said Gascoyne. He even went to the other Nobel laureates in the Foundation with tales about how he was practically starving. In thus exaggerating his condition, he accomplished the almost impossible task of upsetting some of his own staunchest Woods Hole colleagues.

Every year the high point of the Annual Meeting had been the lobster dinner, held in a big tent on the grounds of the Szent-Gyorgyi's house at Penzance Point. In the heyday of the Foundation these had been happy and festive occasions, providing a well-deserved break from the hard work of around-the-clock seminars. In 1985, however, the Szent-Gyorgyis refused to hold the party at their house and then, when it was rescheduled for a room in MBL's Swope Hall, even refused to attend.

Two senior NFCR scientists were dispatched to "Seven Winds" and finally managed to persuade the Szent-Gyorgyis to come, but only on the condition that Frank would make a speech reaffirming the Foundation's support of Albert and his work. Frank did so and when he finished there was much resounding, purposeful applause. Dr. Charles

Pixley remembers Frank handing Albert a copy of this speech. Albert, however, denied having received it. This left tensions as high as ever.

On 18 October 1985, Frank Salisbury called Peter Gascoyne at Woods Hole. The reason for the call, he says, was that communicating with "Prof" by phone had become nearly impossible. What ensued is a matter of acrimonious debate. According to Frank, he merely discussed in a general way the fate of the laboratory during "Prof's" declining years. He regarded Peter as a convenient messenger.

Peter Gascoyne has much more specific recollections, backed up by copious telephone notes taken on this occasion. The time had come to cut back on the size of the Woods Hole laboratory, he recalled Frank saying. "Prof" should have his own little lab, which the Foundation would help set up in his seaside cottage. This might be done for a cost of about $100,000 a year.

According to Peter, Frank told him to start looking for another position and to take the equipment in the laboratory, but not to tell Albert he was doing so. "How can I do that?," Peter says he asked. "What about my loyalty to 'Prof'?"

At this point, he says, Frank told him he had no loyalty to "Prof," but only to NFCR, which paid his salary. The conversation was "bitter," said Gascoyne, "though still well-controlled."

Ironically, although Peter had been wanting to move for some time, he now decided that he *had* to stay to see the struggle through to the end. He had no intention of quitting or taking the equipment without telling "Prof." In fact, his next move was precisely to give Szent-Gyorgyi his interpretation of the phone call.

Soon after this, an article appeared in *The Cape Cod Times,* the local newspaper, that quoted "Prof" as saying that he might soon be leaving his laboratory at MBL. He claimed that NFCR was planning to cut his funding from $300,000 to $100,000 for the coming year. The Foundation, he said, had used him and was now throwing him away.

"Maybe they (the Foundation directors) think I am too old, or no longer of use to them," he complained. "But they have used my name to go before the public to raise a lot of money for my research."[6]

Since the rent alone at MBL was $116,000 a year, this move would force him out of the laboratory, unless MBL itself would be willing to pick up part of the expenses—which they were unwilling to do.

Officials of the Foundation promptly denied that they had ever made such threats, and claimed that Peter Gascoyne had, at best, misunderstood and misinterpreted them. Since Albert's lawyer had complained that the Foundation was using Albert's name to raise money, they revised the history of NFCR. According to a "Brief

History of NFCR" issued at this time, "Frank C. Salisbury . . . recognized that . . . a number of potentially very promising cancer research projects were essentially dormant for lack of recognition and adequate funding." He was aided in this by his wife Tamara and "by a distinguished group of concerned citizens. . . ." It went on like this for six pages, essentially accurate except for one detail: there was no mention of Albert Szent-Gyorgyi!

In vitriolic terms, Albert now expanded on his feelings about NFCR and the Salisburys:

> I faced Hitler. I was expecting to be hanged for years. Then, before Stalin, I expected to go to jail. I am not excited about these little fellows. . . . I am after knowledge and understanding. They are after power and dollars.[7]

"I still have to fight for my very existence with my ten nails," he wrote his grandson David that November.[8] He was terribly riled up by the controversy and yet it momentarily seemed to revitalize him as well.

Frank, in turn, privately suggested that Albert was an inveterate turncoat who had betrayed first the Hungarian army, then the fascists, then the Stalinists, then the U.S. government, and finally the National Foundation for Cancer Research!

Things had reached such a pass that no reconciliation seemed possible. It was hard to believe that these were the same two men who had fallen in "love at first sight" at the inception of their foundation almost fifteen years before. But the one thing Frank could not stand was a challenge to his good name. That was essentially why he had sued *Newsweek*.

Albert, on the other hand, was following his own categorical imperative, to continue to do basic science to the best of his ability. Proud and unyielding, each felt backed into a corner, and seized whatever weapons came to hand. In private, each blamed the other, and especially the other's wife, for starting the whole business. It was not a pretty sight.

In December 1985 Albert presented the Foundation with an ultimatum. Either they would provide him with a written contract for $500,000 a year or he would quit the group and start a new foundation of his own, an "Albert Szent-Gyorgyi Foundation" which would compete directly with NFCR in its fund-raising efforts. His point was to create something that would perpetuate his bioelectronic approach to cancer.

He insisted that the contract run for ten years, to carry him through his one hundred and second year. After such time, he added, the contract could be renegotiated. This sum was to be paid to his estate even if he died. (According to Peter Gascoyne, "Prof" partially suggested this odd provision in order to guarantee his young associate a more secure situation.)[9]

The Foundation insisted that if it were going to commit millions of dollars to the establishment and maintenance of his laboratory, he would have to submit to "peer review" of his work by outside panels:

> The only means by which the officers and directors of NFCR can discharge their fiduciary duty and fulfill their legal and moral obligations regarding the commitment of public funds to this start-up venture is to first evaluate the scientific worth of Dr. Szent-Gyorgyi's proposed research.
> . . . the names of the peer review committee members may not be released. Please be assured, however, that membership will be comprised of world-renowned scientists representing all the scientific disciplines.

The relationship between Albert and the Foundation was now in the hands of the lawyers. The important thing, according to his old friend Prof. Benjamin Kaminer, was that "at the end of his life he had disengaged himself from the Foundation and become once again a "free man." A deadline of 1 June 1986 was set for Albert to complete his proposal forms. Needless to say, Albert Szent-Gyorgyi was not about to start submitting to "peer review," which he considered a humiliating waste of time. He had helped start the Foundation precisely to avoid such paper shuffling. The Foundation countered by informing Albert that his laboratory at Woods Hole would be closed as of 30 September 1986. He himself would be given a retirement stipend. In addition, they would help Peter Gascoyne reestablish himself at some other research institution.

In December 1985, NFCR agreed to drop the *Newsweek* suit. In exchange, the magazine published a letter from the Foundation, explaining the important work it was doing. In addition, in one slim paragraph *Newsweek* apologized for its original article, which it claimed had been misinterpreted. For NFCR, after four years of debilitating struggle, this was the slenderest of pyrrhic victories. By coincidence, it seems, this settlement cut off what could have become Albert's most effective forum for airing his grievances. He certainly could have been one devastating witness for the defense.

As their deadline approached, Albert and his small group of Woods Hole supporters set up their "Albert Szent-Gyorgyi Foundation." They sent out letters to corporate donors, asking them to contribute to the work of the 93-year-old scientist. Albert was optimistic that he would soon be able to function free of Frank and Tamara Salisbury. But there were few takers. Jane McLaughlin, tenaciously loyal to the end, fought to maintain the old laboratory at Woods Hole as it was. Peter was less sanguine. In his early thirties, he had spent ten years in service to "Prof." He now decided to take a job as a visiting scientist at Houston's prestigious M. D. Anderson Cancer Center. NFCR provided $50,000 and transferred equipment from the Woods Hole laboratory for that purpose.

"We still do not have the cure for cancer," Albert wrote his grandson David, "but I am having two substances in synthesis which give me very much hope. It is slow work," he added, "but the hope is alive. I very much hope to solve the cancer problem before the test tube drops out of my hand."

Until April, in fact, he was confident that something would turn up, that the *deus ex machina* would drop down to rescue him as Hopkins had rescued him in Stockholm in 1929, Armour in 1950, and Frank himself in 1972. But this time there was to be no miracle.

In June 1986 Albert became critically ill. For several years he had been suffering from a leukemia-like blood disease, as well as occasional bouts of astronomically high blood pressure. These were kept under control by medication and (he believed) judicious amounts of wheat germ and vitamin C. But he suddenly suffered an attack of kidney disease and what was diagnosed as coungestive heart disease. He called his closest friends and coworkers around him to say goodbye.

Even his grandson David came to visit him in the hospital, where Albert had been taken for a kidney operation. Albert embraced him and tried to convince him, and himself, that the acrimonious family differences had been reconciled and forgiven. Csilla Felker came to visit him as well. Because of his age, he told her, the doctors were afraid to give him the normal dose of anesthetic and he was suffering horrible pain. He complained (in voluble Hungarian) that they were torturing him.

Csilla had brought along her one-year-old child for Albert to see. This lifted him out of his doldrums and he enthused over the baby and the promise it represented. "Look at the future!" he cried, happily. "What a terrible bundle of energy. Such a beautiful little baby. It's like a budding plant that will blossom into a tree." It was, she said, like a spontaneous prose poem, another *Psalmus Humanus,* deeply felt and movingly spoken.

Albert was peaceful and ready to die, but "Marcia and Jane didn't want him to," said Peter, "and so he came back." Although this sounds mystical, Albert's will to live was indeed formidable. Discharged from the hospital, he stayed home that summer, not even attempting to make the short trip to the laboratory. His willingness to make the trip to the lab had always been the critical barometer of his mental as well as physical health. At times he would just sit quietly, while at other moments he was his lucid old self.

Peter Gascoyne went to see him. "Prof" took his hands and stared at him with his bright blue eyes. "We've walked a long way together, a long journey," "Prof" said, thoughtfully. "There's still much to be done. But now it's time for you to journey on alone."

Tears came to Peter's eyes. Albert Szent-Gyorgyi was more than just his lab supervisor. He was his friend, his mentor, and above all his spiritual guide. "If there's anybody on this planet I would trust and lay down my life for," Peter had said defiantly to Frank Salisbury, "It is Albert Szent-Gyorgyi."

"He taught me that it is okay to be original and peaceful about what you do," Peter later reflected. Albert may have had his weaknesses, he added, but after all was said and done, he was an absolutely unique individual, one of the great ones of the earth.

"I'm ready to go on alone, 'Prof,' " Peter finally replied, "As long as you'll remain beside me in spirit."

"Prof" smiled. It was, as Peter said, a "natural ending."

For Albert, however, the end may not have been so natural. The issue for him was simple—not years, but work. All his life he had lived for research, and once past ninety, science became his sustenance. "I either work every day," he told a reporter, "or I die. There is no in-between."

At the June bedside scene he had turned to his granddaughter Lesley and said, "You know my body means nothing. This" (he swept his hand over his body) "can all go, but if I can't work then I can't live. I must always think."[10]

On 1 October however, the doors to Albert's laboratory on the third floor of MBL, where he had worked for nearly forty years, were closed for good. Jane McLaughlin, without a job, tried to occupy herself writing up the results of their latest experiments. Ron Pethig returned to his home base in Wales. Peter Gascoyne sold his house on Cape Cod and moved to Houston. On Tuesday, 21 October, "Prof" went into a coma, and on 22 October 1986, at around 11:30 AM, Albert Szent-Gyorgyi died of kidney failure at his home in Woods Hole. He was ninety-three years old.

"It used to be said in my home town, that the cheapest funeral you could get consisted of taking a candle in your hand and going out, yourself, to the churchyard," he once joked. His own funeral, at his request, was almost that simple. There was no church or memorial services, just a simple graveside ceremony attended by about forty people. He was already buried by the time the story broke on the wire services and in the *New York Times*.

For seventy-five years he had worked at science every day. His first paper had been published in 1913; his last was in preparation at the time of his death. But as he had warned, he could not live without his work and only survived the closing of his laboratory by three weeks.

Eulogizing its most famous full-time scientist, Richard Whitaker, the Interim Director of the Marine Biological Laboratory said, "He was one of the giants of twentieth century science. He made the rest of us look like pygmies."[11] Yet Whitaker was a man of another generation, who hardly knew Albert.

Many old colleagues, including those associated with the National Foundation for Cancer Research, were kept ignorant of his death. The Pollitt family was never formally informed by Marcia but learned of it second-hand. Geoffrey, Michael and Lesley attended the funeral. So did Peter Gascoyne and his wife, Lynn. But David Pollitt did not.

"I was so entirely heartbroken," he later said, "by the terrible family tragedy that I could not be a part of the last ignoble act on Marcia's part—the charade of grief. Did truth ever have a place in this scenario for ten years? It was with immense pain that I stayed away."[12]

In the background (only distantly so, as far as David was concerned) was the question of the estate. In his original will, Albert had left his property (including "Seven Winds") to his grandchildren and his closest associates. He had specifically promised the lovely cottage to the children at Little Nelly's funeral. But with his new marital situation, all that changed. Marcia and her daughter (whom he had adopted) were made principal beneficiaries of his estate.

This decision seemed to occasionally cause him mental grief. "Nothing would give me more pleasure than to help you out," he wrote David, who was struggling to earn a living as a classical musician. "I have worked very hard all my life and hoped that at the end I will be in good material condition and support my grandchildren. This hope did not come true, I am just as poor as ever before."[13]

Toward the end, relations between David and Marcia deteriorated even further. When Albert became critically ill, David said:

> During the few hospital visits, we were never allowed even a moment together alone. Marcia was always present. In addition, communication was very difficult as Marcia did not allow any phones in Grandfather's

room and to insure, in my opinion, no familial influence she took a room close to his in the Massachusetts General Hospital.

Grandfather had an impeccable record as to promptly answering all correspondence. However, it became apparent that not all letters from me ever got there and I had to resort to getting him hand deliveries from a member of his laboratory.[14]

Despite these problems, the family's relationship with Albert managed to survive, albeit in a truncated form. "At no time were we, either as a family or individually, ever estranged from Albert," said Geoffrey. "We were always on the best of terms and in spite of the difficulties I never felt inhibited in my contacts with him."[15]

Albert was particularly attached to David and watched his progress as a musician with great joy. "I wish I could come to your concert and hear the music you produce," he wrote at the age of 92. He signed his last letter, "With the warmest regards and love, your grandfather."[16]

Yet when the will was opened, there was a shock. For not only were the grandchildren not given a share of the house or cottage, but Albert specifically and deliberately excluded them by name from any part of the estate. Almost everything had already been put in trust for Marcia and her daughter. This caused consternation within the family. Disagreements over how to regard this marriage had caused some serious rifts among the Pollitts and their friends over the years, with David taking an increasingly uncompromising line. "The truth hit them in the face in no uncertain terms" after Albert's death, he reflected.[17]

Csilla Felker was among those who had been closest to "Prof" for many years. She attended the funeral service. Looking around she saw hardly anyone she knew. Where, Csilla wondered, were the dozens, even hundreds of people whom Albert had helped along the way, including the many Hungarians like herself who had been given a new life in America through his intervention? "It was like Mozart, in a way," she mused—a hasty burial in an obscure grave.

No one who visited Albert's laboratory on the third floor of MBL could ever forget it. It was a unique place, with solid marble work tables, and high shelves filled with every kind of chemical and glassware. Beyond the tall windows seagulls cruised and there was the smell of ocean, the sound of buoys and the low horn of the Martha's Vineyard ferry. There were sinks and Bunsen burners and various heavy rubber gloves used for God-knows-what purpose and still bearing the imprint of Albert's hands. In the corner were cages for a few dozen white mice. And off to one side was Albert's desk, actually two tables shoved together and piled precariously high with stacks of scientific books, papers and onionskin letters from scholars all over the world. There was Albert's daybook, which recorded every experiment with surprising care and, on the daybook, the glasses that he occasionally wore.

Csilla had worked in this lab, on and off, for ten years. She decided to revisit, thinking perhaps to find in it somehow a reminder of the greatest mind she had ever known. She climbed the echoing stairs, more like those of an old high school than a modern laboratory. At the head of the stairwell was the familiar heavy wooden door. She opened it now, just to have one last look at that place that had fit Albert like one of his well-worn work gloves. But there was nothing there. Nothing. Everything was gone: the bottles, the test tubes, the documents. The room had been swept clean. In fact, there was no sign that Albert Szent-Gyorgyi had ever been there. It was ready for its next tenant. "He had become like a shadow," Csilla said.[18]

And this is probably how Albert would have wanted it. Artists are memorialized by their work. We can say that something of Mozart's personality survives, nearly two hundred years after his death. But a scientist's immortality comes about through a largely anonymous contribution to human knowledge and well-being. The more fundamental the discovery, it sometimes seems, the more anonymous the gift.

If something of Albert Szent-Gyorgyi is remembered it will probably be his intuitive, artistic approach to science. He came to research with the same sort of excitement and verve that ordinary people derive from sports, good food or sex. It turned him on. The pleasure of science far outstripped the other activities of life. Albert combined this verve with an extraordinary intuitive sense. He had excellent hunches. Of course, many of these turned out to be wrong, but he never lost faith in his own ability as an "intellectual dowser." His major discoveries were all made in this way. He had an ability "to see what everyone has seen and think what no one has thought."

Albert's life, to the very end, was driven by the same dichotomies that were present in his earliest days. He was both artist and scientist, rationalist and intuitive genius. His personal relations were equally divided, by the need for warm human contact and the overriding drive to do his research.

As a scientist, he delved into the most minute dimensions of the physical universe, trying to trace life back to the crevices of the molecule. Yet at times he seemed like a pensive child wanting to know what made the grass grow. "The grass and the mower are the same," he concluded.

He was so ambitious that he always placed his life goal just beyond his grasp. He was lauded for his achievements as if they were discreet discoveries. Yet what he was always after was a comprehensive theory of life itself. And this seemed to elude him.

Above all, there was his joy in scientific discovery. At the ecstatic moment of creation utter selflessness and utter selfishness came together to make something wonderful and new. At the moment of discovery, perfection of the life and of the work were one, only to dissolve a moment later into life's typical discord. Or to quote Yeats again, "Genius is a crisis that joins the buried self for certain moments to the daily mind." Albert Szent-Gyorgyi had those moments. They illuminated his life and he lived for them.

Towards the end of his life "Prof" was asked by the author for his credo. He grabbed a piece of paper and scrawled these lines. "Think boldly," he wrote, quite boldly, "Don't be afraid of making mistakes"—here he made an egregious spelling mistake, which he crossed out boldly, and started again—"Don't miss small details, keep your eyes open and be modest in everything except your aims."

NOTES

PREFACE

1. Jeremy Bernstein, "A Portrait of Alan Turing," *The New Yorker,* January 20, 1986.

CHAPTER 1

A CRAVING TO KNOW

1. Budapest was originally two cities, suburban Buda and commercial Pest, brought together by the Chain Bridge and formally merged in 1872. The Szent-Gyorgyis always lived in the busy and glamorous downtown part of Pest. Lenhossek's apartment was in Buda, near what is now the Gellert Hotel. Even today the two parts of the city retain their separate character.

2. The classic description of the agricultural life is G. Illyes' fascinating *People of the Puszta,* (trans. G. F. Cushing, Budapest: Corvina, 1967) a combination exposé/memoir originally written in the 1930s.

3. Albert's father actually had a law degree from Budapest. He never practiced this profession and it meant little. Some sort of college degree was obligatory for members of "good society."

4. "Zur Anatomie und Histologie des Teguments der Analoffnung und des Rectum," *Anatomische Hefte* 49: 305–335 (1913).

CHAPTER 2

RISKY BUSINESS

1. Lenhossek's laboratory was at 93 Ulloi Avenue, on the far eastern side of the city. It is still the pathology department of the University, now headed by a former student of Albert Szent-Gyorgyi, Prof. Tibor Donat.

2. Andrew Szent-Gyorgyi, Albert's younger cousin, now a professor at Brandeis University, recalled a similar laxity when he was a medical student in Budapest during World War II.

3. In the 1970s, according to Albert's colleague, Jane McLaughlin, an American professor wrote to say that the illustrations in these early articles were still the best that had been done on hyaloidal bodies.

4. This was on Esterhazy (now Pushkin) Street, in the rear of the University complex. It was to be an important focus of Albert's career, especially in the period after World War II.

5. Emphasis added. Cited in *Source Book of Medical History*, ed. Clendening (New York: Dover, 1942), pp. 601–602.

6. In the meantime this combination of experimental data with sweeping generalizations went out of fashion, replaced (in the Anglo-American world, at least) by a strict empiricism. The fact that Albert persisted in combining facts with large-scale theories gave much of his own writing a "foreign" ring. Some people saw it as old-fashioned; others as peculiarly Hungarian, or Eastern European; others as possibly influenced by Marxist theory. For a criticism of Albert's too-theoretical approach to biology, see *Science*, 9 February 1979.

In fact, Albert was not directly influenced by Marx or Marxism. It is doubtful he ever read much political theory. But both Claude Bernard and Karl Marx had common roots in the optimistic materialism of the nineteenth century. Some of Bernard's ideas do, in fact, verge on "dialectical materialism." It seems significant that the publisher of one of the few recent English monographs on Bernard's philosophy is the American Institute for Marxist Studies.

"In the writings and scientific thought of Claude Bernard," this pamphlet states, "it is remarkably difficult to separate the experimental from the speculative. Reflection and observation alternate continually, in such mutual support that none of the observations can be classed as purely empirical, nor, in regard to his systemization of knowledge, as purely rational, in the sense of being entirely constituted from abstract thinking," Ernest Kahane, *The Thought of Claude Bernard* (New York: A.I.M.S., 1966). The same might be said about Albert as well.

7. Liddell Hart in "World War I," *Encyclopedia Brittanica*, 14th ed. (Chicago, 1964).

8. A "Privatdocent" is a professional who also teaches part-time at the University. It is not clear whether or not this particular "Privatdocent" was a medical doctor. At times Albert described him as a lawyer, although how and why a lawyer would seek a reputation as a scientist is confusing.

9. Within the family, the mother was called "Big Nelly" and the daughter "Little Nelly." The daughter's name on her birth certificate was Kornelia spelled with a "K" and she initialled documents this way. The mother spelled her name Cornelia with a "C."

10. Liddell Hart, "World War I." Compare this to the United States, which mobilized far fewer men and suffered only eight percent total casualties.

CHAPTER 3

1919

1. He was 53 years old. The cause of death was officially given as "paralysis of the spine."

2. The trusting (some would say naive) Count approached the victorious Allies and asked for talks to settle postwar problems in a rational way. The Allied commander in Belgrade demanded that Hungarian troops first evacuate southern Hun-

gary and most of Transylvania. Then, he said, they could talk. To show his goodwill, Karolyi complied with this rather drastic request. The Allies took this as a sign of weakness. Immediately, Serbian troops occupied the southern part of Hungary, Romanians the east, and soldiers from the newly-proclaimed republic of Czechoslovakia the north. The Hungarian army had been shattered, and Karolyi could do nothing to stop the invaders. The Allies now demanded even further concessions at every point of the compass.

3. There were serious questions at this juncture whether Hungary would even survive as a nation. No one knew what to do, but one group that seemed to have some answers was the Communists. About 100,000 Hungarians had been taken prisoner in Russia and amid the ferment of the Soviet revolution, some of these had become Communists. A Hungarian Group of the Russian Communist Party had been formed at the Hotel Drezden in Moscow on 28 March 1918. Kun was the leader of this group.

4. See Miklos Horthy, *Memoirs* (New York: R. Speller, 1957).

5. The Jews were "demoralized and fearful, not only for the safety of their assets, but also of their lives and limbs." Andrew C. Janos, *The Politics of Backwardness, Hungary 1825–1945*, (Princeton: Princeton University Press, 1982), p. 222.

6. There are still bitter feelings towards Albert among his Hungarian relatives because when Imre came to the United States in the 1950s, Albert refused to receive him. Imre eventually settled in New Hyde Park, New York, became a photographer, and died in the early 1970s. His name is sometimes given as Laszlo or Ladislaw. Albert never showed the least interest in his fate. He had slightly more interest in Pal, and always spoke of his achievements as a musician with pride. He attempted to help Pal emigrate in 1956. Pal left Hungary in the exodus of that year, but settled in West Germany, where he died in the 1960s.

7. Szent-Gyorgyi expressed the same sentiment twenty years later in a letter to Sir Edward Mellanby: "I am plenty nervous when I have to touch an animal, which is much too complicated [a] system for me. A human patient is still much more complicated. The most complex system I know is that consisting of a patient plus a clinician." Medical Research Council (MRC) records, 5 July 1937. This helps explain Szent-Gyorgyi's lifelong aversion to clinical medicine.

8. G. Mansfeld and Albert Szent-Gyorgyi, "Untersuchen uber die Ursche des Herzschlages, "*Pfluger's Archiv fur die gesamte Physiologie des Menschen und der Tiere,* 184; 236–264. Also, Albert Szent-Gyorgyi, "Uber Herzmuskeltonus," *Ibid.,* pp. 266–271.

9. In June 1920 Hungary was forced to sign the treaty of Trianon which left it with about one-third of its prewar area and population. In addition to the ancient coronation city of Pozsony, Hungary also lost control of Transylvania. Three million ethnic Magyars were soon trapped behind foreign borders.

Of the original prewar area of 109,000 square miles the victorious allies left Hungary only 35,000. The prewar population of 20,866,477 was reduced to 7,615,117. It was an almost unprecedented reversal in fortunes for a modern nation. Horthy's popularity was largely based on his pledge to return Hungary to its prewar greatness. His slogan was "No, no, never!" Prof. Bruno Straub recalled starting his school day in the 1930s with the credo, "I believe in one God, one country and the resurrection of Hungary." The seeds of World War II were being planted.

10. The Coris came to the United States in 1922 and became U.S. citizens in 1928. They won the Nobel Prize for their research into the isolation and synthesis of phosphorylase, an enzyme that begins the process of converting glycogen into sugar. Gerty died in 1957, Carl on 22 October 1984, at the age of 87. There is no mention in the standard reference works of Carl Cori having ever studied in Pozsony. He graduated from the German University of Prague in 1920 and was married in the same year. Either these references are incomplete or Szent-Gyorgyi was mistaken in believing that he knew Cori in both Pozsony *and* Prague.

11. See Francis S. Wagner, *Hungarian Contributions to World Civilization* (Center Square, Pa.: Alpha, 1977). Most of the Hungarian Nobel Prize winners were abroad when they won the prize.

CHAPTER 4

DIGGING THE FOUNDATIONS

1. The Tschermaks, like the Lenhosseks, formed a great Central European scientific dynasty. Armin's grandfather was a botanist, his father a famous minerologist. His younger brother, Erich, went down in history as one of the rediscoverers of Mendel's laws of heredity.

2. *Dictionary of Scientific Biography.* This law applied particularly to enzymes and the rate of their activity in the human body. Michaelis "did not care what an enzyme was as long as he could understand how it worked." Isaac Asimov, *Asimov's Biographical Encyclopedia of Science and Technology* (N.Y.: Doubleday, 1964), p. 654. He spent the last summer of his life, in 1949, as Albert's house guest. Even so, "no special intimacy developed."

3. See Robert E. Kohler, *From Medical Chemistry to Biochemistry: The Making of a Biomedical Discipline.* (Cambridge: The University Press, 1982.)

4. That is to say, he made the basic discoveries about the protein keratin which were then exploited by the Toni company. See Asimov, *Biographical Encyclopedia.*

5. "Eine Methode zur experimentellen Prufung der Moleckulartheorie und der Avogadro-Loschmidtschen Zahl." *Zeitschrift fur physikalische Chemie 95; 247–250 (1920).* Pauling's comments in "Albert Szent-Gyorgyi on his 90th birthday," *Foundations of Physics,* vol. 13, No. 9, September 1983.

6. Loewi shared the 1936 Nobel Prize for Physiology or Medicine with Sir Henry Dale. Albert quotes him in a charming essay, "Some Reminiscences of My Life as a Scientist," *Int. J. Quantum Biology Symp.* No. 3, 7–12 (1976), p. 7.

7. M. L. Mitchell, in *Brighter Biochemistry,* June, 1927. See chapter 6 for a discussion of this unique humor magazine published at Cambridge in the 1920s and 30s.

8. A. L. Lehninger, *Biochemistry* (New York: Worth, 1972), p. 379.

9. "Zellatmung. II. Der Oxydationsmechanismus der Milchsaure," *Biochemische Zeitschrift, 157; 50–66 (1925).* Fifth in a series of six papers, "Studien ube die biologische Oxydation," which appeared in that journal in 1924 and 1925.

10. Lehninger, *Biochemistry.*

11. There is a fictional portrait of the effects of uncontrolled Addison's disease in Lawrence Sanders's popular novel, *The Third Deadly Sin* (New York: Berkley, 1985.)

12. From his Nobel Prize acceptance speech in *Nobel Prize Winners in Medicine and Physiology,* translated from Nobelstiftelsen, Stockholm *Physiology or Medicine.* vol. 2 (Amsterdam: published for the Nobel Foundation by Elsevier, 1964–67).

13. "It was already known that those plants which turn brown as the result of damage—about half of all plants—contain a polyphenol . . . besides this a ferment, the polyphenoloxidase, which, with the help of oxygen, oxidizes the polyphenol. There was a complicated interpretation of the working mechanism of this oxidase. It fell to me to show that it is simply a question of the oxidase, along with the oxygen, oxidizing the polyphenol to quinone [compound which results when two opposing hydrogen atoms are replaced by oxygen]. In the intact plant the quinone is again reduced by the hydrogen mobilized from foodstuffs. . . . In the damaged plant the reduction of the quinone cannot keep pace with the mounting oxidation of the phenol, and the quinones remain unreduced and form pigments." *Ibid,* p. 197.

14. *Ibid.*

15. Adrenalin (epinephrine), a secretion of the adrenal medulla, the first known hormone, was discovered in 1897 by John Jacob Abel at Johns Hopkins University. See Bernard Jaffe, *American Men of Science* (New York: Simon and Schuster, 1944).

CHAPTER 5

"I AM SZENT-GYORGYI"

1. Szent-Gyorgyi had never met Prof. Dale. He wrote to him because he was head of the National Institute for Medical Research of the Medical Research Council of Great Britain—in effect, the top government biological researcher.

2. Letter of 2 January 1925. All "MRC" documents are in the library of the Medical Research Council, Regent's Park, London.

3. Letter of 21 January 1925, MRC.

4. *Ibid.* Magnus was considered one of the most brilliant neurophysiologists of his day. A man of broad culture, he was being considered for a Nobel Prize when he died suddenly in 1927, at the age of fifty-three. Szent-Gyorgyi could not remember how they first met. It may have been at the physiological congress in Hamburg. Magnus and Lenhossek were contemporaries and probably friends.

5. This drawing was rediscovered in the 1970s by a librarian at the Medical Research Council, who sent it to Szent-Gyorgyi.

6. On the early hostile reception of biochemistry, and the reasons for it, see Kohler, *From Medical Chemistry to Biochemistry: The Making of a Biomedical Discipline* (Cambridge: The University Press, 1982).

7. In his writings and conversation, Albert always depicted himself as resigning on the spot. The resignation may have been less precipitous, however, for he continued to use his Groningen affiliation on papers until the end of 1926.

8. Albert apparently had planned to go some time in advance. The congress documents list "Dr. and Mrs. A. V. Szent-Gyorgyi" in attendance. When he lost his job Nelly went home to Budapest, however.

9. "Zellatmung. IV. Uber den Oxydationsmechanismus der Kartoffeln," *Biochemische Zeitschrift* 162; 399–412 (1925). Hopkins' speech is found in *Skandanavisches Archives fur Physiologie,* vol. 49, 1926.

CHAPTER 6

A SCIENTIFIC HOME

1. The "Godnose" story quickly made the rounds, and was still being retold in Cambridge almost sixty years later. Harden mistakenly believed the substance was related to sugar acids such as D-glucuronic acid.

2. Albert was already past thirty-three when he arrived in Cambridge. He was enrolled in Fitzwilliam College, an administrative unit set up to enroll independent researchers who had no need of a traditional college.

The Dunn laboratory had opened on 9 May 1924. Sir William Dunn had left a large estate for "the alleviation of human suffering," and Hopkins was one of the executors of the estate. Hopkins became the first director of the biochemistry laboratory, which would soon grow to world prominence.

3. This was in the autumn of 1929. He shared the prize with Christian Eijkman. The source for this anecdote is C. G. King, personal communication 21 February 1984.

4. Hopkins was the first to isolate the amino acid tryptophan from protein and isolated from living tissues the sulfur-containing dipeptide glutathione, showing its importance for oxidation. He showed that the wing pigments of certain butterflies were derived from uric acid. This showed that excretory substances could play a constructive role in certain situations.

5. Joseph Needham of Cambridge was kind enough to guide the author through his own personal set in search of Albert Szent-Gyorgyi's contributions.

6. Joseph Needham, personal communication, 17 May 1984.

7. Lenhossek retired in 1934 and died in 1937. Klebelsberg was an unusual figure, still controversial in Hungary today. (see Chapter 19) He revived the universities, built hundreds of elementary schools, and refused to enforce the *numerus clausus* against the Jewish students. Janos, *Politics of Backwardness*, and Straub, personal communication, May 1984.

8. Letter to Walter Fletcher, 21 June 1929, MRC.

9. Letter to Walter Fletcher, 10 November 1929, MRC.

10. It would not be until 1949, at Hopkins's bidding, that the world's biochemists would form their own organization.

11. Letter to Walter Fletcher, 10 November 1929, MRC.

12. *Ibid.*

13. *Ibid.*

14. *Ibid.* This reference to "a new active principle of the cortex" is intriguing. It is interesting to speculate that Szent-Gyorgyi may have had his hands on cortisone, the still-undiscovered hormone of the adrenal cortex. With his prior commitments, however, he had to return to Europe before he could work out the details of this discovery. "Nick" Kendall received the Nobel Prize for his 1935 discovery of cortisone. Cortisone became the standard treatment for Addison's disease.

15. *Ibid.*

16. Letter to Walter Fletcher, 21 June 1929, MRC.

17. Letter from Dean to Fletcher, 20 June 1929, MRC. There is an unsigned letter in the MRC files which almost certainly is from Fletcher. It is surprisingly intolerant of the idea and unfriendly to Szent-Gyorgyi:

. . .his duty is to his own country. . . . Then again, is it fair for a clever foreigner to sail in and take the bread out of the mouths of your young natives of Cambridge? You are hoping to attract to pathology men of the most diverse origins and training. Will you not lose a chief part of the incentive you can offer if it gets about that profitable posts can be seized by clever foreigners bouncing in from outside? In research his chief function seems to be that of detonator or catalyst. He has a flair without maintained industry.

18. *Science,* 28 August 1931.

CHAPTER 7

A NEW STAR IN THE SKY

1. Zoltan Halasz, *Hungarian Paprika Through the Ages* (Budapest: Korvina, 1963), p. 49. A lively bit of social history.

2. Bruno Straub, personal communication, 2 May 1984.

3. See Janos, *Politics of Backwardness* for background to Klebelsberg's reforms.

4. Letter to Alan Gregg, 22 June 1931, Rockefeller Foundation Archives, RF 1.1./750/2/12.

5. Personal communication, 9 May 1984.

6. Laki, interview with Coughlin, 1982. It is not clear if Laki is referring to Farkos (Wolfgang) Bolyai or his son, Janos—both outstanding mathematicians.

7. The innovation was long-lasting. Students of the technical school that now occupy the building were still playing soccer on this field when the author visited in 1984.

8. Straub, 1984. Klebelsberg was ousted in a political shakeup. His immediate replacement was one of his own subordinates. After the Count's death there was a change of governments. The new prime minister, Gyula Gombos, was the leader of the Right Radicals, "notorious for his fascist, anti-Semitic and militarist views" ("Hungary," *Encyclopedia Brittanica*, 14th ed., 1964) The man referred to in this anecdote was Gombos's minister of education.

9. Letter to Alan Gregg, 22 June 1931, Rockefeller Foundation Archives.

10. Letter to Alan Gregg, 6 December 1931, Rockefeller Foundation Archives.

11. Letter to Alan Gregg, 18 January 1932, Rockefeller Foundation Archives.

12. Ultrasound, at first called "supersound," was discovered by two Americans, R.W. Wood and A.L. Loomis. Loomis was an investment banker on Wall Street who did science as a weekend hobby.

13. A. Szalay, "My First Work in the Wake of a Creative Genius," personal communication, 1984.

14. Letter to Alan Gregg, 22 June 1931, Rockefeller Foundation Archives.

15. Letter to Alan Gregg, 6 December 1931, Rockefeller Foundation Archives.

16. Letter to Lauder Jones, another RF official, 8 October 1931, Rockefeller Foundation Archives.

17. Letter to Alan Gregg, 24 March 1932, Rockefeller Foundation Archives.

18. Robert A. Lambert diary, 25 February 1932, Rockefeller Foundation Archives. Lambert was the Foundation's associate director in Europe for the medical sciences.

19. Robert A. Lambert diary, 26 April 1933, Rockefeller Foundation Archives.

20. Letter to Alan Gregg, 24 March 1932, Rockefeller Foundation Archives.

21. Jones, memo to an otherwise unidentified "I.M.", 1 May 1933, Rockefeller Foundation Archives.

22. Lambert's diary, 26 May 1933, Rockefeller Foundation Archives. Bruno Straub thinks this almost certainly is an exaggeration. Prof. Gyorgyi Ranki adds, "The University professors were relatively wealthy in Hungary during this period." Letter to author, 6 February 1985. The claim was made, naturally, to the RF.

CHAPTER 8

THE BATTLE OVER VITAMIN C

1. *Biochem. Journ.* 22: 1387, 1928.

2. H.M. Miller memo, 7 November 1936. Rockefeller Foundation Archives, RF 1.1./750/2/12.

3. Wayne Martin, *Medical Heroes and Heretics,* (Devin Adair: Old Greenwich, 1977), p. 51.

4. Most experimental animals, such as rats, dogs and chickens, would not succumb to scurvy on *any* diet. Scientists were discovering that almost all animals except man manufactured their own supply. In 1912, however, two German scientists discovered an animal that on a diet of dried hay and oats *would* come down with scurvy: the guinea pig. This was good news for mankind and bad news for the little rodent whose name became synonymous with a subject for medical research. It was subsequently learned that a few other animals, such as the rhesus monkey, the Indian fruit-eating bat and the red-vented bulbul also require an external source of ascorbic acid. See Linus Pauling, *How To Live Longer and Feel Better* (New York: Avon, 1986), p. 78.

5. New York was a prominent center of vitamin C research. There had been an unexpected outbreak of scurvy among city children eventually traced to the copper from water pipes which leeched the vitamin from their bodies. At Columbia University, Prof. H.C. Sherman, a noted nutritionist, had a group of eager students in pursuit of the vitamin. One of these "postdocs" was C.G. King.

6. Letter to Sir Edward Mellanby, 5 July 1937, Medical Research Council. He continues: "A human patient is still much more complicated. The most complex system I know is that consisting of a patient plus a clinician."

7. In the fall of 1929, accompanied by his wife, Hilda, King sailed for England to study for three months with Prof. Hopkins at the Dunn laboratory. The similarity of vitamin C and hexuronic acid apparently was mentioned there:

> After a seminar report on our work in Pittsburgh he [Hopkins] invited me to his office and inquired whether I thought it possible that vitamin C might be the same substance as the adrenal hormone [i.e., hexuronic acid] that Dr. Szent-Gyorgyi had studied in their laboratory. I said, "Yes, of course." C.G. King, "The Isolation of Vitamin C From Lemon Juice," 1979. Paper given as part of a symposium on Nutritional Discoveries of the 1930s, at the annual meeting of the American Institute of Nutrition, 3 April 1979, Dallas, Texas.

In an earlier reminiscence, King gave himself a more active role in the discussion:

> Professor Hopkins somewhat excitedly invited me to his office after the seminar and asked whether I would venture a guess concerning the chemical identity of the vitamin. I replied that its properties and occurrence so far as known correspond with the "hexuronic acid" isolated in

his laboratories. C.G. King, "The Discovery and Chemistry of Vitamin C," *Proceedings of the Nutrition Society*, 1953, vol. 12, no. 3, p. 219.

At the same time, S.S. Zilva declared *ex cathedra* that hexuronic acid could not be vitamin C. See *Nature*, 7 May 1932, p. 690.

8. Svirbely, personal communication, 23 February 1984.

9. King, "Isolation of Vitamin C from Lemon Juice."

10. King, "Discovery and Chemistry of Vitamin C," 222. Notice that King says it was the Szeged group's "first" assay, not their fourth, as Szent-Gyorgyi claimed.

11. W.A. Waugh and C.G. King, "Isolation and Identification of Vitamin C," 97 *Journal of Biological Chemistry*, 325–331, 9 July 1932.

12. *Nature*, 16 April 1932.

13. King, "Discovery and Chemistry of Vitamin C," 219.

14. *Ibid*. Emphasis added.

15. *Ibid*.

16. The author copied the letter by hand from Svirbely's original copy. Svirbely also possessed a number of other documents which support this interpretation. One of them was from a fellow scientist, H.E. Gillander, dated 6 March 1932, in which he said that Glen King still did not know what vitamin C was.

17. This was reported in the Hungarian journal, *Orvosi Hetilap* 76: 259, 12 on 26 March. It was also noted in the German *Monatshefte Ungarisher Mediziner,* and other publications. "In this lecture the identity of vitamin C and 'hexuronic acid' described by myself in 1928, was definitely stated and experimental evidence given," Szent-Gyorgyi later wrote (*Science* 87, 4 March 1938). For conversation with Rockefeller official: RF 1-1/750/2/12.

18. *Food, Drug, Cosmetic Law Journal,* May 1957. In 1941, King and Waugh were finally granted a patent, No. 2,233,417, for their method of isolating vitamin C from lemon juice. This was a pyrrhic victory, since Szent-Gyorgyi had already shown how to easily isolate huge quantities of the vitamin from Hungarian paprika.

19. Albert Einstein, *Ideas and Opinions*, (New York: Crown, 1954).

CHAPTER 9

THE ROAD TO STOCKHOLM

1. Zoltan Halasz, *Hungarian Paprika.*

2. Szalay, "My First Work in the Wake of a Creative Genius."

3. *Ibid.*

4. Halasz, *Hungarian Paprika,* chapter 5.

5. Szalay, "My First Work in the Wake of a Creative Genius."

6. Prof. George Wald informed the author in 1985 that he still had one of these famous samples in its original bottle.

7. Halasz, *Hungarian Paprika.* It is ironic that most of Szent-Gyorgyi's profits from "Pritamin" came from its sales in Germany, where it was widely used by the military, especially the U-boat crews who lacked fresh fruit.

8. Letter of ASG to Fletcher, 6 January 1933, MRC archives.

9. Laki, Interview with Coughlin, 1982.

10. Letter of ASG to Fletcher, 6 January 1933.

11. Letter of Hume to Fletcher, 16 January 1933, MRC.
12. Letter of Dale to Fletcher, 7 February 1933, MRC.
13. Letter of Mellanby to Dale, 7 February 1933, MRC.
14. Letter of Thomson to ASG, 26 May 1933, MRC.
15. Letter of ASG to Thomson, 29 May 1933, MRC.
16. Fodor, personal communication, September, 1983. Fodor is now professor of chemistry at West Virginia University, Morgantown.
17. *New York Times,* 26 March 1933.
18. Letter of ASG to Mellanby, 7 October 1936, MRC.
19. *Ibid.*
20. This is according to the account in *Time,* 8 November 1937. The actual deliberations of Nobel Prize nominating committees are sealed for fifty years. The file on Szent-Gyorgyi was not available in time for inclusion in this book.
21. Hans Krebs, *Reminiscences and Reflections* (Oxford: Clarendon Press, 1981), p. 175. He pointed out that his teacher Warburg won the prize (1931), as did Warburg's teacher Emil Fischer (1902) and Fischer's teacher, Adolph von Baeyer, in 1905. The Prizes only commenced in 1901, but von Baeyer was himself the end point of five earlier generations of great chemists, a direct line of students and teachers dating back directly to Lavoisier in the eighteenth century. Krebs, like Szent-Gyorgyi himself and most other observers, ruled out the influence of nepotism and politics on the science prize committees.
22. *Brighter Biochemistry,* June, 1928.
23. The first three were Philipp Lenard (Physics, 1905); Robert Barany (Physiology or Medicine, 1914); and Richard Zsigmondy (Chemistry, 1925).
24. The other laureates that year were Clinton Joseph Davisson (U.S.) and George P. Thomson (G.B.), physics; Sir Walter Haworth (G.B.) and Paul Karrer (Switz.), chemistry; Roger Martin du Gard (Fr.), literature; and Viscount Cecil of Chelwood (G.B.), peace.
25. "Nobel Prize Winners in Medicine or Physiology."
26. *The Bulletin Index,* Pittsburgh, 18 November 1937.
27. *Ibid.*
28. *Sun Telegraph,* Pittsburgh, 21 November 1937.
29. *Post-Gazette,* Pittsburgh, 19 November 1937.
30. *Post-Gazette,* Pittsburgh, 22 November 1937.
31. *Science,* 10 December 1937, pp. 540–542.

CHAPTER 10

THE NAZI WAVE

1. Krebs was dismissed by no less a personage than the philosopher, Martin Heidegger, who became the Rector at Freiburg. "He was an enthusiastic supporter of Hitler, hailing him on behalf of the University as a saviour, and pledging himself to unswerving loyalty." Krebs, *Reminiscences and Reflections,* p. 70. Warburg himself was part Jewish but was protected by high members of the Nazi regime who thought he had a cure for cancer.
2. Letter, ASG to Krebs, 22 April 1933. *Ibid.* See also related documents in Krebs file, Contemporary Scientific Archives Center (CSAC), Oxford, England.

3. Letter, Krebs to Hopkins, *Ibid.*, 65.

4. Letter, Hopkins to Krebs, 29 April 1933, *Ibid.* Hopkins helped not only Krebs in this way, but later organized a committee to aid persecuted Jewish scientists. Szent-Gyorgyi, too, exerted efforts in the same direction. For instance, he helped Ernst Boris Chain—who later helped develop penicillin—resettle in England. CSAC 92/3/83.

5. Turul was named for a mythical Hungarian bird, similar to a phoenix. This organization was said to be responsible for most of the anti-Semitic riots.

6. This was in 1939. In 1940 Biro's admission to Szeged would have been impossible, for "numerus clausus" was replaced by "numerus nullus" in that year. Henceforth, no Jews were to be accepted into the University. Biro survived the last years of the war in a work camp, and is now Professor of Biochemistry at Budapest. Personal communication, 5 May 1984.

7. Most of the violence came from the right. Ironically, the law students were especially violence-prone. According to Prof. Bruno Straub, who was a Szeged student at the time, they initiated these riots "with the view of closing the university in order to have time for drinking" (letter to author, 10 October 1984). Szent-Gyorgyi agreed: "The law faculty were especially nationalistic; you know they had nothing to do, and were always causing trouble." Biro explained that "nobody wanted to beat his own colleagues. After all, the professor you beat today might sit on your examination committee tomorrow. And so the law students went to the medical faculty to beat up people, while the medical students went to the law school."

8. On 8 December 1933, the *New York Times* reported on a related incident. "This afternoon anti-Semitic students at the University of Szeged tried to force Jewish students [to] take seats on the so-called 'ghetto' benches. When the Jewish students refused, the anti-Semites attacked them and forced them to leave the building. One professor defended the Jewish students and slapped an anti-Semite's face. Two hundred students thereupon stormed the building, demanding satisfaction from the professor, who in the meantime had left the university. The rector closed the university until Monday." According to Straub, this courageous professor was Szent-Gyorgyi's friend Bela Issekutzsen, dean of the medical faculty. Straub, *Ibid.*

9. Fodor, personal communication, 16 September 1983.

10. Wald, personal communication, 15 March 1984.

11. This visit lasted three months according to ASG's recollections, eight weeks according to the RF files.

12. Letter, ASG to Mellanby, 7 February 1937. MRC. Emphasis in original.

13. Letter, ASG to Alan Gregg, 13 September 1936, RFA 1-1/750/2/12.

14. His Vanderbilt lecture series was printed as *On Oxidation, Fermentation, Vitamins, Health and Disease,* The Abraham Flexner Lectures (Baltimore: Williams & Wilkins, 1937).

15. Janos Ladik, personal communication, 16 September 1984. Also Bruno Straub, personal communication 30 April 1984. "Big Nelly" was definitely in the United States in 1938 and after the war as well. Some people in Szeged say they remember her returning there, but the recollections were vague. Her son-in-law does not believe she returned to Hungary before or during the war.

16. "And I still love her," he added, with deep feeling. Marta had been dead almost twenty years when he made these remarks. See Chapter 16.

17. Translated and paraphrased by Prof. Daniel Bagdy, 4 May 1984.

18. Prof. Gyula Juhasz, personal communication, 4 May 1984. Juhasz is a historian with the Hungarian Academy of Sciences. A more likely source of Szent-Gyorgyi's left-wing ideas was the progressive journal, *Szeged Youth.* In fact, a number of prominent leaders of the post-World War II government were to come out of this magazine's circle.

19. Shortly before his death, Horvath put together a booklet of his writings about the theater, including his dramatic aims. After he died his friends and teachers published this as *Orok Szinhaz,* Budapest, 1942. It was dedicated to Szent-Gyorgyi.

CHAPTER 11

MUSCLE MAN

1. Krebs, *Reminiscences and Reflections,* 109, 118.

2. Krebs, "Intermediary Hydrogen-Transport in Biological Oxidation," in *Perspectives in Biochemistry,* Joseph Needham and David Green, eds. (Cambridge: The University Press, 1937).

3. Krebs, *Reminiscences and Reflections,* 109.

4. E. Baldwin, 1948, cited in René Wurmser, "Albert Szent-Gyorgyi and Modern Biochemistry," in *Horizons in Biochemistry* (New York: Academic Press, 1962), M. Kasha and B. Pullman, eds.

5. Hammarsten in *Nobel Prize Winners in Physiology or Medicine.*

6. Lehninger, *Biochemistry, The Molecular Basis of Cell Structure* (New York: Worth, 1972), 340.

7. B. Straub "From Respiration of Muscle to Muscle Actin, 1934–1943," in *Of Oxygen, Fuels and Living Matter,* ed. G. Semenza (New York: John Wiley, 1981).

8. Wurmser, "Albert Szent-Gyorgyi and Modern Biochemistry."

9. Lehninger, *Biochemistry.*

10. Albert Szent-Gyorgyi, "Oxidation and Fermentation," in *Perspectives in Biochemistry.* The volume was dedicated to Hopkins. Szent-Gyorgyi concluded his contribution in this way: "I would like to end by giving expression to my most sincere desire that oxidation and fermentation alike may long continue to interact harmoniously in the cells of our beloved teacher."

11. MRC files.

12. "He is a masterful impressionist, the Monet of modern science." Peter Gascoyne, personal communication, 11 January 1985. See Chapter 20.

13. ATP = adenosine triphosphate. Technically, myosin was called an "adenosinetriphosphatase."

14. Albert Szent-Gyorgyi "Muscle Research," *Scientific American,* June 1949.

15. From the Greek *mys, myos,* for muscle.

16. Albert Szent-Gyorgyi, "Muscle Research."

17. *Ibid.*

18. Straub, "From Respiration. . . ." Straub is here talking about the *early* 1930s, but most of these limitations applied to the late 1930s in Szeged as well.

19. *Albert Szent-Gyorgyi,* "Muscle Research."

20. Albert Szent-Gyorgyi et al, *Studies from Szeged,* (Szeged, 1944).

CHAPTER 12

THE ADVENTURES OF MR. SWENSEN

1. In September 1938, 7,500 square miles of Czechoslovakia were returned to Hungary. It seized more in March 1939. This was no longer "csonka Magyarorszag," or "barebones Hungary." Horthy's slogan "No! No! Never!" was being acted upon. "It worked wonders for bruised Magyar pride," one historian has written. In just three years Hungary doubled in size. Katya Marton, *Wallenberg* (New York: Random House, 1982).

2. "Economic and Political Situation in Europe—Hungary, Part III: The Political Situation," Issued by the Office of European Economic Research, O.S.S., 19 January 1943. N.A. 28304. The report notes that this "democracy" only existed in Budapest and a few other industrial centers. Szeged was primarily agricultural and would not have been included.

3. Adolf Hitler, *Hitler's Secret Conversations, 1941–1942* (New York: Octagon Books, 1972).

4. In April 1941 Hungarian troops joined the Germans in overrunning Belgrade, which had first been pulverized by German bombers flying out of Hungarian air bases. This was what Hitler meant by "helping out in the kitchen." Count Teleki, the conservative, academic Catholic who was serving as Prime Minister, had given his word of honor to the Yugoslavs that he would never attack their country. In fact, he had signed a "Pact of Eternal Friendship" with them just a few months before. When Horthy overruled him, Teleki felt dishonored and committed suicide.

5. Marton, *Wallenberg*.

6. Near the Ukranian town of Voronezh, 140,000 Hungarian soldiers died, and almost all the army's military equipment was lost.

7. Cited in Coughlin's notes for an ASG biography, p. 86. See Preface.

8. *Encyclopedia Britannica*, 14th edition, 1964, "Bethlen." The main reason for Bethlen's pessimism was that the last of Hitler's 270,000 man army had surrendered at Stalingrad only days before.

9. This is disputed by some historians. "Witnesses and historians concur that Szent-Gyorgyi's mission was not expressly endorsed by Kallay." Mario D. Fenyo, *Hitler, Horthy and Hungary: German-Hungarian Relations, 1941–1944* (New Haven: Yale University Press, 1972), p. 123. But Kallay certainly agreed to meet with Szent-Gyorgyi and conveyed his opinions, which were later passed on to Allied intelligence. The effect was the same.

10. Fenyo, *Hitler, Horthy and Hungary*, p. 122.

11. *Ibid.*

12. Dispatch of Steinhardt to Washington, 13 February 1943, cited in Fenyo, *Hitler, Horthy and Hungary*, p. 123.

13. Fenyo, *Hitler, Horthy and Hungary*, p. 124.

14. *Ibid.*

15. C. A. Macartney, *October Fifteenth, A History of Modern Hungary, 1929–1945*, vol. 2. 2nd. ed. (Edinburgh: University Press, 1961), p. 142.

16. See Elyesa Bazna, *I Was Cicero* (New York: Dell, 1964). Also, L. Moyzisch, *Operation Cicero* (New York: Coward-McCann, 1950).

17. Fenyo, *Hitler, Horthy and Hungary*, p. 124. It has been said, in Meszaros's

defense, that he often passed incorrect information to the Abwehr. Also, the German foreign office appears to have known nothing about this connection and considered him, along with Szent-Gyorgyi, of being guilty of "establishing contact with the enemy."

18. *Ibid.*

19. Marton, *Wallenberg,* p. 54.

20. Hitler, *Hitler's Secret Conversation.* Hitler predictably attributed this strength to Horthy's "German blood."

21. Marton, Wallenberg, p. 52.

22. OSS, *Confidential Memo,* N.A. 003412-Y, 4 August 1943.

23. *Minutes,* 17 April 1943; National Archives (NA) Microcopy T-120, roll 618, F-40109-10. Records of this meeting were kept by Hitler's secretary, Schmidt, and recovered, partially burned, after the capture of Berlin.

24. There is no reference to "Schweinhund" in the *Minutes,* but Hitler's worst ravings were excised from the official records. The actual conversation was widely repeated in Budapest at the time. Albert may have heard the story directly from Horthy, when he met him in 1944.

25. N.A. roll 609. F-40098-99.

26. Cited in Fenyo, *Hitler, Horthy and Hungary,* pp. 126–27.

27. Gabor Baross, *Hungary and Hitler* (Astor, Fla. 1970), p. 62.

28. "It was difficult to be a Szent-Gyorgyi at that time," Andrew Szent-Gyorgyi recalled.

29. The city was so crowded because many people believed it would be spared the worst ravages of the war. The exact opposite happened—the worst battles were fought for control of the city, and about ninety percent of the buildings were eventually destroyed. Szeged, by comparison, was barely touched.

30. N.A. Biro, personal communication, 5 May 1984. Rajniss was later executed as a traitor.

31. *New York Times,* 18 January 1940.

32. He probably meant "east." A provisional anti-fascist government had been set up in Debrecen and it was there that the Russians had their temporary headquarters.

33. Szent-Gyorgyi's Nobel Prize medal had been repurchased by the Hungarian government from the Finnish Red Cross. It disappeared in 1945 from its display case in the Budapest history museum and has never been recovered.

CHAPTER 13

CAVIAR FOR BREAKFAST

1. National Archives files, NA L54284, 13 February 1945.

2. Zoltan Bay, personal communication, September 1984.

3. Cited in the notes for the Coughlin biography. (See Preface.) The Marxist terminology is curious.

4. *Ibid.*

5. *Ibid.* The NKVD was the Soviet state security apparatus, predecessor of the KGB.

6. There is a good description of these festivities in Hans Selye, *From Dream to Discovery* (New York: McGraw Hill, 1964), p. 389. Others who attended were Detlev Bronk, Sir Julian Huxley, and of course Selye himself.

7. Letter, Erick Ashby to Dr. O'Brien, RF 1.1/750/2/10, 26 May 1945.

8. Letter, ASG to Alan Gregg, 24 June 1945, Moscow. RF1.1/750/2/10. Szent-Gyorgyi's English had clearly suffered from lack of use.

9. Cegled, or Czegled, is a small city, forty-two miles southeast of Budapest.

10. Speech reprinted in Hungarian in Albert Szent-Gyorgyi, *Egy Biologus Gondolatai* (Budapest: Gondolat, 1970), pp. 132–33. Kindly translated for me by Viktor Polgar, second secretary of the Embassy of the Hungarian People's Republic.

11. It is not certain that Szent-Gyorgyi made two trips to Moscow, as he said. Nobody else recalled a second trip, which would have been logistically difficult under the circumstances. It is possible that the attempt to see Stalin occurred on his first visit in the summer of 1945. He met Stalin briefly at a state banquet, and therefore the idea of writing for a personal audience was not absurd.

12. Whether Szent-Gyorgyi's intuition in this case was correct is difficult to judge. It certainly does not appear to be the case today. Hungary's per capita income was $4,180 in 1982, compared to $2,600 (1976) for the U.S.S.R.

13. RF 1-1/750/2/10.

14. George Weber, "A Genius for Discovery," *Saturday Evening Post,* May/June 1984.

15. George Haydu, personal communication, July 1984.

16. Daniel Bagdy, personal communication, 5 May 1984.

17. Some of the other students of this time included his young cousin, Andrew Szent-Gyorgyi; Zbel Lajtha, the brain biochemist; Eremer Mihalyi; John Gergely; Tamas Erdos and his wife, Agnes Ullman, who later became deputy director of the Pasteur Institute, Paris; and Maria Szekely, who worked with Prof. Sanger at Cambridge. "Uncle" George Rozsa, the mechanical wizard from Szeged, also joined ASG in Budapest.

18. Letter, ASG to Alan Gregg, 30 September 1945.

19. The six members were Szent-Gyorgyi; his physicist friend Zoltan Bay; Paul Gombas, a theoretical physicist; Gyula Illyes, the poet-essayist and author of *People of the Puszta;* Prof. Karacsony, an educator; and the well-known Marxist philosopher, George Lukacs.

20. The Academy was technically the "Academia Scientiarum Naturalium Hungarica." The five journals were to cover mathematics, physics, chemistry, biology, and physiology. The story of the walk-out at the Academy is from Janos Ladik, whose mother was present on the occasion.

21. Zoltan Bay, personal communication, September 1984.

22. On 24 January 1946, Dean John W. M. Bunker wrote to Szent-Gyorgyi that his duties as "Lecturer in Biology" would consist of "selected lectures for students and staff of our Institute, some of which might appropriately be made available to the public or to our sister college and university-personnel." A handwritten note by RF officials on a copy of this letter reads "A.G. [i.e., Alan Gregg], agrees with W.W. [i.e., Warren Weaver] that MIT could handle, with completely adequate stipend, if they so wished; that no necessity of RF aid, etc." RF 1.1./750/2/10.

23. Report on a phone call from Dean Bunker to HMM of the Rockefeller Founda-

tion: "Dr. Szent-Gyorgyi wishes to receive appointment as an honorary lecturer in order to enable him to secure a U.S. visa." *Ibid.* It sounds very much as if ASG were preparing an "escape hatch" for himself from Hungary in case his relations with the new regime soured.

24. Letter of 19 November 1946. RF 1.1/750/2/10.

25. Letter, Karl Compton to Warren Weaver. 26 November 1946. RF 1.1./750/2/10.

26. Letter, ASG to Gregg, 5 December 1946. RF 1.1.750/2/10. According to one RF official, "The American Legation at Budapest had been ready to grant him a visa until it was noted that he was nominally a member of the Hungarian Government, as one of six scientists being coopted to sit on the Hungarian Parliament." Reference therefore had to be made to Washington for permission to grant a visa. The Legation had cabled for permission in October, and again in mid-November, asking that the visa be ready for Szent-Gyorgyi in Paris. But all telephone inquiries to the American Embassy showed no receipt of any such permission request. Memo, 16 November 1946, RF 1.1./750/2/10.

27. Letter, ASG to Gregg, 13 December 1946. RF 1.1./750/2/10.

28. N. A. Biro, personal communication, 5 May 1984.

29. *Ibid.*

30. *Ibid.*

31. It is possible the account was exaggerated in the telling. An RF official who heard the story at the time referred to Rath's treatment as "mild torture." Albert may have been trying to justify the very difficult decision to leave Hungary.

32. G. R. Pomerat diary, 18 September 1947. RF 1.1./750/2/10.

33. *Ibid.*

34. *Ibid.*

CHAPTER 14

IN SEARCH OF DR. SAYGYGI

1. Straub, personal communication, 30 April 1984.

2. G.R. Pomerat diary, 18 September 1947. RF 1.1./750/2/10.

3. Donald Nelson, Alfred A. Streslin, Paul Kestin, and Ralph Colin. Nothing further is known about them.

4. Warren Weaver notes, 26 November 1947. RF 1/750/2/10.

5. No one the author spoke to in Hungary could remember such a play. Straub said he did remember a Russian play about an apathetic scientist staged at this time, but did not think Szent-Gyorgyi was the target.

6. Streslin was the treasurer of the Foundation. "This pretty well fixed me which is not against my will," ASG wrote to Warren Weaver. "My Woods Hole plans assume thus more of a definite outline. By and by I am also getting shaken down, to use your terminology." Letter, ASG to Warren Weaver, 17 December 1947. RF 1.1./750/2/10.

7. Letter, ASG to Warren Weaver, 28 June 1948. RF 1.2/196/1842.

8. Some of the scientists who emigrated at this time were Koloman Laki, G. Rosza, and John Gergely. Andrew Szent-Gyorgyi emigrated on his own during this period. Gergely became the most prominent of the group as a professor at Harvard University and at Massachusetts General Hospital.

9. For example, Cornelius "Dusty" Rhoads, head of Sloan-Kettering Institute, was severely criticized for allowing his face to appear on the cover of *Time,* 27 June 1949. See the author's *The Cancer Syndrome* (New York: Grove Press, 1982), p. 204.

10. "I have invited for this summer Gamow, Teller, Herzfeld, Wycoff, Astbury, Buchthal. I do not know yet who accepts (except Wycoff who did) [but if] they do not come I will invite others, in the first line Michaelis. Moreover I will give my own associates a good holiday and make them profit too [in] the presence of any of these people who will come along." Letter, ASG to Warren Weaver, 28 June 1948, 1-2/196/1842. It is not known which, if any, of these scientists actually came. Michaelis visited in 1949. The invitation to Teller is noteworthy. They would soon be at odds over foreign policy, as Studs Terkel points out in the preface.

11. On 12 May, 8 June, 29 June, and 23 August 1948 according to FBI documents obtained through the Freedom of Information Act.

12. U.S. Department of Justice Application No. D.P. 3131, 13 October 1948.

13. Letter, ASG to Warren Weaver, 11 May 1948. RF 1-2/196/1842.

14. He was, nevertheless, distressed because "my associates, as non-Americans, cannot be civil servants." He therefore decided to house most of them at Woods Hole until they became naturalized citizens.

15. Szent-Gyorgyi also told the story of how Bohr was chosen (by H.H. Dale and others) to present to Winston Churchill the idea of sharing nuclear secrets with the Russians. When Bohr finished an erudite, hour-long presentation, Churchill's only remark was that he had not understood a word Bohr had said. "That was the end of the idea which could have placed mankind on a more hopeful course," Szent-Gyorgyi commented.

16. Letter, ASG to Warren Weaver. 12 October 1950. RG 2-1950.

17. Letter, Warren Weaver to ASG, March 1949. RG 2-1950-200/487/3259.

18. *Ibid.*

19. Letter, Astbury to Clara W. Meyer, 7 November 1950. In RF files. RG 2-1950.

20. Warren Weaver, Diary, 25 September 1950. RG 2-1950.

21. "Despite the fact that muscle is our chief stock in trade and we have been in the business 84 years, we know less about muscle scientifically than we do about any other part of the meat animal." F. W. Specht in *Saturday Evening Post,* 8 March 1952.

22. Straub, personal communication, 30 April 1984.

23. Letter, ASG to Warren Weaver, 11 May 1948. RF 1.2./196/1842.

24. From the Hungarian periodical, *Haladas,* quoted in a dispatch of the American Legation, Foreign Service of the U.S.A., 27 October 1949. N.A. NNF 760050.

25. See C.A. Macartney, "Hungary," *Encyclopedia Britannica,* 14th ed., 1964.

CHAPTER 15

PORTALS OF DISCOVERY

1. Others who worked with him at this time included Eiji Fujimori, Stephen Hajdu, Irv Isenberg, George Karreman, M. Middlebrooks, W.R. Middlebrooks, Helmut Mueller, Gerald Schiffman, Richard Steele, and G. de Villafranca.

2. Michael Kasha, "Four Great Personalities of Science: Personal Recollections of

G.N. Lewis, J. Franck, R.S. Mulliken, and A. Szent-Gyorgyi." Tokyo Science University Lectures, October, 1979.

3. *Ibid.*

4. *Ibid.*

5. According to H.L. Mencken, the "Hole" in Woods Hole, is an archaic word for "a strip of meadow" (*American Language,* 4th ed., N.Y., 1937, p.119n). The author has heard it used locally, however, to describe the swift channel between Elisabeth Islands and the mainland.

6. Kasha, "Four Great Personalities of Science."

7. H.E. Huxley, in *Search and Discovery: A Tribute to Albert Szent-Gyorgyi,* ed. Benjamin Kaminer (N.Y.: Academic Press, 1977).

8. ASG, *Chemistry of Muscular Contraction.*

9. Kasha, *"Four Great Personalities of Science."*

10. The expression "facts are dull things" is attributed to A.V. Hill. Readers might recognize a similarity between this and Lenin's famous quote, "Facts are gray, my friend, but green is the tree of life" in *What is to be Done?*. Lenin himself was quoting Nikolay Chernyshevsky. This primacy of practice over theory, within their mutual interdependence, is one of the tenets of the Marxist philosophy of science.

11. Building on this work, science soon learned a great deal about muscle proteins. It was found, for instance, that there were at least three major components of muscle (myosin, 54 percent; actin, 25 percent; and trypomyosin B, 11 percent) as well as three minor components. The myosin molecule has a wiry "head" which contains the ATPase activity of the molecule, as well as a "light meromyosin" tail, which exists in a double helical form (Albert Lehninger, *Biochemistry,* p. 589.)

12. This same method was later used by others to conserve the motility of sperm, and now plays a major role in animal husbandry, through artificial insemination. Afterwards, glycerol was also used for the preservation of blood in blood banks, until Szent-Gyorgyi's friend Charles Huggins replaced it with dimethyl sulfoxide (DMSO) in 1963.

13. *Time,* 22 March 1954.

14. *Chicago American,* 11 December 1955.

15. Spontaneous mammary tumors—C_3H, transplanted sarcoma 180, and the solid Krebs 2 tumor.

16. *New York Times,* 7 July 1963. The Columbia scientists were headed by Dr. Mary S. Parshley. She also obtained inhibition of sarcoma 180, a type of tumor, in the whole animal using her own extracts of retine. She found that retine also would inhibit the division of other kinds of cells, such as fibroblasts, showing that it was a general growth inhibitor, not just specific to cancer.

17. It was accepted "by the editor without passing through the normal review process to which scientific articles are usually subject." *New York Times,* 28 June 1963.

18. Ivy was a distinguished University of Illinois physician and health administrator who advocated the use of Krebiozen, a controversial cancer treatment derived from horses' serum. It was a medical *cause célèbre* of the 1950s and early 1960s. See Herbert Bailey, *A Matter of Life or Death* (New York: Putnam's, 1958).

19. Bernal was also famous as the premier Marxist historian of science in the

English-speaking world. See his four volume *Science in History* (Cambridge: MIT Press, 1971).

20. Kasha, "Four Great Personalities of Science," 47.

21. Andrew Szent-Gyorgyi in *Search and Discovery,* ed. Benjamin Kaminer.

22. *American Jewish Ledger,* 25 October 1955.

CHAPTER 16

FAMILY MAN

1. In the 1970s, he was on much better terms with these relatives and often had them as guests at "Seven Winds."

2. Like her mother and maternal grandfather, Little Nelly was an excellent skier. In Vienna, on a national ski team tour, she declined to go back, but joined her aunt Sari (pronounced "Shari") in Holland. Big Nelly came to visit them a number of times on their Rhodesian farm. She even stayed for a year, while her daughter took a kind of "prolonged vacation" in Rome, studying art.

3. Greta Cori was almost uniformly described in the press as attending as the *wife* of the Nobel laureate Carl Cori, but she was also a laureate in her own right.

4. "[The Paulings] began a fast-paced Latin rhythm and other guests followed right along until it was time for all to go into the East Room. . . . Earlier in the day, the white-haired scientist had donned slicker and rainhat to parade up and down the White House pavement with other placard-carrying marchers in protest against atmospheric nuclear testing." *Washington Post,* 30 April 1962.

5. Jane McLaughlin adds: "The litigation, concerning the tax exempt status of the Institute for Muscle Research people who received fellowships from the Institute, was a legitimate tax question that took years for the government to answer. The fact that there were no penalties on top of the interest attests to that." Personal communication, 29 January 1985.

6. Kodaly had long been married to a much older woman. When she died he married Sarolta Peczeli, a nineteen year old student whose family he had befriended during World War II. He married her solely so that, under Hungarian law, she and her family could inherit his estate. Percy M. Young, *Zoltan Kodaly* (London: E. Benn, 1964), p. 149. Tunde Felker eventually received her Ph.D. degree in biochemistry from Brown University. Csilla became an art conservator for the Fogg Art Museum.

7. Since these events are still painful to Susan, it seems unnecessary to give her last name. Szent-Gyorgyi's version of these events comes especially from his statements to the National Library of Medicine interviewer in 1967. Susan's version is from personal communication with her, 14 November 1984, 2 July 1986 and 5 October 1986.

8. Albert may not have been visibly bereaved at Nelly's funeral services, but then he always was quite philosophical about the question of death, even his own. His behavior during World War II proves that. The author was with him shortly after he almost was killed in an airplane accident in 1980. (A two-engine plane he was taking from Hyannis to New York got caught in a thunderstorm.) He seemed quite unafraid, and his only concern was for his young companion.

CHAPTER 17

THE 500-TON RAT

1. Coughlin interview, n.d. See Preface.

2. The relationship between the brain and the mind had always been one of his favorite subjects. He told his students in the 1930s that it was the *most important* question, but inaccessible with then-current tools.

3. Here is another similarity to Marxism. This idea is the same as the first law of dialectical materialism, the transformation of quantity into quality. See Frederick Engels, *Dialectics of Nature* (New York: International, 1973), p. 26. This is, of course, ultimately derived from Hegel. At first glance, Szent-Gyorgyi's general schema seems similar to Marx's, especially in his emphasis on conflict as the midwife of new social systems. As noted before, ASG picked up some Marxist ideas along the way, but the differences are significant. Szent-Gyorgyi's thinking may be "dialectical," i.e., it attributes change to the clash of antagonistic, but interdependent parts of a whole; but it is often, in Marxist terms, idealist. In ASG's writing, it is usually *ideas,* not material forces, which cause change.

4. Speech at Harvard, 13 February 1962. Reprinted in Albert Szent-Gyorgyi, *Science, Ethics and Politics,* with an appreciation by Bertrand Russell (New York: Vantage Press, 1963).

5. *New York Times,* 31 March 1965.

6. *New York Times,* 14 December 1965.

7. *New York Times,* 11 March 1966.

8. W. H. Morse for IRS, handwritten note, 12 April 1966, obtained through the Freedom of Information Act.

9. *New York Times,* 29 December 1972.

10. *New York Times,* 3 December 1967.

11. John Malcolm Brinnin, *Dylan Thomas in America* (New York: Viking, 1957). Thomas was of course speaking about himself.

12. He later explained that by using the word "creation" he was simply speaking of the coming-into-being of the physical world, and not endorsing "creation" in a Biblical sense. He never wavered in his belief in evolution.

CHAPTER 18

"DON'T LIE IF YOU DON'T HAVE TO"

1. Zoltan Bay, personal communication, September 1984.

2. *Washington Evening Star,* 29 April 1971.

3. Letter, ASG to Franklin C. Salisbury, 28 May 1971.

4. Letter to author, April 20, 1987.

5. Quoting from one randomly selected letter: "I think I understand cancer now considerably better than I did before. I am more hopeful than before and believe that the problem of cancer is solvable, provided one looks upon it as a scientific and not as a clinical problem. I even think that we may have the cure in sight though much work has to be done still." Letter, ASG to Franklin C. Salisbury, 28 June 1983. NFCR files.

6. In 1985, his title was changed to President and Chief Executive Officer for legal reasons.

7. Letter, ASG to Franklin Salisbury, 7 November 1972. NFCR files.

8. Letter, Franklin Salisbury to ASG, 20 December 1972. NFCR files.

9. He made this decision in May, 1973.

10. Letter, Franklin Salisbury to ASG, 7 May 1973. NFCR files.

11. Letter, ASG to Franklin Salisbury, 26 June 1973. NFCR files. The administrator later denied he ever had any conflict with either ASG or his Foundation.

CHAPTER 19

THE BALLET OF ALBERT SZENT-GYORGYI

1. He made a second trip in January 1978 as part of an official U.S. delegation that returned the Crown and Sceptre of St. Stephen, symbol of Hungarian sovereignty, back to Hungary.

2. There is no independent confirmation of this offer, and several Hungarians spoken to in Hungary and the United States felt that, because of the socialization of agriculture, it is unlikely the offer was ever made in this form.

3. Istvan Kardos, *Scientists Face to Face* (U.K.: Collets, 1978) pp. 351–352. A very interesting collection of interviews.

4. One of the reasons Szent-Gyorgyi wanted to see this biography written was to put forward his views on actin's priority. Another reason was to set the record straight about Prof. King.

5. Straub, "From Respiration. . . ."

6. See, for example, Anne Sayre, *Rosalind Franklin and DNA* (N.Y.: Norton, 1975), and E. F. Keller, *Reflections on Gender and Science* (New Haven: Yale University Press, 1985).

7. Straub has functioned as a spokesperson for the Hungarian regime, representing it in various international conferences. He is an official of the Academy of Sciences.

8. *The Great Soviet Encyclopedia* took a middle road: "In 1942 and 1943, A. Szent-Gyorgyi and F. B. Straub showed that the protein of myofibrils consists of two compounds, myosin and actin." Vol. 17, p. 251.

9. Laki had a heart attack while visiting Szent-Gyorgyi in Woods Hole and died on 12 February 1983.

10. Huggins, at the last minute, was unable to attend, but submitted his paper for the published proceedings. Others at the conference included John T. Edsall, Tamas Erdos, J. Gergely, H. E. Huxley, Irvin Isenberg, Koloman Laki, Fritz Lipmann, Alberte and Bernard Pullman, and Andrew Szent-Gyorgyi.

11. Michael Kasha, Epilogue to *Search and Discovery*.

12. Letter, Geoffrey Pollitt to author, 2 March 1987.

13. Letter, David Pollitt to author, 3 March 1987.

14. Letter, Geoffrey Pollitt, 2 March 1987.

15. Letter, David Pollitt, 3 March 1987.

16. *Ibid.*

17. Letter, Albert Szent-Gyorgyi to Geoffrey Pollitt, 7 November 1978.

18. The author offered Marcia a chance to answer these charges. Her response was a letter from her attorneys stating, "As a general matter, Mrs. Szent-Gyorgyi denies the Pollitts' allegations" but that "because of pending litigation detailed comment . . .

would be inappropriate." Letter from Stanley M. Wheatly of Brown, Rudnick, Freed & Gesmer, 29 April 1987. On March 3, 1987, in fact, Albert's three grandchildren had filed suit in Barnstable (Mass.) Probate Court to overturn his 1984 will. They were principally seeking ownership of the seaside cottage.

19. The author was assistant director of public affairs at Memorial Sloan-Kettering Cancer Center at the time in question (1974–1977). He witnessed some interest in Szent-Gyorgyi's activities at that time, including a perception of the NFCR as a fund-raising competitor.

20. See Ralph W. Moss, *The Cancer Syndrome* (New York: Grove, 1982), Chapter 16.

21. See Peter Stoler, *The War Against The Press* (New York: Dodd Mead, 1986), Chapter 9.

CHAPTER 20

FREE RADICALS

1. Barry Commoner, "Is DNA a Self-Duplicating Molecule—Some Observations on the Present Relationship of Biology to Chemistry and Physics," ed. Michael Kasha and Bernard Pullman, *Horizons in Biochemistry—Albert Szent-Gyorgyi Dedicatory Volume,* (New York: Academic Press, 1962).

2. What we are calling submolecular biology was also described by him in other terms. At different times he called this field biophysics, bioenergetics, electronic biology and quantum biology. It was also called "protometabolism." But whatever it was called, in each case he was grappling both to accurately describe his area and to find a vocabulary which would make it accessible to other scientists.

3. Thomas S. Kuhn, *The Structure of Scientific Revolutions,* 2nd ed. (Chicago: University of Chicago Press, 1970).

4. For a detailed explanation of this theory see Albert Szent-Gyorgyi, *The Living State and Cancer,* (New York: Marcel Dekker, 1978) (a simplified account) and *Electronic Biology and Cancer—A New Theory of Cancer,* (New York: Marcel Dekker, 1976). See also the Kasha and Pullmann *Horizon in Biochemistry* volume. *Submolecular Biology and Cancer, In honor of Albert Szent-Gyorgyi on the occasion of his 85th birthday* (Amsterdam: Excerpta Medica, 1979) contains the proceedings of a symposium held at the Ciba Foundation, London, 25–27 September 1978. It gives an idea of how other scientists viewed the theory. This symposium was chaired by R. J. P. Williams, a professor of chemistry at Oxford. Parts of the present chapter are based on Albert's own contribution to the last-named volume.

5. Peter Gascoyne, personal communication, 11 January 1985.

6. In the last few years "free radicals" have become "complex and controversial" for their putative role in causing cancer, according to H. M. Swartz, "Free Radicals in Cancer," in *Submolecular Biology and Cancer,* 107–130. Some vitamin preparations now promise to guard the body against these molecular marauders. It should be realized that much of the interest in free radicals stems from Szent-Gyorgyi's early work in biophysics. Swartz cites Szent-Gyorgyi, A., Isenberg, I. & Baird, S. L. (1960) on the electron donating properties of carcinogens. *Proc. Natl. Acad. Sci. U.S.A. 46,*

1444–1449 in this regard. Szent-Gyorgyi's influence on the entire field seems to extend beyond and predate this important paper, however.

7. G. Fodor, R. Mujumdar and A. Szent-Gyorgyi (1978). "Electronic properties of some protein-methylglyoxal complexes," *Proc. Natl. Acad. Sci. U.S.A. 75*, 315–318.

8. See Moss, *The Cancer Syndrome*, p. 21 for a discussion of the difficulty of defining cancer.

9. Peter Gascoyne, "Albert Szent-Gyorgyi's Protometabolism: Another Angle," unpublished ms., 1985. Some of the description of "protometabolism" in this chapter comes from this excellent article.

10. Gabor Fodor et al, "The Search for New Cancerostatic Agents," in *Submolecular Biology and Cancer*, 1979. This work formed the basis for Szent-Gyorgyi and Fodor's successful 1986 patent application.

11. These were methoxybenzoquinone (MB) and dimethoxybenzoquinone (d-MB). Another close relative is methoxyhydroquinone (MH). Together these chemicals are collectively called the quinones. It was with mixtures of the various quinones and vitamin C that Szent-Gyorgyi hoped to find a practical solution to cancer.

CHAPTER 21

A NATURAL ENDING

1. "Albert Szent-Gyorgyi: A Special Gift," a 30 minute documentary, produced by Joel Sucher, Steven Fischler and Ralph W. Moss; written by Ralph W. Moss; available from Pacific Street Film Project, 333 Sackett St., Brooklyn, New York, 11231.

2. "Brief History of NFCR," Bethesda, Md. n.d.

3. *New York Times*, 1 November 1986.

4. See Moss, *The Cancer Syndrome*, for a discussion of laetrile and other unconventional cancer therapies.

5. Personal communication, 6 May 1987.

6. "Szent-Gyorgyi May Leave Lab," *Cape Cod Times*, 23 October 1985. See also *Cape Cod Times*, 12 July 1986, for follow-up article.

7. *Cape Cod Times*, 23 October 1985.

8. Letter, Albert Szent-Gyorgyi to David Pollitt, 4 November 1985.

9. Albert's lawyer appears to have suggested that "NFCR commit four million dollars . . . to the establishment and operation of the Albert Szent-Gyorgyi Foundation." Letter of John P. Connors, General Counsel, NFCR to Szent-Gyorgyi's lawyer, Richard G. Babineau, 11 April 1986.

10. Letter, Lesley Pollitt to author, 6 March 1987.

11. Quoted in *Cape Cod Times*, 24 October 1986.

12. Personal communication, March, 1987.

13. Letter ASG to David Pollitt, 4 November 1985.

14. Letter, David Pollitt to author, 3 March 1987.

15. Letter, Geoffrey Pollitt to author, 2 March 1987.

16. Letter, ASG to David Pollitt, 4 November 1985.

17. Personal communication, March 1987.

18. Much of this equipment had, at Albert's request, been given to Jane McLaughlin. Some of the rest went to Houston with Peter Gascoyne.

APPENDIX A
Albert Szent-Gyorgyi's Ancestry

The name "Szent-Gyorgyi" is derived from a familiar English name, Saint George, and the pronunciation in English is similar to "Saint Georgie." It is a popular name in Hungary, since England's patron saint was reputed, in the Middle Ages, to have passed through East-Central Europe. Saint George was an early Christian martyr. According to tradition, he was born in Palestine and martyred at Nicodemia before 323 A.D. The story of his dragon-killing activity dates from the twelfth century, as do the legends of his wandering in Hungary.

The "von" in the name indicated noble birth. It meant that Albert's father, Miklos (Hungarian for "Nicholas") was a member of the aristocracy. "Nagyrapolt" indicated an origin in the municipality of "Great Rapolt." All in all, it was an impressive name for the new baby. Here, it seemed to proclaim, was the scion of an important family, a feudal barony, perhaps, or a branch of the royal Hapsburg line.

In his youth, Albert Szent-Gyorgyi was not above using this impressive name to shore up his tottering fortunes. But in truth, even in 1893 one needed a very good atlas or gazetteer to even locate this "Great Rapolt." It was a small hamlet in the Transylvanian mountains, which at that time were still a part of Hungary. With its 1310 inhabitants it was "great" only in relation to "Kis" or "Little" Rapolt with its 420 souls.

Two or three hundred years before, the Szent-Gyorgyis had been commoners, soldiers. Sometime in the sixteenth or seventeenth century, it is said, one of their ancestors performed a service for King Ferdinand and was rewarded with a title and small tax income (or *portio*) from this Transylvanian town.[1]

According to Maria Szent-Gyorgyi, Albert's cousin and herself a professional archivist, the noble title came from King Ferdinand V (as

Austrian Emperor Ferdinand I). She seems to mean Ferdinand I
(1503–64), the Holy Roman Emperor. Szent-Gyorgyi himself thought
this event took place in the seventeenth century.

A nineteenth century visitor to the region had to traverse "almost
impassable roads, where we found oxen ready to drag us up the
nearly perpendicular rock, and several peasants in attendance to hold
the carriage from falling over."[2]

Not surprisingly, there is no record of any Szent-Gyorgyi ever
actually setting foot in the town or the vicinity. "Von Nagyrapolt" was
a purely honorific title, mostly useful in impressing one's Budapest
neighbors.

"The court had little money," Albert later remarked, "and so they
paid for services with titles. It's cheaper." This title was reaffirmed in
1836 after the family's claim to nobility was called into question by
political enemies.

The main benefit of belonging to the nobility in the nineteenth
century was that one did not have to pay taxes, nor tolls on roads and
bridges. John Paget, a peripatetic Englishman, visited Hungary in
mid-century and wrote about the Hungarian nobility. "They do not
distinguish very clearly between the words 'right' and 'privilege' " he
said, ironically. They were a nobility ripe for revolution.[3]

In 1848 a democratic revolt shook most of Europe, and Hungary
was no exception. Szent-Gyorgyi's grandfather, the family patriarch
Imre, had built his administrative career by faithfully helping the
Austrians rule Transylvania. The Hapsburgs pursued a divide-and-
rule strategy but in that year of revolution there was great popular
pressure on them to finally unite Transylvania with Hungary. Grandfather Imre was therefore instructed to sign a bill declaring the unifica-
tion of the two countries. This caused him great difficulty, for the
Hapsburgs always spoke in Metternichian doubletalk: they usually
meant the exact opposite of what they said. They certainly had no
intention of *signing* such a bill, but they expected their faithful lackey
to bear the onus for failing to carry out their orders, or to "take the
rap" in modern parlance. Imre, however, *did* sign the bill, thereby
incurring the wrath of his Austrian patrons.

Imre was acting under revolutionary influence or pressure. He unexpectedly became a revolutionary hero, and his portrait by the Danish
painter Waldmoeller was hung in the Museum of Fine Arts. He
became one of the leaders of the revolutionary parliament of 1848–
49. His next revolutionary act, however, was a fiasco. He and some
other leading Magyars suspected the duplicitous Austrians of having
removed the famous Crown of St. Stephen from Hungarian soil. This
old golden crown and sceptre was the symbol of Hungarian sov-

ereignty. To remove it would be like removing the U.S. Constitution from its case at the National Archives, or the gold from Fort Knox. It did not seem like a paranoid idea at the time: relations between Austria and Hungary were at a low point. Imre led a delegation from the revolutionary parliament up Castle Hill to see if the crown was still in place. They were probably more embarrassed than relieved to find that it had not been touched.[4]

All of Imre's three sons (Imre, Gyula, and Albert) also joined the abortive revolution. After the failure of the revolution, in 1849, Imre was summoned to the court and told to account for his activities. He was eventually retired on half-pension, lucky to have escaped with his head.

For the rest of the nineteenth century the Szent-Gyorgyis kept out of trouble: they were proper, respectable, and quite dull. There were a number of judges, and an undersecretary in the Department of Justice. One uncle, Otto, was an art dealer who got embroiled in a financial scandal and had to be bailed out by the rest of the family. They scraped together enough money to have him sent to a mental hospital instead of prison.[5]

One of the most interesting of the early Szent-Gyorgyis was an uncle who got fed up with his worldly existence, packed a copy of Horace's poetry and the Bible, and took off for parts unknown. No one ever saw him again. "So evidently there was some queerness in the family," Albert later reflected, approvingly.

Albert's father, Miklos, had been athletic as a youth—a fine runner. By the time Albert was born he was portly, conservative, and fairly rich. The most interesting thing about him was his profession. On Albert's birth certificate he gave his occupation as "financial adviser." In other words, he was a capitalist. What made this unusual was that in nineteenth century Hungary upstanding members of the nobility simply did not go into business of any sort. They were administrators, judges, or generals. Crass money-making was left to the Jews and the Germans, who consequently dominated Hungary's business and professional life. Miklos was a farmer, but he ran his farm as a money-making venture, with a 2,000 acre estate north of Budapest, and an apartment in the capital as well. The land was fifty miles north of Budapest in Nograd country, between the towns of Salgotarjan and Balassagyarmat.

If Albert's creative talent was inherited, it came mainly from the scientific dynasty on his mother's side. They were as interesting as his father's family was dull.

The founder of the dynasty was (the first) Mihaly Lenhossek, born 11 May 1773 in Pozsony. He was a poor cook's apprentice who changed his name from the Slavic Lenhoseg. (He had a good reason: *Seg* in Hungarian means 'ass'.) He attended the University of Vienna and on 16 August 1799 received his doctorate in medicine from the University of Pest. He obtained the friendship of Count Joszef Bathyani, cardinal-primate of Hungary, and wrote a number of influential books on infection and vaccination, as well as attempts to reconcile religion and science. He eventually became professor at Vienna, and rector and dean at Pest. He died on 12 February 1840, one of the most respected figures of his day.

Of the six children he had with N. Nyizsnanzsky (also a Slavic name), only Joszef followed in his footsteps. He was born on 18 March 1818 in Buda. He was famous as the first man to own a microscope in Budapest. In 1858 he published a general work on the histology of the nervous system and another on the fine network of the central nervous system. He also was a Professor of Anatomy and Physiology at Pest, but more on the basis of his father's famous name, it appears, than his own intrinsic talent.

Joszef was more interested in his hobby, the archeology and ethnology of Hungary, than in his academic work. He wrote a book on the prehistory of the Szeged region: *Die Ausgrabungen zu Szeged-Othalon in Hungarn* and won a number of important awards, such as the Monthyou Prize of the French Academy of Sciences. His biological specimens were purchased by the Hunterian Museum in London. Szent-Gyorgyi summed up his grandfather this way, however: "He was not very outstanding in any way. He left no trace in science." He died on 2 December 1888.

He married Emma Bossonyi and they had three children: Zseni, Mihaly and Josefine, or Fini, as she was called (ASG's mother). The reason for the rumor of Emma's Jewish ancestry is as follows: During the German occupation of Hungary in World War II, everyone was required to fill out a form giving the religion of their ancestors. Szent-Gyorgyi filled it out quite explicitly for all his relatives except Emma Bossonyi Lenhossek; next to her name he left a blank. This was rather dangerous under the circumstances and certainly leaves the impression that, rather than lie, he preferred to take whatever risks attended such an omission. Nor was intermarriage between Jews and Gentiles in Hungary unusual in the late nineteenth century. Szent-Gyorgyi himself denied that she was Jewish, but was unable to recall what religion she was, or explain the omission.

The younger Mihaly studied at Budapest, Basel, Wurzburg, and Tubingen. In 1900 Mihaly succeeded his father as Professor of Anatomy and Physiology at Budapest—third in the Lenhossek line to hold that chair.

Albert's mother, Josefine Lenhossek Szent-Gyorgyi, was both intelligent and good-looking. As indicated in Chapter One, she started out with the goal of becoming an opera singer. Her union with Miklos Szent-Gyorgyi was a marriage of convenience. It was not long before Miklos moved to his country estate and she took the Budapest apartment. They would see each other during the summers or on his rare visits to the city. "He always remained a stranger in the family," said Albert.

Except in those summers, Albert and his two brothers were part of a close non-conventional family made up of their mother, their maternal grandmother, and Fini's brother, Mihaly Lenhossek. They occupied a succession of apartments in the best part of Pest, the business and cultural center of town. The first apartment was at 10 Staczio Street, then, a year or two later, at 10 Baross Avenue. After this they lived at 2 Kalvin Square. The house was demolished by bombs during World War II.

NOTES

1. John Paget, *Hungary and Transylvania* (London: J. Murray, 1839), p. 249.

2. Transylvania became part of Romania after World War I, through the Trianon Treaty. It was seized by Hungary during World War II, but then later returned to Romania. See Chapter 10.

3. Paget, *Hungary and Transylvania,* p. 15.

4. There is poetic justice in the fact that Albert himself accompanied U.S. Secretary of State Cyrus Vance when he returned the crown and sceptre to Hungary in January, 1978. The crown had been stolen at the end of World War II, made its way into American hands, and was returned as a gesture of American-Hungarian friendship.

5. Andrew Szent-Gyorgyi, personal communication, July, 1984.

APPENDIX B

Excerpts from *The Crazy Ape*

On 20 February 1970 the *New York Times* published excerpts from Albert Szent-Gyorgyi's book, *The Crazy Ape*. The *Times* described the subject of the book as "man imperiled by the technological revolution of his own making." These statements caused such a sensation at the time that the *Sunday Times* picked up the story and reprinted it in full several days later. Here are the excerpts from the interview in that article:

Man is a very strange animal. In much of the world half the children go to bed hungry and we spend a trillion on rubbish—steel, iron, tanks. We are all criminals. There is an old Hungarian poem: "If you are among brigands and you are silent, you are a brigand yourself."

Any race that does not adapt, will have to disappear. The dinosaurs disappeared, and man may have to disappear too.

On his new book: "It is a revolutionary book because it's only 40 pages—it can be read in two hours. The trouble with books is that they cannot be read. Who the hell has the time to read 300 pages? There is nothing you cannot say in two hours if it is essential."

On what he would do if he were twenty: "I would share with my classmates rejection of the whole world as it is—all of it. Is there any point in studying and work? Fornication—at least that is something good. What else is there to do? Fornicate and take drugs against this terrible strain of idiots who govern the world."

On the powers of science: "You have only to wish it and you can have a world without hunger, disease, cancer and toil . . . wish anything and it can be done. Or else we can exterminate ourselves. . . .

301

"At present we are on the road to extermination. American society is death-oriented. If you watch and if you read the newspapers, a great part of it is taken up by war, by killing, by murder, atomic bombs, MIRV's, gases, bacterial agents, napalm, defoliants, asphyxiating agents, and we have war. All our ideas are death-oriented. . . .

"The only way we can survive is to make a new beginning. There is one factor that makes a new beginning very difficult—that the human brain freezes up for new ideas at a certain age, around 40. And our whole government is over this age. . . . Our government is a gerontocracy. They cannot really assimilate new ideas.

"The only people who can make the turn is youth—our present youth. And if we live long enough, if your human kind is not exterminated, they will make the turn. . . .

"So I wish that instead of expressing themselves with superficial symbols the whole youth of the world would come together and hammer out the constitution of the future world, which they can then implement, not to freeze up before they have thought what the world should be like."

APPENDIX C

"Psalmus Humanus and Six Prayers"[1]

Psalmus Humanus

My Lord, Who are You?
Are You my stern Father,
Or are You my loving Mother
In whose womb the Universe was born?
Are You the Universe itself?
Or the Law which rules it?
Have You created life only to wipe it out again?
Are You my maker, or did I shape You,
That I may share my loneliness and shun my responsibility?

God! I don't know who You are
But I am calling to You, for I am in trouble,
Frightened of myself and my fellow men!
You may not understand my words,
But comprehend my wordless sounds.[2]

First Prayer: God

My Lord!
You are greater than the world You created,
And Your house is the Universe.

I shaped You to my own image
Thinking You vicious, greedy and vain,
Desirous of my praise and sacrifices,
Revengeful of my petty trespasses,
Needful of the houses I build you
While my fellow men I let go without food and shelter.

God! Let me praise You by improving my corner of Your Creation
By filling this little world of mine
With light, warmth, good will and happiness.

Second Prayer: The Leaders

My Lord!
We elect leaders to lead us,
And give You servants to serve You.

But the leaders don't lead us to You,
They don't listen to our mute voices of craving for peace,
They are corrupted by power, lead man against man,
And the servants we give You don't serve You,
They serve power and bless our guns,
Torture and kill my fellow men in Your name.

God! Give us leaders who are Your servants,
Who lead us to You, lead us to peace,
Lead man to man.

Third Prayer: The Heart and the Mind

My Lord!
You have given me a heart capable of love and thirsty for love,
You have given me a mind capable of clear thought and creativeness,

And I have filled my heart with fear and hatred,
And my heart corrupts my mind and makes it build monstrous
instruments of murder

To destroy Your world, myself and my fellow men,
And damage the sacred stuff life is made of.

God! Clean my heart, lift my mind,
And make me my brother's brother.

Fourth Prayer: Energy and Speed

My Lord!
You have revealed to us the secret energies of matter
To ease our toil and elevate life,
You have taught us to travel faster than the sound we make
That distance should no more separate man from man.

We toil to press these energies into shells
In which to send them to the distant corners of the earth,
To bring misery and destruction to our fellow men,
Leaving the earth scorched and barren of life.

God! Let me not destroy the temple of life,
Let me use my knowledge to my advantage, to elevate life,
Lend dignity to the short span of my existence.

Fifth Prayer: The Earth

My Lord!
You have given us this lovely globe to live on,
Hidden untold treasures in its bowels,
Enabled us to comprehend Your work,
Ease our toil, ban hunger and disease.

We are digging up those treasures to squander them,
To build them into formidable machines of destruction,
With which to destroy what other men have built
Which will turn against me, destroy me and my children.

God! Let us be Your partners in creation
By understanding and improving Your work,
Making this globe of ours a safe home
For wealth, happiness and harmony.

Sixth Prayer: Children

My Lord!
You have separated the sexes that in their mutual search
The deepest chords of our souls may vibrate in the highest harmonies.
Out of the search spring our children, lovely children
Who come to us with clean and empty minds.

And I fill these minds with my hatreds, fears and prejudices,
My bomb shelters teach them the darkness of life and the futility of
endeavor,
And when they grow up, ready for noble deeds,
I make them study organized manslaughter,
Wasting their best years in moral stagnation.

God! Save my children,
Save their minds

That my corruption may not corrupt them,
Save their lives
That the weapons I forge against others may not destroy them,
That they may be better than their elders,
That they may build a world of their own,
A world of beauty, decency, harmony, good will and equity,
That peace and love may reign,
For ever.

NOTES

1. Written by Albert in the summer of 1964 and recorded by him recitative style to musical accompaniment composed and played by Agi Jambor. First performed at the MBL Club, Woods Hole, on 16 August 1964 and recorded by the Fassett Recording Studio, Boston, Mass., #F-SGJ-1.

2. This refers to the music on the recording.

INDEX